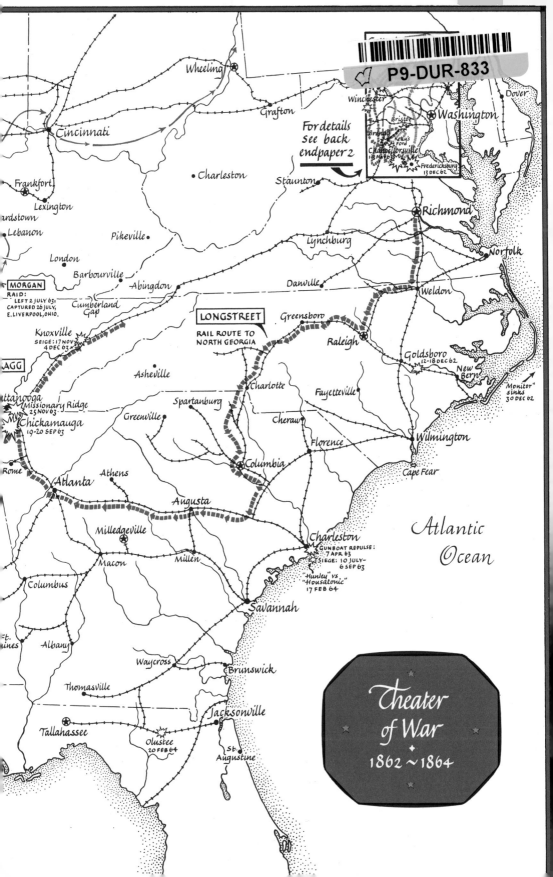

Wheeling

Winchester

Washington

Dover

Grafton

Bristol

Brandy

Kelly's Ford

Chancellorsville
1-6 MAY 63

Fredericksburg
13 DEC 62

Cincinnati

Charleston

Staunton

For details
see back
endpaper 2

Frankfort

Lexington

Pikeville

Richmond

ardstown

Lynchburg

Norfolk

Lebanon

Barbourville

Abingdon

Danville

Weldon

London

MORGAN
RAID:
LEFT 2 JULY 63;
CAPTURED 26 JULY,
E. LIVERPOOL, OHIO.

Cumberland
Gap

LONGSTREET

RAIL ROUTE TO
NORTH GEORGIA

Greensboro

Raleigh

Goldsboro
12-18 DEC 62

New
Bern

Knoxville
SEIGE: 17 NOV-
4 DEC 63

AGG

Asheville

Charlotte

Fayetteville

"Monitor"
sinks
30 DEC 62

ttanooga
Missionary Ridge
25 NOV 63

Chickamauga
19-20 SEP 63

Spartanburg

Greenville

Cheraw

Florence

Wilmington

Rome

Athens

Columbia

Cape Fear

Atlanta

Augusta

Atlantic
Ocean

Milledgeville

Millen

Charleston
GUNBOAT REPULSE:
7 APR 63
SEIGE: 10 JULY-
6 SEP 63

Macon

Columbus

"Hunley" vs.
"Housatonic"
17 FEB 64

t.
nes

Albany

Waycross

Savannah

Brunswick

Thomasville

Jacksonville

Tallahassee

Olustee
20 FEB 64

St.
Augustine

Theater
of War
◆
1862 ~ 1864

The Civil War
A Narrative

ALL THESE WERE HONOURED IN THEIR GENERATIONS

AND WERE THE GLORY OF THEIR TIMES

THERE BE OF THEM

THAT HAVE LEFT A NAME BEHIND THEM

THAT THEIR PRAISES MIGHT BE REPORTED

AND SOME THERE BE WHICH HAVE NO MEMORIAL

WHO ARE PERISHED AS THOUGH THEY HAD NEVER BEEN

AND ARE BECOME AS THOUGH THEY HAD NEVER BEEN BORN

AND THEIR CHILDREN AFTER THEM

BUT THESE WERE MERCIFUL MEN

WHOSE RIGHTEOUSNESS HATH NOT BEEN FORGOTTEN

WITH THEIR SEED SHALL CONTINUALLY REMAIN

A GOOD INHERITANCE

AND THEIR CHILDREN ARE WITHIN THE COVENANT

THEIR SEED STANDETH FAST

AND THEIR CHILDREN FOR THEIR SAKES

THEIR SEED SHALL REMAIN FOR EVER

AND THEIR GLORY SHALL NOT BE BLOTTED OUT

THEIR BODIES ARE BURIED IN PEACE

BUT THEIR NAME LIVETH FOR EVERMORE

Ecclesiasticus xliv

THE
Civil War
A Narrative

— ★ ★ —

FREDERICKSBURG
to CHANCELLORSVILLE

— ★ ★ —

The Longest Journey

By SHELBY FOOTE

RANDOM HOUSE · NEW YORK

CONTENTS

★ ✗ ☆

☆

Fredericksburg
to
Chancellorsville

☆

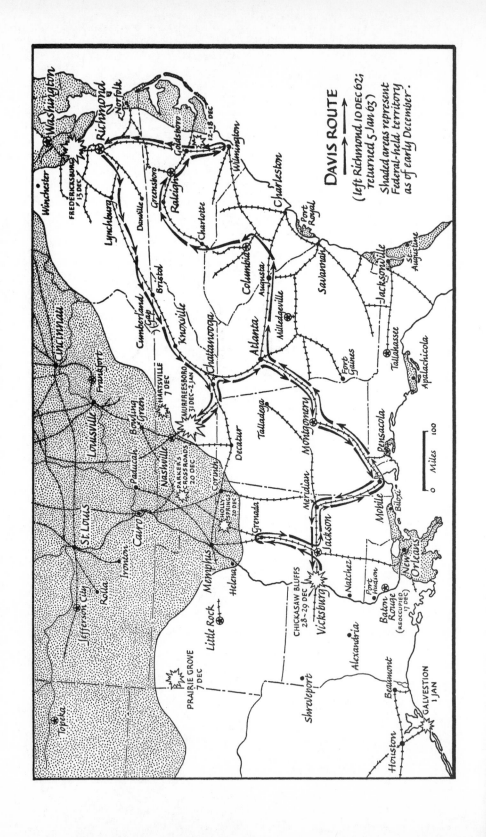

DAVIS ROUTE

(left Richmond 10 DEC 62;
returned 5 JAN 63)

Shaded areas represent
Federal-held territory
as of early December.

0   Miles   100

Washington
Richmond
Norfolk
Winchester
FREDERICKSBURG 13 DEC
Lynchburg
Danville
Greensboro
Goldsboro 12-18 DEC
Raleigh
Wilmington
Charlotte
Charleston
Port Royal
Columbia
Augusta
Milledgeville
Savannah
Jacksonville
St. Augustine
Tallahassee
Apalachicola
Cincinnati
Frankfort
Cumberland Gap
Bristol
Knoxville
Chattanooga
Atlanta
Fort Gaines
Louisville
Paducah
Bowling Green
HARTSVILLE 7 DEC
MURFREESBORO 31 DEC–2 JAN
Nashville
PARKER'S CROSSROADS 20 DEC
Decatur
Talladega
Montgomery
Pensacola
St. Louis
Cairo
Ironton
Corinth
HOLLY SPRINGS 20 DEC
Grenada
Meridian
Jackson
Mobile
Biloxi
New Orleans
Memphis
Helena
Natchez
Port Hudson
Baton Rouge (REOCCUPIED 17 DEC)
Jefferson City
Rolla
Little Rock
CHICKASAW BLUFFS 28-29 DEC
Vicksburg
Alexandria
Topeka
PRAIRIE GROVE 7 DEC
Shreveport
Beaumont
Houston
GALVESTON 1 JAN

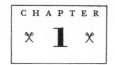

The Longest Journey

★ ✗ ☆

"AFTER AN ABSENCE OF NEARLY TWO YEARS," Jefferson Davis told the legislators assembled under the golden dome of his home-state capitol on the day after Christmas, 1862 — twenty months and two weeks, to the day, since the guns of Charleston opened fire on Sumter to inaugurate the civil war no one could know was not yet halfway over — "I again find myself among those who, from the days of my childhood, have ever been the trusted objects of my affection, those for whose good I have ever striven and whose interests I have sometimes hoped I may have contributed to subserve. . . . I left you to assume the duties which have devolved upon me as the representative of the new Confederacy. The responsibilities of this position have occupied all my time, and have left me no opportunity for mingling with my friends in Mississippi or for sharing in the dangers which have menaced them. But, wherever duty may have called me, my heart has been with you, and the success of the cause in which we are all engaged has been first in my thoughts and prayers."

In February of the year before, he had left for Montgomery, Alabama, to assume his role as President of the newly established provisional government, believing, as he said now, "that the service to which I was called could be but temporary." A West Pointer and an authentic hero of the Mexican War, he had considered his primary talent — or, as he termed it, his "capacity" — to be military. He had thought to return to the duty he found congenial, that of a line officer in the service of his state, "to lead Mississippians in the field, and to be with them where danger was to be braved and glory won. . . . But it was decided differently. I was called to another sphere of action. How, in that sphere, I have discharged the duties and obligations imposed on me, it does not become me to constitute myself the judge. It is for others to decide that question. But, speaking to you with that frankness and that confidence with which I have always spoken to you, and which partakes of the nature of thinking aloud, I can say with my hand upon my heart that whatever I have done has been done with the sincere purpose of promoting the noble cause in which we are engaged. The period which has elapsed since I left you is short; for the time which may appear long in the life of a man is short in the history of a nation. And in that short period remarkable changes have been wrought in all the circumstances by which we are surrounded."

Remarkable changes had indeed been wrought, and of these the most immediately striking to those present, seated row on row beneath him or standing close-packed along the outer aisles, was in the aspect of the man who stood before them, tall and slender, careworn and oracular, in a mote-shot nimbus of hazy noonday sunlight pouring down from the high windows of the hall. When they had seen him last on this same rostrum, just short of twenty-three months ago this week, he had not appeared to be within a decade of his fifty-two years of age. Now, though, he was fifty-four, and he looked it. The "troubles and thorns innumerable" which he foretold on his arrival in Montgomery to take the oath of office, back in the first glad springtime of the nation, had not only come to pass; they had also left their marks — as if the thorns, being more than figurative, had scored his brow and made of him what he had never seemed before, a man of sorrows. The gray eyes, one lustrous, the other sightless, its stone gray pupil covered by a film, were deeply sunken above the jut of the high cheekbones, and the thin upper lip, indicative of an iron will and rigid self-control, was held so tightly against the teeth, even in repose, that you saw their shape behind it. The accustomed geniality was there, the inveterate grace and charm of manner, along with the rich music of the voice, but the symptoms of strain and overwork were all too obvious. These proceeded, it was said, not only from having had to await (as he was awaiting even now) the outcome of battles in which he could have no active part, whatever his inclination, but also, it was added, from a congenital inability to relegate authority, including the minor paperwork which took up such a disproportionate share of his existence.

Other changes there were, too, less physical and therefore less immediately obvious, but on closer inspection no less profound. In this case, moreover, the contrast between now and then was emphasized by mutuality, involving others besides Davis. It was two-sided; reciprocal, so to speak. Arriving in Jackson to accept his appointment as commander of Mississippi troops after his farewell to the Senate in January of what had presently turned out to be the first year of the conflict some men had still believed could be avoided, he had been met at the station by Governor J. J. Pettus, whom he advised to push the procurement of arms. "We shall need all and many more than we can get," he said, expressing the conviction that blood would soon be shed. "General, you overrate the risk," the governor protested, and Davis replied: "I only wish I did." So thoroughly had this prediction been fulfilled in the past twenty months — Kentucky and Missouri irretrievably gone, along with most of Tennessee and the northwest quarter of Virginia, New Orleans fallen, Nashville and Memphis occupied, and North Mississippi itself aswarm with bluecoats — that now it was Governor Pettus who was calling for reassurance, and calling for it urgently, from the man to whom he previously had offered it so blandly.

"You have often visited the army of Virginia," he wired Richmond in early December. "At this critical juncture could you not visit the army of the West? Something must be done to inspire confidence."

By way of reinforcement for this plea there came a letter from Senator James Phelan, whose home lay in the path of the invaders. "The present alarming crisis in this state, so far from arousing the people, seems to have sunk them in listless despondency," he wrote. "The spirit of enlistment is thrice dead. Enthusiasm has expired to a cold pile of damp ashes. Defeats, retreats, sufferings, dangers, magnified by spiritless helplessness and an unchangeable conviction that our army is in the hands of ignorant and feeble commanders, are rapidly producing a sense of settled despair. . . . I imagine but one event that could awaken from its waning spark the enthusiastic hopes and energy of Mississippians. Plant your own foot upon our soil, unfurl your banner at the head of the army, tell your own people that you have come to share with them the perils of this dark hour. . . . If ever your presence was needed as a last refuge from an 'Iliad of woes,' this is the hour. It is not a point to be argued. [Only] you can save us or help us save ourselves from the dread evils now so imminently pending."

Flattering as this was, in part — especially the exhortation to "unfurl your banner," which touched the former hero of Buena Vista where his inclination was strongest and his vanity was most susceptible — the senator's depiction of regional gloom and fears, tossed thus into the balance, added weight to the governor's urgent plea that the Commander in Chief undertake the suggested journey to his homeland and thereby refute in the flesh the growing complaint that the authorities in Richmond were concerned only for the welfare of the soldiers and civilians in Virginia, where if anywhere the war was being won, rather than for those in the western theater, where if anywhere the war was being lost. Not that the danger nearest the national capital was slight. Major General Ambrose Burnside, a month in command of the Army of the Potomac as successor to Major General George McClellan, who had been relieved for a lack of aggressiveness, was menacing the line of the Rappahannock with a mobile force of 150,000 men, backed by another 50,000 in the Washington defenses. To oppose this host General Robert E. Lee had something under 80,000 in the Army of Northern Virginia moving toward a concentration near Fredericksburg, where the threat of a crossing seemed gravest, midway of the direct north-south hundred-mile line connecting the two capitals. That the battle, now obviously at hand, would be fought even closer to the Confederate seat of government appeared likely, for Davis wrote Lee on December 8: "You will know best when it will be proper to make a masked movement to the rear, should circumstances require you to move nearer to Richmond."

Something else he said in this same letter. Hard as it was for him to leave the capital at a time when every day might bring the battle that would perhaps decide his country's fate, he had made up his mind to heed the call that reached him from the West. "I propose to go out there immediately," he told Lee, "with the hope that something may be done to bring out men not heretofore in service, and to arouse all classes to united and desperate resistance." After expressing the hope that "God may bless us, as in other cases seemingly as desperate, with success over our impious foe," he added, by way of apology for not having reviewed the Virginian's army since it marched northward on the eve of Second Manassas: "I have been very anxious to visit you, but feeble health and constant labor have caused me to delay until necessity hurries me in the opposite direction." He sent the letter by special courier that same December 8; then, two days later, he himself was off.

He left incognito, aboard a special car and accompanied by a single military aide, lest his going stir up rumors that the capital was about to be abandoned in the face of the threat to the line of the Rappahannock. His planned itinerary was necessarily roundabout: not only because the only direct east-west route was closed to him by the Federal grip on the final hundred miles of the Memphis & Charleston Railroad, but also because he had decided to combine the attempt to restore morale among the distraught civilians of the region, as suggested by Governor Pettus and Senator Phelan, with a personal inspection of the two main armies charged with the defense of the theater bounded east and west by the Blue Ridge Mountains and the Mississippi River. The Army of Tennessee, the larger of the two, northwest of Chattanooga and covering that city by pretending to threaten Nashville, was under General Braxton Bragg; the other, the Army of Mississippi under Lieutenant General John C. Pemberton, covered Vicksburg. Both were menaced by superior forces, or combinations of forces, under Major Generals William S. Rosecrans and Ulysses S. Grant, and Davis had lately appointed General Joseph E. Johnston to co-ordinate the efforts of both armies in order to meet the double menace by operating on interior lines, much as Lee had done for the past six months in Virginia, on a smaller scale but with such success as had won for Confederate arms the admiration of the world.

Johnston's was the more difficult task, albeit one on which the survival of the nation was equally dependent. Whether it could be performed — specifically, whether it could be performed by Johnston — remained to be seen. So far, though, the signs had appeared to the general himself to be anything but promising. Pemberton was falling back under pressure from Grant in North Mississippi, and Bragg's preparations for the defense of Middle Tennessee, though they had not yet been tested by Federal pressure, did not meet with the new commander's approval when he inspected them this week. In fact, he found in them full justification for a judgment he had delivered the week before, when he first established headquarters in Chattanooga. "Nobody ever assumed a command under more unfavorable circumstances," he wrote to a friend back East. "If Rosecrans had disposed our troops himself, their disposition could not have been more unfavorable to us."

Davis did not share the Virginian's gloom; or if he did he did not show it as he left Richmond, December 10, and rode westward through Lynchburg and Wytheville and across the state line to Knoxville, where, beginning his attempt to bolster civilian morale by a show of confidence, he made a speech in which he characterized "the Toryism of East Tennessee" as "greatly exaggerated." Joined by Lieutenant General Edmund Kirby Smith, the department commander whose march north in August and September had cleared the region of bluecoats and delivered Cumberland Gap, but whose strength had been reduced by considerably more than half in the past month as a result of orders to reinforce Bragg in the adjoining department, the President reached Chattanooga by nightfall and went at once to pay a call on Johnston.

He found him somewhat indisposed, waiting in his quarters. Short of stature, gray and balding, a year older than Davis despite the fact that he had been a year behind him at West Point, the general had a high-colored, wedge-shaped face, fluffed white side whiskers, a grizzled mustache and goatee, eyes that crinkled attractively at their outer corners when he smiled, and a jaunty, gamecock manner. Mrs Johnston, in attendance on her husband, was able to serve their visitor a genuine cup of coffee: the "real Rio," she reported proudly to a friend next day, describing the event. She claimed nonetheless the saddest heart in Chattanooga. Whatever Davis might have accomplished elsewhere on this arduous first day of the journey he had undertaken "to arouse all classes to united and desperate resistance," he obviously had had little success in her direction. "How ill and weary I feel in this desolate land," she added in the letter to her friend in the Old Dominion, which she so much regretted having left, "& how dreary it all looks, & how little prospect there is of my poor husband doing ought than lose his army. Truly a forlorn hope it is."

The general himself was far from well, suffering from a flare-up of the wound that had cost him his Virginia command, six months ago at Seven Pines, and from a weariness brought on by his just-completed inspection of the Army of Tennessee. So Davis, postponing their strategy conference until such time as he would be able to see for himself the condition of that army, left next day for Bragg's headquarters at Murfreesboro, ninety miles away and only thirty miles from Nashville.

It was a two-day visit, and unlike Johnston he was heartened by what he saw. Serenaded at his hotel by a large and enthusiastic crowd, he announced that he entertained no fears for the safety of Richmond, that Tennessee would be held to the last extremity, and that if the people would but arouse themselves to sustain the conflict, eventual if not immediate foreign intervention would assure a southern victory and peace on southern terms. His listeners, delighted by a recent exploit beyond the northern lines by Colonel John H. Morgan, did not seem to doubt for a moment the validity of his contentions or predictions. Whatever dejection he might encounter in other portions of the threatened region, he found here an optimism to match his own. The thirty-seven-year-old Morgan, with four small regiments of cavalry and two of infantry — just over 2000 men in all, most of them Kentuckians like himself — had crossed the icy Cumberland by starlight, in order to strike at dawn on Sunday, December 7, a Union force of equal strength in camp at Hartsville, forty miles upstream from Nashville. Another enemy force, three times his strength, was camped nine miles away at Castalian Springs, within easy hearing distance of his guns, but had no chance to interfere. After less than an hour of fighting, in which he inflicted more than 300 casualties at a cost of 125, Morgan accepted the surrender of Colonel Absalom B. Moore of Illinois. By noon he was back across the Cumberland with 1762 prisoners and a wagon train heavily loaded with captured equipment and supplies, riding hard for Murfreesboro and the cheers that awaited him there. "A brilliant feat," Joe Johnston called it, and recommended that Morgan "be appointed brigadier general immediately. He is indispensable."

Davis gladly conferred the promotion in person when he arrived, receiving from Morgan's own hands in return one of the three sets of enemy infantry colors the cavalryman had brought home. A formal review of one corps of the Army of Tennessee next day, followed that evening by a conference with Bragg and his lieutenants, was equally satisfying, fulfilling as it did the other half of the President's double-barreled purpose. "Found the troops there in good condition and fine spirits," he wired the Secretary of War on December 14, after his return to Chattanooga the night before. "Enemy is kept close in to Nashville, and indicates only defensive purposes."

This last had led to a strategic decision, made on the spot and before consultation with Johnston. As Davis saw it, comparing Pemberton's plight with Bragg's, the Mississippi commander was not only more gravely threatened by a combination of army and naval forces, above and below the Vicksburg bluff; he was also far more heavily outnumbered, and with less room for maneuver. Practically speaking, despite the assurance lately given the serenaders, the loss of Middle Tennessee would mean no more than the loss of supplies to be gathered in the region; whereas the loss of Vicksburg would mean the loss of the Mississippi River throughout its length, which in turn would mean the loss of Texas, West Louisiana, Arkansas, and the last tenuous hope for the recovery of Missouri. Consequently, in an attempt to even the odds — east and west, that is; North and South the odds could never be evened, here or elsewhere — Davis decided to reinforce Pemberton with a division from Bragg. When the latter protested that this would encourage Rosecrans to attack him, he was informed that he would have to take his chances, depending on maneuver for deliverance. "Fight if you can," Davis told him, and if necessary "fall back beyond the Tennessee."

Bragg took the decision with such grace as he could muster; but not Johnston. When Davis returned to Chattanooga with instructions for the transfer to be ordered, the Virginian protested for all he was worth against a policy which seemed to him no better than robbing Peter to pay Paul. Both western armies, he declared, were already too weak for effective operations; to weaken either was to invite disaster, particularly in Tennessee, which he referred to as "the shield of the South." But in this matter the President was inflexible. Apparently reasoning that if the general would not do the job for which he had been sent here — a balancing and a taking of calculated risks in order to make the most of the advantage of operating on interior lines — then he would do it for him, Davis insisted that the transfer order be issued immediately. This Johnston did, though with a heavy heart and still protesting, convinced that he would be proved right in the end.

Whatever Davis's reaction was on learning thus that one of his two ranking commanders was opposed to availing himself of the one solid advantage strategically accruing to the South, he had other worries to fret him now: worries that threatened not a long-range but an immediate collapse, not of a part but of the whole. On his return from Murfreesboro he heard from the War Department that the national capital was menaced from two directions simultaneously. A force of undetermined strength was moving inland from coastal North Carolina against Goldsboro and the vital Weldon Railroad, and Burnside was across the Rappahannock. "You can imagine my anxiety," Davis wrote his wife, chafed by distance and the impossibility of being in two places at once. "If the necessity demands, I will return to Richmond, though already there are indications of a strong desire for me to visit the further West, expressed in terms which render me unwilling to disappoint the expectation." Presently, however, his anxiety was relieved. The Carolina invasion, though strongly mounted, had been halted at the Neuse, well short of the vital supply line, and Lee had inflicted another staggering defeat on the main northern army, flinging it back across the Rappahannock. Davis was elated at the news, but Johnston's reaction was curiously mixed. "What luck some people have," he said. "Nobody will ever come to attack me in such a place."

After a day of rest and conferences, political as well as military, Davis left Chattanooga late on the afternoon of December 16, accompanied by Johnston, who would be making his first inspection of the western portion of his command. However, with the Memphis & Charleston in Federal hands along the Tennessee-Mississippi line, their route at first led south to Atlanta, where they spent the night and Davis responded to another serenade. Continuing south to Montgomery next morning, he spoke at midday from the portico of the Alabama capitol, where he had delivered his first inaugural a week after being notified of his unexpected election to head the newly established Confederate States of America. That was nearly two years ago. Whatever thoughts he had as to the contrast between now and then, as evidenced by the demeanor of the crowd that gathered to hear him, he kept to himself as he and Johnston rode on that night to Mobile, where he spoke formally for the second time that day. Next morning, December 19, they reached Jackson, but having agreed to return for a joint appearance before the Mississippi legislature on the day after Christmas, they only stayed for lunch and left immediately afterwards for Vicksburg.

This too was a two-day visit, and mainly they spent it inspecting the town's land and water defenses, which had been extended northward a dozen miles along a range of hills and ridges overlooking the Yazoo and its swampy bayous — Chickasaw Bluffs, the range was called, or sometimes Walnut Hills — and southward about half that far to Warrenton, a hamlet near the lower end of the tall red bluff dominating the eastern shank of the hairpin bend described at this point by a whim of the Mississippi. To an untrained eye the installations might look stout indeed, bristling with guns at intervals for nearly twenty miles, but Johnston was not pleased by what he saw. To his professional eye, they not only left much to be desired in the way of execution; their very conception, it seemed to him, was badly flawed. Nor was he any slower to say so now than he had been eight months ago at Yorktown, in a similar situation down the York-James peninsula from Richmond. "Instead of a fort requiring a small garrison," which would leave the bulk of available troops free to maneuver, he protested, the overzealous engineers had made the place into "an immense intrenched camp, requiring an army to hold it." Besides, scattered as they were along the high ground north and south "to prevent the bombardment of the town, instead of to close the navigation of the river to the enemy," the batteries would not be able to concentrate their fire against naval attack. In these and other matters Johnston expressed his discontent. Davis, a professional too, could see the justice in much of this, and though he did not order the line contracted, he moved to strengthen it by wiring the

War Department of the "immediate and urgent necessity for heavy guns and long-range fieldpieces at Vicksburg."

Two bits of news, one welcome, one disturbing, reached them here in the course of their brief visit. The first was that a Federal ironclad, the *Cairo*, had been sunk up the Yazoo the week before, the result of an experiment with torpedoes by Commander Isaac N. Brown, builder and skipper of the *Arkansas*, which single-handedly had raised the midsummer naval siege by an all-out attack on the two enemy fleets before she steamed downriver to her destruction in early August. The other news was that Major General Nathaniel P. Banks, whose troops were escorted upriver from New Orleans by the deep-draft fleet under Rear Admiral David G. Farragut, had reoccupied Baton Rouge, abandoned three months before by his predecessor, Major General Benjamin F. Butler. Whatever comfort the bluff's defenders found in the mishap encountered by the Yankees in their probe of the Yazoo was more than offset by the news that they were approaching in strength from the opposite direction. Johnston, for one, was convinced that, in addition to the 9000-man division already on the way from Bragg, another 20,000 troops would be required if Vicksburg and Port Hudson, another strong point on another bluff three hundred miles downriver, were to be held against the combined forces of Grant and Banks. What was more, he thought he knew just where to get them: from the adjoining Transmississippi Department, commanded by Lieutenant General Theophilus H. Holmes.

"Our great object is to hold the Mississippi," Johnston told Davis. In this connection, he firmly believed "that our true system of warfare would be to concentrate the forces of the two departments" — his and Holmes's — "on this side of the Mississippi, beat the enemy here, then reconquer the country beyond it, which [the Federals] might have gained in the meantime."

Davis had already shown his appreciation of this "true system" by recommending, a month before he left Richmond and two weeks before Johnston himself had been assigned to the western command, that Holmes send reinforcements eastward to assist in the accomplishment of the "great objective." Since then, unfortunately, and by coincidence on the December 7 of Morgan's victory at Hartsville, the Arkansas army under Major General Thomas C. Hindman, the one mobile force of any size in the department beyond the river, had fought and lost the Battle of Prairie Grove, up in the northwest corner of the state. This altered considerably Holmes's ability to comply with the request. However, instead of pointing out this and other drawbacks to Johnston's argument — 1) that to lose the Transmississippi temporarily might be to lose it permanently, as a result of losing the confidence of the people of the region; 2) that the Confederacy, already suffering from the strictures of the Federal blockade, could not afford even a brief stoppage of the flow of supplies from Texas and the valleys of the Arkansas and the Red; and 3) that the transfer east of men in gray would result in a proportional transfer of men in blue, which would lengthen rather than shorten the odds on both sides of the river unless the blow was delivered with unaccustomed lightning speed — Davis was willing to repeat the recommendation in stronger terms. Accordingly, on this same December 21, he wrote to Holmes in Little Rock, apprising him of the growing danger and urging full co-operation with Johnston's plan as set forth in that general's correspondence, which was included. It was a long letter, and in it the President said in part: "From the best information at command, a large force is now ready to descend the Mississippi and co-operate with the army advancing from Memphis to make an attack upon Vicksburg. Large forces are also reported to have been sent to the lower Mississippi for the purpose of ascending the river to attempt the reduction of Port Hudson. . . . It seems to me then unquestionably best that you should reinforce Genl Johnston." After reminding Holmes that "we cannot hope at all points to meet the enemy with a force equal to his own, and must find our security in the concentration and rapid movement of troops," Davis closed with a compliment and an admonition: "I have thus presented to you my views, and trusting alike in your patriotism and discretion, leave you to make the application of them when circumstances will permit. Whatever may be done should be done with all possible dispatch."

Johnston's enthusiasm on reading the opening paragraphs of the letter, which was shown to him before it was given to a courier bound for Little Rock, was considerably dampened by the close. Judging perhaps by his own reaction the week before, when he protested against the detachment of a division from Bragg for this same purpose, he did not share the President's trust in the "patriotism and discretion" Holmes was expected to bring to bear, and he noted regretfully that, despite the final suggestion as to the need for haste, "circumstances" had been left to govern the application of what Davis called his "views."

Two days later, moreover, the general's gloom was deepened when they returned to Jackson and proceeded north a hundred miles by rail to Grenada, where Pemberton had ended his southward retreat in the face of Grant's advance and had his badly outnumbered field force hard at work in an attempt to fortify the banks of the Yalobusha River while his cavalry, under Major General Earl Van Dorn, probed for Grant's rear in an attempt to make him call a halt, or anyhow slow him down, by giving him trouble along his lengthening supply line. Here as at Vicksburg, Johnston found the intrenchments "very extensive, but slight — the usual defect of Confederate engineering." Nor was he pleased to discover, as he said later, that "General Pemberton and I advocated opposite modes of warfare." He would have continued the retreat to a better position farther south, hoping for a stronger concentration; but as usual Davis discounted the advantage of withdrawal and sided with the commander who was opposed to delaying a showdown.

Christmas Day they returned to Jackson, which gave the President time for an overnight preparation of the speech he would deliver tomorrow before his home-state legislature. This was not so large a task as might be thought, despite the fact that he would speak for the better part of an hour. In general, what he would say here was what he had been saying for more than two weeks now, en route from Virginia, through Tennessee, Georgia, and Alabama, and elsewhere already in Mississippi. His overnight task was mainly one of consolidating his various impromptu responses to serenades and calls for "remarks" from station platforms along the way, albeit with added emphasis on his home ties and the government's concern for the welfare of the people in what he called "the further West."

That was why he began by addressing his listeners as "those who, from the days of my childhood, have ever been the trusted objects of my affection," and adding: "Whatever fortunes I may have achieved in life have been gained as a representative of Mississippi, and before all I have labored for the advancement of her glory and honor. I now, for the first time in my career, find myself the representative of a wider circle of interest, but a circle of which the interests of Mississippi are still embraced. . . . For, although in the discharge of my duties as President of the Confederate States I had determined to make no distinction between the various parts of the country — to know no separate state — yet my heart has always beat more warmly for Mississippi, and I have looked on Mississippi soldiers with a pride and emotion such as no others inspired."

Flanked on the rostrum by Governor Pettus and Senator Phelan, he waited for the polite applause to subside, then launched at once into an excoriation of the northern government: not only its leaders but also its followers, in and out of the armies of invasion.

"I was among those who, from the beginning, predicted war . . . not because our right to secede and form a government of our own was not indisputable and clearly defined in the spirit of that declaration which rests the right to govern on the consent of the governed, but because I saw that the wickedness of the North would precipitate a war upon us. Those who supposed that the exercise of this right of separation could not produce war have had cause to be convinced that they had credited their recent associates of the North with a moderation, a sagacity, a morality they did not possess. You have been involved in a war waged for the gratification of the lust of power and aggrandizement, for your conquest and your subjugation, with a malignant ferocity and with a disregard and a contempt of the usages of civilization entirely unequaled in history. Such, I have ever warned you, were the characteristics of the northern people. . . . After what has happened during the last two years, my only wonder is that we consented to live for so long a time in association with such miscreants and have loved so much a government rotten to the core. Were it ever to be proposed again to enter into a Union with such a people, I could no more consent to do it than to trust myself in a den of thieves. . . . There is indeed a difference between the two peoples. Let no man hug the delusion that there can be renewed association between them. Our enemies are a traditionless and homeless race. From the time of Cromwell to the present moment they have been disturbers of the peace of the world. Gathered together by Cromwell from the bogs and fens of the north of Ireland and England, they commenced by disturbing the peace of their own country; they disturbed Holland, to which they fled; and they disturbed England on their return. They persecuted Catholics in England, and they hung Quakers and witches in America."

He spoke next of the conscription act, defending it against its critics; reviewed the recent successes of Confederate arms, sometimes against odds that had amounted to four to one; recommended local provision for the families of soldiers in the field; urged upon the legislators "the necessity of harmony" between the national government and the governments of the states; then returned to a bitter expression of his views as to the contrast between the two embattled peoples.

"The issue before us is one of no ordinary character. We are not engaged in a conflict for conquest, or for aggrandizement, or for the settlement of a point of international law. The question for you to decide is, Will you be slaves or will you be independent? Will you transmit to your children the freedom and equality which your fathers transmitted to you, or will you bow down in adoration before an idol baser than ever was worshipped by Eastern idolators? Nothing more is necessary than the mere statement of this issue. Whatever may be the personal sacrifices involved, I am confident that you will not shrink from them whenever the question comes before you. Those men who now assail us, who have been associated with us in a common Union, who have inherited a government which they claim to be the best the world ever saw — these men, when left to themselves, have shown that they are incapable of preserving their own personal liberty. They have destroyed the freedom of the press; they have seized upon and imprisoned members of state legislatures and of municipal councils, who were suspected of sympathy with the South; men have been carried off into captivity in distant states without indictment, without a knowledge of the accusations brought against them, in utter defiance of all rights guaranteed by the institutions under which they live. These people, when separated from the South and left entirely to themselves, have in six months demonstrated their utter incapacity for self-government. And yet these are the people who claim to be your masters. These are the people who have determined to divide out the South among their Federal troops. Mississippi they have devoted to the direst vengeance of all. 'But vengeance is the Lord's,' and beneath His banner you will meet and hurl back these worse than vandal hordes."

Having attempted thus to breathe heat into what Senator Phelan had called "a cold pile of damp ashes," Davis spoke of final success as certain. "Our people have only to be true to themselves to behold the Confederate flag among the recognized nations of the earth. The question is only one of time. It may be remote, but it may be nearer than many people suppose. It is not possible that a war of the dimensions that this one has assumed, of proportions so gigantic, can be very long protracted. The combatants must soon be exhausted. But it is impossible, with a cause like ours, that we can be the first to cry, 'Hold, enough.' " He spoke of valor and determination, of his pride in the southern fighting man, and assured his listeners that the Confederacy could accomplish its own salvation. This last led him into a statement unlike any he had made before:

"In the course of this war our eyes have often been turned abroad. We have expected sometimes recognition, and sometimes intervention, at the hands of foreign nations; and we had a right to expect it. Never before in the history of the world have a people so long a time maintained their ground, and shown themselves capable of maintaining their national existence, without securing the recognition of commercial nations. I know not why this has been so, but this I say: 'Put not your trust in princes,' and rest not your hopes on foreign nations. This war is ours; we must fight it out ourselves. And I feel some pride in knowing that, so far, we have done it without the good will of anybody."

When the applause that echoed this had died away he defined what he believed to be the "two prominent objects in the program of the enemy. One is to get possession of the Mississippi River, and to open it to navigation, in order to appease the clamors of the [Northwest] and to utilize the capture of New Orleans, which has thus far rendered them no service. The other is to seize upon the capital of the Confederacy, and hold this but as proof that the Confederacy has no existence." The fourth full-scale attempt to accomplish the latter object had just been frustrated by Lee at Fredericksburg, he informed the legislature, "and I believe that, under God and by the valor of our troops, the capital of the Confederacy will stand safe behind its wall of living breasts." As for the likelihood that the Unionists might accomplish the first-mentioned object, Davis admitted that this had caused him grave concern, and was in fact the reason for his present visit.

"This was the land of my affections," he declared. "Here were situated the little of worldly goods I possessed." He had, he repeated, "every confidence in the skill and energy of the officers in command. But when I received dispatches and heard rumors of alarm and trepidation and despondency among the people of Mississippi; when I heard, even, that people were fleeing to Texas in order to save themselves from the enemy; when I saw it stated by the enemy that they had handled other states with gloves, but Mississippi was to be handled without gloves — every impulse of my heart dragged me hither, in spite of duties which might have claimed my attention elsewhere. When I heard of the sufferings of my own people, of the danger of their subjugation by a ruthless foe, I felt that if Mississippi were destined for such a fate, I would wish to sleep in her soil." However, now that he had seen for himself the condition of the army and the people of his homeland, "I shall go away from you with a lighter heart . . . anxious, but hopeful."

In closing he spoke as a man who had kept a vigil through darkness into dawn, so that now he stood in sunlight. "I can, then, say with confidence that our condition is in every respect greatly improved over what it was last year. Our armies have been augmented; our troops have been instructed and disciplined. The articles necessary for the support of our troops and our people, and from which the enemy's blockade has cut us off, are being produced by the Confederacy. . . . Our people have learned to economize and are satisfied to wear homespun. I never see a woman dressed in homespun that I do not feel like taking off my hat to her, and although our women never lose their good looks, I cannot help thinking that they are improved by this garb. I never meet a man dressed in homespun but I feel like saluting him. I cannot avoid remarking with how much pleasure I have noticed the superior morality of our troops and the contrast which in this respect they present to the invader. On their valor and the assistance of God I confidently rely."

The applause that followed had begun to fade, when suddenly it swelled again, provoked and augmented by loud calls for "Johnston! Johnston!" At last the general rose and came forward, modestly acknowledging the cheers, which were redoubled. When they subsided he spoke with characteristic brevity and the self-effacement becoming to a soldier. "Fellow citizens," he said. "My only regret is that I have done so little to merit such a greeting. I promise you, however, that hereafter I shall be watchful, energetic, and indefatigable in your defense." That was all; but it was enough. According to one reporter, the applause that burst forth as he turned to resume his seat was "tremendous, uproarious, and prolonged." Apparently the general was more popular than the Chief Executive, even in the latter's own home state.

Despite this evidence of enthusiastic support from the civilians of the region, now that he had completed his military inspection Johnston was more dissatisfied than ever with the task which had been thrust into his hands. His command, he told Davis as soon as they were alone, was "a nominal one merely, and useless. . . . The great distance between the Armies of Mississippi and Tennessee, and the fact that they had different objects and adversaries, made it impossible to combine their action." The only use he saw for his talents, he continued in a subsequent account of the interview, was as a substitute commander of one of the armies, "which, as each had its own general, was not intended or desirable." In short, he told the President, he asked to be excused from serving in a capacity "so little to my taste."

Davis replied that distance was precisely the factor which had caused Johnston to be sent here. However far apart the two armies were, both were certainly too far from Richmond for effective control to be exercised from there; someone with higher authority than the two commanders should be at hand to co-ordinate their efforts and "transfer troops from one army to another in an emergency." Unpersuaded, still perturbed, the general continued to protest that, each being already "too weak for its object," neither army "could be drawn upon to strengthen the other," and with so much distance between the two, even "temporary transfers" were "impracticable." In point of fact, he could see nothing but ultimate disaster resulting from so unorthodox an arrangement. Once more Davis disagreed. Johnston was not only here; he was *needed* here. He must do the best he could. Or as the general put it, his "objections were disregarded."

On this discordant note the two men parted, Johnston to establish a new headquarters in the Mississippi capital and Davis to visit his eldest brother Joseph at his new plantation near Bolton, on the railroad west of Jackson. Their previous holdings on Davis Bend, just below Vicksburg — Joseph's, called The Hurricane, and his own, called Brierfield — had been overrun and sacked by Butler's men during their abortive upriver thrust, made in conjunction with Farragut's fleet the previous summer: which, incidentally, was why Davis had used the past tense in reference to "the little of worldly goods I possessed," and which, in part, was also why he referred to the Federals as "worse than vandal hordes."

In the course of his two-day visit with his septuagenarian brother, good news reached him on December 27 which seemed to indicate that Johnston's unwelcome burden already had been made a good deal lighter than he had protested it to be. Grant's army in North Mississippi was in full retreat; Van Dorn had broken loose in its immediate rear and burned its forward supply base at Holly Springs, capturing the garrison in the process, while Brigadier General Nathan Bedford Forrest, even farther in the northern commander's rear, was wrecking vital supply lines and creating general havoc all over West Tennessee. The following day, however, on the heels of these glad tidings, came word that Vicksburg itself was under assault by Major General William Tecumseh Sherman, who had come downriver from Memphis with the other half of Grant's command, escorted by Rear Admiral David Porter's ironclad fleet, and was storming the Chickasaw Bluffs. With the main body off opposing Grant, this was the worst of all possible news, short of the actual capture of the place; but on the 29th the President's anxiety was relieved and his spirits lifted by word that Sherman's repulse had been accomplished as effectively and as decisively, against even longer odds, as Burnside's had been at Fredericksburg two weeks before. What was more, the means by which it had been done went far toward sustaining Davis's military judgment, since the victory had been won in a large part by two brigades from the division he had recently detached, under protest, from the Army of Tennessee.

Vicksburg, then, had been delivered from the two-pronged pressure being applied from the north. If Bragg could do even partly as well in keeping Rosecrans out of Chattanooga, and if the garrison at Port Hudson could stop Banks and Farragut in their ascent of the Mississippi, the multiple threats to the western theater would have been smashed all round, or anyhow blunted for a season, despite the dire predictions made only that week by its over-all commander. One thing at any rate was certain. The President's long train ride back to Richmond would be made in a far more genial atmosphere, militarily speaking, than he had encountered at successive stops in the course of the outward journey.

He left Jackson on the last day of the year, and after speaking again that evening from a balcony of the Battle House in Mobile, received while retracing in reverse his route through Alabama and Georgia a double — indeed, a triple — further measure of good tidings. "God has granted us a happy New Year," Bragg wired from Murfreesboro. Rosecrans had ventured out of his intrenchments to attack the Army of Tennessee, which had then turned the tables with a dawn assault, jackknifing the Union right against the Union left. Not only was Chattanooga secure, but from the sound of the victorious commander's dispatch, Nashville itself might soon be recovered. "The enemy has yielded his strong position and is falling back," Bragg exulted. "We occupy whole field and shall follow him."

The pleasure Davis felt at this — augmented as it was by information that John Morgan had outdone himself in Kentucky on a Christmas raid, wrecking culverts, burning trestles, and capturing more than two thousand men, while Forrest and Van Dorn were returning safely from their separate and equally spectacular raids, the former after escaping a convergence designed for his destruction at Parker's Crossroads, deep inside the enemy lines — was raised another notch by word that a Federal reconnaissance force, sent upriver by Banks from Baton Rouge, had turned tail at the unexpected sight of the guns emplaced on Port Hudson's bluff and steamed back down without offering a challenge. And when this in turn was followed by still a third major item in the budget of good news, the presidential cup ran over. Major General John B. Magruder, recently arrived to take command of all the Confederates in Texas, had improvised a two-boat fleet of "cotton-clads" and had retaken Galveston in a New Year's predawn surprise attack, destroying one Yankee deep-water gunboat and forcing another to strike its colors. With the surrender of the army garrison in occupation of the island town, Texas was decontaminated. The only bluecoats still on her soil were Magruder's prisoners.

Leaving Mobile, Davis again visited Montgomery and Atlanta, but passing through the latter place he proceeded, not north to Chattanooga, but eastward to Augusta, where he spent the night of January 2. Next morning he entered South Carolina for the first time since the removal of the government to Richmond, back in May, and after a halt for a speech in Columbia, the capital, went on that night across the state line to Charlotte. At noon the following day he spoke in Raleigh, the North Carolina capital, then detoured south to Wilmington, the principal east coast port for blockade-runners, where he received the first really disturbing military news that had reached him since he left Virginia, nearly a month before. Instead of "following" the defeated Rosecrans, as he had said he would do, Bragg had waited a day before resuming the offensive, and then had been repulsed; whereupon, having been informed that the enemy had been reinforced — and bearing in mind, moreover, the Commander in Chief's recent advice: "Fight if you can, and fall back [if you must]" — he fell back thirty miles to a better defensive position on Duck River, just in front of Tullahoma and still protecting Chattanooga, another fifty-odd miles in his rear. As at Perryville, three months ago, he had won a battle and then retreated. Not that Murfreesboro was not still considered a victory; it was, at least in southern eyes. Only some of the luster had been lost. Davis, however, placing emphasis on the odds and the fact that Chattanooga was secure, counted it scarcely less a triumph than before. In response to a Wilmington serenade, tendered just after he received word that Bragg had fallen back, he spoke for a full hour from his hotel balcony. Employing what one hearer called "purity of diction" and a "fervid eloquence" to match the enthusiasm of the torchlight serenaders, he characterized recent events as a vindication of the valor of southern arms, and even went so far as to repeat the words he had spoken to a similar crowd from a Richmond balcony on the jubilant morrow of First Manassas: "Never be humble to the haughty. Never be haughty to the humble."

That was a Sunday. Next day, January 5, he covered the final leg of his long journey, returning to Richmond before dark. He was weary and he looked it, and with cause, for in twenty-five days he had traveled better than twenty-five hundred miles and had made no less than twenty-five public addresses, including some that had lasted more than an hour. However, his elation overmatched his weariness, and this too was with cause. He knew that he had done much to restore civilian morale by appearing before the disaffected people, and militarily the gains had been even greater. Though mostly they had been fought

against odds that should have been oppressive, if not completely paralyz-
ing, of the several major actions which had occurred during his absence
from the capital or on the eve of his departure — Prairie Grove and
Hartsville, Fredericksburg and Goldsboro, Holly Springs and Chickasaw Bluffs, Galveston and Murfreesboro — all were resounding victories except the first and possibly the last. Taken in conjunction with
the spectacular Christmas forays of Morgan and Forrest, the torpedoing
of the *Cairo* up the Yazoo River, and Grant's enforced retreat in North
Mississippi, these latest additions to the record not only sustained the
reputation Confederate arms had gained on many a field during the year
just passed into history; they also augured well for a future which only
lately had seemed dark. Defensively speaking, indeed, the record could
scarcely have been improved. Of the three objectives the Federals had
set for themselves, announcing them plainly to all the world by moving
simultaneously against them as the year drew to a close, Vicksburg had
been disenthralled and Chattanooga remained as secure as Richmond.

Davis himself had done as much as any man, and a good deal
more than most, to bring about the result that not a single armed enemy
soldier now stood within fifty air-line miles of any one of these three
vital cities. It was therefore a grateful, if weary, President who was met
by his wife and their four children on the steps of the White House, late
that Monday afternoon of the first week of the third calendar year of
this second American war for independence.

✗ 2 ✗

Of all these various battles and engagements, fought in all these various
places, Fredericksburg, the nearest to the national capital, was the largest — in numbers engaged, if not in bloodshed — as well as the grandest
as a spectacle, in which respect it equaled, if indeed it did not outdo, any
other major conflict of the war. Staged as it was, with a curtain of fog
that lifted, under the influence of a genial sun, upon a sort of natural
amphitheater referred to by one of the 200,000 participants, a native of
the site, as "a champaign tract inclosed by hills," it quite fulfilled the
volunteers' early-abandoned notion of combat as a picture-book affair.
What was more, the setting had been historical long before the armies
met there to add a bloody chapter to a past that had been peaceful up to
now. John Paul Jones had lived as a boy in the old colonial town that
gave its name and sacrificed the contents of its houses to the battle. Hugh
Mercer's apothecary shop and James Monroe's law office were two
among the many points of interest normally apt to be pointed out to
strangers by the four thousand inhabitants, most of whom had lately
been evacuated, however, by order of the commander of the army
whose looters would presently take the place apart and whose corpses

would find shallow graves on its unwarlike lawns and in its gardens. Here the widowed Mary Washington had lived, and it was here or near here that her son was reported to have thrown a Spanish silver dollar across the Rappahannock. During the battle itself, from one of the dominant hills where he established his forward command post, R. E. Lee would peer through rifts in the swirling gunsmoke in an attempt to spot in the yard of Chatham, a mansion on the heights beyond the river, the old tree beneath whose branches he had courted Mary Custis, granddaughter of the woman who later married the dollar-flinging George and thus became the nation's first first lady.

Yet it was Burnside, not Lee, who had chosen the setting for the impending carnage. Appointed to succeed his friend McClellan because of that general's apparent lack of aggressiveness after the Battle of Antietam, he had shifted the Army of the Potomac eastward to this point where the Rappahannock, attaining its head of navigation, swerved suddenly south to lave the doorsteps of the town on its right bank. Washington lay fifty miles behind him; Richmond, his goal, lay fifty miles ahead. Mindful of the President's admonition that his plan for eluding Lee in order to descend on the southern capital would succeed "if you move very rapidly, otherwise not," he had indeed moved rapidly; but, as it turned out, he had moved to no avail. Though he had successfully given Lee the slip, the pontoons he had requisitioned in advance from Harpers Ferry, altogether necessary if he was to cross the river, did not reach the Fredericksburg area until his army had been massed in jump-off positions for more than a week; by which time, to his confoundment, Lee had the opposite ridges bristling with guns that were trained on the prospective bridge sites. Burnside was so profoundly distressed by this turn of events that he spent two more weeks looking down on the town from the left-bank heights, with something of the intentness and singularity of purpose which he had displayed, back in September at Antietam, looking down at the little triple-arched bridge that ever afterwards bore his name as indelibly as if the intensity of his gaze had etched it deep into the stone. Meanwhile, by way of increasing his chagrin as Lee's butternut veterans clustered thick and thicker on the hills across the way, it was becoming increasingly apparent, not only to the northern commander but also to his men, that what had begun as a sprint for Richmond had landed him and them in coffin corner.

He had troubles enough, in all conscience, but at least they were not of the kind that proceeded from any shortage of troops. Here opposite Fredericksburg, ready to execute his orders as soon as he could decide what those orders were going to be, Burnside had 121,402 effectives in his six corps of three divisions each. Organized into three Grand Divisions of two corps each, these eighteen divisions were supported by 312 pieces of artillery. Nor was that all. Marching on Dumfries, twenty miles to the north, were two more corps with an effective strength of 27,724 soldiers and 97 guns. In addition to this field force of nearly 150,000 men, supported by more than 400 guns, another 52,000 in the Washington defenses and along the upper Potomac were also included in his nominal command; so that his total "present for duty" during this second week of December — at any rate the first part of it, before the butchering began — was something over 200,000 of all arms. He did not know the exact strength of the rebels waiting for him beyond the town and at other undetermined positions downriver, but he estimated their strength at just over 80,000 men.

In this — unlike McClellan, who habitually doubled and sometimes even tripled an enemy force by estimation — he was not far off. Lee had nine divisions organized into two corps of about 35,000 each, which, together with some 8000 cavalry and artillery, gave him a total of 78,511 effectives, supported by 275 guns. He had, then, not quite two thirds as many troops in the immediate vicinity as his opponent had. By ordinary, as he had lately told the Secretary of War, he thought it preferable, considering the disparity of force, "to attempt to baffle [the enemy's] designs by maneuvering rather than to resist his advance by main force." However, he found his present position so advantageous — naturally strong, though not so formidable in appearance as to rule out the possibility of an attempted assault — that he was determined to hold his ground, despite the odds, in the belief that the present situation contained the seeds of another full-scale Federal disaster.

Except for two detached brigades of cavalry, his whole army was at hand. So far, though, he had effected the concentration of only one corps, leaving the other spread out downstream to guard the crossings all the way to Port Royal, twenty miles below. The first corps, five divisions under Lieutenant General James Longstreet — "Old Peter," his men called him, adopting his West Point nickname; Lee had lately dubbed him "my old warhorse" — was in position on the slopes and crest of a seven-mile-long range of hills overlooking the mile-wide "champaign tract" that gave down upon the town and the river, its flanks protected right and left by Massaponax Creek and the southward bend of the Rappahannock. Forbidding in appearance, the position was even more formidable in fact; for the range of hills — in effect, a broken ridge — was mostly wooded, affording concealment for the infantry, and the batteries had been sited with such care that when Longstreet suggested the need for another gun at a critical point, the artillery commander replied: "General, we cover that ground now so well that we comb it as with a fine-tooth comb. A chicken could not live on that field when we open on it."

The other corps commander, Lieutenant General Thomas Jonathan Jackson — "Old Jack" to his men, redoubtable "Stonewall" to the world at large — had three of his four divisions posted at eight-mile intervals downstream, one on the south bank of Massaponax Creek, one at Skinker's Neck, and one near Port Royal, while the fourth was held at Guiney Station, on the Richmond, Fredericksburg & Potomac Railroad, eight miles in rear of Longstreet's right at Hamilton's Crossing. Despite the possibility that Burnside might swamp Longstreet with a sudden assault, outnumbering him no less that three-to-one, Lee accepted the risk of keeping the second corps widely scattered in order to be able to challenge the Union advance at the very outset, whenever and wherever it began. Jackson, on the other hand, would have preferred to fight on the line of the North Anna, a less formidable stream thirty miles nearer Richmond, rather than here on the Rappahannock, which he believed would be an effective barrier to pursuit of the beaten Yankees when they retreated, as he was sure they would do, under cover of their superior artillery posted on the dominant left-bank heights. "We will whip the enemy, but gain no fruits of victory," he predicted.

In point of fact, whatever validity Jackson might have as a prophet, Lee not only accepted the risk of a sudden, all-out attack on Longstreet; he actually preferred it. Though he expected the crossing to be attempted at some point downriver, in which case he intended to challenge it at the water's edge, it was his fervent hope that Burnside could be persuaded — or, best of all, would persuade himself — to make one here. In that case, Lee did not intend to contest the crossing itself with any considerable force. The serious challenge would come later, when the enemy came at him across that open, gently undulating plain. He had confidence that Old Peter, securely intrenched along the ridge, his guns already laid and carefully ranged on check points, could absorb the shock until the two closest of Stonewall's divisions could be summoned.

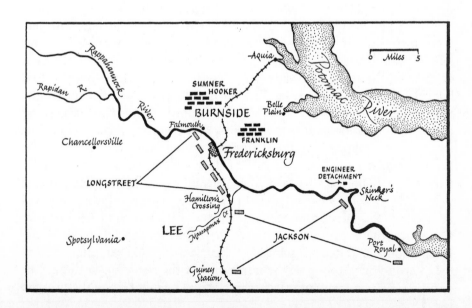

Their arrival would give the Confederate infantry the unaccustomed numerical wealth of six men to every yard of their seven-mile line: which Lee believed would be enough, not only to repulse the Federals, but also to enable the graybacks to launch a savage counterstroke, in the style of Second Manassas, that would drive the bluecoats in a panicky mass and pen them for slaughter against the unfordable river, too thickly clustered for escape across their pontoon bridges and too closely inter-mingled with his own charging troops for the Union artillery to attempt a bombardment from the opposite heights. It was unlikely that Burnside would thus expose his army to the Cannae so many Southerners believed was overdue. It was, indeed, almost too much to hope for. But Lee did hope for it. He hoped for it intensely.

Burnside, too, was weighing these possibilities, and it seemed to him also that the situation was heavy with the potentials of disaster: much more so, in fact, than it had been before he shifted his army east-ward in November from the scene of Pope's late-August rout. Though so far he had escaped direct connection with a military fiasco, he had not been unacquainted with sudden blows of adversity in the years before the war. Once as a newly commissioned lieutenant on his way to the Mexican War he had lost his stake to a gambler on a Mississippi steamboat, and again in the mid-50's he had failed to get a government contract for the manufacture of a breech-loading rifle he had invented and put his cash in after leaving the army to devote full time to its pro-motion, which left him so broke that he had to sell his sword and uni-forms for money to live on until his friend McClellan gave him a job with the land office of a railroad, where he prospered. Between these two financial upsets, he had received his worst personal shock when a Kentucky girl, whom he had wooed and finally persuaded to accom-pany him to the altar, responded to the minister's final ceremonial ques-tion with an abrupt, emphatic "No!" Hard as they had been to take, these three among several lesser setbacks had really hurt no one but himself, nor had they seriously affected the thirty-eight-year-old gen-eral's basically sunny disposition. But now that he had the lives of two hundred thousand men dependent on his abilities, not to mention the possible outcome of a war in which his country claimed to be fighting for survival, he did not face the likelihood of failure with such equanim-ity as he had shown in those previous trying situations. Formerly a hearty man, whose distinctive ruff of dark brown whiskers described a flamboyant double parabola below a generous, wide-nostriled nose, a pair of alert, dark-socketed eyes, and a pale expanse of skin that ex-tended all the way back to the crown of his head, he had be-come increasingly morose and fretful here on the high left bank of the Rappahannock. "I deem it my duty," he had advised his superiors during the interim which followed the nonarrival of the pontoons at the climax of his rapid cross-country march, "to say that I cannot make the promise of probable success with the faith that I did when I supposed that all the parts of the plan would be carried out."

This was putting it rather mildly. Yet, notwithstanding his qualms, he had evolved a design which he believed would work by virtue of its daring. His balloons were up, despite the blustery weather, and the observers reported heavy concentrations of rebels far downstream. He had intended to throw his bridges across the river at Skinker's Neck, ten miles beyond Lee's immediate right, then march directly on the railroad in the southern army's rear, thus forcing its retreat to protect its supply line. However, the balloon reports convinced him that Lee had divined his purpose, and this — plus the difficulty of concealing his preparations in that quarter, which led him to suspect that he would be doing nothing more than side-stepping into another stalemate — caused him to shift the intended attack back to the vicinity of Fredericksburg itself, where he could use the town to mask the crossing. It was a bold decision, made in the belief that, of all possible moves, this was the one his opponent would be least likely to suspect until it was already in execution: which, as he saw it from the Confederate point of view, would be too late. The troops below were Jackson's, the renowned "foot cavalry" of the Army of Northern Virginia, but a good part of them were as much as twenty miles away. By the time they arrived, if all went as Burnside intended, there would be no other half of their army for them to support; he would have crushed it, and they would find that what they had been hastening toward was slaughter or surrender.

Accordingly, early on December 9, a warning order went out for Grand Division commanders to report to army headquarters at noon, by which time they were to have alerted their troops, supplied each man with sixty rounds of ammunition, and begun the issue of three days' cooked rations. They would have the rest of today to get ready, he told them, and all of tomorrow. Then, in the predawn darkness of Thursday, December 11, the engineers would throw the six bridges by which the infantry and cavalry would cross for the attack, followed at once by such artillery as had been assigned to furnish close-up support. The crossing would be made in two general areas, one directly behind the town and the other just below it, with three bridges at each affording passage for the left and right Grand Divisions, commanded respectively by Major Generals William B. Franklin and Edwin V. Sumner. The center Grand Division, under Major General Joseph Hooker, would lend weight to the assault by detaching two of its divisions to Franklin and the other four to Sumner, giving them each a total of approximately 60,000 men, including cavalry and support artillery. Burnside's intention — not unlike McClellan's at Antietam, except that the flanks were reversed — was for Franklin's column to attack and carry the lower end of the ridge on which the Confederates were intrenched, then wheel and sweep northward along it while the enemy was being held in place by attacks delivered simultaneously by Sumner on the right. It was simple enough, as all such designs for destruction were meant to be. In fact, Burnside apparently considered it so readily comprehensible as to require little or no incidental explanation when the three generals reported to him at noon.

One additional subterfuge he would employ, but that was all. The engineers at Skinker's Neck, assisted by a regiment of Maine axmen, would be kept at work felling trees and laying a corduroy approach down to the riverbank at that point, as if for the passage of infantry with artillery support. The sound of chopping, along with the glow of fires at night, would help to delude the rebels in their expectation of a crossing there. However, even this was but a strengthening of the original subterfuge, the shifting of the main effort back upstream, on which the ruff-whiskered general based his belief, or at any rate his hope, that he would find Lee unprepared and paralyze him with his daring.

That was a good deal more than any of the northern commander's predecessors had been able to do, but Burnside's gloom had been dispelled; his confidence had risen now to zenith. As he phrased it in a dispatch telegraphed to Washington near midnight, outlining his attack plan and divulging his expectations, "I think now that the enemy will be more surprised by a crossing immediately in our front than in any other part of the river. The commanders of Grand Divisions coincide with me in this opinion, and I have accordingly ordered the movement. ... We hope to succeed."

Lee was indeed surprised, though not unpleasantly. Already a firm believer in the efficacy of prayer, he might have seen in this development a further confirmation of his faith. Nor was the surprise as complete as Burnside had intended. On Wednesday night, December 10, a woman crept down to the east bank of the Rappahannock and called across to the gray pickets that the Yankees had drawn a large issue of cooked rations — always a sign that action was at hand. Then at 4.45 next morning, two hours before dawn, two guns boom-boomed the prearranged signal that the enemy was attempting a crossing here in front of Fredericksburg. At once the Confederate bivouacs were astir with men turning out of their blankets to take the posts already assigned them along the ridge overlooking the plain that sloped eastward to the old colonial town, still invisible in the frosty darkness.

In it there was one brigade of Mississippi infantry, bled down to 1600 veterans under Brigadier General William Barksdale, a former congressman with long white hair and what one of his soldiers called "a thirst for battle glory." He had had his share of this in every major engagement since Manassas, but today was his best chance to slake that thirst; for Lee, being unwilling to subject the town to shelling, had left

to these few Deep South troops the task of contesting the crossing — not
with any intention of preventing it, even if that had been possible in the
face of all those guns on the dominant heights, but merely to make it as
costly to the Federals as he could. Barksdale received the assignment
gladly, posting most of his men in stout brick houses whose rear walls,
looking out upon the river, they loopholed so as to draw their beads
with a minimum of distraction in the form of return fire from the
men they would be dropping when the time came. Shortly after midnight, hearing sounds of preparation across the way — the muffled tread
of soldiers on the march, the occasional whinny of a horse or bray of
a mule, the clank of trace-chains, and at last the ponderous rumble of
what he took to be pontoons being brought down from the heights
— he knew the time was very much at hand. After sending word of this
to his superiors, he saw to it that the few remaining civilians, mostly
women and children, with a sprinkling of old men, either hastened
away to the safety of the hills or else took refuge in their cellars.

He was in no hurry to open fire, preferring not to waste ammunition in the darkness. Long before daylight, however, his men could
hear the Federal engineers at work: low-voiced commands, the clatter
of lumber, and at intervals the loud crack of half-inch skim ice as another pontoon was launched. This last drew closer with every repetition
as the bridge was extended, unit by six-foot unit, across the intervening
four hundred feet of water. At last, judging by the sound that the pontoniers had reached midstream, the waiting riflemen opened fire. They
aimed necessarily by ear, but the result was satisfactory. After the first
yelp of pain there was the miniature thunder of boots on planks, diminishing as the runners cleared the bridge; then silence, broken presently by the boom-boom of the two guns passing the word along the
ridge that the Yanks were coming.

Soon they returned to the bridge-end, working as quietly as
possible since every sound, including even the squeak of a bolt, was
echoed by the crack of rifles from the western bank. It was perilous
work, but it was nothing compared to the trouble brought by a misty
dawn and a rising sun that began to burn the fog away, exposing the
workers to aimed shots from marksmen whose skill was practically
superfluous at a range of two hundred feet. A pattern was quickly established. The pontoniers would rush out onto the bridge, take up their
tools, and work feverishly until the fire grew too hot; whereupon they
would drop their tools and run the gauntlet back to bank. Then, as
they got up their nerve again, their officers would lead or chevy them
back onto the bridge, where the performance would be repeated. This
went on for hours, to the high delight of the Mississippians, who jeered
and hooted as they shot and waited, then shot and waited to shoot some
more.

By 10 o'clock the northern commander's patience had run out.

The movement was already hours off schedule; Longstreet's signal guns had announced Lee's alertness, and Jackson's lean marchers might well be on the way by now. Rifle fire having proved ineffective against the snipers behind the brick walls of the houses along the riverbank, Burnside ordered his chief of artillery, Brigadier General Henry Hunt, to open fire with the 147 heavy-caliber guns posted on Stafford Heights, frowning down on the old town a hundred feet below. The response was immediate and uproarious, and it lasted for more than an hour, Hunt having instructed his gun crews to maintain a rate of fire of one shot every two minutes. Seventy-odd solid shot and shells a minute were thrown until 5000 had been fired. During all that time, a correspondent wrote, "the earth shook beneath the terrific explosions of the shells, which went howling over the river, crashing into houses, battering down walls, splintering doors, ripping up floors."

As a spectacle of modern war it was a great success, and it was also quite successful against the town. It wrecked houses, setting several afire; it tore up cobblestones; it shook the very hills the armies stood on. But it did not seem to dampen the spirits or influence the marksmanship of the Mississippians, who rose from the rubble and dropped more of the pontoniers, driving them again from the work they had returned to during the lull that followed the bombardment. When Barksdale sent a message asking whether he should have his men put out the fires, Longstreet replied: "You have enough to do to watch the Yankees." Back at Lee's observation post, the sight of what the Union guns had done to the Old Dominion town so riled the southern commander that he broke out wrathfully against the cannoneers and the officers who had given them orders to open fire. "Those people delight to destroy the weak and those who can make no defense," he said hotly. "It just suits them!" However, when he sent to inquire after the welfare of Barksdale's men and to see if there was anything they wanted, that general sent back word that he had everything he needed. But he added, "Tell General Lee that if he wants a bridge of dead Yankees, I can furnish him with one."

It was well past noon by now. Hunt, admitting that his guns could never dislodge the rebels, suggested that infantry use the pontoons as assault boats in order to get across the river and pry the snipers out of the rubble with bayonets. A Michigan regiment drew the duty, supported by two others from Massachusetts, and did it smartly, establishing a bridgehead in short order. During the street fighting, which used up what was left of daylight, the bridges were laid and other regiments came to their support. Barksdale's thirst was still unslaked, however. When he received permission to withdraw, he declined and kept on fighting, house to house, until past sundown. Not till dusk had fallen was he willing to call it a day, and even then he had trouble persuading some of his men to agree. This was particularly difficult in the case of the rear-guard company, whose commander somehow discovered in the course of the engagement that the Federal advance was being led by a Massachusetts company whose commander had been his classmate at Harvard. The Mississippi lieutenant called a halt and faced his men about, determined to whip his blue-clad friend then and there, until his colonel had him placed in arrest in order to continue the withdrawal. It was 7 o'clock by the time the last of Barksdale's veterans crossed the plain to join their admiring comrades on the ridge, leaving Fredericksburg to the bluecoats they had been fighting for fifteen hours.

Not until well after dark did Lee order Jackson to bring his two nearest divisions to Longstreet's support, and not even then did he summon the other two from Port Royal and Skinker's Neck, where the Maine axmen on the opposite bank had kindled campfires around which they were resting from their daylong chopping. Pleased though he was with the day's work — his eyes had lighted up at each report that a new attempt to extend the bridge had been defeated — Lee simply could not believe that his hopes had been so completely fulfilled that the enemy was concentrating everything for an attack against the ridge where his guns had been laid for weeks now and his infantry was disposed at ease in overlapping lines of battle.

Across the way, on Stafford Heights, Burnside too was pleased. Despite delays that had been maddening, he had his six bridges down at last (the three lower ones, below the town, had been down since noon, but he had hesitated to use them so long as the Fredericksburg force of unknown strength was in position on their flank) and his army was assembled for the crossing. Besides, he had received balloon reports at sundown informing him that the other half of the rebel army was still in its former positions down the river, with no signs of preparation for a move in this direction. The delay, it seemed, had cost him nothing more than some nervous twinges and a few expendable combat engineers; Lee might be caught napping yet. So confidently did the ruff-whiskered general feel next morning, when observers reported Jackson's troops still in position at Skinker's Neck and Port Royal, twenty miles away, that he decided he could afford to spend another day assembling his army on the west bank of the Rappahannock for the assault across the empty plain and against the rebel ridge.

Fog shrouded the entire valley while the long blue lines of men came steeply down to the riverbank and broke step as they crossed the swaying bridges. On the heights above, the Union guns fired blindly over their heads, in case the Confederates attempted to challenge the crossing. They did not. At noon, however, the fog lifted; Lee, with a close-up view of the bluecoats massed in their thousands beyond the plain, saw at once that this was no feint, but a major effort. He sent for Jackson's other two divisions, instructing them to begin their long marches immediately in order to arrive in time for the battle, which he now saw would be fought tomorrow. Beyond that he could do no more.

Though he was outnumbered worse than three-to-two, and knew it, he was in good spirits as he rode on a sundown inspection of his lines. Returning to headquarters, he seemed pleased that the Federals on the flat were about to charge him. "I shall try to do them all the damage in our power when they move forward," he said.

Down in the town, meanwhile, the Union soldiers had been having themselves a field day. Cavalrymen ripped the strings from grand pianos to make feed troughs for their horses, while others cavorted amid the rubble in women's lace-trimmed underwear and crinoline gowns snatched from closets and bureau drawers. Scarcely a house escaped pillage. Family portraits were slashed with bayonets; pier glass mirrors were shattered with musket butts; barrels of flour and molasses were dumped together on deep-piled rugs. It was all a lot of fun, especially for the more fortunate ones who found bottles of rare old madeira in the cellars. Gradually, though, the excitement paled and the looters began to speculate as to why the rebs had made no attempt to challenge the crossing today, not even with their artillery. Some guessed it was because they had no ammunition to spare, others that they were afraid of retaliation by "our siege guns." One man had a psychological theory: "General Lee thinks he will have a big thing on us about the bombardment of this town. He proposes to rouse the indignation of the civilized world, as they call it. You'll see he won't throw a shell into it. He is playing for the sympathies of Europe." Still another, a veteran private, had a different idea. "Shit," he said. "They *want* us to get in. Getting out won't be quite so smart and easy. You'll see."

★　★　★

They would see; but not just yet. Day broke on a fog so thick that the sun, which rose at 7.17 beyond the Union left, could not pierce it, but rather gave an eerie, luminous quality to the mist that swathed the ridge where Lee's reunited army awaited the challenge foretold by sounds of preparation on the invisible plain below; "an indistinct murmur," one listener called it, "like the distant hum of myriads of bees."

Longstreet held the Confederate left. Four of his five divisions were on line, commanded north to south by Major Generals Richard Anderson, Lafayette McLaws, George Pickett, and John Bell Hood; the fifth and smallest, a demi-division under Brigadier General Robert Ransom, was in reserve. Jackson, on the right, had posted Major General A. P. Hill's large division along his entire front, backed by a second line of two close-packed divisions under Brigadier Generals William Taliaferro and Jubal Early, which in turn was supported by Major General D. H. Hill's division, just arrived from Port Royal after an all-night march. Major General J. E. B. Stuart's cavalry guarded the flank, extending it southward from Hamilton's Crossing to Massaponax Creek. Since this end of the ridge was considerably lower than the other, and consequently much less easy to defend, Lee had assigned five miles of the line to Longstreet and only two to Jackson, who thus had no less than ten men to every yard of front and could distribute them in depth. It was no wonder, then, that he replied this morning to a staff officer's expression of qualms about the enemy strength and the lowness of the ridge in this direction: "Major, my men have sometimes failed to take a position, but to defend one, never! I am glad the Yankees are coming."

Lee and Longstreet stood on an eminence known thereafter as Lee's Hill because that general had set up his forward command post here, about midway of Longstreet's line, with an excellent view — or at any rate what would be an excellent view, once the curtain of fog had lifted — of the lines in both directions, including most of Jackson's line to the south, as well as of Fredericksburg and the snow-pocked plain where the blue host was massing under cover of their guns on Stafford Heights, preparing even now to give the lower ridge across the way a long-range pounding. Today as yesterday, however, the southern commander was in good spirits. Tall and comely — nothing less, indeed,

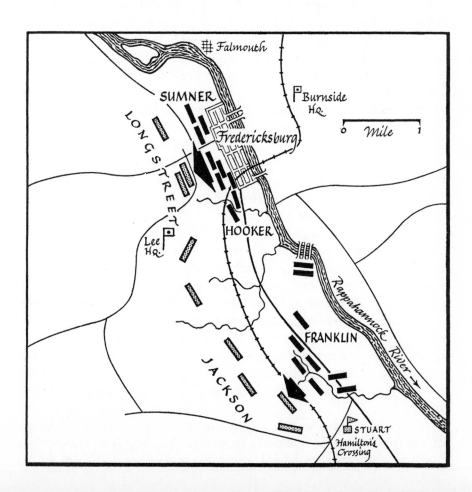

than "the handsomest man in Christendom," according to one who saw him there this morning — neatly dressed, as always, with only the three unwreathed stars on the collar of his thigh-length gray sack coat to show his rank, he gave no sign of nervousness or apprehension. Above the short-clipped iron-gray beard and beneath the medium brim of a sand-colored planter's hat, his quick brown eyes had a youthfulness which, together with the litheness of his figure and the deftness of his movements, disguised the fact that he would be fifty-six years old next month.

His companion seemed to share his confidence, if not his handsomeness of person, though he too was prepossessing of appearance. A burly, shaggy man, six feet tall, of Dutch extraction and just past forty-one, Longstreet gave above all an impression of solidity and dependability. His men's great fondness for him was based in part on their knowledge of his concern for their well-being, in and out of combat. Yesterday, for example, when some engineers protested to him that the gun crews were ruining their emplacements by digging them too deep, Old Peter would not agree to order them to stop. "If we only save the finger of a man, that's good enough," he told the engineers, and the cannoneers kept digging. Often phlegmatic, this morning he was in an expansive mood: especially after he and Lee were joined by the third-ranking member of the army triumvirate, who came riding up from the south. It was Jackson, but a Jackson quite unlike the Stonewall they had known of old. Gone were the mangy cadet cap and the homespun uniform worn threadbare since its purchase on the eve of the Valley Campaign, through the miasmic nightmare of the Seven Days, the suppression of the "miscreant Pope" at Cedar Mountain and Second Manassas, the invasion of Maryland and the hard fight at Sharpsburg. Instead he wore a new cap bound with gold braid, and more braid — "chicken guts," Confederate soldiers irreverently styled the stuff — looped on the cuffs and sleeves of a brand-new uniform, a recent gift from Jeb Stuart. Even his outsized boots were brightly polished. For all his finery, he looked as always older than his thirty-eight years. His pale blue eyes were stern, his thin-lipped mouth clamped forbiddingly behind the scraggly dark-brown beard; but this had not protected him from the jibes of his men, who greeted him with their accustomed rough affection as he rode among them. "Come here, boys!" they yelled. "Stonewall has drawed his bounty and bought hisself some new clothes." Others shook their heads in mock dismay at seeing him tricked out like some newly commissioned quartermaster lieutenant. "Old Jack will be afraid for his clothes," they said, doleful amid the catcalls, "and will not get down to work."

He had ridden all this way, exposing himself to all that raillery, for a purpose which he was quick to divulge. Turning aside Longstreet's banter, he muttered that the finery was "some doing of my friend Stuart,

I believe," and passed at once to the matter that had brought him here. He wanted permission to attack. If his men surged down the ridge and onto the plain before the fog had lifted, he explained, they would be hidden from the guns on Stafford Heights and could fling the startled bluecoats into the river. Lee shook his head. He preferred to have the superior enemy force worn down by repeated charges and repulses, in the style of Second Manassas, before he passed to the offensive. Stonewall had his answer. As he turned to leave, Longstreet began to bait him again. "General, do not all those multitudes of Federals frighten you?" Old Peter's humor was heavy-handed, but Jackson had no humor at all. "We shall see very soon whether I shall not frighten *them*," he said as he put one foot in the stirrup. But Longstreet kept at him. "Jackson, what are you going to do with all those people over there?" Stonewall mounted. "Sir, we will give them the bayonet," he said, and he turned his horse and rode away.

By 10 o'clock the fog had begun to thin. It drained downward, burned away by the sun, layer by upper layer, so that the valley seemed to empty after the manner of a tub when the plug is pulled. Gradually the town revealed itself: first the steeples of two churches and the courthouse, then the chimneys and rooftops, and finally the houses and gardens, set upon the checkerboard of streets. Dark lines of troops flowed steadily toward two clusters, one within the town, masked by the nearer buildings, the other two miles down the Richmond Stage Road, which ran parallel to the river and roughly bisected the mile-wide plain. Already the more adventurous Federal batteries had opened, arching their shells through sunlit rifts in the thinning mist, but the Confederates made no reply until 10.30 when Lee passed the word: "Test the ranges on the left." Longstreet's guns began to roar from Marye's Heights, the tall north end of the long ridge, directly opposite the center of the town, where the first of the two clusters of blue-clad men was thickening. All the fog was gone by now, replaced by brilliant sunlight. The drifting smoke made shifting patterns on the plain. High over Stafford Heights, where the long-range guns were adding their deeper voices to the chorus of the Union, two of Burnside's big yellow observation balloons bobbed and floated, the men in their swaying baskets looking down on war reduced to miniature.

First blood was drawn in a brief dramatic action staged in front of the Confederate right. Here the fog had rolled away so rapidly that the scene was exposed as if by the sudden lift of a curtain, showing a three-division Federal corps advancing westward in long lines so neatly dressed that watchers on the ridge could count the brigades and regiments — ten of the former, forty-six of the latter, plus eleven batteries of artillery — each with its attendant colors rippling in the sunlight. From Lee's Hill, the southern commander was surprised to see two horse-drawn guns, toy-sized in the distance, go twinkling out to the old stage road and go into position in the open, within easy range of the left flank of the 18,000 Federals, which was thrown into some disorder and came to a milling halt as the two guns began to slam their shots endwise into the blue ranks, toppling men like tenpins.

They had been brought into action by Stuart's chief of artillery, twenty-four-year-old Major John Pelham of Alabama, who in his haste to join the southern army had left West Point on the eve of graduation in '61. He had often done daring things, similar to this today, but never before with so large an audience to applaud him. As the men of both armies watched from the surrounding heights, he fired so rapidly that one general involved in the blue confusion estimated his strength at a full battery. Four Union batteries gave him their undivided attention, turning their two dozen guns against his two. One, a rifled Blakely, was soon disabled and had to be sent to the rear, but Pelham kept the other barking furiously, a 12-pounder brass Napoleon, and shifted his position each time the enemy gunners got his range. The handsome young major was in his glory, wearing bound about his cap, at the request of a British army observer, a necktie woven of red and blue, the colors of the Grenadier Guards. When Stuart sent word for him to retire, Pelham declined, though he had lost so many cannoneers by then that he himself was helping to serve the gun. "Tell the general I can hold my ground," he said. Three times the order came, but he obeyed only when his caissons were nearly empty. Back at Hamilton's Crossing, he returned the smoke-grimed necktie-souvenir to the English visitor, blushing with pleasure and embarrassment at the cheers. Lee on his hill took his glasses down, smiling as he exclaimed: "It is glorious to see such courage in one so young!"

While the Federals remained halted on the plain, recovering the alignment Pelham had disturbed, their artillery began to pound the lower ridge in earnest, probing the woods in an attempt to knock out Jackson's hidden batteries before the battle passed to the infantry. The Confederate gunners made no reply, being under orders not to disclose their positions until the enemy came within easy range. At last he did, and the graybacks got their revenge for the punishment they had had to accept in silence. When the advance came within 800 yards, all of Stonewall's guns cut loose at once. The blue flood stopped, flailed ragged along its forward edge, and then reversed its flow.

The Union guns resumed the argument, having spotted their targets by the smoke that boiled up through the trees, but the infantry battle now shifted northward to where the bluecoats had been massing under cover of the town. At 11.30 they emerged and began to surge across the plain toward Marye's Heights, less than half a mile away. A thirty-foot spillway, six feet deep, lay athwart their path, however, and the rebel gunners caught them close-packed as they funneled onto three bridges whose planks had been removed but whose stringers had been left in place, apparently to lure them across in single file. "Hi! Hi! Hi!" the Federals yelled as they pounded over, taking their losses in order to gain the cover of a slight roll or "dip" of ground that hid them from the guns on the heights beyond.

"It appeared to us there was no end of them," a waiting cannoneer observed. But Longstreet was not worried; he had a surprise in store for them. Along the base of Marye's Heights ran a road, flanked by stone walls four feet high, which Brigadier General T.R.R. Cobb had had his Georgians deepen, throwing the spoil over the townward wall, to add to its effectiveness as a breastwork and to hide it from the enemy. This was the advance position of the whole army, and as such it might be outflanked or enfiladed. However, when Cobb was given permission to fall back up the hill in case that happened, he replied grimly in the spirit of Barksdale and Pelham: "Well, if they wait for me to fall back, they will wait a long time."

Presently he got the chance to begin to prove his staunchness; for the Federals leaped to their feet in the swale and made a sudden rush, as if they intended to scale the heights whose base was only 400 yards away. High up the slope the guns crashed, darting tongues of flame, and the Georgians along the sunken road pulled trigger. It was as if the charging bluecoats had struck a trip wire. When the smoke of that single rifle volley rolled away, all that were left in front of the wall were writhing on the ground or scampering back to safety in the swale. After a wait, they rose and came forward again, deploying as they advanced. This time the reaction was less immediate, since they knew what to expect; but it was no different in the end. The guns on the slope and the rifles down along the wall broke into a clattering frenzy of smoke and flame, and more men were left writhing as others fell back off the blasted plain and into the swale. Again they rose. Again, incredibly, they charged. They came forward, one of them afterwards recalled, "as though they were breasting a storm of rain and sleet, their faces and bodies being only half turned to the storm, with their shoulders shrugged." Another observed that "everybody, from the smallest drummer boy on up, seemed to be shouting to the full extent of his capacity." Like the first and second, except that more men fell because it lasted longer, this third charge broke in blood and pain before a single man got within fifty yards of the wall. The survivors flowed back over the roll of earth and into the "dip," where reinforcements were nerving themselves for still a fourth attempt.

"They are massing very heavily and will break your line, I am afraid," Lee told Longstreet. But Old Peter did not believe it. He was ready for the whole Yankee nation, provided it would come at him from the direction this portion of it had done three times already, and he said so: "General, if you put every man now on the other side of the Potomac in that field to approach me over that same line, and give me plenty of ammunition, I will kill them all before they reach my line. Look to your right; you are in some danger there," he said. "But not on my line."

It was true; Lee's line was in considerable danger southward. While Sumner's men were charging the sunken road, repeatedly and headlong, taking their losses, Franklin was taking stock of the situation as Pelham's brass Napoleon and Jackson's masked batteries had left it when they disrupted his first and second advances. Both had been tentative, at best, but now he believed he knew what he had to deal with. However, as in Pleasant Valley preceding the battle on Antietam Creek, he was inclined to be circumspect: an inclination which had not been lessened here on the Rappahannock by Burnside's instructions that, once he was over the river "with a view to taking the heights," he was to be "governed by circumstances as to the extent of your movements." Further instructions had arrived this morning, warning him to keep his attack column "well supported and its line of retreat open." Accordingly, before going forward for the third time, he took care to protect the flank in Stuart's direction. The attack was delivered by the same corps, commanded by Major General John F. Reynolds, whose three divisions were under Major General George G. Meade and Brigadier Generals Abner Doubleday and John Gibbon. Doubleday was ordered to wheel left, guarding the bruised flank (sure enough, Pelham came out promptly and began to pound him) while the other two went forward in an attempt to storm the ridge. Gibbon, on the right, got as far as the railroad embankment, where he ran into murderous point-blank fire, was himself wounded, and had to be brought out on a stretcher. He was followed shortly by his men, who were not long in discovering that the Johnnies had drawn them into a trap.

That left Meade, whose division was the smallest of the three. Out of 60,000 soldiers available for the intended assault on the Confederate right, Franklin managed to get only these 4500 Pennsylvanians into slugging contact with the enemy, but they did what they could to make up in spirit for what they lacked in weight. Charging first to the railroad, then beyond it, they struck a boggy stretch of ground, about 500 yards in width, which A. P. Hill had left unmanned in the belief that it was impenetrable. It was not. Meade's troops slogged through it, burst upon and scattered a second-line brigade of startled rebels, and were still driving hard toward the accomplishment of Franklin's assignment — that is, to get astride the lower ridge and then sweep northward along it, dislodging men and guns as he went — when they themselves were struck in front and on both flanks by a horde of screaming graybacks.

These were Early's men, from over on the right. Told that Hill's line had been pierced, they came on the run, hooting as they passed the fugitives: "Here comes old Jubal! Let old Jubal straighten out that fence!" Then they struck. The Pennsylvanians were driven back through the boggy gap and out again across the open fields, where the pursuers stabbed vengefully at their rear and Confederate guns to the left and right tore viciously at their flanks. Unsupported, heavily outnumbered, thrown off balance by surprise, they paid dearly for their daring; more than a third of the men who had gone in did not come out again. There was no safety for the survivors until they regained the cover of their artillery, which promptly drove the pursuers back with severe losses and shifted without delay to the rebel batteries, blanketing them so accurately with shellbursts that the fire drew an indirect compliment from Pelham himself, who happened to be visiting this part of the line at the time. "Well, you men stand killing better than any I ever saw," he remarked as he watched the cannoneers being knocked about.

At any rate, the break had been repaired, the line restored. Lee on his hill had seen it all, the penetration and repulse on Jackson's front, coincident with the bloody disintegration of the third attack on Longstreet. The ground in front of both was carpeted blue with the torn bodies of men who had challenged unsuccessfully the integrity of his line. Beyond the river, Stafford Heights were ablaze with guns whose commanding elevation and heavier metal enabled them to rake the western ridge almost at will. Even now, one of them put a large-caliber shell into the earth at the southern commander's feet, but it did not explode. A British observer saw "antique courage" in Lee's manner as he turned to Longstreet, lowering his glasses after a long look at the blasted plain where still more Federals were massing to continue their assault over the mangled remains of comrades who had tried before and failed. "It is well that war is so terrible," the gray-bearded general said. "We should grow too fond of it."

If the assault was to be resumed after the comparative lull that settled over the field about 3.30, following the double failure at opposite ends of the line, it would have to be launched against that portion of the ridge where Longstreet's men were ranked four-deep in the sunken road, their rifles cocked and primed for firing at whatever came at them across the fields beyond their breast-high wall of stone and dirt. To the south, Franklin had shot his bolt with Meade's quick probe of the hole in Jackson's front: in reaction to which he was not unlike a man who has managed to salvage a good part of one hand after groping about in the dark and finding a bear trap. There might be other holes, for all he knew, but after that one costly venture the commander of the left Grand Division seemed less concerned about finding than he was about avoiding them. Whoever might deliver another attack, it was not going to be Franklin. That left Sumner and Hooker. Burnside sent them instructions to continue the assault with their right and center

Grand Divisions, in hopes that the Confederates along the ridge could be breached or budged or somehow thrown into confusion as a prelude to their downfall.

Sumner, a crusty veteran of forty-four years' service, nearly forty of which had been spent accomplishing the slow climb from second lieutenant to colonel, was altogether willing, despite his heavy losses up to now. So was Hooker, whose nickname was "Fighting Joe." Shortly before 4 o'clock, the men crouched in the swale caught sight of what they thought was their best chance to storm the ridge. A whole battalion of rebel artillery began a displacement from the slopes of Marye's Heights. Quickly the word passed down the Union line; men braced themselves for the order to charge. It came and they surged forward, followed this time by several batteries, which ventured out to within 300 yards of the fuming wall, adding the weight of their metal to the attack but losing cannoneers so fast that the guns could only be served slowly. As it turned out, this was worse than ever. The artillery displacement they had spotted was not the beginning of a retreat, as they had supposed, but a yielding of the position to a fresh battalion, which arrived with full caissons in time to aid in contesting this fourth assault. Down in the sunken road, Tom Cobb had been hit by a sharp-shooter firing from the upper story of a house on the edge of town; he had bled to death by now; but his men were still there, reinforced by several regiments of North Carolinians from Ransom's reserve division. Shoulder to shoulder along the wall, they loosed their volleys, then stepped back to reload while the rank behind stepped up to fire. So it went, through all four ranks, until the first had reloaded and taken its place along the wall, which flamed continuously under a mounting bank of smoke as if the defenders were armed with automatic weapons. This attack, like the three preceding it, broke in blood. The Federals fell back, leaving the stretch of open ground between the swale and a hundred yards of the wall thick-strewn with corpses and writhing men whose cries could be heard above the diminishing clatter of musketry.

While the carnage was being continued here ("Oh, great God!" a division commander groaned in anguish from his lookout post in the cupola of the courthouse. "See how our men, our poor fellows, are falling!") Jackson was burning to take the offensive against the inactive bluecoats at the other end of the line: so much so, indeed, that according to one observer "his countenance glowed, as from the glare of a great conflagration." If all those thousands of Federals on the plain could not be persuaded to approach the ridge, he ached to go down after them. "I want to move forward," he said impatiently; "to attack them — drive them into the river yonder," and as he spoke he threw out his arm, by way of lending emphasis to his words. The risk was great, he knew, for a repulse would expose his men to annihilation by the guns on the opposite heights. But at last, out of urgency, he devised a plan by which he hoped to nullify his prediction that the Confederates would "gain no fruits" from their victory. If the counterstroke were preceded by a bombardment, he believed, the enemy might be so stunned that the sudden charge across the plain might be made without undue sacrifice of life, and if it were launched just at sundown he could withdraw under cover of darkness in case it failed.

So conceived, it was so ordered. However, the almanac put sunset at 4.34; there was little time for preparation. Word was passed to the four divisions assigned to the attack, and as they got ready for the jump-off Stonewall's batteries went forward, out into the open, to begin their work of stunning or confusing the enemy. Instead, it was they who were stunned and confused, and in short order. Beyond the river, Stafford Heights seemed to buck and jump in flame and thunder as the guns on the crest redoubled their fire at the sight of these easy targets down below. Jackson quickly recalled his badly pounded artillerymen and canceled the attack, which he now saw would be shattered as soon as the infantry emerged from the woods. At that, the demonstration was not without its effect: especially on Franklin, who had already notified Burnside that "any movement to my front is impossible at present. . . . The truth is, my left is in danger of being turned. What hope is there of getting reinforcements across the river?" Of his eight divisions, only three had been employed offensively, and one whole corps of 24,000 men, the largest in the army, saw no action at all; yet he was asking after reinforcements. At the height of Jackson's abortive demonstration, orders came from Burnside for Franklin to take the offensive, but he declined. He was in grave danger here, he repeated. Besides, there was no time; the sun was down behind the western ridge.

Sunset did not slow the tempo of the fighting to the north, where a fifth major assault on Marye's Heights had been repulsed in much the same manner as all the others, though the officers in charge had attempted a somewhat different approach. Their instructions were for the men to veer northward when they left the swale and thus confront the sunken road from the right, which perhaps would enable them to lay down an enfilade as they gained the flank and bore down at an angle. But it did not work out that way. As the men went forward, attempting to bear off to the right, they encountered a marsh that forced them back to the left and a repetition of the direct approach to the stone wall, which seemed thus to draw them like a magnet. From behind it, all this while, the rebels — many of whom were shoeless, without overcoats or blankets to protect them from the penetrating mid-December chill — taunted the warmly clad Federals coming toward them in a tangle-footed huddle after their encounter with the bog: "Come on, blue belly! Bring them boots and blankets! Bring 'em hyar!" And they did bring them, up to within fifty yards of the flame-stitched wall at any rate. There the forward edge of the charge was frayed and broken, the survivors crawling or running to regain the protection of the swale, which by now they were convinced they never should have left.

Sumner had done his best, or worst but the carnage was by no means over. Hooker's men had crossed the river, under orders to continue the assault, and the commander of one of his divisions, Brigadier General Andrew Humphreys, believed he knew a way to get his troops up to and over the wall, so they could come to grips with the jeering scarecrows in the sunken road. While they were deploying in the dusk he rode among them, telling them not to fire while they were charging. It was obvious by now, he said, that firing did the rebels little damage behind their ready-made breastwork; it only served to slow the attack and expose the attackers to more of the rapid-fire volleys from beyond the wall. The object was to get there fast — much as a man might hurry across an open space in a shower of rain, intending to be as dry as possible when he reached the other side — then rely on the bayonet to do the work that would remain to be done when they got there.

They went forward in the twilight, stumbling over the human wreckage left by five previous charges. Prone men, wounded and unwounded, called out to them not to try it; some even caught at their legs as they passed, attempting to hold them back; but they ignored them and went on, beckoned by voices that mocked them from ahead, calling them blue-bellies and urging them to bring their boots and blankets within reach. Humphreys sat his horse amid the bullets, a slim veteran of aristocratic mien. He had left West Point in '31, two years behind R. E. Lee, and his record in the peacetime army had been a good one; yet his advancement since then, it was said, had been delayed because of suspicions aroused by his prewar friendship with Jefferson Davis. Now he was out to prove those suspicions false. As he watched he saw the stone wall become "a sheet of flame that enveloped the head and flanks of the column." Its formations unraveled by sudden attrition, the charge was brought to a stumbling halt about forty yards from the wall. For a moment the Federals hung there, beginning to return the galling fire; but it was useless, and they knew it. Despite the shouts and pleas of their officers — including Humphreys, who remained mounted yet incredibly went unhit — the men turned and stumbled back through the gathering darkness. Or anyhow the survivors did, having added a thousand casualties to the wreckage that cluttered the open slope, ghastly under the pinkish yellow flicker of muzzle-flashes still rippling back and forth along the crest of the stone wall.

"The fighting is about over," a Union signal officer reported at 6 o'clock from the heights across the way; "only an occasional gun is heard."

It was over, as he said, but not as the result of instructions from Burnside. Hooker was the one who finally called a halt to the carnage.

"Finding that I had lost as many men as my orders required me to lose," he later declared in his official report, "I suspended the attack."

Burnside himself took a much less gloomy view of the state of affairs when he crossed the river late that night for an inspection of the front. Unquestionably a great deal of blood had been shed — far more, in fact, than he would know until he received the final casualty returns — but he had little doubt that a continuation of today's work would break Lee's line tomorrow. At any rate he was determined to try it, and he sent out orders to that effect, alerting his front-line commanders. Recrossing the Rappahannock at 4 o'clock in the morning, he got off a wire to Washington: "I have just returned from the field. Our troops are all over the river. We hold the first ridge outside the town, and 3 miles below. We hope to carry the crest today."

★ ★ ★

Once more Lee had divined his opponent's purpose. "I expect the battle to be renewed at daylight," he wired Richmond, three hours after the final assault had failed, and this opinion was reinforced within another three hours by the capture, shortly before midnight, of a courier bearing orders to Burnside's front-line commanders for tomorrow's continuation of the attack. But Sunday's dawn, December 14, brought only the soup-thick fog of yesterday, without the familiar hum of preparation from down on the curtained plain. Indeed, even after the rising sun had burned away the mist, the only change apparent to the eye was in the lines along the western ridge. Expecting a turning movement, Lee had instructed his men to improve their fortifications in order to free all but a comparative handful for action on the flanks. So well had they plied their tools, these soldiers who six months ago had sneered at digging as cowardly work "unfit for a white man" and in derision had dubbed their new commander "the King of Spades," that Lee remarked with pleasure at the sight: "My army is as much stronger for these new intrenchments as if I had received reinforcements of 20,000 men."

No longer in need of prodding, or even suggestion, they kept digging. As the sun rose higher, so did the parapets. But the observers on Lee's Hill discerned no corresponding activity among the Federals on the plain, portions of whose forward edge were carpeted solid blue with the thick-fallen dead and wounded. The only sign of preparation was that the near ends of the east-west streets of Fredericksburg had been barricaded, as if in expectation of receiving, not delivering, an attack. The morning wore on. Noon came and went: then afternoon: and still no sign that the bluecoats were about to launch the assault that had been ordered in the dispatch captured the night before. As the shadows lengthened, Lee turned at last to Longstreet, who had been acquainted with the northern commander in the peacetime army. "General," he said, "I am losing faith in your friend General Burnside."

He was by no means alone in this, although the principal loss of faith in Old Peter's friend had occurred within the luckless commander's own ranks. Refreshed by a short sleep, and still convinced that he would break Lee's line by continuing yesterday's headlong tactics, Burnside had risen early that morning, only to be confronted by Sumner, who had been five years in the army before his present chief was born. He was known to be no quitter; in fact, so pronounced was his fondness for personal combat, Burnside had ordered the old man to remain at his left-bank headquarters yesterday, lest he get himself killed leading charges. Today, though, he was quite unlike himself in this respect.

"General," he said, obviously unstrung by all he had seen the day before, if only from a distance, "I hope you will desist from this attack. I do not know of any general officer who approves of it, and I think it will prove disastrous to the army."

Burnside was taken aback, having expected to encounter a different spirit. However, as he later wrote, "Advice of that kind from General Sumner, who had always been in favor of an advance whenever it was possible, caused me to hesitate." To his further dismay, he found his other Grand Division commanders of the same opinion. Franklin did not surprise him greatly in this regard — ironically, that general had served him on the left at Fredericksburg in much the same fashion as he himself had served McClellan on the left at Antietam — but when Hooker, the redoubtable Fighting Joe, was even more emphatic than Sumner in advising no renewal of the attack, he knew the thing was off. His first reaction was one of frantic despair. He had a wild impulse to place himself at the head of his old corps and lead an all-out, all-or-nothing charge against the sunken road, intending to break Lee's line or else be broken by it. Dissuaded from this, he retired to his tent, bitter with the knowledge that all yesterday's blood had been shed to no advantage: except to the rebels, who would be facing that many fewer men next time the two armies came to grips. A corps commander, Major General W. F. Smith, followed him into the tent and found him pacing back and forth, distracted. "Oh, those men! Oh, those men!" he was saying. What men? Smith asked, and Burnside replied: "Those men over there," pointing across the river, where portions of the plain were carpeted blue: "I am thinking of them all the time!"

Sunset closed a day that had witnessed nothing more than a bit of long-range firing on one side and a great deal of digging on the other. Such spectacle as there was, and it was much, came after nightfall. A mysterious refulgence, shot with fanwise shafts of varicolored light, predominantly reds and blues — first a glimmer, then a spreading glow, as if all the countryside between Fredericksburg and Washington were afire — filled a wide arc of the horizon beyond the Federal right. It was the aurora borealis, seldom visible this far south and never before seen by most of the Confederates, who watched it with amazement. The Northerners might make of it what they chose by way of a portent (after all, these were the *Northern* Lights) but to one Southerner it seemed "that the heavens were hanging out banners and streamers and setting off fireworks in honor of our great victory."

As if to rival this gaudy nighttime aerial display, morning brought a terrestrial phenomenon, equally amazing in its way. The ground in front of the sunken road, formerly carpeted solid blue, had taken on a mottled hue, with patches of startling white. Binoculars disclosed the cause. Many of the Federal dead had been stripped stark naked by shivering Confederates, who had crept out in the darkness to scavenge the warm clothes from the bodies of men who needed them no longer.

That afternoon, as a result of a request by Burnside for a truce during which he could bury his dead and relieve such of his wounded as had survived two days and nights of exposure without medicine for their hurts or water for their fever-parched throats, the men of both armies had a nearer view of the carnage. No one assigned to one of the burial details ever forgot the horror of what he saw; for here, close-up and life-size, was an effective antidote to the long-range, miniature pageantry of Saturday's battle as it had been viewed from the opposing heights. Up close, you heard the groans and smelled the blood. You saw the dead. According to one who moved among them, they were "swollen to twice their natural size, black as Negroes in most cases." They sprawled "in every conceivable position, some on their backs with gaping jaws, some with eyes as large as walnuts, protruding with glassy stare, some doubled up like a contortionist." Here, he wrote — approaching incoherency as the memory grew stronger — lay "one without a head, there one without legs, yonder a head and legs without a trunk; everywhere horrible expressions, fear, rage, agony, madness, torture; lying in pools of blood, lying with heads half buried in mud, with fragments of shell sticking in oozing brain, with bullet holes all over the puffed limbs."

Not even amid such scenes as this, however, did the irrepressible rebel soldier's wry sense of humor — or anyhow what passed for such; mainly it was a biting sense of the ridiculous — desert him. One, about to remove a shoe from what he thought was a Federal corpse, was surprised to see the "corpse" lift its head and look at him reproachfully. "Beg pardon, sir," the would-be scavenger said, carefully lowering the leg; "I thought you had gone above." Another butternut scarecrow, reprimanded by a Union officer for violating the terms of the truce by picking up a fine Belgian rifle that had been dropped between the lines, looked his critic up and down, pausing for a long stare at the polished boots the officer was wearing. "Never mind," he said dryly. "I'll shoot you tomorrow and git them boots."

So he said. But as the thing turned out, neither he nor anyone else was going to be doing any shooting on that field tomorrow: not unless the Confederates started shooting at each other. Night brought a storm of sleet and driving rain, with a hard wind blowing eastward off the ridge and toward the river. When the fog of December 16 rolled away, the plain was empty. A hurried and red-faced investigation disclosed the fact that not a single live, unwounded Federal remained on the west bank of the Rappahannock. Covered by darkness, the sound of their movements drowned by the howling wind, the bluecoats had made a successful withdrawal in the night, taking up their pontoons after such a good job of salvaging equipment that one signal officer proudly reported that he had not left a yard of wire behind.

Burnside was distressed that a campaign which had opened so auspiciously should have so ignominious a close. What was more, reports of the battle were appearing by now in the northern papers, and the correspondents, ignoring the general's plea that they not treat "the affair at Fredericksburg" as a disaster, pulled out all the descriptive stops and figuratively threw up their hands in horror at the bungling and the bloodshed. An account in the New York *Times* so infuriated Burnside that he summoned the reporter to his tent and threatened to run him through with his sword. By ordinary a mild-natured man, he was souring under the goads of criticism, such as those made by two of his own colonels: one that he and his men had been committed piecemeal — "handed in on toasting forks," he phrased it — and the other that the defeat had been "owing to the heavy fire in front and an excess of enthusiasm in the rear." Nor was his temper soothed when he read such comments as the following, from an Ohio journal: "It can hardly be in human nature for men to show more valor, or generals to manifest less judgment, than were perceptible on our side that day."

In truth, the casualties were staggering: especially by contrast. The Federals had lost 12,653 men, the Confederates well under half as many: 5309. The latter figure was subsequently adjusted to 4201, just under one third of the former, when it was found that more than a thousand of those reported missing or wounded had taken advantage of the chance at a Christmas holiday immediately after the battle.

Longstreet was not unhappy with the results, despite the bloodless withdrawal. Suffering fewer than 2000 casualties, he had inflicted about 9000, and he was looking forward to a repetition of the tactics which had made this exploit possible. But Jackson, whose losses were not much less than his opponent's on the right, was far from satisfied, even though 11,000 stands of arms had been gleaned from the field after the departure of the Yankees. "I did not think a little red earth would have frightened them," he said. "I am sorry they are gone. I am sorry that I fortified." Lee agreed, saying of Burnside and the punishment that general had absorbed: "Had I divined that was to have been his only effort, he would have had more of it."

That evening he wrote his wife, "They went as they came — in the night. They suffered heavily as far as the battle went, but it did not go far enough to satisfy me." His anger had been aroused by the evidence of rabid vandalism he saw when he rode into Fredericksburg that afternoon. So had Jackson's. "What can we do?" a staff officer asked helplessly when he saw how thoroughly the Federals had taken the town apart. "Do?" Stonewall replied promptly. "Why, shoot them."

The stern-lipped Jackson's ire would never cool (later he expanded this remark; "We must do more than defeat their armies," he said. "We must destroy them") but Lee's was influenced considerably by the advent of the season of the Nativity. On Christmas Day he wrote his wife: "My heart is filled with gratitude to Almighty God for His unspeakable mercies with which He has blessed us in this day, for those He has granted us from the beginning of life, and particularly for those He has vouchsafed us during the past year. What should have become of us without His crowning help and protection? Oh, if our people would only realize it and cease from vain self-boasting and adulation, how strong would be my belief in final success and happiness to our country! But what a cruel thing is war; to separate and destroy families and friends, and mar the purest joys and happiness God has granted us in this world; to fill our hearts with hatred instead of love for our neighbors, and to devastate the fair face of this beautiful world. I pray that, on this day when only peace and good-will are preached to mankind, better thoughts may fill the hearts of our enemies and turn them to peace." But he added a sort of postscript in a letter to his youngest daughter, remarking that he was "happy in the knowledge that General Burnside and his army will not eat their promised Christmas dinner in Richmond today."

✕ 3 ✕

Near the far end of the thousand-mile-long firing line that swerved and crooked its way between North and South — westward across northern Virginia, East and Middle Tennessee, North Mississippi, central Arkansas, and thence on out to Texas — Theophilus Holmes, with less rank and not one half as many soldiers in a department better than twenty times as large, had troubles which, in multiplicity at any rate, made Lee's seem downright single. From his Transmississippi headquarters in Little Rock the lately appointed North Carolinian looked apprehensively north and west and south; he was threatened from all those quarters; while from the east he was being jogged by repeated pleas and suggestions from Johnston and the President, not to mention such comparatively minor figures as Pemberton and the Secretary of War, that he send his hard-pressed and outnumbered troops to the aid of his fellow department commander on the opposite bank of the big river that ran between them. A grim-featured man, deaf as a post, at fifty-seven Holmes was the oldest of the Confederate field commanders. Moreover, his rigidity of face, indicative of arteriosclerosis, was matched by a rigidity of mind which augured ill in a situation that called for nothing so much as it called for flexibility.

By way of compensation for this drawback, he had under him three major generals whose outstanding characteristic, individually and collectively, was the very flexibility he lacked. John Magruder, Richard Taylor, and Thomas Hindman, respectively in charge of Texas, West Louisiana, and Arkansas, were remarkable men, battle tested and of proved resourcefulness. In this regard the last was not the least accomplished of the three. A prewar Helena lawyer, thirty-four years old, Hindman had preceded his present chief to his home state, and within six months of his arrival in late May, stepping into the vacuum left by Van Dorn's April crossing of the Mississippi with all the men and weapons that could be salvaged from the defeat at Elkhorn Tavern, had created and equipped, by strict enforcement of the new conscription act and the establishment of factories and foundries where none had been before, an army of 20,000 recruits, armed and uniformed more or less in accordance with regulations and supported by 46 guns. This in itself was about as close to a miracle of improvised logistics as any general ever came in the whole war, but Hindman expected to accomplish a great deal more before he was through. Dapper, jaunty, dandified, addicted to patent leather boots and rose-colored kidskin gloves, frilled shirt fronts and a rattan cane, perhaps by way of compensation for his Napoleonic five feet two of height, he was accustomed to getting what he wanted, whether it was a fine brick house, a seat in Congress, or a wife whose father had sought to keep her from him by locking her away in a convent: all of which he had won, despite the odds, by extending his credit, demolishing opponents from the stump, and scaling the convent wall. What he had in mind just now, though, was not only the scourging of all bluecoats from the soil of Arkansas — including Helena, where the Federal commander of the force in occupation had taken over the fine brick house for his headquarters — but also the recovery of Missouri.

Arriving in mid-August to find the diminutive Arkansan already far along with his plans, Holmes had been infected by his enthusiasm and had approved his preparations for a counterinvasion. It was gotten under way at once. By October Hindman's advance, a combined command of cavalry and Indians, was across the Missouri border, but suffered a repulse at the hands of a superior Union force under Brigadier

General John M. Schofield, in command of three divisions styled the Army of the Frontier. The Indians scattered like chaff before a fan, and the cavalry fell back to the security of the Boston Mountains, skirmishing as they went. Hindman, coming forward to Fort Smith with the main body, was not discouraged by this turn of events. Indeed, as he saw it, the Federals were being lured to their destruction in the wilds of northwest Arkansas. Accordingly, he crossed the Arkansas river and concentrated his infantry at Van Buren. All he wanted, he told Holmes, was a chance to hit the Yankees with something approaching equal strength, after which he would "move into Missouri, take Springfield, and winter on the Osage at least."

Presently he got that chance, and at odds considerably better than he had dared even to hope for. Schofield, believing in mid-November that hostilities had ended for the winter, left the largest of his three divisions near Fayetteville under Brigadier General James G. Blunt, with the assignment of blocking the path of another Confederate incursion, and withdrew to Springfield with the other two, which he placed under Brigadier General Francis J. Herron while he himself took off on sick leave. Hindman, with a mobile force of 11,500 men and 22 guns, was preparing to take advantage of this chance to strike at Blunt, who had 7000 men and 20 guns, when word came from Holmes (who by now had received instructions from the Secretary of War, urging the necessity for reinforcing Vicksburg) for him to return posthaste to Little Rock with all his men, in preparation for an eastward march across the Mississippi. Hindman protested for all he was worth. To fall back would cost him heavily in desertions, he knew, since many of his conscripts were natives of the region through which they would be retreating. Besides, he told Holmes, "to withdraw without fighting at all would . . . so embolden the enemy as to insure his following me up." Without waiting for a reply he put his army in motion on December 3, intending to precede the retrograde movement with an advance and a victory that would leave the Federals in no condition to pursue. Slogging next day through the brushy Boston Mountains, the highest and most rugged section of the Ozark chain, he printed and distributed an address to his soldiers, designed to steel their arms for the strike at Blunt. "Remember that the enemy you engage has no feeling of mercy or kindness toward you," he told them. "His ranks are made up of Pin Indians, free negroes, Southern tories, Kansas jayhawkers, and hired Dutch cut-throats. These bloody ruffians have invaded your country; stolen and destroyed your property; murdered your neighbors; outraged your women; driven your children from their homes, and defiled the graves of your kindred. If each man of you will do what I have here urged upon you, we will utterly destroy them."

Blunt now had his troops in bivouac about twenty miles southwest of Fayetteville, near the hamlet of Cane Hill, from which he had driven the grayback cavalry that week. When he got word that Hindman was across the Arkansas with an estimated 25,000 men he reacted according to his nature, rejecting the notion of retreat. A Maine-born Kansan who had practiced medicine en route in Ohio, he was a militant abolitionist and a graduate of the border wars. Round-faced, stocky, pugnacious in manner, he was thirty-six years old and no part of his training had prepared him for running from rebels, whatever their numbers. Determined to hold his ground, he wired for reinforcements and began to organize his position for defense.

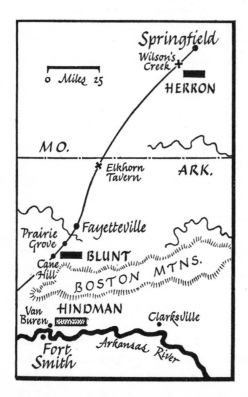

The trouble with this was that the only reinforcements available were the two small divisions under Herron, a scant 6000 men with 22 guns, and they were back near Springfield, well over a hundred miles away, whereas Hindman's camp at Van Buren was little more than a third that distance from Cane Hill, so that the chances were strong that the rebels would arrive before the reinforcements did. However, this was leaving two factors out of account. The first was that Hindman's route of march lay through the mountains; his men would be climbing and descending about as much as they would be advancing along the rugged trails. The other factor was Frank Herron. An adopted Iowan, already in command of two divisions at the age of twenty-five, he intended to accomplish a great deal more in the way of fulfilling his military ambitions before returning to civilian life as head of the Dubuque bank established for him by his wealthy Pennsylvania parents. Just now, more than anything, he wanted a chance to command those two divisions in actual battle, and he got it much sooner than he had expected. At 8 o'clock on the morning of December 3 — by which hour, unknown to him or Blunt, Hindman had put his army on the road for its trek across the Boston Mountains — Herron received the summons from Cane Hill, one hundred and thirty miles from his present camp on the somber fields where the Battle of Wilson's Creek had been fought and lost by Nathaniel Lyon, almost a year and a half ago. Drums and bugles sounded assembly and the men fell in to receive instructions for the march. It would be made without tents or baggage, they were told, except for knapsacks which would be hauled in wagons. By noon they were headed south, and before they stopped at dawn next morning, slogging at route step down the pike, they had made twenty miles. After a short rest they were off again. Across the state line on December 5, munching hardtack and raw bacon as they walked, they skirted the granite slopes of Pea Ridge and saw the nine-months-old scars on the Elkhorn Tavern, where Van Dorn had come to grief. At midnight the following day, having covered better than one hundred blistering miles of road, the head of the column entered Fayette-ville, where the weary marchers slept in the streets, sprawled around fires they kindled and fed by ripping pickets from front-yard fences. Another twenty miles tomorrow and they would be at Cane Hill with Blunt, ready for whatever came at them from beyond the mountains whose foothills they could presently see by the glimmer of dawn on Sunday, December 7.

The first sign they had that they were not going to make it — at least not on schedule — came later that morning, twelve miles down the pike, when they encountered long-range cannonfire as they were approaching Illinois Creek. Soon they saw that the Confederates had drawn a line of battle around the hilltop village of Prairie Grove, a couple of miles beyond the creek, blocking the path of the road-worn bluecoats eight miles short of their goal. Herron shook out a regiment of skirmishers and advanced them to the protection of the creekbank, where to his horror he discovered that his men were so weary that once they were off their feet they promptly dropped to sleep with rebel shells and bullets whistling and twittering over their heads. Undaunted, he built up his firing line and put his batteries in position, partly by way of returning the hostile fire, but mostly by way of letting Blunt know from the racket that he had arrived, or almost arrived, and needed help. The trouble was, with all those graybacks swarming in his front, he was not even sure that Blunt and his men were still in existence. For all he knew, Hindman might have gobbled them up while he himself was on the march from Wilson's Creek.

Hindman had not gobbled up Blunt; he had gone around him. Approaching Cane Hill late the afternoon before, after a march across the shoulder of the mountains in weather so cold that water froze in the men's canteens and icicles tinkled on the beards of the horses, he had put his troops in position for a dawn attack, only to learn that Herron was on the way, already approaching Fayetteville with a force which, once it was joined to Blunt's, would give the Federals the ad-vantage of numbers, both in men and guns. In command of a brigade at Shiloh, where he had been wounded and commended for gallantry, Hindman decided to profit from the example of that battle by prevent-ing what had caused its loss, the arrival of Buell after Grant had been pushed to the edge of desperation. That is, he would strike at the reinforcements first, then turn on the main body. Accordingly, he built up the campfires along his outpost line, left a skeleton brigade of cavalry to keep up the bluff next morning, and set off after moonset on a circuitous march with 10,000 men to intercept and defeat the blue column hurrying southward out of Fayetteville. That was how it came about that Herron encountered long-range cannonfire at the crossing of Illinois Creek and the bristling line of battle at Prairie Grove, eight miles short of a junction with Blunt at Cane Hill.

Blunt had spent the morning in constant expectation of being swamped by the rebels maneuvering boldly to his front, apparently in overwhelming numbers. Near noon, however, hearing the sudden boom of guns from across the hills to his left rear, he realized that he had been outflanked; whereupon he fell back hastily to Rhea's Mills, six miles north, in order to protect his trains. Finding them secure he turned southeast in the direction of the booms and at 4 o'clock reached Prairie Grove, where he came upon the battle still in full swing after nearly five hours of doubtful contest. Two rounds from his lead battery announced his arrival — announced it all too emphatically, in fact, for both shots landed among Herron's skirmishers, causing them to think that they were being flanked by their foes instead of being supported by their friends. Herron had been holding his own despite the weariness of his foot-sore men. Two charges against the ridge had failed, breaking in blood against the rim of the rebel horseshoe line, but Hindman had had no better luck in attempting a counterattack with his green conscripts, who fell apart whenever he ordered them forward. The fighting continued, left and right, muzzle flashes stabbing the early darkness. Despite their superiority of numbers, especially in guns — 42 to 22, now that the Union forces were united — Blunt's fresh troops could make no more of a penetration of the rebel line than Herron's weary ones had been able to achieve. Gradually the firing died to a sputter. Then it stopped. The battle was over.

Losses in killed, wounded, and missing totaled 1317 for the Confederates and 1251 for the Federals. Of the latter only 333 were from Blunt's command, indicating how much heavier a proportion of the conflict Herron's men had borne, despite the fact that both laid claim to a lion's share in having brought the victory about. Hindman's only claim in that respect was the not inconsiderable one that he had managed to hold his ground throughout the fighting. Whether he had also accomplished his main objective — to shock the enemy into immobility, escaping pursuit while he fell back southward in compliance with the previous orders from Holmes — would soon be known; for he retreated that night under cover of darkness, wrapping the iron tires of his gun and caisson wheels with blankets to muffle the sound of his withdrawal. The ruse worked, and so did another he tried next morning. Not only did Blunt not hear him go, but at dawn he also granted a request for a truce, which Hindman sent forward under a white flag, to allow for tending the wounded and burying the dead. Discovering presently that the Confederate main body had departed in the night, Blunt canceled the truce, on grounds that the rebels were gleaning abandoned arms from the field, and prepared to follow. By that time, however, Schofield was on the scene. Up from his sickbed and furious that his army had been committed to battle in his absence, he censured both commanders: Blunt for not withdrawing to meet the reinforcements hurrying toward him, and Herron for attacking with troops so badly blown that some of them were found dead on the field, not from wounds but from exhaustion and exposure after their long march from Wilson's Creek. If Schofield's purpose in this was to prevent his subordinates' advancement by discrediting their valor, that purpose failed. By way of showing its appreciation for a victory won by northern arms as the year drew to a close — a victory which presently shone the brighter by contrast with the several full-scale disasters that developed elsewhere along the thousand-mile-long firing line before the month was out — the government promptly awarded major general's stars not only to Blunt but also to Herron, who then succeeded Lew Wallace as the youngest man to hold that rank in the U.S. Army. Moreover, as soon as these promotions came through, both men would outrank their present commander.

Hindman's discomfort was considerably increased in late December, when Schofield finally unleashed his cavalry for a forced march against the Confederates who, down to about 4000 men as a result of straggling and desertions, had taken sanctuary behind the Arkansas River. Three days after Christmas the blue riders struck Van Buren, destroying five steamboats at the wharf and all of the supplies of corn and bacon Hindman had gathered over the months in order to keep his army from starvation. Once more he was thrown into dispirited retreat, losing still more soldiers as he went. The Federals withdrew to Fayetteville, and thence on back to comfortable winter quarters in Missouri, but now there was no question of Hindman's returning to Little Rock with the prospect of marching his army to the relief of Vicksburg. Practically speaking he had no army. So much of it as did not lie in shallow graves at Prairie Grove was scattered over northern Arkansas, hiding from conscription agents in Ozark coves and valleys.

Thus it was that the battle lost in northwest Arkansas had repercussions far beyond the theater it was fought in. Holmes had opposed the eastward transfer from the start, protesting that the march led through a region barren of supplies and would require no less than thirty days. "Solemnly, under the circumstances," he had informed the Adjutant General earlier that month, "I regard the movement ordered as equivalent to abandoning Arkansas." All the same, against his better judgment, he had been preparing to go along with the plan. But now, with Hindman's army practically out of existence and only the local reserves to protect Little Rock itself against an advance from occupied Helena, he had what he considered the best of specific reasons for declining to comply with the government's wishes. On December 29, the day after Schofield's cavalry hit Van Buren, he wrote Johnston in reply to the correspondence the President had forwarded from Vicksburg during his inspection of that place the week before: "My information from Helena is to the effect that a heavy force of the enemy has passed down the Mississippi on transports. . . . Thus it seems very certain that any force I can now send from here would not be able to reach Vicksburg, and if at all not before such a reinforcement would be useless, while such a diversion would enable the enemy to penetrate those portions of the Arkansas Valley where the existence of supplies of subsistence and forage would afford them leisure to overrun the entire state and gradually reduce the people to . . . dependence."

★　★　★

It was bad enough that the Yankees were steaming down the Mississippi, but they were also steaming up it — simultaneously. Banks had reoccupied Baton Rouge in mid-December and now was giving every sign that he intended to continue the northward penetration, shortening the stretch of river necessarily rebel-held if Holmes was to keep open the supply lines vital to the feeding and reinforcement, if not indeed to the survival, of all the armies of the South. Since the loss of the armed ram *Arkansas*, three months back, the Confederacy had had no vestige of a navy with which to oppose this two-pronged challenge designed for her riving and destruction; the threat would have to be stopped, if at all, not on the river itself, but from its banks. On the east bank the responsibility was Pemberton's, and to help him meet it he had two stout high-ground bastions one hundred air-line miles apart, commanding bends of the river at Vicksburg and Port Hudson. On the west bank it was Richard Taylor's, who had nothing: not only no lofty fortresses bristling with heavy-caliber guns emplaced to blow the Union ironclads out of the water, but also no army. In fact, on his arrival from Virginia in late August, he had found that his total force consisted of two troops of home-guard cavalry, a scattering of guerillas hidden from friends and foes in the moss-hung swamps and bayous, and a battalion of mounted infantry just arrived from Texas — in all, fewer than 2000 effectives for the defense of the whole Department of Louisiana. Nonetheless, Holmes had confidence that this second of his three major generals would be ingenious and tireless in his efforts to reduce the nearly immeasurable odds, and this confidence was not misplaced.

Commander of a division used as shock troops by Stonewall Jackson throughout the Shenandoah Valley campaign, Taylor had been one of the stars of that amazing chapter in military history, and had found in that experience ample compensation for his lack of formal training in the art of war. Gripped on the eve of the Seven Days by a strange paralysis of the legs, which seemed to portend the close of a promising career and a denial of any further share in winning his country's independence, this son of Zachary Taylor had recovered in time to receive his present assignment, together with a promotion, from his brother-in-law Jefferson Davis. Happy over what in fact would be a home-coming, for he had commanded Louisianians in the Valley and had spent his antebellum years on a Louisiana plantation, he came West with an enthusiasm that was only slightly dampened by the discovery of conditions in his new department, as of August 20, when he established headquarters in Alexandria. Undismayed by the shortage of soldiers, which kept him from any immediate accomplishment of big things — such as the retaking of New Orleans, which was very much a part of his plans for the future — he decided to be content at first with small ones. Within two weeks of his arrival he mounted a surprise attack that captured a four-gun battery and two companies of infantry at Bayou des Allemands, a Federal post near his plantation home, fifty miles downriver from Donaldsonville and less than half that far above New Orleans. If he could not retake the Crescent City just yet, he could at least draw near it — and profitably, too.

Slight though it was, this first success gained locally by Confederate arms in the four months since the fall of the South's first city was heartening indeed to the people of the district. Not even the recapture of the post in late October, when the resurgent Louisianians were driven away by a Federal amphibious force that included four regiments of infantry and a quartet of light-draft gunboats, detracted from the brilliance of that first strike. What was more, Taylor was planning others of still larger scope. Denied access to the Lafourche, that fertile region lying between the Mississippi and the Atchafalaya, he moved into the Teche country, which lay between the Atchafalaya basin and the Gulf of Mexico, and here, despite the fact that his government, as he said, "had no soldiers, no arms or munitions, and no money within the limits of the district," he set about the task of raising, equipping, and training the army with which he hoped, in time, not only to capture but also to hold the series of fortified posts that blocked the path between him and his goal, New Orleans. Meanwhile, intent on preventing further enemy penetrations, he had to disperse what forces he had in order to meet threats from all directions. With few trained subordinates and almost no telegraph or railway lines, the problem of central control was well-nigh insoluble. However, now that December had come on and the year drew toward a close, Taylor went far toward solving it. By using relays of fast-stepping mules and an ambulance in which he could sleep while traveling, the thirty-six-year-old general managed to employ what might have been his immobile hours for visits to the various scattered points in his large department. "Like the Irishman's bird," he subsequently wrote, "I almost succeeded in being in two places at the same time."

In this respect, as well as in several others, he was easily distinguishable from his opposite number, the newly arrived commander of all the Union forces in the region. Ten years Taylor's senior, of humbler birth but with much larger accomplishments in public life, having been a three-term governor of Massachusetts and speaker of the national House of Representatives, Nathaniel Banks was nothing like the Irishman's bird and had nothing like his opponent's nighttime mobility — though the fact was, he had perhaps an even greater need for it if he was to carry out the multiple assignment given him by his superiors when he set out from Hampton Roads on his voyage down and around the coast to relieve his fellow Bay State politician, Benjamin Butler, as military ruler of New Orleans and commander of the Department of the Gulf. Vicksburg and Mobile were his primary objectives, he was told, and after the fall of the former place had opened the Mississippi to Union traffic throughout its length he was to move up the Red in order to gain control of northern Louisiana and, eventually, Texas. It was a large order, particularly for a general who not only had not a single battlefield victory to his credit, but rather had been whipped twice already in open contest — once at Winchester, in the Shenendoah Valley, and again at Cedar Mountain, both times by Stonewall Jackson, whose lean marchers had captured so many of his supplies that they had dubbed him "Commissary" Banks — but he apparently had no doubt that it could be filled and that he was the man to fill it. He docked at New Orleans, December 14, and took over formally next day from Butler, who issued an address to his army — "I greet you, my brave comrades, and say farewell!" it began, and ended: "Farewell, my comrades! Again, Farewell!" — and promptly departed for Washington to take the government to task for having made what seemed to him an improvident substitution.

Banks wasted no time on speeches. On the day he took command he issued orders for one of the divisions he had brought along to proceed at once upriver, without unloading from its transports, and to reoccupy Baton Rouge, which Butler had abandoned after repulsing an all-out attack on the place in early August. Two days later, when the Louisiana capital fell without even a show of resistance, Banks was greatly pleased at having made so prompt and effective a beginning toward fulfilling his government's outsized expectations. Including the reinforcements still arriving after their long voyage from New York and Fort Monroe, he had 36,508 effectives in his department, exclusive of navy personnel, and he felt that these were ample for the accomplishment of his task. What was more, he reported that he had found in Farragut, who was to be his partner in continuing the bold upriver thrust, a sailor who was "earnest for work." After a conference with the Tennessee-born admiral he added that he was delighted with his enthusiasm and frankness, and that he looked forward to "a most satisfactory result from our mutual labors." Banks was feeling chipper, and he said so. "All the indications of our campaign are auspicious," he notified Washington on December 18, the day after the fall of Baton Rouge, "and I hope to make good the most sanguine expectations in regard to my expedition."

There were, however, two previously unsuspected matters for concern, one military, one civil, and both grave. The first was the presence, thirty-five miles above Baton Rouge, which in turn was a hundred miles above New Orleans, of the fortifications at Port Hudson. Neither his Washington superiors nor Banks himself, until he arrived, had known of the existence of any such obstacle south of Vicksburg, another 250 winding miles upstream; yet intelligence reports informed him now that the Confederates had no less than 12,000 troops in the place, strongly intrenched on the landward side and with 21 heavy guns emplaced on the high bluff, waiting to sink or blow sky high whatever came their way across the chocolate-colored surface of the river. This in itself, placing as it did a new complexion on the problem of ascent, was enough to give Banks pause. But the other concern, the civil one, was even more disturbing in its way, since it showed that the command of the department was going to be a far more complex occupation than he had supposed, early that month, when he set out from Virginia. Less than two weeks after his arrival, for example, he received a note from one C. A. Smith, commission agent for certain northern interests, and Andrew Butler, whose brother Ben had set him up in business when he took over as military ruler of New Orleans. "Dear Sir," it read. "If you will allow our commercial program to be [carried] out as projected previous to your arrival in this department, giving the same support and facilities as your predecessor, I am authorized on [receiving] your assent to place at your disposal $100,000."

In the course of his rise from bobbin boy to the top of the heap in Massachusetts politics Banks no doubt had encountered other offers of this nature, but hardly one that was made so blatantly or with such apparent confidence in his basic corruptibility. "It was no temptation," he told his wife. "I thank God every night that I have no desire for dishonest gains." All the same, he felt obliged to report to Washington "that as much, or more, attention has been given to civil than to military matters," including the training of his army, and that, in consequence, the troops were "not in condition for immediate service." Though he declared on Christmas Eve, "We hope to move up the river at the close of the week," he was still in New Orleans after New Year's, complaining that he was cramped by a shortage of siege artillery. "The enemy's works at Port Hudson have been in progress many months and are formidable," he explained. "Our light field guns would make no impression on them." In fact, having learned by now of the reverses lately suffered by the column supposed to be working its way southward out of Memphis while he moved northward from New Orleans, he was beginning to "feel some anxiety as to the defenses of this city. . . . The enemy is concentrating all available forces on the river, and in the event of disasters North will not fail to turn their attention to this quarter."

So it was that, now in January — while Taylor kept busy raising and training an army in the bayous, lulled to sleep each night in his ambulance by the clopping of hoofs as he traveled the moon-drenched roads of the Teche and dreamed of retaking the South's first city — Banks stayed where he was, bedeviled by itchy-handed speculators, made apprehensive by rebel successes upriver, and fretted by shortages while he continued his preparations for the upstream movement which he had assured his superiors in December would be launched without delay.

Another part of his assignment, albeit one that was no more than incidental, he had also placed in the way of execution, though so far on a scale that was small indeed. Its conception was provoked by the shortage of cotton for the textile mills of New England, 3,252,000 of whose 4,745,750 spindles had fallen idle by the middle of the year, with the result that production was down to less than one fourth of normal before its close. New Orleans having failed to yield more than a comparative handful of bales, the hungry manufacturers had cast their eyes on Texas. What they had in mind was conquest and colonization; they saw their chance to make of it what one observer called "another and a fairer Kansas," where Yankee know-how and industry, replacing the slovenly farming methods now employed, would produce more cotton in a single year than had previously been grown in all the history of the vast Lone Star expanse. That way, the idle spindles would be fed, the mill hands would return to work, and the owners would get rich. First, however, the army would have to clear the path for immigration, and in this connection Banks had in his entourage a Texas Unionist, Andrew Jackson Hamilton, upon whom the War Department, at the behest of the New England manufacturers, had conferred the rank of brigadier general, together with appointment as military governor of Texas. He would take office, preparing the way for the textile-sponsored "colonists," when and if Banks won control of some portion of the state for him to govern.

So far, all there was for him in this regard was Galveston harbor, seized two months ago by the navy and now being patrolled by gunboats of the West Coast Blockading Squadron, part of Farragut's command. Texas was far down on the list of Banks's assigned objectives; though his department had been enlarged to include that state, its occupation was scheduled to follow the opening of the Mississippi and the conquest of the Red River Valley in northwest Louisiana; but at Hamilton's urging he agreed to send a Massachusetts regiment to take and hold the island town at once, thus giving the newly appointed governor at least the shadow of a dry-land claim to his high title. Accordingly, an advance party of three companies left New Orleans on December 22, before they had had time for more than a hurried look at the sights of the city, and landed at Galveston on Christmas Eve. There, under the muzzles of the gunboats anchored in the harbor, they set to work barricading the wharf as a precaution against attack from the landward side while awaiting the arrival of the rest of the infantry by sea, together with attached units of cavalry and field artillery.

They had need for greater caution than they suspected, for this action brought them into immediate contact with the first in rank of Holmes's three major generals, John Magruder. Known to be unpredictable and tricky, he was also first in reputation; "Prince John" he had been called in the old army, partly because of his aristocratic manner and his fondness for staging amateur theatricals, partly too because of his flared mustache, luxuriant sideburns, gaudy clothes, and imperial six-feet-two of height. As flamboyant in the Transmississippi as he had been in his native Virginia — where, previous to becoming somewhat unstrung in the jangle of the Seven Days, he had put on such a show of strength with a handful of men that McClellan had been awed into immobility before Yorktown — his ache for distinction and love of flourish were no less pronounced in the Lone Star state. The difference here, eight months later, was that Magruder was thinking offensively. For some time now, in fact ever since his assignment to command the District of Texas, Arizona, and New Mexico on October 10, five days after the Union flotilla steamed in and put Galveston under its guns, he had had it in mind not only to liberate the island town, less than fifty miles southeast of his Houston headquarters, but also to sink or capture the warships riding insolently at anchor in the harbor. So far as Prince John was concerned, the addition of those three companies of Massachusetts infantry, now barricading the wharf against attack, only fattened the prize within his grasp and added to the glory about to be won.

Nor was his plan for making a naval assault deterred by his lack of anything resembling a navy. If he had none then he would build one, or at any rate improvise one, and he did so in short order. Workmen off the Houston docks piled bales of cotton around the paddle boxes and decks of the *Bayou City*, a two-story side-wheel Mississippi steamboat, and the stern-wheeler *Neptune*, a smaller vessel. The former was armed with a rifled 32-pounder, located forward of her stacks, and the latter's bow was faced with railroad iron to stiffen her punch as a ram.

Their crews were army volunteers, including some 300 riflemen stationed about the decks as sharpshooters. These two "cotton-clads" would stage the naval assault, descending Buffalo Bayou to come booming down on the five Union gunboats, *Westfield, Harriet Lane, Owasco, Clifton,* and *Sachem,* which had a combined displacement of over 3000 tons and mounted a total of 28 guns, mostly heavy. For the land attack there were in all about 500 men; Texans under Colonel Tom Green, who had led them at Valverde, they were survivors of Brigadier General Henry Sibley's nightmare expedition up the Rio Grande, back in the spring. Magruder divided them into three assault columns, taking the center one himself. By New Year's Eve his preparations were complete. He gave the signal and the attack got under way, bringing in the new year with a bang.

Crossing from the mainland by the unguarded bridge, he struck the barricade shortly after midnight — only to find that his scaling ladders were too short. All he could do was work his men up close and keep exchanging shots with the defenders, who had turned out at the first alarm and were laying down a heavy fire. Everything depended now on the untried two-boat navy. The first the Federals knew of its existence was when lookouts on the *Westfield,* Commander W. B. Renshaw's flagship, spotted two ungainly-looking steamboats, apparently overloaded with cotton bales, driving hard toward the anchored flotilla. Attempting to take evasive action, the *Westfield* went aground on Pelican Island Bar, removed from the fight as effectively as if she had been sunk. Aboard the *Bayou City,* bearing down on the *Harriet Lane,* the gun captain of the 32-pounder shouted: "Well, here goes for a New Year's present!" and pulled the lanyard. The first shot missed, as did the second, and on the third the gun exploded at the breech, killing him and four of its crew; whereupon the *Neptune* came up, churning the water in her wake, and struck the *Lane* such a tremendous thump that she broke her own nose and had to run up on the flats to keep from sinking. Afloat as ashore, the battle seemed lost by mishap or miscalculation.

By now, however, the *Bayou City* had pulled up alongside the *Lane,* her upper-deck riflemen firing down on the rattled bluejackets while a boarding party swarmed over the bulwarks and began slashing at the survivors in the style of John Paul Jones. In the course of this melee the Union skipper was killed and his lieutenant ran up the white flag of surrender; observing which, the other three nearby captains did the same. Across the way, still hard aground, Renshaw saw that the *Westfield* was next on the rebel target list. Determined not to have her fall into enemy hands, he ordered the crew to abandon ship while he lowered into an open magazine a barrel of turpentine equipped with a slow fuze which he set and started before he turned to go. That was his last act on earth or water, for the fuze was defective or wrongly set.

Before he made it out of range, a flame-shot column of black smoke roared skyward and the *Westfield* blew apart, her wreckage enveloped in fire and steam.

Watching this abrupt disintegration of the naval support for the defenders of the wharf, the Texans in front of the barricade took heart and the Federals behind it were dejected; so much so, indeed, that the three Massachusetts companies, warned by a step-up in the firing that an assault was about to be launched, surrendered in a body. But the commanders of the gunboats *Clifton*, *Owasco*, and *Sachem*, claiming that this forcing of the issue ashore was in violation of the naval "truce" — for so they had considered it, they later affirmed by way of rebuttal to the outrage expressed by the rebels — hauled down their white flags and made a sudden run for open water. The Confederates, unable to pursue out into the Gulf, could do nothing but howl in protest at foul play. They had lost 143 killed and wounded. Including captives the Federals had lost about 600 soldiers and sailors: plus, of course, two gunboats and the town. At a single stroke, boldly conceived and boldly delivered, Magruder had cleared Texas of armed bluecoats. Nor did he intend to grant them another foothold. Moving his headquarters triumphantly to Galveston, he notified his government next day: "We are preparing to give them a warm reception should they return."

The navy might (and in fact did, the following week, withdrawing the 2000-ton screw steamer *Brooklyn* and six gunboats from the blockade squadron off Mobile and bringing them to Galveston, where they were careful however to maintain station well outside the harbor and thus beyond reach of another eruption of Magruder's cotton-clads) but Banks had no intention of returning, not even with a token force. He counted himself lucky that the whole Bay State regiment, together with its artillery and cavalry supports, had not landed in time to be gobbled up, and he brought the still-loaded transports back to New Orleans, turning a deaf ear to Would-Be-Governor Hamilton's disgruntled protestations. That gentleman and his party — a sizable group, characterized by one critic as "friends, patrons, and creditors," who had meant to be front runners in the intended Lone Star colonization — returned instead to Washington, complaining bitterly that they had been "deliberately and purposely humbugged."

Though Holmes of course was quick to congratulate Magruder, whose amphibious coup made the one bright spot in the entire Transmississippi as the new year came in, Hamilton's dejection and disgust were not matched by any corresponding elation on the part of the overall commander of the Confederate Far West. Though he had managed, on the face of it, to achieve a sort of balance within the limits of his department — defeat in northwestern Arkansas, stalemate in West Louisiana, victory in coastal Texas — he knew that it was precarious in nature, tenuous at best and, in consideration of the odds, most likely temporary.

Nor was the maintenance of that shaky balance only dependent on what occurred within the borders of the monster region. Cut off, Holmes and all those under him would be left as it were to wither on the vine; so that what happened beyond or along those borders was equally important, and this was true in particular as to what happened along the eastern border, the Mississippi itself, down which he had reported the "heavy force" of Union ironclads and transports steaming the week before past Helena. It was headed, according to his conjecture, for Vicksburg, the linchpin whose loss might well result in the collapse of the whole Confederate wagon.

✗ 4 ✗

Haste made waste and Grant knew it, but in this case the haste was unavoidable — unavoidable, that is, unless he was willing to take the risk of having another general win the prize he was after — because he was fighting two wars simultaneously: one against the Confederacy, or at any rate so much of its army as stood between him and the river town that was his goal, and the other against a man who, like himself, wore blue. That was where the need for haste came in, for the rival general's name was John McClernand. A former Springfield lawyer and Illinois congressman, McClernand was known to have political aspirations designed to carry him not one inch below the top position occupied at present by his friend, another former Springfield lawyer and Illinois congressman, Abraham Lincoln. Moreover, having decided that the road to the White House led through Vicksburg, he had taken pains to see that he traveled it well equipped, and this he had done by engaging the preliminary support, the active military backing, not only of his friend the President, but also of the Secretary of War, the crusty and often difficult Edwin M. Stanton. With the odds thus lengthened against him, Grant — when he belatedly found out what his rival had been up to — could see that this private war against McClernand might well turn out to be as tough, in several ways, as the public one he had been fighting for eighteen months against the rebels.

In the first place, he had not even known that he had this private war on his hands until it was so well under way that his rival had already won the opening skirmish. McClernand had gone to Washington on leave in late September, complaining privately that he was "tired of furnishing brains" for Grant's army. Arriving in the capital he appealed to Lincoln to "let one volunteer officer try his abilities." His plan was to return to his old political stamping ground and there, by reaching also into Indiana and Iowa, raise an army with which he would descend the Mississippi, capture Vicksburg, "and open navigation to New Orleans." Lincoln liked the sound of that and took him to see Stanton, who liked it too. McClernand left Washington in late October, armed with a confidential order signed by Stanton and indorsed by Lincoln, giving official sanction to his plan. By early November Grant was hearing rumors from upriver in Illinois: rumors which were presently reinforced by a dispatch from General-in-Chief Henry W. Halleck, whom the three former lawyers had not taken into their confidence. Memphis, which was in Grant's department, was to "be made the depot of a joint military and naval expedition on Vicksburg." Alarmed at hearing the rumors confirmed, Grant wired back: "Am I to understand that I lie still here while an expedition is fitted out from Memphis, or do you want me to push south as far as possible?" Halleck was something of a lawyer, too, though he now found himself at cross-purposes with the men who had not let him in on the secret. "You have command of all troops sent to your department," he replied, " and have permission to fight the enemy where you please."

Grant considered himself unleashed. Organizing his mobile force of about 40,000 effectives into right and left wings, respectively under Major General W. T. Sherman and Brigadier General C. S. Hamilton, with the center under Major General J. B. McPherson, he began to move at once, southward along the Mississippi Central Railroad from Grand Junction. Ordinarily he would have preferred to wait for reinforcements, but not now. "I feared that delay might bring McClernand," he later explained. Vicksburg was 250 miles away, and as he saw it the town belonged to the man who got there first. By mid-November he was in Holly Springs, where he set up a depot of supplies and munitions, then continued on across the Tallahatchie, leapfrogging his headquarters to Oxford while the lead division was fording the Yocknapatalfa, eight miles north of Water Valley, which was occupied during the first week of December. The movement had been rapid and well coordinated; so far, it had encountered only token resistance from the rebels, who were fading back before the advance of the bluecoats. Presently Grant discovered why. Pemberton — whose strength he considerably overestimated as equal to his own — was avoiding serious contact while seeking a tactical advantage, and at last he found it. He called a halt near Grenada, another twenty-five miles beyond Water Valley, and put his gray-clad troops to work improving with intrenchments a position of great natural strength along the Yalobusha. Approaching Coffeeville on December 5, midway between Water Valley and Grenada, the Federal cavalry was struck a blow that signified the end of easy progress. Still 150-odd miles from Vicksburg, Grant could see that the going was apt to be a good deal rougher and slower from here on.

Something else he could see as well, something that disturbed him even more. While he was being delayed in the piny highlands of north-central Mississippi, facing the rebels intrenched along the high-banked Yalobusha, McClernand might come down to Memphis, where advance contingents of his expedition were awaiting him already, and ride the broad smooth highway of the Mississippi River down to Vicksburg unopposed: in which case Grant would not only have lost his private war, he would even have helped his opponent win it by holding Pemberton and the greater part of the Vicksburg garrison in position, 150 miles away, while McClernand captured the weakly defended town with little more exertion than had been required in the course of the long boat ride south from Cairo. That was what rankled worst, the thought that he would have helped to pluck the laurels that would grace his rival's brow. But as he thought distastefully of this, it began to occur to him that he saw here the possibility of a campaign of his own along these lines. "You have command of all troops sent to your department," Halleck had told him, and presumably this included the recruits awaiting McClernand's arrival at Memphis. So Grant, still at his Oxford headquarters on December 8, sent a note to Sherman, whose command was at College Hill, ten miles away: "I wish you would come over this evening and stay tonight, or come in the morning. I would like to talk with you."

Sherman did not wait for morning. Impatient as always, he rode straight over, a tall red-haired man with a fidgety manner, concave temples, glittering hazel eyes, and a scraggly, close-cropped beard. "I never saw him but I thought of Lazarus," one observer was to write. A chain smoker who, according to another witness, got through each cigar "as if it was a duty to be finished in the shortest possible time," he was forty-two, two years older than the comparatively stolid Grant and once his military senior, too, until Donelson brought the younger brigadier fame and a promotion, both of which had been delayed for Sherman until Shiloh, where he fought under — some said, saved — his former junior. He felt no resentment at that. In fact, he saw Grant as "the coming man in this war." But he had never had better reason for this belief than now at Oxford, when he was closeted with him and heard his plan for the sudden capture of Vicksburg with the help of a kidnaped army.

As usual in military matters, geography played a primary part in determining what was to be done, and how. Various geographic factors made Vicksburg an extremely difficult nut to crack. First there was the bluff itself, the 200-foot red-clay escarpment dominating the hairpin bend of the river at its base, unscalable for infantry and affording the guns emplaced on its crest a deadly plunging fire — as Farragut, for one, could testify — against whatever naval forces moved against or past it. As for land forces, since they could not scale the bluff itself, even if they had been able to approach it from the front, their only alternative was to come upon it from the rear; that is, either to march overland down the Mississippi Central to Grenada, as Grant was now attempting to do, and thence along the high ground lying between the Yazoo and the Big Black Rivers, or else debark from their transports somewhere short of the town and make a wide swing east, in order to approach it from that direction. However, the latter was nearly impossible, too, because of another geographic factor, the so-called Yazoo-Mississippi alluvial delta. This incredibly fertile, magnolia-leaf-shaped region, 200 miles in length and 50 miles in average width, bounded east and west by the two rivers that gave it its compound name, and north and south by the hills that rose below and above Memphis and Vicksburg, was nearly roadless throughout its flat and swampy expanse, was subject to floods in all but the driest seasons, and — except for the presence of a scattering of pioneers who risked its malarial and intestinal disorders for the sake of the richness of its forty-foot topsoil, which in time, after the felling of its big trees and the draining of its bayous, would make it the best cotton farmland in the world — was the exclusive domain of moccasins,

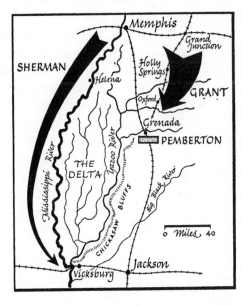

bears, alligators, and panthers. It was, in short, impenetrable to all but the smallest of military parties, engaged in the briefest of forays. An army attempting to march across or through it would come out at the other end considerably reduced in numbers and fit for nothing more strenuous than a six-month rest, with quinine as the principal item on its diet. Anyhow, Grant did not intend to try it that way. He had his eye fixed on the mouth of the Yazoo, twelve miles above Vicksburg, and it seemed to him that an amphibious force could ascend that river for a landing on the southeast bank, which would afford the troops a straight shot at the town on the bluff. True, there were hills here, too — the Walnut Hills, they were called, the beginning of the long ridge known as the Chickasaw Bluffs, which lay along the left bank of the Yazoo, overlooking the flat morass of the delta — but they were by no means as forbidding as the heights overlooking the Mississippi, a dozen miles below. It was Grant's belief that determined men, supported by the guns of the fleet, could swarm over these comparatively low-lying hills, brushing aside whatever portion of the weakened garrison tried to stop them, and be inside the town before nightfall of the day they came ashore.

That was why he had sent for Sherman, who seemed to him the right man for the job. Sherman happily agreed to undertake it, and Grant gave him his written orders that same evening. He was to return at once to Memphis with one of his three divisions, which he would combine with McClernand's volunteers, already waiting there. This would give him 21,000 troops, and to these would be added another 12,000 to be picked up at Helena on the way downriver, bringing his total strength to four divisions of 33,000 men, supported by Porter's fleet. Grant explained that he himself would continue to bristle aggressively along the line of the Yalobusha "so as to keep up the impression of a continuous move," and if Pemberton fell back prematurely he would "follow him even to the gates of Vicksburg," in which event he and Sherman would meet on the Yazoo and combine for the final dash into the town. Delighted with the prospect, Sherman was off next day for Memphis, altogether mindful of the need for haste if he was to forestall both McClernand and Pemberton. "Time now is the great object," he wired Porter. "We must not give time for new combinations."

He did not make it precisely clear whether these feared "combinations" were being designed in Richmond or in Washington — whether, that is, they threatened the successful prosecution of Grant's public or his private war. By mid-December, however, Grant's worries in regard to the latter were mostly over. Sherman was in Memphis, poised for the jump-off, and McClernand's men had become organic parts of the army the redhead was about to take downriver. There was still one danger. McClernand outranked him; which meant that if he arrived before Sherman left, he would assume command by virtue of seniority. But Grant considered this unlikely. Sherman was thoroughly aware of the risk and would be sure to avoid the consequences. Besides, with Halleck's telegram in his files as license for the kidnap operation, Grant felt secure from possible thunder from on high. "I doubted McClernand's fitness," he later wrote, "and I had good reason to believe that in forestalling him I was by no means giving offense to those whose authority to command was above both him and me."

The arrival of a telegram from Washington on the 18th, instructing him to divide his command (now and henceforward to be called the Army of the Tennessee) into four corps, with McClernand in charge of one of those assigned to operations down the Mississippi — which meant of course that, once he joined it, he would be in charge of the whole column by virtue of his rank, unless Grant himself came over and took command along the river route — did not disturb the plans Grant had described in a letter home, three days ago, as "all complete for weeks to come," adding: "I hope to have them all work out just as planned." Sherman was ready to leave, he knew, and in fact would be gone tomorrow, before McClernand could possibly arrive from Illinois. Blandly he wired his new subordinate word of the Washington order, which dispelled McClernand's illusion that his command was to be an independent one. Instructing him to come on down to Memphis, Grant even managed to keep a straight face while remarking: "I hope you will find all the preliminary preparations completed on your arrival and the expedition ready to move."

★ ★ ★

McClernand found no such thing, of course. All he found when at last he reached Memphis on December 29 were the empty docks his men had departed from, ten days ago under Sherman, and Grant's telegram, delayed eleven days in transmission. Nor did Grant's own plans, "all complete for weeks to come," work out as he had intended and predicted. In both cases — entirely in the former and largely in the latter — the cause could be summed up in three two-syllable nouns: Nathan Bedford Forrest.

"He was the only Confederate cavalryman of whom Grant stood in much dread," a friend of the Union general's once remarked. Then he told why. "Who's commanding?" Grant would ask on hearing that gray raiders were on the prowl. If it was some other rebel chieftain he would shrug off the threat with a light remark; "but if Forrest was in command he at once became apprehensive, because the latter was amenable to no known rules of procedure, was a law unto himself for all military acts, and was constantly doing the unexpected at all times and places."

Grant's apprehensions were well founded as he looked back over his shoulder in the direction of his main supply base at Columbus, Kentucky; or, more specifically, since the far-off river town was adequately garrisoned against raiders, as he traced on the map the nearly two hundred highly vulnerable, not to say frangible, miles of railroad which were his sole all-weather connection with the munitions and food his army in North Mississippi required if it was to continue to shoot and eat. Without that base and those railroads, once he had used up the reserve supplies already brought forward and stored at Holly Springs, his choice would lie between retreat on the one hand and starvation or surrender on the other. Just now, moreover, the reason his apprehensions were so well founded was that Forrest was looking — and not only looking, but moving — in that direction, too: as Grant learned from a dispatch received December 15 from Jackson, Tennessee, a vital junction about midway of his vulnerable supply line. "Forrest is crossing [the] Tennessee at Clifton," the local commander wired. Four days later, Jackson itself was under attack by a mounted force which the Federal defenders estimated at 10,000 men, with Forrest himself definitely in charge.

Pemberton had begun it by appealing to Bragg in late November for a diversion in West Tennessee, which he thought might ease the pressure on his front, and Bragg had responded by sending Forrest instructions to "throw his command rapidly over the Tennessee River and precipitate it upon the enemy's lines, break up railroads, burn bridges,

destroy depots, capture hospitals and guards, and harass him generally."
Receiving these orders December 10 at Columbia, forty miles south of
Nashville, Forrest was off next day with four regiments of cavalry and a
four-gun battery, 2100 men in all, mostly recruits newly brigaded under
his command and mainly armed with shotguns and flintlock muskets.
Four days later and sixty miles away, he began to cross the Tennessee at
Clifton on two flatboats which he had built for the emergency and
which he afterwards sank in a nearby creek in case he needed them coming back. Deep in enemy country, with the bluecoats warned of his crossing while it was still in progress, he encountered on the 18th, near Lexington, two regiments of infantry, a battalion of cavalry, and a section
of artillery, all under Colonel Robert G. Ingersoll, who had been sent
out to intercept him. The meeting engagement was brief and decisive.
Falling back on the town, Ingersoll took up what he thought was a good
defensive position and was firing rapidly with his two guns at the rebels
to his front, when suddenly he "found that the enemy were pouring in
on all directions." The fight ended quite as abruptly as it had begun.
"If he really believed that there is no hell," one grayback later said of
the postwar orator-agnostic, "we convinced him that there was something mightily like it." Captured along with his two guns and 150 of his
men, while the rest made off "on the full run" for Jackson, twenty-five
miles to the west, Ingersoll greeted his captors with aplomb: "Is this
the army of your Southern Confederacy for which I have so diligently
sought? Then I am your guest until the wheels of the great Cartel are put
in motion."

Following hard on the heels of the fugitives, who he knew would
stumble into Jackson with exaggerated stories of his strength, Forrest
advanced to within four miles of the place and began to dispose his
"army" as if for assault, maneuvering boldly along the ridge-lines and
beating kettledrums at widely scattered points to keep up the illusion, or,
as he called it, "the skeer." It worked quite well. Convinced that he was
heavily outnumbered, though in fact he had about four times as many
troops inside the town as the Confederates had outside it, Brigadier General Jeremiah Sullivan prepared to make a desperate house-to-house defense. All next day the rebel host continued to gather, waxing bolder
hour by hour. When dawn of the 20th showed the graybacks gone,
Sullivan took heart and set out after them, pushing eastward — into
emptiness, as it turned out, for Forrest had swung north. Today in fact,
having thrown the Federal main body off his trail, he began in earnest to
carry out his primary assignment, the destruction of the sixty miles of
the Mobile & Ohio connecting Jackson and Union City, up near the
Kentucky line. The common complaint of army commanders, that cavalry could seldom be persuaded to get down off their horses for the
hard work that was necessary if the damage to enemy installations was
to be more than temporary, was never leveled against Forrest's men.

Besides forcing the surrender of the several blue garrisons in towns along the line, they tore up track, burned crossties and trestles, and wrecked culverts so effectively that this stretch of the M&O was out of commission for the balance of the war. In Union City on Christmas Eve, resting his troopers after their four-day rampage with axes and sledges, Forrest reported by courier to Bragg that, at a cost so far of 22 men, he had killed or captured more than 1300 of the enemy, "including 4 colonels, 4 majors, 10 captains, and 23 lieutenants." That he considered this no more than a respectable beginning was shown by his closing remark: "My men have all behaved well in action, and as soon as rested a little you will hear from me in another quarter."

His problem now, after paroling his captives and sending them north to Columbus to spread bizarre reports of his strength — reports that were based on bogus dispatches, which he had been careful to let them overhear while their papers were being made out at his headquarters — was, first, what further damage to inflict and, second, how to get back over the river intact before the various Federal columns, still chasing phantoms all over West Tennessee, converged on him with overwhelming numbers. The first was solved on Christmas Day, when he marched southeast out of Union City and spent the next two days administering to the Nashville & Northwestern the treatment already given the M&O. Reaching McKenzie on the 28th in an icy, pelting rain, he headed south across the swampy bottoms of the swollen Obion River, and now began his solution of the second part of his problem. Instead of trying to make a run for the Tennessee, with the chance of being caught half-over and hamstrung, he decided to brazen out the game by thrusting in among the Federals attempting a convergence, and by vigorous blows, struck right or left at whatever came within his reach, stun them into inaction or retreat, while he continued his movement toward the security of Middle Tennessee.

The fact was, he had little to fear from the direction of Columbus. Brigadier General Thomas A. Davies, commander of the 5000 bluecoats gathered there, had been so alarmed by demonstrations within ten miles of the town on Christmas Eve, as well as by the parolees coming in next day with reports of 40,000 infantry on the march from Bragg, that he had spiked the guns at New Madrid and Island Ten, throwing the powder into the Mississippi to keep it out of rebel hands, and now was concentrating everything in order to protect the $13,000,000 worth of supplies and equipment being loaded onto steamboats at the Columbus wharf for a getaway in case Forrest broke his lines. Conditions were scarcely better, from the Union point of view, 250 miles downriver at Memphis, where the citizens had become so elated over rumors that their former alderman was coming home, along with thousands of his troopers, that Major General S. A. Hurlbut, perturbed by their reaction and the fact that his garrison was down to a handful since the departure of

Sherman, telegraphed Washington: "I hold city by terror of heavy guns bearing upon it and the belief that an attack would cause its destruction." Grant, however, was of a different breed. He was thinking not of his safety, but of the possible destruction of Forrest and his men. "I have directed such a concentration of troops that I think not many of them will get back to the east bank of the Tennessee," he informed a subordinate. Nor was this opinion ill-founded. One superior blue force was coming south from Fort Henry, another north from Corinth, and both were now much closer to the Clifton crossing than Forrest was. So, for that matter, were Jere Sullivan and his three brigades, two of which were back by now from their goose chase east of Jackson and headed north. Undiscouraged by his lack of luck so far, he believed he knew just where the raiders were, and he intended to bag them. "I have Forrest in a tight place," he wired Grant on December 29. "My troops are moving on him from three directions, and I hope with success."

Forrest was indeed in a tight place, and that place was about to get tighter. Emerging from the flooded Obion bottoms, which he had crossed by an abandoned causeway, he paused on December 30 to let Sullivan's unsuspecting lead brigade go by him, then resumed his march past Huntingdon and toward Clarksburg, nearing which place on the morning of the last day of the year he encountered the other brigade, forewarned and drawn up to meet him at Parker's Crossroads. By way of precaution he had sent four companies to guard the road from Huntingdon and warn him in case the lead brigade turned back, and now, secure in the belief that his rear was well protected against surprise, he settled down to a casualty-saving artillery duel with the blue force to his front. It lasted from about 9 o'clock until an hour past noon, by which time he had captured three of the enemy guns and 18 wagonloads of ammunition and had driven the skirmishers back on their supports. He had in fact ceased firing, in response to several white flags displayed along the Union line, and was sending in his usual demand for "unconditional surrender to prevent the further effusion of blood," when an attack exploded directly in his rear. For the first last only time in his career, Forrest was completely surprised in battle. His reaction was immediate. Quickly resuming the fight to his front, he simultaneously charged rearward, stalling the surprise attackers with blows to the head and flanks, and withdrew sideways before his opponents recovered from the shock. It was smartly done — later giving rise to the legend that his response to a staff officer's flustered question, "What shall we do? What shall we do?" was: "Charge both ways!" — but not without sacrifice. The captured guns were abandoned, along with three of his own, for lack of horses to draw them, as well as the 18 wagonloads of ammunition. Three hundred men who had been fighting afoot were taken, too, while trying to catch their mounts, which had bolted at the sudden burst of gunfire from the rear. Sullivan, coming up from behind Jackson with his third brigade next day, was elated. "Forrest's army completely broken up," he wired Grant. "They are scattered over the country without ammunition. We need a good cavalry regiment to go through the country and pick them up."

So he said. But while he and his three brigades were waiting for that "good regiment," Forrest and his troopers were riding hard for the Tennessee and eluding the columns approaching cautiously from Corinth and Fort Henry. All in high spirits on New Year's Day — except possibly the captain who by now had been verbally blistered for taking yesterday's rear-guard companies up the wrong road and thus permitting the Federals to march past him unobserved — they reached Clifton about midday, raised the sunken flatboats, and were across the icy river before dawn. The basis for their high spirits was a sense of accomplishment. They had gone out as green recruits, miserably armed, and had returned within less than three weeks as veterans, equipped with the best accouterments and weapons the U.S. government could provide. In the course of a brief midwinter campaign, which opened and closed with a pontoonless crossing of one of the nation's great rivers, and in the course of which they more than made up in recruits for what they lost in battle or on the march, they had killed or paroled as many men as they had in their whole command and had kept at least ten times their number of bluecoats frantically busy for a fortnight. Besides the estimated $3,000,000 they had cost the Federals in wrecked installations and equipment, they had taken or destroyed 10 guns and captured 10,000 rifles and a million badly needed cartridges. Above all, they had accomplished their primary assignment by cutting Grant's lifeline, from Jackson north to the Kentucky border. They saw all this as Forrest's doing, and it was their pride, now and for all the rest of their lives — whether those lives were to end next week in combat or were to stretch on down the years to the ones they spent sunning their old bones on the galleries of crossroads stores throughout the Deep and Central South — that they had belonged to what in time would be known as his Old Brigade.

Pemberton was highly pleased, not only with the results of this cavalry action outside the limits of his department, but also with another which had been carried out within those limits and which he himself had designed as a sort of companion piece or counterpart to the raid-in-progress beyond the Tennessee line. Both had a profound effect on the situation he had been facing ever since he called a halt and began intrenching along the Yalobusha, preparatory to coming to grips with Grant's superior army: so profound an effect, indeed, that it presently became obvious that if he and Grant were to come to grips, it would be neither here nor now. Like that of the first, the success of this second horseback exploit — which in point of fact was simultaneous rather than sequential, beginning later and ending sooner — could also be summed up in three nouns, though in this case the summary was even briefer, since all three were single-syllabled: Earl Van Dorn.

"Buck" Van Dorn, as he had been called at West Point and by his fellow officers in the old army, had leaped at the chance for distinction, not only because it was part of his nature to delight in desperate ventures, but also because he was badly in need just now of personal re-

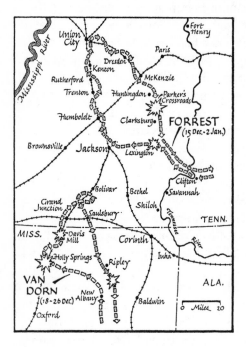

demption. After a brilliant pre-Manassas career in Texas, he had been called to Virginia, then reassigned to Arkansas, where his attempt at a double envelopment had been foiled disastrously at Elkhorn Tavern. Crossing the Mississippi after Shiloh, he had suffered an even bloodier repulse at Corinth in October, which gave him so evil a reputation in his home state that a court had been called to hear evidence of his bungling. Although he was cleared by the court, the government soon afterwards promoted Pemberton over the head upon which the public was still heaping condemnations. The accusation that he was "the source of all our woes," Senator Phelan wrote President Davis, was "so fastened in the public belief that an acquittal by a court-martial of angels would not relieve him of the charge." Van Dorn was depressed, but he was not without hope. A court-martial of angels was one thing; a brilliant military exploit, characterized by boldness and attended by great risk, was quite another. So when Pemberton summoned him to army headquarters and gave him his assignment — an all-out raid on Grant's communications and supply lines, including the great depot lately established at Holly Springs — the diminutive Mississippian saw in it the opportunity to retrieve his reputation and bask once more in the warmth of his countrymen's affection. Always one to grasp the nettle danger, he embraced the offered chance without delay.

He left Grenada on December 18 with 3500 cavalry, heading east at first to skirt Grant's flank, then north as if for a return to Corinth. Next day, however, he turned west beyond New Albany and came thundering into Holly Springs at dawn, December 20. The Federal commander there, Colonel R. C. Murphy, had been placed in a similar uncomfortable position in September at Iuka, which he had abandoned without a fight or even destruction of the stores to keep them from falling into enemy hands. Grant had forgiven him then because of his youth and inexperience, and now he was given another chance to prove his mettle. He did no better. In fact, despite advance warning that a heavy column of graybacks was moving in his direction, he did far worse. This time, he lost not only the stores in his charge but also the soldiers, 1500 of whom were captured and paroled on the spot by the jubilant rebels, caracoling their horses at the sight of the mountains of food and equipment piled here for Grant's army. "My fate is most mortifying," he reported that night amid the embers which were all that remained of the million-dollar depot of supplies. "I have done all in my power — in truth, my force was inadequate."

Grant reacted "with pain and mortification" at the news of his loss and ordered Murphy dismissed from the service, as of "the date of his cowardly and disgraceful conduct." With Forrest loose on the railroad north of Jackson that same day, and his own wife spared embarrassment at Holly Springs only because she had left to join him in Oxford the day before, Grant began to design combinations of forces in North Mississippi, not unlike those already sent out after Forrest in West Tennessee, to accomplish Van Dorn's destruction before he could return to safety behind the Yalobusha. "I want those fellows caught, if possible," he said.

The trouble with this was that by the time the various columns could be put in motion Van Dorn was no longer in North Mississippi. Instead of racing for home, and perhaps into the arms of superior forces already gathering in his rear, he pushed on northward into Tennessee. Before he left his native state, however, the commander of a small outpost at Davis Mill, twenty miles north of Holly Springs and just south of the Tennessee line, gave him — and, incidentally, Murphy — a lesson in how well an "inadequate" force could hold its own against "overwhelming" numbers. His name was Colonel W. H. Morgan and he had less than 300 men for the defense of a point made critical by the presence of a trestle by which the Mississippi Central crossed Wolf River. Hearing that the raiders were coming his way, he converted an old sawmill into a blockhouse, reinforcing its walls with cotton bales and crossties, and a nearby Indian mound into a moated earthwork, both of which covered the railroad approach with converging fire. About noon of the 21st, the Confederates came up and launched a quick assault, which was repulsed. After a two-hour long-range skirmish, finding the fire too hot for a storming party to reach and ignite the trestle, let alone cross the river, the attackers sent forward, under a flag of truce, a note asking whether the defenders were ready to surrender. Morgan replied with what he later termed "a respectful but decided negative," and the Confederates withdrew, leaving 22 dead and 30 wounded on the field, along with another 20 prisoners who had ventured up too close to be able to pull back without exposing themselves to slaughter. Morgan's loss was 3 men slightly wounded.

Except for the further damage it did to his former opinion that one Southerner was worth ten Yankee hirelings in a scrap, Van Dorn was not greatly disturbed by this tactical upset. In the course of his approach to the fight, and even while it was in progress, he had done the railroad enough damage to be able to afford to let the trestle go. Bypassing Morgan's improvised blockhouse, he crossed upstream and pushed on northward between Grand Junction and LaGrange, where he tore up sections of the Memphis & Charleston for good measure. Near Bolivar on the 23rd, he circled Middleburg, still ripping up track and wrecking culverts, and headed back south on Christmas Eve, riding through Van Buren and Saulsbury to re-enter Mississippi. South of Ripley on Christmas Day, he had a brush with one of the converging Union colums, but pressed on without delay, through Pontotoc and thence on back to Grenada, which he reached by midafternoon of December 28. He had carried out his mission in fine style, destroying Grant's reserve supplies of food, forage, and munitions. What was more, at least from a particular point of view, he had refurbished his tarnished reputation. Households which formerly had mentioned his name only with frowns of disapproval or downright scowls of condemnation now drank his health with shouts of joy and praised him to the skies.

Pemberton, then, was delighted at the manner in which Van Dorn had achieved redemption; but not Grant, who paid the bill which thus was added to all that Forrest was costing him simultaneously. With Columbus in a panic, Memphis cowed by heavy guns, his communications disrupted, and his supply line almost a continuous wreck from Holly Springs north to the Kentucky border, he was stymied and he knew it. Van Dorn having destroyed his supplies on hand and Forrest having made it impossible for him to bring up more, he could neither move forward nor stand still. There was no way he could go but back, and this he proceeded to do, meanwhile solving the problem of immediate subsistence by sending out "all the wagons we had, under proper escort, to collect and bring in all supplies of forage and food from a region of fifteen miles east and west of the road from our front back to Grand Junction." At the news of this, the broad smiles caused by Van Dorn's coup faded from the faces of the people around Oxford. Their former mocking question, "What will you do now?" was changed to: "What are we to do?" Grant replied that he had done his best to feed his soldiers from their own northern resources, but now that these had been cut off "it could not be expected that men, with arms in their hands, would starve in the midst of plenty." In short, as he said later, "I advised them to emigrate east, or west, fifteen miles and assist in eating up what we left."

To his amazement — for he had thought the pickings would be slim and had lately advised his government that an army could not "subsist itself on the country except in forage"; "Disaster would result in the end," he had predicted — the wagons returned heavy-laden with hams, corn on the cob, field peas and beans, sweet and Irish potatoes, and fowls of every description, accompanied by herds of beef on the hoof. "It showed that we could have subsisted off the country for two months instead of two weeks without going beyond the limits designated," he subsequently wrote, adding: "This taught me a lesson."

The knowledge thus gained might prove to be of great use in the future, but for the present one thing still bothered him beyond all others. This was the thought that, putting it baldly, he was leaving his friend Sherman in the lurch. He had promised to hold Pemberton in position, 150 miles from Vicksburg, while Sherman was storming its thinly held defenses; yet Pemberton was already hurrying troops in that direction, as Grant knew, and might well arrive in time to smother the attackers in the Yazoo bottoms. However, there was little Grant could do about it now, except depend on Sherman to work out his own salvation. Out of touch as he was, because of his ruptured communications, Grant did not even know whether Sherman had left Memphis yet — or, if so, whether he was still in command of the river expedition; McClernand, in event of delay, might have arrived in time to take over. All Grant could do was send a courier to Memphis with a message addressed to "Commanding Officer Expedition down Mississippi," advising him, whoever he was, "that farther advance by this route is perfectly impracticable" and that he and his men were falling back, while Pemberton did likewise. Whether this would arrive in time to forestall disaster, he did not know.

★ ★ ★

Sherman was already downriver, and so far his only thought of disaster had been the intention to inflict it. "You may calculate on our being at Vicksburg by Christmas," he wrote Grant's adjutant on December 19, the day he left Memphis. "River has risen some feet, and all is now good navigation. Gunboats are at mouth of Yazoo now, and there will be no difficulty in effecting a landing up Yazoo within twelve miles of Vicksburg." Two days later at Helena, where he picked up his fourth division, he received from upriver his first intimation that Grant might be having trouble in the form of rebel cavalry, which was reported to have captured Holly Springs. If this was so, then Sherman's first letter most likely had not got through to Oxford; nor would a second. Nevertheless, he refused to be disconcerted, and wrote again. "I hardly know what faith to put in such a report," he said, "but suppose whatever may be the case you will attend to it."

All was indeed "good navigation" for the fifty-odd army transports and the 32,500 soldiers close-packed on their decks, steaming rapidly toward their destiny below, as well as for the naval escort of three ironclads, two wooden gunboats, and two rams. But for the rest of Porter's fleet — three ironclads and two "tinclads," so called because their armor was no more than musket-proof — the going had been less easy. Sent downriver two weeks before, they had succeeded in clearing the Yazoo from its mouth upstream to Haines Bluff, where a stout Confederate battery defined the limit of penetration, 23 winding miles from the point of entrance. This had not been accomplished without cost, however, for the defenses were in charge of Isaac Brown, and Brown was known to be hungry for vengeance because of the recent loss above Baton Rouge of the steam ram *Arkansas*, which he had built up this same river the summer before and with which he had charged and sundered the two flotillas then besieging Vicksburg. He had no warship now, but he had notions about torpedoes, five-gallon whiskey demijohns packed with powder, fuzed with artillery friction tubes, and each suspended a few feet below a float on the muddy surface. On December 12 the five-boat Union reconnaissance squadron appeared up the Yazoo, shelling the banks and fishing up Brown's torpedoes as it advanced. Approaching Haines Bluff, the ironclad *Cairo* made contact with one of the glass demijohns at five minutes before noon, and at 12.03 she was out of sight, all but the tips of her stacks, in thirty feet of water.

Celerity and good discipline made it possible for the crew to abandon ship within the allowed eight minutes. No lives were lost, but the *Cairo*'s skipper, Lieutenant Commander T. O. Selfridge, Jr., a young man with a lofty forehead and luxuriant sideburns, was greatly disturbed by the loss of his boat and the possible end of his career as well, depending on the admiral's reaction to the news. Steaming back down the Yazoo aboard one of the tinclads, he found Porter himself at the mouth of the river, just arrived from Memphis, and stiffly requested a court of inquiry. "Court!" the admiral snorted. "I have no time to order courts. I can't blame an officer who puts his ship close to the enemy. Is there any other vessel you would like to have?" Without waiting for an answer he turned abruptly to the flag captain standing beside him on the bridge. "Breese, make out Selfridge's orders to the *Conestoga*."

Porter was like that, when he chose to be. Just short of fifty and rather hard-faced, with a hearty manner and a full dark beard, he had been given his present assignment, together with the rank of acting rear admiral, over the heads of eighty seniors. For the present, though, despite this cause for self-congratulation, the heartiness and bluster were cover for worry. Most of his old sailors had broken down, with the result that his heavy boats were half-manned, while ten light-draft vessels were laid up for lack of crews, and he was complaining to Washington that a draft of new men, lately arrived from New York, were "all boys and very ordinary landsmen." Characteristically, however, in a letter written this week to Sherman, after protesting of these and other matters, including a shortage of provisions, fuel, medicines, and clothing — not to mention the loss of the *Cairo* — he closed by observing: "I expected that the government would send men from the East, but not a man will they send or notice my complaints, so we will have to go on with what we have."

Reaching Milliken's Bend, on the west bank of the Mississippi ten miles above the mouth of the Yazoo, Sherman landed a brigade on Christmas Day and sent it out to wreck a section of the railroad connecting Vicksburg and Monroe, Louisiana. Next morning, while the brigade was returning, its mission accomplished, the rest of the armada proceeded downstream, entered the Yazoo, and steamed up its intricate channel. A light gunboat and an ironclad led the way, followed by twenty transports, each with two companies of riflemen charged with returning the fire of snipers. Then came another ironclad and twenty more transports, similarly protected. So it went, to the tail of the 64-boat column, until a landing was made at Johnson's Farm, on the Vicksburg shore of the Yazoo ten miles above its mouth. Alertness had paid off, or else it had been unnecessary. "Some few guerilla parties infested the banks," Sherman explained, "but did not dare to molest so strong a force as I commanded." It occurred to some of his soldiers, though, that the rebels were going to let geography do their fighting for them. Wide-eyed as the Illinois and Indiana farmboys were in this strange land, that seemed altogether possible. First there had been the big river itself — or himself; the Old Man, natives called the stream, taking their cue from the Indians, who had named it the Father of Waters — the tawny, mile-wide Mississippi, so thick with silt that recruits could almost believe the steamboat hands who solemnly assured them that if you drank its water for as much as a week "you will have a sandbar in you a mile long." Then had come the smaller stream, with its currentless bayous and mazy sloughs, whose very name was the Indian word for death. And now there was this, the land itself, spongelike under their feet as they came ashore, desolate as the back side of the moon and brooded over by cypresses and water oaks with long gray beards of Spanish moss. North was only a direction indicated by a compass — if a man had one, that is, for otherwise there was no north or south or east or west; there was only the brooding desolation. If this was the country the rebs wanted to take out of the Union, the blue-coated farmboys were ready to say good riddance.

The molestation Sherman had said the Confederates did not dare to attempt began the following day, December 27, against the navy. Commander William Gwin, a veteran of all the river fights since Fort Henry, took his ironclad *Benton* upstream to shell out some graybacks lurking in the woods on the left flank, but got caught in a narrow stretch of the river and was pounded by a battery on the bluffs. Three of the more than thirty hits came through the *Benton*'s ports, cutting her crew up badly, and Gwin, who refused to take cover in the shot-proof pilothouse — "A captain's place is on the quarterdeck," he protested when urged to step inside — was mortally wounded by an 8-inch solid that took off most of his right arm and breast, exposing the ribs and lung in a sudden flash of white and scarlet. Meanwhile the army was having its share of opposition, too, as it floundered about in the Yazoo bottoms and tried to get itself aligned for the assault on the Walnut Hills. The four division commanders, Brigadier Generals A. J. Smith, M. L. Smith, G. W. Morgan, and Frederick Steele, were in the thick of things next morning, dodging bullets like all the rest, when suddenly their number was reduced to three by a sniper who hit the second Smith in the hip joint and retired him from the campaign.

These two high-placed casualties only added to a confusion that was rife enough already. Johnson's Farm, which was little more than a patch of cleared ground in the midst of swampy woods, was separated from the hills ahead by a broad, shallow bayou, a former bed of the Yazoo, and hemmed in on the flanks by two others, Old River Bayou on the right and Chickasaw Bayou on the left. All three looked much alike to an unpracticed eye, so that there was much consequent loss of direction, misidentification of objectives, and countermarching of columns. A bridge ordered constructed over the shallow bayou to the front was built by mistake over one of the others, too late to be relaid. Whole companies got separated from their regiments and spent hours ricocheting from one alien outfit to another. As a result of all this, and more, it was Monday morning, December 29, before the objectives could be assigned and pointed out on the ground instead of on the inadequate maps. Sherman's plan for overrunning the hilltop defenses was for all four divisions to make "a show of attack along the whole front," but to concentrate his main effort at two points, half a mile apart, which seemed to him to afford his soldiers the best chance for a penetration. One of these was in front of Morgan's division, and when Sherman pointed it out to him and told him what he wanted, Morgan nodded positively. "General, in ten minutes after you give the signal I'll be on those hills," he said.

His timing was a good deal off. Except for one brigade, which "took cover behind the [opposite] bank, and could not be moved forward," as Sherman later reported in disgust, Morgan not only did not reach "those hills," he did not even get across the bayou, in ten or any other number of minutes after the signal for attack was given by the batteries all along the Federal line. Presently, however, it was demonstrated that, all in all, this was perhaps the best thing to have done in the situation in which their red-headed commander had placed them. A brigade of Steele's division, led by Brigadier General Frank Blair, Jr., a former Missouri congressman and brother of the Postmaster General, got across in good order and excellent spirits, only to encounter a savage artillery crossfire that sent it staggering back, leaving 500 killed, wounded, and captured at the point where it had been struck. One regiment kept going but was stopped by the steepness of the bluff and a battery firing directly down the throats of the attackers. With their hands they began to scoop out burrows in the face of the nearly perpendicular hillside, seeking overhead cover from enemy riflemen who held their muskets out over the parapet and fired them vertically into the huddled, frantically digging mass below. Indeed, so critical was their position, as Sherman later said, "that we could not recall the men till after dark, and then one at a time." He added, in summation of the day's activities: "Our loss had been pretty heavy, and we had accomplished nothing, and had inflicted little loss on our enemy."

"Pretty heavy" was putting it mildly, as he would discover when he found time for counting noses, but the rest of this estimation was accurate enough. Federal losses reached the commemorative figure 1776, of whom 208 were killed, 1005 were wounded, and 563 were captured or otherwise missing. The Confederates lost 207 in all: 63 killed, 134 wounded, and 10 missing.

Unwilling to let it go at that — "We will lose 5000 men before we take Vicksburg," he had said, "and may as well lose them here as anywhere else" — Sherman decided to reload Steele's division aboard transports and move it upstream for a diversionary strike in the vicinity of Haines Bluff, which might induce the defenders to weaken their present line. Porter was no less willing than before. Moreover, by way of disposing of Brown's remaining torpedoes, he conceived the idea of using one of the rams to clear the path. "I propose to sent her ahead and explode them," he explained. "If we lose her, it does not matter much." Colonel Charles R. Ellet, youthful successor to his dead father as commander of the former army vessels, did not take to this notion of a sacrificial ram. With Porter's consent, he added a 45-foot boom extending beyond the prow and equipped it with pulleys and cords and hooks for fishing up the floats and demijohns. Ram and transports set out by the dark of the moon on the last night of the year, while Sherman alerted his other three divisions for a second all-out assault on the Walnut Hills as soon as they heard the boom of guns upstream. What came instead, at 4 a.m. on New Year's Day, was a note from Steele, explaining that the boats were fog-bound and could not proceed. So Sherman called a halt and took stock. He had been waiting all this time for some word from Grant, either on the line of the Yalobusha or here on the Yazoo, but there had been nothing since the rumor of the fall of Holly Springs. From Vicksburg itself, ten air-line miles away, its steeples visible from several points along his boggy front, he had been hearing for the past three days the sound of trains arriving and departing. It might be a ruse, as at Corinth back in May. On the other hand, it might signify what it sounded like: the arrival from Grenada or Mobile or Chattanooga, or possibly all three, of reinforcements for the rebel garrison. Also, rain had begun to fall by now in earnest, and looking up he saw watermarks on the trunks of trees "ten feet above our heads." In short, as he later reported, seeing "no good reason for remaining in so unenviable a position any longer," he "became convinced that the part of wisdom was to withdraw."

Withdraw he did, re-embarking his soldiers the following day and proceeding downriver without delay. There was more room on the decks of the transports now, and Sherman was low in spirits: not because he was dissatisfied with his direction of the attempt — "There was no bungling on my part," he wrote, "for I never worked harder or with more intensity of purpose in my life" — but because he knew that the journalists, whom he had snubbed at every opportunity since their spreading of last year's rumors that he was insane, would have a field day writing their descriptions of his repulse and retreat. Presently he was hailed by Porter, who signaled him to come aboard the flagship. Sherman did so, rain-drenched and disconsolate.

"I've lost 1700 men," he said, "and those infernal reporters will publish all over the country their ridiculous stories about Sherman being whipped."

"Pshaw," the admiral replied. "That's nothing; simply an episode of the war. You'll lose 17,000 before the war is over and think nothing of it. We'll have Vicksburg yet, before we die. Steward! Bring some punch."

When he got the red-head settled down he gave him the unwelcome news that McClernand was at hand, anchored just inside the mouth of the Yazoo and waiting to see him. Sherman, who could keep as straight a face as his friend Grant when so inclined, afterwards remarked of his rival's sudden but long-expected appearance on the scene: "It was rumored he had come down to supersede me."

McClernand, too, had news for him when they met later that day. Grant was not coming down through Mississippi; he had in fact been in retreat for more than a week, leaving Pemberton free to concentrate for the defense of Vicksburg. Sherman suggested that this meant that any further attempt against the town with their present force was hopeless. Indeed, in the light of this disclosure, he began to consider himself most fortunate in failure, even though it had cost him a total of 1848 casualties for the whole campaign. "Had we succeeded," he reasoned, "we might have found ourselves in a worse trap, when General Pemberton was at full liberty to turn his whole force against us."

Dark-bearded McClernand agreed that the grapes were sour, at least for now. Next day, January 3, he and Sherman withdrew their troops from the Yazoo and rendezvoused again at Milliken's Bend, where McClernand took command.

"Well, we have been to Vicksburg and it was too much for us and we have backed out," Sherman wrote his wife from the camp on the west bank of the Mississippi. Reporting by dispatch to Grant, however, he went a bit more into detail as to causes. "I attribute our failure to the strength of the enemy's position, both natural and artificial, and not to his superior fighting," he declared; "but as we must all in the future have ample opportunities to test this quality, it is foolish to discuss it."

Pemberton would have agreed that it was foolish to discuss it, not for the reason his adversary gave, but because he considered the question already settled. The proof of the answer, so far as he was concerned, had been demonstrated in the course of the past two weeks, during which time he had stood off and repulsed two separate Union armies, each superior in numbers to his own. What was more, he had gained new confidence in his top commanders: in Van Dorn, whose lightning raid, staged in conjunction with Forrest's in West Tennessee, had abolished the northward menace: in the on-the-spot Vicksburg defenders, Major General Martin L. Smith and Brigadier General Stephen D. Lee, who with fewer than 15,000 soldiers, most of whom had arrived at the last minute from Grenada, had driven better than twice as many bluecoats out of their side yard, inflicting in the process about nine times as many casualties as they suffered: and in himself, who had engineered the whole and had been present for both repulses. Not that he did not expect to have to fight a return engagement. He did. But he considered that this would be no more than an occasion for redemonstrating what had been proved already.

"Vicksburg is daily growing stronger," he wired Richmond soon after New Year's. "We intend to hold it."

✕ 5 ✕

Rosecrans too was aware that haste made waste, but unlike Grant he was having no part of it. In reply to Halleck's frequent urgings that he move against Bragg and Chattanooga without delay — it was for this, after all, that he had been appointed to succeed his fellow Ohioan, Don Carlos Buell, whose characteristic attitude had seemed to his superiors to be one of hesitation — he made it clear that he intended to take his time. He would move when he got ready, not before, and thus, as he put it, avoid having to "stop and tinker" along the way. His policy, he explained in a series of answers to the telegraphic nudges, was "to lull [the rebels] into security," then "press them up solidly" and "endeavor to make an end of them." When Halleck at last lost patience altogether, informing the general in early December that he had twice been asked to designate a successor for him — "If you remain one more week in

Nashville," he warned, "I cannot prevent your removal" — Rosecrans set his heels in hard and bristled back at the general-in-chief: "I need no other stimulus to make me do my duty than the knowledge of what it is. To threats of removal or the like I must be permitted to say that I am insensible."

"Old Rosy" the men called him, not only because of his colorful name, but also because of his large red nose, which one observer classified as "intensified Roman." He was a tall, hale man, a heavy drinker but withal an ardent Catholic; he carried a crucifix on his watch chain and a rosary in his pocket, and he so delighted in small-hours religious discussions that he sometimes kept his staff up half the night debating such fine points as the distinction between profanity, which he freely employed, and blasphemy, which he eschewed. One such discussion achieved marathon proportions, going on for ten nights running, and though this was hard on the staff men, who missed their sleep, Rosecrans considered the problem solved beforehand by the fact that, like himself, they were all blond; "sandy fellows," he remarked upon occasion, were "quick and sharp," and, being more industrious by nature than brunets, required less rest — although he, for his own part, often slept till noon on the day following one of the all-night sessions devoted to eschatology or the question of how many angels could stand tiptoe on a pinpoint. Like Bardolph, whom he so much resembled in physiognomy, he could swing rapidly from gloom to equanimity or from abusiveness to affability. The bristly reply to Halleck was characteristic, for he would often flare up on short notice; but he was likely to calm down just as fast. All of a sudden, on the heels of an outburst of temper, he would be all smiles and congeniality, stroking and cajoling the very man he had been reviling a moment past, and if this was sometimes confusing to those around him, it was also a rather welcome relief from the dour and noncommittal Buell. Rosecrans was forty-three, two years younger than his present opponent Bragg, who had graduated five years ahead of him at West Point, where each had stood fifth in his class. Sometimes he seemed older than his years, sometimes not, depending on his mood, but in general he was liked and even admired, especially by the volunteers, who found him approachable and amusing. For instance, he would stroll through the camps after lights-out, and if he saw a lamp still burning in one of the tents he would whack on the canvas with the flat of his sword. The response, if not blasphemous, would at any rate be profane and abusive. Prompt to apologize when they saw the red-nosed face of their general appear through the tent flap, the soldiers would explain that they had thought he was some rowdy prowling around in the dark. He took it well, including the muffled laughter that followed the extinguishing of the lamp on his departure, and the result was a steady growth of affection between him and the men of the army which Halleck was protesting he was slow to commit to battle.

That army's present over-all strength was 81,729 effectives, divided like Grant's into Left Wing, Center, and Right Wing, commanded respectively by Major Generals T. L. Crittenden, George Thomas, and Alexander McCook, all veterans of the bloody October fight at Perryville, Kentucky, under Buell. By mid-December — Halleck having more or less apologized for the previous nudgings by explaining that they had not been intended as "threats of removal or the like," but merely as expressions of the President's "great anxiety" over the fact that, Middle Tennessee being the Confederacy's only late-summer gain which had not been erased, pro-Southern members of the British parliament, scheduled to convene in January, might find in this apparent stalemate persuasive arguments for the intervention France was already urging — Rosecrans became more optimistic, despite the drouth which kept the Cumberland River too shallow for it to serve as a dependable supply line. "Things will be ripe soon," he assured his nervous superiors on the 15th, and followed this dispatch with another, put on the wire within an hour: "Rebel troops say they will fight us. . . . Cumberland still very low; rain threatens; will be ready in a few days."

The few days stretched on to Christmas, and still he had not moved. By then, however, he had received encouraging reports from scouts and spies beyond the rebel lines. In the first place, Morgan and Forrest were on the prowl, and though normally this would have been considered alarming information, in this case it was not so, for the former was now so far in his rear as not to be able to interfere with any immediate action south or east of Nashville, while the latter was clean outside his department. Whatever harm they might do in Kentucky and West Tennessee (which, as it turned out, was considerable) Rosecrans could wish them Godspeed, so long as they kept their backs in his direction. Moreover, he had learned of the visit to Murfreesboro by Jefferson Davis and the subsequent detachment of one of Bragg's six divisions to Pemberton. Now if ever was the time to strike, and the Union commander was ready. Orders went out Christmas Day for the advance to begin next morning in three columns: Crittenden on the left, marching down the Murfreesboro turnpike through La Vergne and paralleling the Nashville & Chattanooga Railroad; McCook in the middle, cross-country through Nolensville; Thomas on the right, due south through Brentwood, then eastward across McCook's rear to take his rightful position in the center. Each of the three "wings" was well below its normal three-divisional strength because of guard detachments. Thomas, for example, had left a whole division on garrison duty at Nashville, in case Morgan or Forrest turned back or some other pack of raiders struck in that direction while the main body was attending to Bragg, and Crittenden and McCook were almost equally reduced by piecemeal detachments on similar duty elsewhere along the lines of supply and communication. The result was that Rosecrans had barely

44,000 troops in his three columns — Crittenden 14,500, Thomas — 13,500, McCook 16,000 — or only a little more than half of his total effective strength. But he was not ruffled by this reduction of the numerical odds in his favor; he knew that he was still a good deal stronger than his opponent. What was more, his deliberate preparations had paid off. Not only would he be free of the necessity to "stop and tinker" for lack of engineering equipment; he had within reach "the essentials of ammunition and twenty days' rations." Thus he had notified Washington on Christmas Eve, while planning the movement of his eight attack divisions, and he added in regard to the enemy, thirty miles southeastward down the pike: "If they meet us, we shall fight tomorrow; if they wait for us, next day."

It was neither "tomorrow" nor the "next day" — which was in fact the day he actually got started. Nor was it the day after that, or the day after that, or even the day after that. Still, Rosecrans was not unduly perturbed. Delay had already gained him much, including the loss by the Confederates of one infantry division and two brigades of cavalry; further delay might gain him more. Such was not the case, as it turned out, but what fretted him most just now was the slashing efficiency of the cavalry retained by Bragg, which cost the advancing Federals portions of their wagon train, as well as isolated detachments of their own horsemen assigned to protect the flanks and rear of the main body, slogging forward in three columns. As these drew near Murfreesboro on the 29th and 30th, consolidating at last to form a continuous line of battle along the west bank of the south fork of Stones River, two miles short of the town, they began to encounter infantry resistance, spasmodic at first and then determined, which seemed to promise fulfillment of the vow Rosecrans had passed along to Halleck two weeks before: "Rebel troops say they will fight us." However, he had followed this with a vow of his own, which he also believed was moving toward fulfillment: "If we beat them, I shall try to drive them to the wall."

Bragg had 37,713 effectives, well under half as many as his opponent, but he had them all at hand, with the result that the attackers were only about fifteen percent stronger than the defenders. Not that he considered himself committed to the tactical defensive. If the opportunity arose he intended to hit Rosecrans first, and hard. By way of preparation, however, he wanted him within reach, and therefore he gave his outpost commanders instructions to offer the advancing blue columns no more than a token resistance. "General Bragg sent us word not to fight them too much, but to let them come on," one gray cavalryman afterwards recalled.

In the course of the four-day Federal approach march — which was impeded, but not "too much," by the nearly 4000 troopers under

Brigadier General Joseph Wheeler — Bragg assembled his 34,000 infantry at Murfreesboro, the center of the wide arc along which his five divisions had been disposed so as to cover the roads out of Nashville. Lieutenant General Leonidas Polk's two-division corps was there already, and Lieutenant General William J. Hardee's came in on December 28 from Triune, fifteen miles west. With the arrival next day of Major General John McCown's division from Readyville, a dozen miles east, the concentration was complete, and the army formed for combat astride Stones River, which was fordable at practically all points because of the drouth. Hardee was on the right, northwest of the town and with a bend of the river to his front; Polk was on the left, due west of the town and with another bend of the river to his rear; McCown was in reserve behind the center, which

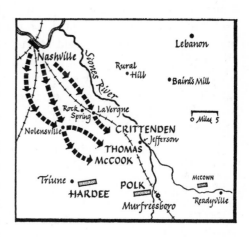

was pierced by the Nashville turnpike and the Nashville & Chattanooga Railroad, pointing arrow-straight in the direction from which Rosecrans was expected. Except for Wheeler's horsemen, who, now that the consolidation of the infantry had been effected with time to spare, were turned loose with a vengeance on the flanks and rear of the still approaching Federals, the Confederates settled down to wait for the opening of the battle everyone knew was about to be fought.

Many of them — particularly the officers, whose opportunities were larger in this respect — were still suffering from the aftereffects of a Christmas which they had celebrated with the fervor of men who knew only too well that the chances were strong that it would be their last. "I felt feeble," a Georgia lieutenant wrote in his diary the morning after, "but, being anxious to be with my men, reported for duty." Things had been that way for weeks now. Murfreesboro, a former state capital named for a colonel in the Revolution, was a lively place whose citizens, decidedly pro-rebel no matter which army happened to be in occupation, afforded their gray-clad defenders entertainments and amusements of all kinds, including horse races, balls, whist parties, and midnight gatherings in their parlors. President Davis's visit, two weeks before, had been the occasion for much rejoicing and pride, but all agreed that the social high point of the season had been the marriage on December 14, the day after the President's departure, of John Morgan and a local belle. Spirited in her defense of all things southern, when she heard some northern officers disparaging the raider during the Union occupation the previous summer, she told them off so

roundly that one of the bluecoats asked her name. "It's Mattie Ready
now," she said. "But by the grace of God one day I hope to call myself
the wife of John Morgan." Hearing the story, the widower cavalryman came to call on her as soon as the town was again in southern hands,
and in due time — for the young lady was apparently as skilled in her
brand of tactics as the colonel was in his — they became engaged. Because of the size of the guest list, which included Bragg and his ranking
commanders, Morgan's fellow officers and kinsmen from Kentucky,
and a host of civilians invited from round about by the bride's family,
the wedding was held in the courtroom of the Murfreesboro courthouse, Leonidas Polk officiating and wearing over the uniform of a Confederate lieutenant general the vestments of an Episcopal bishop. Thus
it was that Mattie Ready, by the grace of God, became Mrs John
Hunt Morgan.

Within a week, apparently not content with his exploit at Hartsville earlier that month, the bridegroom was off on what would be
known as his Christmas Raid, a twofold celebration of his marriage and
the brigadier's commission recently handed him by the President himself. His goal, assigned by Bragg, was Rosecrans' supply line, specifically
the Louisville & Nashville Railroad north of Bowling Green, with
particular attention to be paid to the great trestles at Muldraugh's Hill.
He left Alexandria, thirty miles northeast of Murfreesboro, on December 21 with 2500 horsemen, crossed the Cumberland the following
day, and re-entered his home state the day after that. Passing through
Glasgow on the 24th, he forded the Green on Christmas Day, skirmishing as he went and taking prisoners by the hundreds, and struck suddenly north of Munfordville to lay siege to the Federal garrison at
Elizabethtown, which surrendered on the 27th, opening the way to
Muldraugh's Hill, where the garrison also surrendered. After burning
the trestles, enormous structures five hundred feet long and eighty
feet tall, he continued east through Bardstown to Springfield, then
turned south, skirting heavily garrisoned Lebanon and fighting off pursuers for a getaway through Campbellsville, Columbia, and Burkes-
ville, to reach Smithville, Tennessee, on January 5, fifteen miles southeast of his starting point at Alexandria. In two weeks, having covered
better than 400 miles, he had fought four engagements and numerous
skirmishes. At a total cost of 2 men killed and 24 wounded, plus about
300 stragglers — victims not of enemy guns but of the weather, which
was bitter, and of confiscated bourbon — he had destroyed the vital
railroad trestles and four important bridges, along with an estimated
$2,000,000 in Union stores, and had torn up more than twenty miles
of L&N track, while capturing and paroling 1887 enemy soldiers.

Joe Wheeler, West Point '59, was not to be outdone by Morgan
or Forrest, who were his subordinates as a result of Bragg's appointment
of the twenty-six-year-old Georgian as commander of all the cavalry

in the Army of Tennessee. Unleashed on the night of December 29, after screening the concentration of the gray infantry in his rear and delaying the advance of the blue columns to his front, he rode north on the Lebanon pike with 2000 troopers, then swung west to Jefferson, where he attacked a brigade of infantry on the march and gobbled up a 20-wagon segment of Crittenden's supply train. At La Vergne by noon, halfway to Nashville and well in the Union rear, he captured and burned McCook's whole train of 300 wagons, packed with stores valued by Wheeler at "many hundred thousands of dollars," and paroled 700 prisoners, including the teamsters and their escort. "The turnpike, as far as the eye could reach, was filled with burning wagons," a Federal officer reported when he rode through the town next morning and surveyed the ruin the graybacks left behind. "The country was over-spread with disarmed men [and] broken-down horses and mules. The streets were covered with empty valises and trunks, knapsacks, broken guns, and all the indescribable débris of a captured and rifled army train." Wheeler and his horsemen were over the southwest horizon by then, having taken two more trains, one at Rock Spring and another at Nolensville. Beyond there, more prisoners were paroled while the weary raiders snatched a few hours' sleep before swinging back into their saddles and heading east for Murfreesboro to rejoin the infantry drawn up along Stones River. Completing his two-day circuit of Rose-crans — in the course of which he had captured more than a thousand men, destroyed all or parts of four wagon trains, brought off enough rifles and carbines to arm a brigade, remounted all of his troopers who needed fresh horses, and left a train of devastation along both flanks and around the rear of the entire Union army — Wheeler made contact with Bragg's left at 2 a.m. on the last day of the year, in time for a share in the battle which was now about to open.

A certain amount of reshuffling had occurred during his absence. Rosecrans, coming forward with his main body on the 30th while Wheeler was clawing at his flanks and rear, put his three corps in line, left to right, Crittenden and Thomas and McCook, the first opposite Hardee, the second opposite Polk, and the third — the largest of the three — opposite nothing more than a thin line of skirmishers extend-ing the rebel left. Because of skillful screening by the gray cavalry during the approach march, the Federal commander was not aware of the opportunity he had created for a lunge straight into Murfreesboro around the Confederate flank; but Bragg was, and he moved at once to correct his dispositions, shifting McCown's reserve division from its post behind the center to a position on Polk's left, extending his line of battle southward to meet the threat. Rosecrans meanwhile was plan-ning and issuing orders for an attack. His intention was to execute a right wheel, sending Crittenden forward on the north, with instructions to pivot on the left of Thomas, who would also move forward in sequence to assist in the capture of the town, cutting the rebels off from their supplies and setting them up for annihilation. McCook was thus to serve as anchor man. "If the enemy attacks you," Rosecrans told him, "fall back slowly, refusing your right, contesting the ground inch by inch. If the enemy does not attack you, you will attack him, not vigorously but warmly." As an added piece of deception, McCook was ordered about 6 p.m. to build a line of fires beyond his right, simulating a prolongation of his line so as to draw Bragg's attention away from the main effort at the far end of the field.

The southern commander was indeed deceived, and quite as thoroughly as Rosecrans had intended, but his reaction was something different from what the northern commander had hoped for. Or, rather, it was what he had hoped for, only more so. When Bragg observed the fires and heard sounds of movement on the Federal right, not only did he take the bait, but he proceeded, so to speak, to run away with it. Devising an offensive of his own to meet what he conceived to be a new threat to his left, he instructed Hardee, whose two divisions were under Major Generals John C. Breckinridge and Patrick R. Cleburne, to leave the former posted where it was, guarding the river crossings on the right, and move the latter southward to a position in support of McCown, who had been shifted earlier that day. Hardee himself was to come along, moreover, and take command of these two divisions on the left for a slashing assault on the Federals seemingly massed in that direction. Bragg's plans called for a right wheel by both corps on the west bank of Stones River, with the pivot on Polk's right division near the Nashville pike, the brigades attacking in rapid sequence from left to right, obliquing northward as they advanced, in order to throw the bluecoats back against the stretch of river whose crossings were covered by Breckinridge's guns and infantry.

Just before tattoo, while this additional shift was being completed under cover of darkness and orders were going out for the assault next morning, the military bands of both armies began to play their respective favorite tunes. Carrying sweet and clear on the windless wintry air, the music of any one band was about as audible on one side of the line as on the other, and the concert thus became something of a contest, a musical bombardment. "Dixie" answered the taunting "Yankee Doodle"; "Hail Columbia" followed "The Bonnie Blue Flag." Finally, though, one group of musicians began to play the familiar "Home Sweet Home," and one by one the others took it up, until at last all the bands of both armies were playing the song. Soldiers on both sides of the battle line began to sing the words, swelling the chorus east and west, North and South. As it died away on the final line — "There's no-o place like home" — the words caught in the throats of men, who, bluecoat and butternut alike, would be killing each other tomorrow in what already gave promise of being one of the bloodiest battles in that fratricidal war.

★　★　★

As at First Manassas, a year and a half ago, both commanders had identical plans of battle: in this case, an advance on the left to strike the enemy right. Here as there, if they had moved simultaneously, the two armies might have grappled and swung round and round, like a pair of dancers clutching each other and twirling to the accompaniment of cannon. So it might have been, but it was not. For one thing, the lines were closer together on the south than on the north, and there was no natural obstacle such as the river to delay the Confederate attack in its initial stages. For another, with his usual attention to preparatory matters, Rosecrans had told his generals to advance as soon as possible after breakfast; whereas Bragg, with less concern for the creature comforts, had called for a dawn assault, and that was what he got.

McCown went forward in the steely twilight before sunrise, Cleburne following 400 yards behind. Between them they had 10,000 men and McCook had 16,000, but the latter were still preparing breakfast when the rebel skirmishers, preceding a long gray double line of infantry extending left and right, shoulder to shoulder as far as the eye could reach, broke through the cedar thickets and bore down on them, yelling. Coming as it did, with all the advantage of surprise, the charge was well-nigh irresistible. A Tennessee private later recalled that his brigade, in the front rank of the attackers, "swooped down on those Yankees like a whirl-a-gust of woodpeckers in a hail storm." The fact was, in this opening phase, everything went so smoothly for the aggressors that even their mistakes seemed to work to their advantage. When McCown, who had had little combat experience, having been left behind in command of Knoxville during the invasion of Kentucky, drifted wide because he neglected to oblique to the right as instructed, Pat Cleburne, whose soldierly qualities had grown steadily since Shiloh despite the wounds he had taken at Richmond and Perryville, moved neatly forward into the gap without even the need to pause for alignment. Advancing on this extended front the two divisions swept everything before them, their captures including several front-line batteries taken before the cannoneers could leap to their posts and get a round off. Such knots of bluecoats as managed to form for individual resistance in clumps of cedar or behind outcroppings of rock, finding themselves suddenly outflanked on the left or right, cried as they had cried under Buell twelve weeks before: "We are sold! Sold again!" and broke for the rear, discarding their weapons as they ran.

McCook's three divisions, on line from right to left under Brigadier Generals R. W. Johnson, Jefferson Davis, and Philip Sheridan, caught the full force of the initial assault. Johnson and Davis were under personal clouds, the former because he had been captured by Morgan early that month and exchanged on the eve of battle, the latter because of his assassination of Major General William Nelson in a Lousiville hotel lobby back in September; but they had little chance to earn redemption here. Johnson's division, on the far right of the army, practically disintegrated on contact, losing within the opening half-hour more than half its members by sudden death, injury, or capture. Davis, next in line, fared scarcely better, though most of his men at least had. time to put up a show of resistance before falling back, dribbling skulkers as they went. That left Sheridan. As pugnacious here as he had been at Perryville, where he first attracted general attention, the bandy-legged, bullet-headed Ohioan was determined to yield no ground except under direct pressure, and only then when that pressure buckled his knees. "Square-shouldered, muscular, wiry to the last degree, and as nearly insensible to hardship and fatigue as is consistent with humanity" — thus a staff man saw him here, on the eve of his thirty-second birthday — he rode his lines, calling on his men to stand firm while the storm of battle drew nearer, then broke in fury against his front.

Polk's corps, with its two divisions under Major Generals J. M. Withers and Benjamin Cheatham, had taken up the assault by now, and it was Withers who struck Sheridan first — and suffered the first Confederate repulse. The Federals were in a position described by one of its defenders as "a confused mass of rock, lying in slabs, and boulders interspersed with holes, fissures, and caverns which would have made progress over it extremely difficult even if there had been no timber." But there was timber, a thick tangle of cedars whose trunks "ran straight up into the air so near together that the sunlight was obscured." Fighting here, with all that was happening on the right or left hidden from them "except as we could gather it from the portentous avalanches of sound which assailed us from every direction," Sheridan's men repulsed three separate charges by Withers. Then Cheatham came up. A veteran of Mexico and all the army's battles since Belmont, where he had saved the day, Cheatham was forty-two, a native Tennessean, and had earned the distinction of being the most profane man in the Army of Tennessee, despite the disadvantage in this respect of having as his corps commander the distinguished and watchful Bishop of Louisiana. "Give 'em hell, boys!" he shouted as he led his division forward. Polk, who was riding beside him, approved of the intention if not of the unchurchly language. "Give them what General Cheatham says, boys!" he cried. "Give them what General Cheatham says!"

That was what they gave them, though they received in return a goodly measure of the same. Sheridan, down to his last three rounds and having lost the first of his three brigade commanders, his West Point classmate Brigadier General Joshua Sill — he would lose the other two before the day was over — fell back under knee-buckling pressure from Cheatham in front and Cleburne on the flank, abandoning eight guns in the thicket for lack of horses to draw them off. He then replenished his ammunition and took a position back near the Nashville turnpike, facing south and east alongside Brigadier General J. S. Negley's division, one of the two belonging to Thomas, who had been forced to give ground during the struggle. It was now about 10 o'clock; Bragg's initial objectives had been attained, along with the capture of 28 guns and no less than 3000 soldiers. The enemy right had been driven three miles and the center had also given way, until now the Union line of battle resembled a half-closed jackknife, most of it being at right angles to its original position. Bragg was about to open the second phase, intending to break the knife at the critical juncture of blade and handle; after which would come the third phase, the mop-up.

Rosecrans meanwhile had used to good advantage the interlude afforded him by Sheridan's resistance, though it was not until the battle had been raging for more than an hour that he realized he was face to face with probable disaster. For some time, indeed, having joined Crittenden on the left so as to supervise the opening attack, he assumed that what was occurring on the right — the uproar being considerably diminished by distance and acoustical peculiarities — was in accordance with his instructions to McCook, whereby Bragg had been deceived

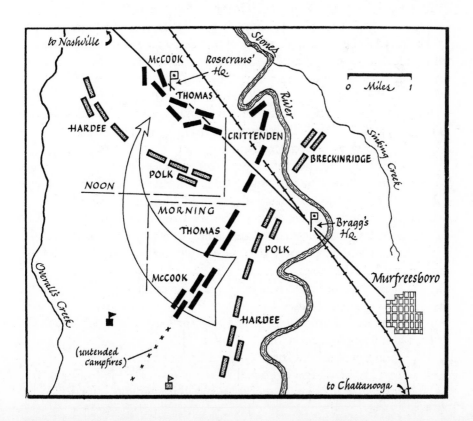

into stripping the flank about to be assaulted, in order to bolster the flank beyond which the untended campfires had been kindled the night before. One of Crittenden's divisions was already crossing Stones River, and he was preparing to follow with the other two. Not even the arrival of a courier from McCook, informing Rosecrans that he was being assailed and needed reinforcements, changed the Federal commander's belief in this regard.

"Tell General McCook to contest every inch of ground," he told the courier, repeating his previous instructions. "If he holds them we will swing into Murfreesboro with our left and cut them off." To his staff he added, with apparent satisfaction: "It's working right."

Discovering presently, however, that it was "working" not for him but for Bragg, who was using his own battle plan against him and had got the jump in the process — with the result that McCook, far from being able to conduct an inch-by-inch defense, had lost control of two of his three divisions before he was able to conduct a defense that was even mile-by-mile — Rosecrans reacted fast. To one observer he seemed "profoundly moved," but that was putting it rather mildly. Even his florid nose "had paled and lost its ruddy luster," the officer added, the glow apparently having been transferred to his eyes, which "blazed with sullen fire." Canceling the advance on the left, he told Crittenden to send the two uncrossed divisions of Brigadier Generals John Palmer and Thomas Wood to reinforce the frazzled right. Brigadier General Horatio Van Cleve's division was to be recalled from the opposite bank of the river and sent without delay after the others, except for one brigade which would be left to guard against a crossing, in case the rebels tried to follow up the withdrawal in this quarter. Crittenden passed the word at once, and: "Goodbye, General," Wood replied as he set out in the direction of the uproar, which now was swelling louder as it drew nearer. "We'll all meet at the hatter's, as one coon said to another when the dogs were after them."

Rosecrans had no time for jokes. His exclusive concern just now was the salvation of his army, and it seemed to him that there was only one way for this to be accomplished. "This battle must be won," he said. He intended to see personally to all the dispositions, especially on the crumbling right, but first he needed a feeling of security on the left — if for no other purpose than to be able to forget it. Accordingly, accompanied by his chief of staff, he rode to the riverbank position of the one brigade Van Cleve had left behind to prevent a rebel crossing, and inquired who commanded.

"I do, sir," a colonel said, stepping forward. He was Samuel W. Price, a Union-loyal Kentuckian.

"Will you hold this ford?" Rosecrans asked him.

"I will try, sir," Price replied.

Unsatisfied, Rosecrans repeated: "Will you hold this ford?"

"I will die right here," the colonel answered stoutly.

Still unsatisfied, for he was less interested in the Kentuckian's willingness to lay down his life than he was in his ability to prevent a rebel crossing, the general pressed the question a third time: "Will you hold this ford?"

"Yes, sir," Price said.

"That will do," Rosecrans snapped, and having at last got the answer he wanted, turned his horse and galloped off.

As he drew near the tumult of battle, which by now was approaching the turnpike on the right, he received another shock in the form of a cannonball which, narrowly missing him, tore off the head of his chief of staff, riding beside him, and so bespattered Rosecrans that whoever saw him afterwards that morning assumed at first sight that he was badly wounded. "Oh, no," he would say, in response to expressions of concern. "That is the blood of poor Garesché." However, this did nothing to restrict or slow his movements; he would not even pause to change his coat. "At no one time, and I rode with him during most of the day," a signal officer afterwards reported, "do I remember of his having been one half-hour at the same place." To Crittenden, whose troops he was using as a reserve in order to shore up the line along the turnpike, he "seemed ubiquitous," and to another observer he appeared "as firm as iron and fixed as fate" as he moved about the field, rallying panicked men and hoicking them into line. "This battle must be won," he kept repeating.

Arriving in time to meet Sheridan, who had just been driven back, he directed him to refill his cartridge boxes from the ammunition train and to fall in alongside Negley and Major General Lovell Rousseau, commanding Thomas's other division. As a result of such stopgap improvisations, adopted amid the confusion of retreat, there was much intermingling of units and a resultant loss of control by division and corps commanders. Some of Crittenden's brigades were on the right with McCook, who had set up a straggler line along which he was doing what he could to rally the remnants of Johnson and Davis, and some of McCook's brigades were on the left with Crittenden, who was nervously making his dispositions on unfamiliar ground. Between them, with his two divisions consolidated and supported by Van Cleve, George Thomas was calm as always, whatever the panic all around him. Where his left joined Crittenden's right there was a salient, marking the point where the half-closed knife blade joined the handle, and within this angle, just east of the pike and on both sides of the railroad, there was a slight elevation inclosed by a circular four-acre clump of cedars, not unlike the one Sheridan had successfully defended against three separate all-out rebel assaults that morning. Known locally as the Round Forest, this tree-choked patch of rocky earth was presently dubbed "Hell's Half-Acre" by the soldiers; for it was here that Bragg seemed most determined to score a breakthrough, despite the heavy concentration of artillery of all calibers which Rosecrans had massed on the high ground directly in its rear.

He struck first, and hard, with a brigade of Mississippians from Withers. They surged forward across fields of unpicked cotton, yelling as they had yelled at Shiloh, where they had been the farthest to advance, and were staggered by rapid-fire volleys from fifty guns ranked hub to hub on the high ground just beyond the clump of dark-green trees. At that point-blank range, one cannoneer remarked, the Federal batteries "could not fire amiss." Deafened by the uproar, the Confederates plucked cotton from the fallen bolls and stuffed it in their ears. Still they came on — to be met, halfway across, by sheets of musketry from the blue infantry close-packed under cover of the cedars; whereupon, some regiments having lost as many as half a dozen color-bearers, the Mississippians wavered and fell back, leaving a third of their number dead or wounded in the furrows or lying crosswise to the blasted rows. Next to try it, about noon, was a Tennessee brigade from Cheatham, which lately had helped throw Sheridan out of a similar position. They charged through the rattling dry brown stalks, yelling with all the frenzy of those who had come this way before, but with no better luck. They too were repulsed, and with even crueler losses. More than half of the men of the 16th Tennessee were casualties, while the 8th Tennessee lost 306 out of the 424 who had started across the fields in an attempt to drive the bluecoats out of the Round Forest.

Bragg was by no means resigned, as yet, to the fact that this could not be done. Though he had no reserves at hand — McCown and Cleburne were still winded from their long advance, around and over the original Federal right, and Withers and Cheatham had just been fought to a frazzle by the newly established left — the five-brigade division of Breckinridge, the largest in the army, was still posted beyond the river, having contributed nothing to the victory up to this point except the shells its batteries had been throwing from an east-bank hill which the former Vice President had been instructed to hold at all costs, as "the key to the position." So far, he had had no trouble doing this, despite an early-morning cavalry warning that a large body of enemy troops had crossed the river well upstream and was headed in his direction. This was of course Van Cleve's division, whose advance had been spotted promptly, but whose subsequent withdrawal had gone unnoticed or at any rate unreported; so that when Bragg's order came, about 1 o'clock, for him to leave one brigade to guard the right while he marched to the support of Polk and Hardee with the other four, Breckinridge was alarmed and sent back word that it was he who needed reinforcements; the enemy, in heavy force, was moving upon him even now, intending to challenge his hold on "the key to the position." Bragg's reply was a peremptory repetition of the order, which left the Kentuckian no choice except to obey. He sent two brigades at 2 o'clock, and followed with the other two himself, about an hour later.

That way, they came up piecemeal, and piecemeal they were fed into the hopper. The Federals, allowed an hour or more in which to improve their dispositions in the Round Forest and replenish the ammunition for the guns posted just behind it, caught the third wave of attackers much as they had caught the first and second, naked in the open fields, with devastating effect. Here again there was no lack of valor. One defender said of the charge that it was "without doubt the most daring, courageous, and best-executed attack which the Confederates made on our line between pike and river." But it broke in blood, as the others had done, and the survivors fell back across the fields, leaving their dead and wounded behind with the dead and wounded Tennesseans and Mississippians. Again there was a lull, until about 4 o'clock, when the last two brigades arrived from Breckinridge and the fourth gray wave rolled out across the fields of cotton.

"The battle had hushed," a Union brigadier reported, "and the dreadful splendor of this advance can only be conceived, as all descriptions must fall vastly short." While the attackers moved forward, "steadily, and, as it seemed, to certain victory," he added, "I sent back all my remaining staff successively to ask for support, and braced up my own lines as perfectly as possible." The bracing served its purpose; for though the defenders suffered heavily, too — it was here that Sheridan lost the third of his three brigade commanders — the charge was repulsed quite as decisively as the others. The sun went down at 4.30 and the racket died away. After eleven hours of uproar, a mutual hush fell over the glades and copses, and the brief winter twilight faded into the darkness before moonrise.

Bragg's losses had been heavy — about 9000 — but he had reason to believe that the enemy's, which included several thousand prisoners, had been much heavier. Moreover, in thus reversing the usual casualty ratio between attacker and defender, he had not only foiled the attempt to throw him out of his position covering Murfreesboro and Chattanooga; he had overrun the original Union position at every point where he had applied pressure, driving major portions of the blue line as far as three miles backward and taking guns and colors in abundance as he went. By all the logic of war, despite their stubborn stand that afternoon in the Round Forest, the Federals were whipped, and now they would have to accept the consequences. As Bragg saw it, they had little choice in this respect. They could stay and suffer further reverses, amounting in the end to annihilation; or they could retreat, hoping to find sanctuary in the Nashville intrenchments. Perhaps because it was the one he himself would have chosen, he believed the latter course to be the one Rosecrans was most likely to adopt. At any rate, this opinion seemed presently to have been confirmed by the arrival of outpost reports informing him that long lines of wagons had been heard rumbling through the darkness behind the Union lines and along the Nashville pike. Elated by this apparent chance to catch the northern army strung out on the roads and ripe for slaughter, Bragg prepared to follow in the morning. Proudly reviewing today's accomplishments while anticipating tomorrow's, he got off a wire to Richmond before he went to bed: "The enemy has yielded his strong position and is falling back. We occupy whole field and shall follow him. . . . God has granted us a happy New Year."

He was mistaken, at least in part. The rumble of wagons, northwestward along the turnpike, had not signified an attempt on the part of the Federal commander to save his trains before the commencement of a general retreat, but rather was the sound made by a long cavalcade of wounded — part of today's total of about 12,000 Union casualties — being taken back to the Tennessee capital for treatment in the military hospitals established there as another example of foresight and careful preparation. Not that Rosecrans had given no thought to a withdrawal. He had indeed. In fact, in an attempt to make up his mind as to the wisdom of retreating, he was holding a council of war to debate the matter and share the responsibility of the decision, even as Bragg was composing his victory message. It was a stormy night, rain beating hard on the roof of the cabin which Rosecrans had selected the day before as his headquarters beside the Nashville pike, never suspecting that the battle line would be drawn today practically on its doorstep. All three of his corps commanders were present, along with a number of their subordinates, and all presented a rather bedraggled aspect, "battered as to hats, tousled as to hair, torn as to clothes, and depressed as to spirits." An adjutant in attendance described them thus, and added: "If there was a cheerful-expressioned face present I did not see it."

After a long silence, broken only by the drumming of rain on shingles, Rosecrans began the questioning, addressing the several generals in turn, clockwise as they sat about the room. "General McCook, have you any suggestions for tomorrow?" Smooth-shaven and round-faced, the thirty-one-year-old McCook was somewhat more subdued tonight than he had been on the night after Perryville — where, as here, his had been the corps that was surprised and routed — but he showed by his reply that at least a part of his rollicking nature still remained. "No," he said. "Only I would like for Bragg to pay me for my two horses lost today." Others were gloomier and more forthright, advising retreat as the army's best way out its predicament. Characteristically, George Thomas had fallen asleep in his chair before the discussion got well under way. When the word "retreat" came through to him, he opened his eyes. "This army doesn't retreat," he muttered, and fell back into the sleep he had emerged from. The discussion thus interrupted was resumed, but it led to no clear-cut decision before the council broke up and the commanders returned to their units. Except for incidental tactical adjustments, specifically authorized from above, they would hold their present positions through tomorrow, unless they received alternate instructions before dawn.

Still undecided, Rosecrans rode out for a midnight inspection of his lines, in the course of which he looked out across the fields and saw an alarming sight. On the far side of Overall's Creek, which crossed the turnpike at right angles and covered his right flank and rear, firebrands were moving in the night. The explanation was actually simple: Federal cavalrymen, suffering from the cold, had disobeyed orders against kindling fires and were carrying brands from point to point along the outpost line: but Rosecrans, never suspecting that his orders would be flaunted in this fashion, assumed that they were rebels. "They have got entirely in our rear," he said, "and are forming line of battle by torchlight!" With retreat no longer even a possibility, let alone an alternative — or so at any rate he thought — he returned at once to army headquarters and, adopting the dramatic phraseology of the Kentucky colonel which he had rejected that morning beside the upper Stones River ford, sent word for his subordinates to "prepare to fight or die."

Except for the surgeons and the men they worked on, blue and gray, whose screams broke through the singing of the bone saws, both sides were bedded down by now amid the wreckage and the corpses, preparing to sleep out as best they could the last night of the year. Simultaneously, from a balcony of the Mobile Battle House, Jefferson Davis lifted the hearts of his listeners with a review of recent Confederate successes, unaware that even as he spoke the list was about to be lengthened by John Magruder, whose two-boat navy of cotton-clads was steaming down Buffalo Bayou to recapture Galveston. Lee's Army of Northern Virginia still occupied the field of its two-weeks-old long-odds victory on the southwest bank of the Rappahannock, and the Federal invaders from coastal North Carolina were back beneath the shelter of their siege guns, licking the wounds they had suffered in their repulse along the Neuse. In North Mississippi, where Van Dorn was resting his troopers after their exploits in Holly Springs and beyond the Tennessee line, Grant was in retreat on Memphis, while Sherman, three hundred winding miles downriver, was counting his casualties under Chickasaw Bluff and preparing to give it one more try before falling back down the Yazoo to meet the general whose army he had kidnaped and depleted to no avail. Forrest and Morgan, the former moving east from Parker's Crossroads, the latter riding south through Campbellsville, both having eluded their pursuers, were returning in triumph from disruptive raids on their respective home regions in West Tennessee and Kentucky. In all these scattered theaters, where so recently the Confederacy had seemed at best to be approaching near-certain disaster, fortune had smiled on southern arms; yet nowhere did her smile seem broader than here, southeast of Nashville and northwest of vital Chattanooga, where Bragg with such alacrity had snatched up the gage flung down by Rosecrans and struck him smartly with it, first on the flank, a smashing blow, and then between the eyes. Now both rested from their injuries and exertions. Wrapped in their blankets, those who had them, the soldiers of both armies huddled close to fires they had kindled against orders. The waxing moon set early and the wind veered and blew coldly from the north; the screams of the wounded died away with the singing of the bone saws. Unlike the night before, on the eve of carnage, there were no serenades tonight, no mingled choruses of "Home Sweet Home," for even the bandsmen had fought in this savage battle, and expected to have to fight again tomorrow, bringing in the new year as they had ushered out the old.

★   ★   ★

So they thought; but they were wrong, at least so far as the schedule was concerned. Though there were tentative skirmishes, fitful exchanges of artillery fire, and some readjustment of the tactical dispositions on both sides, New Year's Day saw nothing like the carnival of death that had been staged on New Year's Eve. In point of fact, the two armies were rather like two great jungle cats who, having fought to mutual exhaustion, were content — aside, that is, from the more or less secret hope on the part of each that the other would slink away — to eye one another balefully, limiting their actions to licking their wounds and emitting only occasional growls and rumbles, while storing up strength to resume the mortal contest.

Considerably surprised, in the light of last night's cavalry reports of a withdrawal, to find the enemy not only still there, but still there in line of battle, Bragg sent Polk forward about midmorning to discover what effect a prod would have. He soon found out. Though the troops moved unopposed into the Round Forest, which Rosecrans had ordered evacuated so as to straighten out his line, and which in turn gave validity to the bishop's subsequent claim that "the opening of the new year found us masters of the field," Polk encountered resistance just beyond it too stiff to permit his men to emerge from the woods on the far side. All he had gained for his pains were more blue corpses, along with the unwelcome task of digging their graves in order to rid his nostrils of their stench. Likewise, on the Union left, Rosecrans advanced Van Cleve's division — now under Colonel Samuel Beatty; Van Cleve had caught a bullet in the leg — beyond Stones River, retracing the route it had taken the previous morning by moving today into the vacuum created by the withdrawal of Breckinridge the afternoon before, and occupied a hill overlooking the ford. These were the only major read-adjustments, North or South, though the Federals were reinforced by a brigade arrived from Nashville, accompanied as one officer said by "an army of stragglers" picked up along the pike. For the most part, the soldiers on both sides roved the field, looking for fallen comrades among the wounded and the slain. The search for food was even more intensive, and for once, as a result of Wheeler's depredations in the course of his prebattle ride around the Union forces, the Yankees were worse off in this respect than the rebels. One brigade commander later recorded that he made his supper off a piece of raw pork and a few crackers he found in his pocket. No food had ever tasted sweeter, he declared. Even so high-ranking an officer as Crittenden was not exempt from want, but as he went to bed, complaining of hunger pangs, he was delighted to hear his orderly say he could get him "a first-rate beefsteak." The Kentuckian accepted the offer gladly, and presently, when the promised meal was brought, consumed it with gusto — only to learn next morning that the "beefsteak" had been cut from a horse that had been killed in the battle. "I didn't know this at the time I ate it," he afterwards explained, somewhat ruefully.

Day ended; night came down. Although Rosecrans had no apparent notion of resuming the offensive, or indeed any definite plan at all beyond holding onto the ground he had fallen back to, he was pleased to have had this day-long opportunity to consolidate his forces and recover in some measure from the shock to his army and his nervous system. Bragg on the other hand seemed to have no more of a plan than his opponent. Convinced that he had won a victory, he apparently did not know what to do with it beyond setting various details to work collecting the arms and matériel scattered about the field and paroling the thousands of captives he had taken the day before. What he mainly wanted, still, was for the enemy to admit defeat by retreating, and thus substantiate his claim; then he would follow, as he had promised in his wire to Richmond, hoping to catch the blue mass in motion on the pike and tear its flanks and rear, which now were inaccessible to him beyond the guns parked hub to hub behind the long lines of close-spaced bayonets weaving in and out of the cedar brakes and among the gray outcroppings of rock that scarred the landscape. The prospect was altogether grim. After nightfall, however, he was again encouraged by cavalry reports that well-guarded Federal trains were in motion on the roads leading back to Nashville. If this meant what Bragg hoped it did, that the Unionists were finally admitting they were whipped and were preparing to retire, bag and baggage, he would be up and after them tomorrow.

Tomorrow's dawn showed the prospect unimproved. Whatever might be moving along the rearward roads, the bayonets defining the Union front glinted quite as close-spaced as ever and the guns frowned every bit as grim. In fact, as Bragg conducted a personal inspection of his lines that morning, combining with it a long-range binocular reconnaissance of the enemy position, he began to perceive that, despite his bloodless occupation of the Round Forest, which increased his claim to the honors of the field, it was his own army which was in the graver danger as a result of yesterday's tactical readjustments. The advance of Van Cleve's division, which put it in possession of the hill just east of the river, gave him particular concern. Artillery emplaced on that height could fire across the stream and enfilade Polk's flank if he attempted to advance. With this in mind, Bragg decided the enemy guns must be dislodged. Accordingly he sent for Breckinridge, whose troops had returned to their east-bank position north of Murfreesboro, along a ridge about a mile short of the hill overlooking the ford. When the former Vice President reached army headquarters, under a large sycamore that stood alongside the Nashville pike just west of the wrecked bridge that had spanned Stones River, Bragg told him what he wanted. He was going to resume the offensive by sending Polk forward, he explained. First, though, he wanted Van Cleve's men flung off the dominant height. This was admittedly a tough assignment, he continued, but to protect the attackers from the added strain of having to repulse a counterattack, he was directing that the movement be made less than an hour before sundown, which would give the Federals no time to reorganize or bring up reinforcements before dark. Then next morning Polk could jump off, not only with his flank secure, but also with the enemy mouse-trapped out of position to his front.

Breckinridge, who was not yet forty-two despite his distinguished prewar career in national politics — a hearty-looking man with a prominent forehead, somewhat bulging eyes, a plump but firm jaw, and the swooping dark mustache of a Sicilian brigand, he was a leading contender among the many candidates for the title of the handsomest general in the southern army — protested at once and for all he was worth. The hill was well-nigh impregnable, he said, and Van Cleve's division had now been reinforced by two brigades from Palmer; besides which, he added, guns from the main Union line across the river would tear his flank as he advanced, thus exposing his men to the very horror he would be sparing Polk's if he was successful, which was doubtful. Warming to the subject, he took up a stick and began to draw in the soft dirt a map that emphasized the difficulty of the terrain. Bragg stopped him in mid-sketch. The Kentuckian had delayed the battle two days ago with similar protests which had turned out to be ill-founded, and the army commander was having no more of that. "Sir," Bragg said curtly, "my information is different. I have given the order to attack the enemy in your front and expect it to be obeyed."

That was that, and Breckinridge returned to his troops, most of whom were Bluegrass natives like himself, exiles from their homeland since midwinter nearly a year ago; "my poor orphans," he sometimes called them, jokingly but not without an undertone of sadness and homesickness. Rejoining them he sought out his friend Brigadier General William Preston — now commanding one of his brigades, but formerly chief of staff to his brother-in-law Albert Sidney Johnston, who had died in his arms at Shiloh — to whom he now addressed himself concerning the assignment he had just been given. "General Preston," he said, speaking formally and with a tone that strangely combined dejection and determination, "this attack is made against my judgment and by the special orders of General Bragg. Of course we all must try to do our duty and fight the best we can. But if it should result in disaster and I be among the slain, I want you to do justice to my memory and tell the people that I believed this attack to be very unwise and tried to prevent it." And having thus unburdened his mind he ordered his five brigades to form for the assault.

Across the way, Crittenden was inspecting his dispositions along the west bank of Stones River, accompanied by his chief of artillery Captain John Mendenhall, when he looked over the ford near the base of the occupied hill beyond and saw the graybacks forming in heavy columns along the ridge to the south, obviously preparing for a blow at Beatty, who commanded not only Van Cleve's division but also the two brigades of reinforcements which had joined him that morning. It was now about 3.30; the sun was within an hour of the landline. According to Mendenhall, "The general asked me if I could not do something to relieve Colonel Beatty with my guns." The Indiana-born West Pointer could indeed, and he moved to do so promptly. Assembling within the next half hour a total of 58 pieces of various calibers, he stationed 37 of these on the crest of a west-bank hill, cradled by a bend of the stream and overlooking the opposite bank, and placed the other 21 along its eastern base for flat-trajectory fire that would catch the rebel columns end-on as they charged across the rolling slopes beyond the river. Then he waited; but not for long.

The five Confederate brigades, with a total effective strength of 4500 men, started down off their sheltering ridge at 4 o'clock, moving steadily across the valley which lay between them and the hill from whose crest Beatty's cannoneers and riflemen soon took them under fire. As at Baton Rouge five months ago, where they had fought in isolation while the rest of Bragg's army was preparing to set out for their native Bluegrass, the Kentuckians did not falter as they swung down the long slope of the intervening valley, crossed its floor, and began to climb the other side. Halfway up the face of the hill, taking heavier losses now at closer range, they fired their first volleys and then, beginning to yell, broke into a run for the crest. The bluecoats did not wait for them, but whirled and fled from the threat of contact, and the attackers came on after them, yelling now with shrill screams of triumph as they topped the rise and pursued the defenders down the rearward slope.

However, they could not close the gap created by the quick retreat, and this gave Mendenhall the chance he had been waiting for all this time, to shoot at his foes without injuring his friends. At the signal "Fire!" his 58 double-shotted guns began to roar in chorus, flinging more than a hundred rounds a minute against the flank of the butternut mass across the way. "Thinned, reeling, broken under that terrible hail" — thus one reporter described the instantaneous effect — the graybacks milled in confusion, scarcely knowing at first what had struck them. When they saw what it was, they attempted to change front to the left and move against the fuming hill beyond the ford; but to no avail. "The very forest seemed to fall before our fire," one Federal observer wrote — without exaggeration, for men in the gray ranks were actually crushed under fallen limbs that were torn from the trees by exploding shells when they tried to find shelter in a patch of woods — "and not a Confederate reached the river." Shattered, they changed front again to the left, of one accord, and ran for the ridge that had marked their line of departure. A Union colonel, watching this sudden turn of events, was the amused witness of a double, simultaneous retreat. "It was difficult to say which was running away the more rapidly," he later reported, "the division of Van Cleve to the rear, or the enemy in the opposite direction."

Breckinridge watched his men come stumbling back through the dusk that followed sunset of the brief winter day. They had been gone just seventy minutes in all, and of their number 1700 had fallen: which meant that better than one man out of every three who descended the slope did not return unhurt. As their commander, who had protested the slaughter in advance and done what he could to prevent it, watched them close ranks to fill the gaps as they formed their line behind their own ten guns on the ridge, his eyes filled with tears. "My poor orphans! My poor orphans!" he exclaimed.

The lament for the fallen need not have been limited to the Confederate right, nor indeed to either side of the line of battle; for the overall Federal losses had been even heavier. According to final reports and computations, in two days of conflict — the day-long struggle of the 31st and the sunset repulse on the 2d — only a dozen less than 25,000 casualties had been suffered by the two armies. (Which, incidentally, indicated something of the fury of western fighting. With fewer than half as many troops involved, the butcher bill at Murfreesboro, Tennessee, was more than one-third greater than the one presented at Fredericksburg, Virginia, three weeks back.) The South lost 1294 killed, 7945 wounded, and 2500 captured or missing, a total of 11,739. The North lost 1730 killed, 7802 wounded, and 3717 captured or missing, a total of 13,249. The over-all total thus was 24,988: which was to say, and more could scarcely *be* said, that the battle had been bloodier than Shiloh or Sharpsburg.

At any rate, though neither commander yet recognized the fact, the carnage was over. Polk, who had learned of the sunset assault only just before it was launched, when Bragg came to his headquarters for a better view of the action across the river, had protested almost as vehemently as Breckinridge had done, but with no more success; Bragg's mind was quite made up. And now that the attack had met with predicted disaster, the blue defenders returned to the abandoned hill in greater strength than ever, reinforced by another whole division. Tactically, all was as it had been before the assault was launched, only more so; Polk would be less able to advance tomorrow than he had been today. Whether the enemy was under a similar disadvantage he did not know, but his two division commanders were not only doubtful that such was the case, they were also doubtful that their troops were in any fit condition to block the way: as was shown by a letter they wrote, shortly after midnight, and sent through channels to Bragg. "We deem it our duty to say to you frankly," Cheatham and Withers declared, "that, in our judgment, this army should be promptly put in retreat. . . . We do fear great disaster from the condition of things now existing, and think it should be averted if possible." Polk added his endorsement to the unusual document: "I greatly fear the consequences of another engagement at this place in the ensuing day. We could now, perhaps, get off with some safety and some credit, if the affair is well managed," and forwarded it to Bragg. Waked at 2 a.m., the grim-faced commander sat up in bed and read the letter halfway through, then stopped and told the aide who had disturbed his sleep: "Say to the general we shall maintain our position at every hazard."

When he rose at daylight, however, he began to discover how great that hazard was. Rain was falling steadily and the river was rising fast, threatening to isolate the two wings of his army. Moreover, unlike the previous ones, this morning's cavalry reports gave no hint of signs in the night that the enemy was considering withdrawal, but rather informed him that another fresh brigade of reinforcements had just arrived on the Union right, accompanying a train of supplies from the Tennessee capital. By now, too, his staff had found time to study the papers captured when McCook's headquarters were overrun, which indicated an effective strength of nearly 70,000 bluecoats to his front. This gave Bragg pause, and having paused he wavered. At 10 o'clock that morning he sent for Polk and Hardee, who found him in a different frame of mind from the one he had shown eight hours ago, when he was roused out of sleep to read the letter advising retreat. With the enemy heavily reinforced, as he believed and later wrote in his report, "Common prudence and the safety of my army, upon which even the safety of our cause depended, left no doubt on my mind as to the necessity of my withdrawal from so unequal a contest." The retrograde movement got under way that night, January 3, and was conducted with such skill that not even a rear-guard action was fought with the unsuspecting Federals, who seemed no more anxious to pursue than Bragg had been to stay. He himself went to Winchester, fifty miles southeast, planning to establish a new line along Elk River. Polk was instructed to fall back on Shelbyville, Hardee on Tullahoma, respectively twenty-three and thirty-five miles from Murfreesboro, but when the former reached his goal and reported that the bluecoats had not ventured beyond Stones River, Bragg ordered Hardee to stop at Wartrace, on line with Polk. Returning at once to establish headquarters at Tullahoma, on the railroad about midway between Nashville and Chattanooga, he began to organize a new defensive position along the Duck, whose rich valley offered much in the way of subsistence and adequate camp sites, including level fields for the daily hours of close-order drill in which he placed great store as a disciplinarian.

His pride in his army and its conduct during the battle — which was in a way a coda to the Kentucky excursion, launched soon after he took command at Tupelo, Mississippi, back in June — was expressed in his report, where he listed with satisfaction the capture of 6273 prisoners and enemy colors in abundance, along with 31 cannon and 6000 small arms, as well as "a large amount of other valuable property, all of which was secured and appropriated to proper uses." Moreover, he declared by way of final proof of moral superiority over his antagonist, "the army retired to its present position behind Duck River without giving or receiving a shot." Within the ranks of that army, however, though the men agreed that they had won a victory, there were fewer signs of elation. The retreat was made in wretched weather, and as they plodded southward through the mud, alternately drenched with rain and pelted with sleet, bent beneath the weight of their sodden packs, it seemed to them that the Perryville technique — fight; win; fall back — had been repeated. "What does he fight battles for?" they grumbled, beginning to discern a discouraging pattern to their efforts under Bragg. Similarly at home, as one civilian diarist recorded, "It was small surcease to the sob of the widow and the moan of the orphan that 'the retreat to Tullahoma was conducted in good order.'"

Rosecrans, on the other hand — who had not made a single offensive move since the explosive attack on his right wing at dawn of the 31st, who had allowed a foe he claimed was beaten to withdraw from his immediate front without so much as a threat of molestation, and who was so cautious in pursuit that his eventual movement to the east bank of Stones River, from which he had withdrawn on the night of January 3 lest the rising waters expose his troops to destruction in detail, amounted to practically no pursuit at all — was praised not only by those below and above him in the army, but also by the public at large, including the Ohio legislature, which tendered him before the month was out a resolution of thanks "for the glorious victory resulting in the capture of Murfreesboro and the defeat of the rebel forces at that place." Cheered by his soldiers as he rode among them, he received equally gratifying responses to the dispatches by which he announced his victory to the authorities in Washington. "God bless you, and all of you," the President replied, and the Secretary of War (who had said of Rosecrans' appointment at the outset, "Well, you have made your choice of idiots. Now you can await the news of a terrible disaster") was quite expansive, wiring: "The country is filled with admiration of the gallantry and heroic achievement of yourself and the officers and troops under your command. . . . There is nothing you can ask within my power to grant to yourself or your noble command that will not be cheerfully given." Even Halleck, who had prodded and nudged him for weeks beyond endurance, eventually joined the chorus of praise, though not before he had waited a few days for verification in Confederate newspapers smuggled across the border. "Rebel accounts fully confirm your telegrams from the battlefield," he wired, and added: "You and your brave army have won the gratitude of your country and the admiration of the world. . . . All honor to the Army of the Cumberland — thanks to the living and tears for the lamented dead."

Bragg, he knew, was playing a cagey game at Tullahoma ("We shall fight him again at every hazard if he advances, and harass him daily if he does not," the terrible-tempered general was telling his superiors even now) but Rosecrans was firm in his intentions and had already reverted to the use of vigorous phrases he had been employing two weeks back, on the eve of battle. "We shall press them as rapidly as our means of traveling and subsistence will permit," he notified Stanton on January 5. Next day, though he was still at Murfreesboro, he boldly repeated words he had used at Nashville in mid-December: "I now wish to press them to the wall."

★ ★ ★

When Davis returned to Richmond that same January 5, to be met on the portico of the White House by his wife and their four children — three sons and a daughter, stair-stepped at two-year intervals so that their ages ranged from just past one to almost eight — Mrs Davis, observing that her husband was near exhaustion, insisted that he retire at once to rest from the exertions of his journey. Presently, however, they heard the thump and blare of drums and horns and the cheers of a crowd that had gathered in front of the house to welcome him back with a serenade. Weary though he was, and despite his desire to be alone with his family — "Every sound is the voice of my child and every child renews the memory of a loved one's appearance," he had written home from Tennessee, "but none can equal their charms, nor can any compare with my own long-worshipped Winnie" — he felt that he could not ignore the shouts of the crowd or fail to acknowledge the courtesy being tendered.

The cheers were redoubled as the big front door swung ajar once more and the President came out onto the steps. Captain J. B. Smith's Silver Band played "Listen to the Mocking Bird" and several other airs which the crowd enjoyed while waiting for the speech they had come to hear. Davis did not disappoint them. Carried forward perhaps by a sort of verbal secondary inertia, he spoke as he had been speaking now for more than three weeks, to similar crowds and with similar words, in the course of his nearly three-thousand-mile trip to "the further West" and back.

"I am happy to be welcomed on my return to the capital of the Confederacy — the last hope, as I believe, for the perpetuation of that system of government which our forefathers founded — the asylum of the oppressed, and the home of true representative liberty." His voice, as he thus began, showed the strain to which it had been exposed, but as usual it gathered strength as he continued, reverting to the deeds of olden days in the Old Dominion, where the earlier Revolution had been proclaimed and, finally, won. Now once more, he told these latter-day Virginians, "anticipating the overthrow of that government which you had inherited, you assumed to yourselves the right, as your fathers had done before you, to declare yourself independent, and nobly have you advocated the assertion which you have made. Here, upon your soil, some of the fiercest battles of the Revolution were fought, and upon your soil it closed by the surrender of Cornwallis. Here again are men of every state; here they have congregated, linked in the defense of a most sacred cause. They have battled, they have bled upon your soil, and it is now consecrated by blood which cries for vengeance against the insensate foe of religion as well as of humanity, of the altar as well as of the hearthstone." Thus he repeated the bitterness he had voiced in his home state, ten days ago. Nor, with first-hand accounts of the sack of Fredericksburg now added to the list of northern depredations — not the least of them being the recently issued Emancipation Proclamation, which, as he saw it, incited the slaves to the murder of their masters — had that reaction been tempered by second thought. Rather, the bitterness had increased: as he now showed. "It is true," he told his listeners, "you have a cause which binds you together more firmly than your fathers were. They fought to be free from the usurpations of the British crown, but they fought against a manly foe. You fight against the offscourings of the earth."

Applauded, he passed on to a brief review of recent Confederate successes in the field, which he predicted would bring discord to northern councils, and then returned to his condemnation, not only of the conduct of the Federal armies of invasion, but also of the men who had sent them South. "Every crime which could characterize the course of demons has marked the course of the invader . . . from the burning of defenseless towns to the stealing of silver forks and spoons." In this last he had particular reference to Ben Butler, known as "Beast" Butler and "Spoons" Butler as a result of his alleged brutality and deftness in the exercise of his authority in command of the occupation of New Orleans, and Davis made the charge explicit, asserting that the Massachusetts general had "exerted himself to earn the excoriations of the civilized world, and now returns [to Washington] with his dishonors thick upon him to receive the plaudits of the only people on earth who do not blush to think he wears the human form. . . . They have come to disturb your social organization on the plea that it is a military necessity. For what are they waging war? They say to preserve the Union. Can they preserve the Union by destroying the social existence of a portion of the South? Do they hope to reconstruct the Union by striking at everything which is dear to man? — by showing themselves so utterly disgraced that if the question was proposed to you whether you would combine with hyenas or Yankees, I trust every Virginian would say: 'Give me the hyenas.' "

"Good! Good!" his listeners cried, and there was laughter. They wanted more along these lines.

But Davis spoke calmly now, as if to refute the charge made by his critics that he was cold in his attitude toward the people, unconcerned for their welfare, and anxious to avoid commingling with them — as if, indeed, he had brought back East from his journey West an increased awareness of the warmth and strength proceeding from contact with those who looked to him for leadership not only as their President but also as a man. "My friends, constant labor in the duties of office, borne down by care, and with an anxiety which has left me scarcely a moment for repose, I have had but little opportunity for social intercourse among you. I thank you for this greeting, and hope the time may come soon when you and I alike, relieved of the anxieties of the hour, may have more of social intercourse than has heretofore existed." Flushed with confidence as a result of the victories won by the nation's armies in the course of his trip, he added: "If the war continues we shall only grow stronger and stronger as each year rolls on. Compare our condition today with that which existed one year ago. See the increasing power of the enemy, but mark that our own has been proportionately greater, until we see in the future nothing to disturb the prospect of the independence for which we are struggling. One year ago, many were depressed and some were despondent. Now deep resolve is seen in every eye; an unconquerable spirit nerves every arm. And gentle woman, too;

who can estimate the value of her services in this struggle? ... With such noble women at home, and such heroic soldiers in the field, we are invincible."

He waited for the applause to die away, and then concluded his remarks, once more on a personal note. "I thank you, my friends, for the kind salutation tonight; it is an indication that at some future time we shall be better acquainted. I trust we shall all live to enjoy some of the fruits of the struggle in which we are engaged. My prayers are for your individual and collective welfare. May God prosper our cause, and may we live to give to our children untarnished the rich inheritance which our fathers gave us. Good night!"

CHAPTER
✗ 2 ✗

Unhappy New Year

★ ✗ ☆

NEW YEAR'S 1863 WAS FOR ABRAHAM LINCOLN
perhaps the single busiest day of his whole presidential life, and it came
moreover at dead center of what was perhaps his period of deepest gloom
and perplexity of spirit. Not only was there political division within his
party, and even within his own official family, but with the possible exception of Rosecrans, whose battle was in mid-career and appeared
worse than doubtful, all his hand-picked commanders had failed him utterly, through enemy action or their own inaction, in his hopes for a mul-
tifaceted early-winter triumph in which he himself had assigned them the
parts they were to play in putting a quick end to rebellion. One by one,
sometimes two by two, they had failed him. Burnside and his fellow generals on the Rappahannock, having blundered into defeat at Fredericksburg, were engaged in a frenzy of backbiting such as not even the highly
contentious Army of the Potomac had ever known before. Grant, according to the New York *Times*, remained "stuck in the mud of northern Mississippi, his army of no use to him or anybody else." Banks,
caught in a toil of imported New Orleans cotton speculators, was stymied by a previously unsuspected fort on the Mississippi, two hundred
and fifty miles downstream from his assigned objective. And McClernand,
from whom the Commander in Chief had perhaps expected most, was apparently the worst off of all. He not only had done nothing with his
army; the last Lincoln had heard from him, he could not even find it.

Nor had these and other failures of omission and commission gone
unnoticed by the country at large, the voters and investors on whose
will and trust the prosecution of the war depended. The Democrats, still
on the outside looking in, but with substantial gains in the fall elections to
sharpen their appetite for more, had seen to that: especially Ohio Representative Clement L. Vallandigham, who was savagely pointing out,
from the vantage point of his seat in Congress, the administration's errors. "Money you have expended without limit," he told Republicans in

the House, "and blood poured out like water. Defeat, debt, taxation, and sepulchers — these are your only trophies." Others, less violent but no less earnest, including his disaffected former allies, were accusing the President in a similar vein; so that now, perhaps, with his own critics crying out against him, he could feel more sympathy for James K. Polk than he had felt when he spoke against him in Congress, fifteen years ago this month, in the midst of another war. "I more than suspect already," the youthful Lincoln had declared from a seat in the rear of the House, "that he is deeply conscious of being in the wrong; that he feels the blood of this war, like the blood of Abel, is crying to heaven against him; that originally having some strong motive . . . to involve the two countries in a war, and trusting to escape scrutiny by fixing the public gaze upon the exceeding brightness of military glory . . . he plunged into it and has swept on and on, till, disappointed in his calculation . . . he now finds himself he knows not where. . . . His mind, tasked beyond its power, is running hither and thither, like some tortured creature on a burning surface, finding no position on which it can settle down and be at ease. . . . He is a bewildered, confounded, and miserably perplexed man. God grant he may be able to show there is not something about his conscience more painful than all his mental perplexity!"

The words rebounded from the target, boomeranged down the years, and came back in other forms to strike the sender. Orestes Brownson, the prominent Boston author and former transcendentalist, wrote of Lincoln: "His soul seems made of leather, and incapable of any grand or noble emotion. Compared with the mass of men, he is a line of flat prose in a beautiful and spirited lyric. He lowers, he never elevates you. You leave his presence with your enthusiasm dampened, your better feelings crushed, and your hopes cast to the winds. You ask not, can this man carry the nation through its terrible struggles? but can the nation carry this man through them, and not perish in the attempt?" Brownson was of no uncertain mind where Lincoln was concerned. "He is thickheaded; he is ignorant; he is tricky, somewhat astute, in a small way, and obstinate as a mule. . . . He is wrong-headed, the attorney not the lawyer, the petty politician not the statesman, and, in my belief, ill-deserving of the soubriquet of Honest. I am out of all patience with him," he added, rather anticlimactically, and inquired: "Is there no way of inducing him to resign, and allow Mr Hamlin to take his place?" Senator William Pitt Fessenden, a Maine Republican high in the party's councils, replied in somewhat the same vein when told that he should be a member of the cabinet in order to be at Lincoln's elbow and give the nation the full benefit of his advice. "No friend of mine should ever wish to see me there," he answered. "You cannot change the President's character or conduct. He remained long enough in Springfield, surrounded by toadies and office-seekers, to persuade himself that he was specially chosen by the Almighty for this crisis, and well chosen. This conceit has never yet been beaten out of him, and until it is, no human wisdom can be of much avail. I see nothing for it but to let the ship of state drift along, hoping that the current of public opinion may bring it safely into port." Similarly, a Boston philanthropist, railroad magnate J. M. Forbes, convinced that Lincoln was badly off the track, was asking: "Can nothing be done to reach the President's ear and heart? I hear he is susceptible to religious impressions; shall we send our eloquent divines to talk to him, or shall we send on a deputation of mothers and wives, or can we, the conservators of liberty, who have elected him, combine with Congress in beseeching him to save the country?"

In point of fact, one such group of "eloquent divines" as Forbes suggested did come to call on Lincoln at this time, protesting with considerable heat the lack of progress in the war; but he gave them little satisfaction beyond a brief, short-tempered lecture comparing the administration's predicament to that of a tightrope walker in mid-act. "Gentlemen," he told them, "suppose all the property you were worth was in gold, and you had put it in the hands of Blondin to carry across the Niagara River. Would you shake the cable or keep shouting out to him, 'Blondin, stand up a little straighter!' 'Blondin, stoop a little more!' 'Go a little faster'; 'Lean a little more to the north'; 'Lean a little more to the south'? No. You would hold your breath as well as your tongue, and keep your hands off until he was safe over. The government is carrying an immense weight. Untold treasures are in their hands. They are doing the very best they can. Don't badger them. Keep silence, and we'll get you safe across." The visit, he said afterwards, made him "a little shy of preachers" for a time. "But the latchstring is out," he added, "and they have the right to come here and preach to me if they will go about it with some gentleness and moderation."

Gentleness and moderation were easier to prescribe than they were to practice. An infinitely patient man, he was beginning to lose patience: with the result that some who formerly had complained that he lacked firmness were now protesting that he had assumed the prerogatives of a dictator, spurning their counsels and high-handedly overruling their objections. It was true in some respects. His accustomed tact sometimes failed him under pressure nowadays, and he gave short answers, though rarely without the saving grace of humor, the velvet glove that softened the clutch of the iron hand. This was evident, for example, in a clash with Secretary of the Treasury Salmon P. Chase about this time. An economist came to Lincoln with a plan for issuing greenbacks. Lincoln heard him out, liked the notion, but told him: "You must go to Chase. He is running that end of the machine." The man left, then presently returned, saying that the Secretary had dismissed him with the objection that the proposal was unconstitutional. Lincoln grimaced. "Go back to

Chase," he said, "and tell him not to bother himself about the Constitution. Say that I have that sacred instrument here at the White House, and am guarding it with great care."

Such brusque, not to say cavalier, treatment of his highly respected Treasury chief was prologue to an even rougher handling of that dignitary in mid-December, when he tripped him neatly from behind as he tried a sprint up several rungs of the political ladder. This was a time of crisis and division, in the cabinet as in the nation at large. One member, Secretary of the Interior Caleb Blood Smith, who had received his appointment as the result of a convention bargain, was leaving to accept a judgeship Lincoln had offered him in his native Indiana; his post would go to John Palmer Usher, another Hoosier, at present the Assistant Secretary. The other six members were split on the question of whether to admit West Virginia as a state under an act just passed by Congress, divorcing Virginia's northwest counties from the Old Dominion and validating the rump government set up in Charleston during the Sumter furor. Three cabinet officers — Chase, Stanton, and Secretary of State William H. Seward — wanted Lincoln to sign the bill, converting slave soil into free soil by the stroke of a pen, and incidentally adding good Republican votes on whatever questions Congress might decide needed settling in the future; while three others — Secretary of the Navy Gideon Welles, Attorney General Edward Bates, and Postmaster General Montgomery Blair — recommended that he veto it, on grounds that the act was in a sense a ratification of secession. Though he could not reconcile their views, Lincoln quickly solved the problem to his own approximate satisfaction. "The division of a state is dreaded as a precedent," he reasoned. "But a measure made expedient by a war is no precedent for times of peace. It is said that the admission of West Virginia is secession, and tolerated only because it is *our* secession. Well, if we call it by that name, there is still difference enough between secession against the Constitution and secession in favor of the Constitution." On the last day of the year, though he did so with a wry face, he signed the bill. West Virginia would become in June a full-fledged state of the Union, the thirty-fifth, not discounting the eleven who had no representation in Congress pending the settlement of their claim to have abolished their old ties.

Seward and Chase had voted together on the issue, but that was rare. In general they were diametrically opposed, as they had been in the old days when they were rivals for the office which, by a fluke, had gone to Lincoln. Chase, who was jealous of Seward's position as the President's chief adviser, wanted not only the seat closest to the one at the head of the table, but also, as time would show, the principal seat itself. In this connection, noting the way the wind blew, he had aligned himself with the radicals in Congress, the so-called Jacobins who had come to see Seward as the stumbling block in the way of adoption of their notions as to how the war should be fought and the country run, just as Chase had come to see him as a hurdle that would have to be removed or overleaped if he was to fulfill his own ambitions. By way of undoing their common adversary, he fanned the flames of the radicals' hatred by reporting Seward's every private opposition to their aims (the New Yorker, for example, had delayed the promulgation of the Preliminary Emancipation Proclamation by advising Lincoln to wait for a more propitious season before releasing it to the world; than which, indeed, there could be no crime greater in radical eyes) as well as by giving them a blow-by-blow account of every cabinet crisis, omitting nothing that served to thicken the atmosphere of discord and indecision. So it was that at last, on December 17 — four days after the Fredericksburg fiasco, which seemed to them to prove emphatically that the prosecution of the war was in quite the wrong hands — all but one of the thirty-two Republican senators met in secret caucus on Capitol Hill and passed unanimously the following resolution, by way of advice to the leader of their party: *"Resolved, that . . . the public confidence in the present administration would be increased by a change in and partial reconstruction of the cabinet."* It was Seward they were after, Seward alone, and lest there be any doubt on that score a committee of nine was appointed to present the resolution to Lincoln and explain to him just what it was they meant.

The one abstaining senator was New York's Preston King, who went at once to Seward and warned his former senatorial colleague that the Jacobins, "thirsty for a victim" in the wake of recent misfortunes, had selected his neck for the ax. Seward reacted fast when he learned thus of the resolution about to be presented. "They may do as they please about me," he said, "but they shall not put the President in a false position on my account." Accordingly he took a sheet of paper, and having scrawled a few words across it —"Sir, I hereby resign from the office of Secretary of State, and beg that my resignation be accepted immediately" — sent it forthwith to the White House. Lincoln was shocked. "What does this mean?" he asked as he put on his hat and set out for Seward's house, which was just across the street. Seward explained what had happened, along with what was about to happen, and added that he personally would be glad to get from under the burden of official duties and political harassment. "Ah yes, Governor," Lincoln said, shaking his head. "That will do very well for you, but I am like the starling in Sterne's story. 'I can't get out.'" He pocketed the resignation and went sadly back across the White House lawn.

At any rate, next morning when the committee spokesman called, he knew what to expect. He set the time for the presentation at 7 o'clock that evening; he would receive the full committee then. This was a crisis, not only for Lincoln but also for the nation, and he knew it. "If I had yielded to that storm and dismissed Seward," he said later, "the thing would have all slumped over one way, and we should have been left with a scant handful of supporters." Knowing what had to be done was a quite different thing, however, from knowing how to do it. Ben Wade of Ohio, George W. Julian of Indiana, Zachariah Chandler of Michigan: these and others like them were men of power and savage purpose, accomplished haters who would be merciless in revenging even an imagined slight, let alone an outright rebuff. Whatever Lincoln did had better be done without incurring their personal enmity. Besides, he not only had to avoid their anger; he also needed their support. What he required just now was someone to draw their wrath, someone to serve him much as a billygoat serves the farmer who places him in a barnlot to draw fleas. By evening, not without a certain sense of political and even poetical justice, he had chosen the someone. All that remained was to make him serve, and that could be done quite simply by branding him, in the eyes of all, for what he was.

The nine committeemen were prompt; Lincoln received them in his office. By way of a beginning, seventy-one-year-old Jacob Collamer of Vermont, who had been elected spokesman, read the resolution and followed it with a paper which summed up the conclusions reached in caucus the day before. The war should be prosecuted vigorously; cabinet members should be "cordial, resolute, unwavering" in their devotion to the principles of the Republican majority; the cabinet itself, once it had been stripped and rebuilt so as to contain only such stalwarts, should have a larger voice in the running of the government. Wade rose next, a vigorous man with "burning" eyes and bulldog flews, protesting hotly that the President had "placed the direction of our military affairs in the hands of bitter and malignant Democrats." He spoke at length, going somewhat afield from the central issue, and was followed by Fessenden, who agreed that the war was "not sufficiently in the hands of its friends," then brought the discussion back on target by charging specifically "that the Secretary of State [is] not in accord with the majority of the cabinet and [has] exerted an injurious influence upon the conduct of the war." Others had their say along these lines, also at considerable length, but Lincoln kept his temper and said little. After three hours of listening, however, he suggested that the meeting adjourn until the following night. The senators agreed. Alone at last, he saw clearly, as he presently remarked, that if he let these men have their way "the whole government must cave in; it could not stand, could not hold water; the bottom would be out."

He knew what to do and, by now, how to do it; but he was saddened. "What do those men want?" he asked his friend Senator Orville Browning of Illinois next day. "I hardly know, Mr President," Browning replied, "but they are exceedingly violent...." Lincoln knew well enough what they wanted, though, and he said so: "They wish to get rid of me — and I am sometimes half disposed to gratify them." Browning protested, but Lincoln shook his head. "We are now on the brink of destruction," he said. "It appears to me the Almighty is against us, and I can hardly see a ray of hope." Again Browning protested. Though he was not a member of the committee, he had attended the caucus and had voted for the resolution: which, he explained defensively, "was the gentlest thing that could be done. We had to do that, or worse." The trouble he said was Seward. While he personally had a high regard for the Secretary, others were saying that the New Yorker had the President under his thumb. "Why should men believe a lie," Lincoln broke in, "an absurd lie, that could not impose on a child, and cling to it and repeat it in defiance of all evidences to the contrary?" His sadness deepened. "The committee is to be up to see me at 7 o'clock. Since I heard last night of the proceedings of the caucus I have been more distressed than by any event of my life."

If this was so, it did not show in his manner when he welcomed the committeemen that evening for a second round of grievance presentations. Before the discussion got under way, however, he announced to the assembled senators that he had thought it fitting to have the cabinet officers — minus Seward, of course, since even aside from the fact that his resignation was pending, that would have been too indelicate — present to answer the charge that there was discord among them and that the President seldom followed or even asked for their advice. Whereupon the door opened and the six gentlemen in question filed into the room. Lincoln had invited them at the cabinet meeting that morning, after telling them of the matter afoot and of Seward's submission of his resignation. Mostly they had welcomed the chance to confront their accusers, although two of their number — Chase in particular — had protested that they "knew of no good that could come of an interview." In the end, however, the two — the other was Bates — had been obliged to go along with the majority. Now here they were, face to face with critics whose accusations were based, at least in part, on information supplied in private by Chase in order to curry favor with them. Already he was squirming, as if the fleas had jumped at the sight of his large, handsome person: but the worst was still to come.

If Chase and some of the senators were embarrassed by the confrontation, Lincoln certainly was not. He began the proceedings by reading aloud yesterday's bill of particulars, admitting as he went along that he had not consulted the cabinet on all affairs of state or war, and that he had not always followed their advice, even when he had sought it; but in the main, he said, he had valued and used their abilities, individually and collectively. As for discord, he did not think it reasonable to expect seven such independent-minded men to agree on every issue that came before them; but here again, he said, he thought they worked together mainly as a unit, and certainly he himself had no complaint. He paused, then turned to the six cabinet members present, beginning to poll them one by one. Did they or did they not agree with his statement of the case? They did; or so they said, one by one; until he came to Chase. Chase, as it turned out, also agreed, though not without considerable hemming and hawing by way of preamble. He would never have come to the meeting, he said, if he had known he was "to be arraigned." He seemed angry. He seemed to feel that he was being "put upon"— as indeed he was. In the end, with Wade and the others watching balefully, he admitted that matters of prime importance had usually come before the cabinet, though perhaps "not so fully as might be desired," and that there had been "no want of unity in the cabinet, but a general acquiescence in public measures." Thus he wound up, and the Jacobins watched him cold-eyed, contrasting what he said now, in the presence of Lincoln and his colleagues, with what he had said in private. The President did not prolong his suffering. Having more or less settled these two points of contention, he shifted the talk to the question of Seward, defending his chief minister against yesterday's charges, and then began to poll the committeemen on their views. At that point Fessenden recoiled. "I do not think it proper," he said, "to discuss the merits or demerits of a member of the cabinet in the presence of his associates." Chase was quick to agree. "I think the members of the cabinet should withdraw," he said. In solemn procession they did so, some amused, some disgruntled, and one, at least, discredited in the eyes of men whose favor he had sought.

Like Simon Cameron a year ago, the Treasury chief had learned the hard way what it meant to tangle with Lincoln. Cameron was in Russia now, a victim of political decapitation, and Chase was determined to avoid such punishment. He would forestall the headsman by submitting, however regretfully, his resignation. This was exactly what Lincoln wanted: as was shown next morning, December 20, when he came into his office and found Chase, Welles, and Stanton grouped around the fire. Chase began to complain of yesterday's damage to his dignity. It had affected him most painfully, he said, for it seemed to indicate a lack of confidence. In fact — he hesitated — he had written out his resignation at home the night before. . . . Lincoln's reaction to this was not at all what the Secretary had expected. His expression was one of downright joy.

"Where is it?" he said eagerly.

"I brought it with me," Chase replied, taking a letter from his inside coat pocket.

"Let me have it," Lincoln said, and he put out a long arm.

Chase drew back, but not in time. Lincoln already had hold of the paper, and the Secretary suffered the added shock of having it snatched from his grasp. Reading it quickly through, Lincoln laughed; "a triumphal laugh," Welles called it in his diary. "This cuts the Gordian knot," he exclaimed. "I can dispose of this subject now without difficulty. I see my way clear." Stanton, who had been guilty of some of the same backstairs maneuvers — though he did not know whether the President suspected him, or what he might do if he did — remarked stiffly that he was prepared to tender his resignation, too. But Lincoln already had what he had been working toward. "You may go to your department," he said gaily. "I don't want yours. This"— he held up Chase's letter —"is all I want; this relieves me; the case is clear; the trouble is ended. I will detain neither of you longer."

His satisfaction was obvious, amounting to delight. What he had had in mind all along, and had achieved through skillful handling, was a balance: Chase's resignation against Seward's, which the Jacobins were still urging him to accept. Now, however, with Chase's inseparably included —"If one goes, the other must," he presently notified the senators; "they must hunt in couples"— they would be much less insistent; for, whatever their disgust with the Treasury chief's performance the day before, they still believed that he could be useful to them within the administration's private councils. Lincoln himself described the situation with a metaphor out of his boyhood in Kentucky, where he had seen farmers riding to market with a brace of pumpkins lodged snugly in a bag, one at each end in order to make a balanced load across the horse's withers. "Now I can ride," he said. "I have got a pumpkin in each end of my bag." Accordingly, he sent polite, identical notes to the two ministers, declining to accept their resignations and requesting them to continue as members of his official family. Seward, who had watched the maneuvers with amusement from a seat behind the scene, agreed at once; but Chase held off, still suffering from the fleabites, which were no less painful for being figurative. "I will sleep on it," he said. However, after a day of meditation and prayer — for it was a Sunday and he was intensely religious, spending a good part of each Sabbath on his knees — he agreed to remain at his post, as Lincoln had confidently expected.

Here was a case of double salvation, in more ways than one. Within the confines of his office in the White House, Lincoln had planned and fought a three-day battle as important to the welfare of the nation, and the progress of the war through united effort, as many that raged in the open field with booming guns and casualties by the thousands. In addition to retaining the services of Seward and Chase, both excellent men at their respective posts, he had managed to turn aside the wrath of the Jacobins without increasing their bitterness toward himself or incurring their open hatred, which might well have been fatal. Nor was that all. Paradoxically, because of the way he had gone about it, in avoiding the disruption of his cabinet he had achieved within it a closer harmony than had obtained before. This was partly because of the increased respect his actions earned him, but it was also because of the effect the incident had on the two ministers most intimately concerned. For all his loyalty to Lincoln through the storm, Seward had not previously abandoned the notion that he was the man directly in line for his job. Now, though, with all but one of the senators in his own party having expressed a desire to see him removed from any connection with the executive branch of the government, the presidential itch was cured. From that hour, his devotion to his duties was single-minded and his loyalty acquired an added zeal. So much could hardly be said for Chase, exactly, but he too had been sobered, and his ambition taken down a notch, by the cold-eyed looks the radical leaders had given him while he squirmed. It was no wonder, then, that Lincoln indulged in self-congratulation when he reviewed the three-day maneuver. "I do not see how I could have done better," he remarked.

Few would disagree with this assessment, even among the frock-coated politicians he had bested, whether senators or members of his cabinet. In point of fact, whatever shocks they had suffered along the way, there should have been little surprise at the outcome; for the matter had been essentially political, and politics (or statesmanship, if you will, which he once defined as the art of getting the best from men who all too often were intent on giving nothing better than their worst) was a science he had mastered some time back. The military art was something else. Whether Lincoln would ever do as well as Commander in Chief of the nation's armies as he had done as its Chief Executive was more than doubtful — particularly in the light of current testimony as to the condition of the largest of those armies, still on the near bank of the Rappahannock attempting to recover from the shock of its mid-December blood bath.

"Exhaustion steals over the country. Confidence and hope are dying," the Quartermaster General wrote privately this week to its commander. "The slumber of the army since [the attack at Fredericksburg] is eating into the vitals of the nation. As day after day has gone, my heart has sunk and I see greater peril to our nationality in the present condition of affairs than I have seen at any time during the struggle." Complaints were heard from below as well as above, and though these were not addressed to Burnside personally, accusing fingers were leveled in his direction and even higher. "Our poppycorn generals kill men as Herod killed the innocents," a Massachusetts private declared, and a Wisconsin major called this winter "the Valley Forge of the war." A bitterness was spreading through the ranks. "Alas my poor country!" a New York corporal wrote home. "It has strong limbs to march and meet the foe, stout arms to strike heavy blows, brave hearts to dare. But the brains, the brains — have we no brains to use the arms and limbs and eager hearts with cunning? Perhaps Old Abe has some funny story to tell, appropriate to the occasion. . . . Mother, do not wonder that my loyalty is growing weak," he added. "I am sick and tired of disaster and the fools that bring disaster upon us."

There was a snatch of doggerel, sung to the tune of the old sea chanty "Johnny, Fill up the Bowl," making the rounds:

> *Abram Lincoln, what yer 'bout?*
>   *Hurrah! Hurrah!*
> *Stop this war. It's all played out.*
>   *Hurrah! Hurrah!*
> *Abram Lincoln, what yer 'bout?*
> *Stop this war. It's all played out.*
> *We'll all drink stone blind:*
> *Johnny, fill up the bowl!*

Veterans in the Army of the Potomac took up the refrain, "all played out," and made it their own. Once they had pretended cynicism as a cover for their greenness and their fears, but now they felt they had earned it and they found the phrase descriptive of their outlook through this season of discontent. "The phrensy of our soldiers rushing to glory or death has, as our boys amusingly affirm, *been played out*," a regimental chaplain wrote. "Our battle-worn veterans go into danger when ordered, remain as a stern duty so long as directed, and leave as soon as honor and duty allow." Case-hardened by their recent experience over the river, particularly in the repeated fruitless assaults on the stone wall at the base of Marye's Heights, they had no use for heroic postures or pretensions nowadays. When they saw magazine illustrations showing mounted officers with drawn sabers leading smartly aligned columns of troops unflinchingly through shellbursts, they snickered and jeered and whooped their motto: "All played out!"

Lincoln already knew something of this, but he learned a good deal more on December 29 when two disgruntled brigadiers hurried from Falmouth to Washington on short-term passes, intending to warn their congressmen of what they believed was imminent disaster. Burnside was planning to recross the Rappahannock any day now, having issued three days' cooked rations the day after Christmas, along with orders for the troops to be held in readiness to move on twelve hours' notice. What alarmed the two brigadiers — John Newton and John Cochrane, the latter a former Republican congressman himself — was that the army, which they were convinced was in a condition of near-mutiny, would come apart at the seams if it was called upon to repeat this soon the tragic performance it had staged two weeks ago in the same arena, and therefore they had come to warn the influential Bay State senator Henry Wilson, chairman of the Senate Military Committee, in hopes that he could get the movement stopped. In the intensity of their concern, as they discovered when they reached the capital, they had failed to take into account the fact that Congress was in recess over the holidays; Wilson had gone home. Undeterred, they went to see the Secretary of State, a former political associate of Cochrane's. When Seward heard their burden of woes he took them straight to the President, to whom — though they were somewhat daunted now, never having intended to climb this

high up the chain of command — they repeated, along with hasty assurances that the basis for their admittedly irregular visit was patriotism, not
hope for advancement, their conviction that if the Army of the Potomac
was committed to battle in its present discouraged state it would be utterly destroyed. Not only would it be unable to hold the line of the Rappahannock; it would not even be able to hold the line of the river from
which it took its name. Lincoln, who had known nothing of the pending
movement, and scarcely more of the extent of the demoralization Cochrane and Newton claimed was rampant, was infected with their fears and
got off a wire to Burnside without delay: "I have good reason for saying
that you must not make a general movement without first letting me
know of it."

Burnside, though his infantry had already been alerted for a
downstream crossing while his cavalry was in motion for a feint upstream —"a risky expedition but a buster," one trooper called the plan —
promptly complied with the President's telegram by canceling the movement, but he was angered and saddened by the obvious lack of confidence on the part of his superiors. The army, too — whatever its glad-
ness over the postponement of another blood bath — was aggrieved as it
filed back into its camps, feeling mistrusted and mistrustful. "Such checks
destroy the enthusiasm of any army," the same trooper dolefully protested.

Yet it was at this point, near the apparent nadir of its self-confidence and pride, with disaffection evident in all of its components, from
the commander down to the youngest drummer boy, that the one truly
imperishable quality of this army first began to be discerned, like a gleam
that only shone in darkness. If men could survive the unprofitable
slaughter of Fredericksburg — the patent bungling, the horror piled on
pointless horror, and the disgust that came with the conclusion that their
comrades had died less by way of proving their love for their country
than by way of proving the ineptness of their leaders — it might well be
that they could survive almost anything. There were those who saw this.
There were those who, unlike Newton and Cochrane, did not mistake
the vociferous reaction for near-mutiny, who knew that griping was not
only the time-honored prerogative of the American soldier, from Valley
Forge on down, but was also, in its way, a proof of his basic toughness
and resilience. "The more I saw of the Army of the Potomac," one correspondent wrote from the camps around Falmouth, "the more I wondered
at its invincible spirit, which no disaster seemed able to destroy." A *Harper's Weekly* editor perhaps overstated the case —"All played out!" the
soldiers who read it doubtless jeered — but was also thinking along these
lines in an issue that came out about this time: "Like our forefathers the
English, who always began their wars by getting soundly thrashed by
their enemies, and only commenced to achieve success when it was

thought they were exhausted, we are warming to the work with each mishap."

Lincoln thought so, too, what time he managed to shake off the deep melancholy that was so much a part of his complex nature. He probed and, probing, he considered what emerged. As of the first day of the year which was opening so inauspiciously, the Union had 918,211 soldiers under arms, whereas the Confederacy had 446,622, or a good deal less than half as many. At several critical points along the thousand-mile line of division the odds were even longer — out in Middle Tennessee, for instance, or down along the Rappahannock — and the troubled Commander in Chief found solace in brooding on the figures, even those that reached him from the field of Fredericksburg. "We lost fifty percent more men than did the enemy," a member of the White House staff remarked after hearing his chief discuss the outcome of the fighting there, "and yet there is sense in the awful arithmetic propounded by Mr Lincoln. He says that if the same battle were to be fought over again, every day, through a week of days, with the same relative results, the army under Lee would be wiped out to the last man, [while] the Army of the Potomac would still be a mighty host. The war would be over, the Confederacy gone." There was error here. Northern losses in the battle had exceeded southern losses, not by fifty, but by considerably better than one hundred percent. And yet there was validity in Lincoln's premise as to the end result, and especially was there validity in the conclusion the staff man heard him draw: "No general yet found can face the arithmetic, but the end of the war will be at hand when he shall be discovered."

Scott and McDowell, Pope and McClellan, and now Burnside: none of these was the killer he was seeking. Already he saw that this search was perhaps after all the major problem. All else — while, like Blondin, Lincoln threaded his way, burdened by untold treasures — was, in a sense, a biding of time until the unknown killer could be found. Somewhere he existed, and somewhere he would find him, this unidentified general who could face the grim arithmetic being scrawled in blood across these critical, tragic pages of the nation's history.

★   ★   ★

These and other matters were much on the President's mind when he woke on January 1. After an early-morning conference with Burnside, who had come up from Falmouth to ask in person just what the Commander in Chief's "good reason" had been for not allowing him to handle his own army as he saw fit, Lincoln spent the usual half hour with his barber, then got into his best clothes and went downstairs for the accustomed New Year's White House reception. For three hours, beginning at 11 o'clock, it was "How do you do?" "Thank you." "Glad to see you." "How do you do?" as the invited guests — high government officials, members of the diplomatic corps, and other important dignitaries, foreign and domestic — having threaded their way through the crowd of uninvited onlookers collected on the lawn, alighted from their carriages, came into the parlor, and filed past Lincoln for handshakes and refreshments. At 1 o'clock the long ordeal was over; he went back upstairs to his office for the day's — or, some would say, the century's — most important business, the signing of the Emancipation Proclamation.

Throughout the ninety-nine days since September 23, when the preliminary announcement of intention had been made, there had been much speculation as to whether he would issue or withdraw the final proclamation. Some were for it, some against. His friend Browning, for example, reflecting the view of constituents in the President's home state, thought it "fraught with evil, and evil only." The senator believed that the "useless and mischievous" document would serve "to unite and exasperate" the South, and to "divide and distract us in the North." Lincoln himself, if only by his neglect of the subject while the hundred days ticked off, had seemed to see the point of this objection. In his December message to Congress he had barely mentioned the projected edict, but had reverted instead to his original plan for compensated emancipation, a quite different thing indeed. Alarmed by this apparent failure of nerve, Abolitionists looked to their hero Senator Charles Sumner of Massachusetts, who went to Lincoln three days after Christmas for a straight talk on the matter. He found him hard at work on the final draft of the proclamation, writing it out in longhand. "I know very well that the name connected with this document will never be forgotten," Lincoln said, by way of explanation for his pains, and Sumner returned to his own desk to reassure a qualmish friend in Boston: "The President says he would not stop the Proclamation if he could, and he could not if he would. . . . Hallelujah!"

So it was. Seward brought the official copy over from the State Department, where a skilled penman had engrossed it from Lincoln's final draft, just completed the night before. All it lacked was the President's signature. He dipped his pen, then paused with it suspended over the expanse of whiteness spread out on his desk, and looked around with a serious expression. "I never in my life felt more certain that I was doing right," he said, "than I do in signing this paper. But I have been receiving calls and shaking hands since 9 o'clock this morning, till my arm is stiff and numb. Now this signature is one that will be closely examined, and if they find my hand trembled they will say, 'He had some compunctions.' But anyway it is going to be done." Slowly and carefully he signed, not the usual *A. Lincoln*, but his name in full: *Abraham Lincoln*. The witnesses crowded nearer for a look at the result, then laughed in relief of nervous tension; for the signature, though "slightly tremulous," as Lincoln himself remarked, was bold and clear. Seward signed next, the quick, slanting scrawl of the busy administrator, and the great seal was affixed, after which it went to its place in the State Department files (where it later was destroyed by fire) and in the hearts of men, where it would remain forever, though some of them had doubted lately that it would even be issued.

★ ★ ★

It was one thing to claim that by the stroke of a pen the fetters had been struck from the limbs of five million slaves and that their combined worth of more than a billion dollars was thereby automatically subtracted from enemy assets. It was quite another, however, to translate the announcement into fact, especially considering its peculiar limitations. All of Delaware, Maryland, Kentucky, Tennessee, and Missouri were exempt by specific definition within the body of the edict, along with those portions of Virginia and Louisiana already under Federal control. Lincoln himself explained that the proclamation had "no constitutional or legal justification, except as a military measure. The exemptions were made because the military necessity did not apply to the exempted localities." He freed no slave within his reach, and whether those beyond his reach would ever be affected by his pronouncement was dependent on the outcome of the war, which in turn depended on the southward progress of his armies. Just now that progress, East and West — once more with the possible exception of Middle Tennessee, where the issue remained in doubt — was negligible at best and nonexistent for the most part. Nor did the signs in either direction give promise of early improvement. Here in the East, in fact, if this morning's conference with Burnside was any indication of what to expect, the outlook was downright bleak.

The ruff-whiskered general had arrived in a state of acute distress, obviously fretted by more than the discomforts of his all-night ride from Falmouth, and Lincoln was distressed in turn to see him so. He liked Burnside — almost everyone did, personally — for his courage, for his impressive military bearing, and for what one subordinate called his "single-hearted honesty and unselfishness." All these qualities he had, and Lincoln, with a feeling of relief after weeks of trying to budge the balky McClellan, had chosen him in expectation of aggressiveness. The Indiana-born Rhode Islander had certainly given him that at Fredericksburg, in overplus indeed, but with a resolution so little tempered by discretion that critics now were remarking that he waged war in much the same way some folks played the fiddle, "by main strength and awkwardness." He himself was the first to admit his shortcomings. He had done so from the start, and recently in testimony given under oath before a congressional committee he had taken on his shoulders the whole blame for the late repulse. This was in a way disarming; it had the welcome but unfamiliar sound of natural modesty, so becoming in a truly capable man. However, there were those who saw it merely as further proof of his unfitness for the job he had accepted under protest. Burnside, they said, had not only admitted his incompetency; he had sworn to it.

When he opened the New Year's conference by asking what lay behind the telegram advising him not to move against the enemy without notifying Washington beforehand, Lincoln told him of the interview with the two brigadiers, in which they had stated that the army lacked confidence in its commander and was in no fit shape to be committed. Bristling at this evidence of perfidy from below, Burnside demanded to know their names, but Lincoln declined to divulge them for fear of the reprisal which he now saw would be visited upon their heads. This further increased the general's depression. It might well be true, he said, that his army had no faith in him; certainly not a single one of his senior commanders had approved of the movement he had canceled at Lincoln's suggestion. In fact, he added, plunging deeper into gloom, "It is my belief that I ought to retire to private life." When Lincoln demurred, Burnside's spirits rose a bit: enough, at least, to allow a sudden shift to the offensive. However low his own stock might have fallen, he said earnestly, he wanted the President to know that in his opinion neither Stanton's nor Halleck's was any higher. A man was apt to be a poor judge of his own usefulness and the loyalty of his subordinates, but of one thing he was sure. Neither the Secretary of War nor the general-in-chief had the confidence of the army — or of the country either for that matter, he quickly added, though he admitted that Lincoln was probably better informed on this latter point than he was. At any rate it was his belief that they too should be removed. . . . Lincoln expressed no opinion as to whether he could spare Stanton or Halleck, but he assured the unhappy Burnside that he valued his services highly. He urged him to return at once to his command and do the best he could, as he was sure he had done invariably in the past. Burnside replied that his plan was still to cross the Rappahannock, somewhere above or below Fredericksburg, and attack the rebels on their own ground. Lincoln said that was what he wanted, too, but prudence sometimes had to be applied, especially when risky ventures were involved. Whereupon, having secured this approval, however qualified, the general took his leave, apparently in a somewhat better frame of mind.

Still the fact remained that he was returning to his army with the intention of requiring it to pursue a course of action which, by his own admission, did not have the approval of the ranking subordinates who would be charged with its execution. The situation was, to say the least, loaded with possibilities of disaster. Here, Lincoln saw, was where the general-in-chief would fit into the picture; here was where Halleck could begin to perform the principal duty for which he had been summoned to the capital almost six months ago. He could go down to Falmouth for a first-hand look at the lay of the land and a talk with the disaffected corps commanders, then come back and submit his recommendations as to whether Burnside should be given his head or halted and replaced. Accordingly, before going upstairs to dress for the New Year's reception, Lincoln took out a sheet of paper and wrote the owl-eyed general a letter explaining what it was he wanted him to do. "If in such a difficulty as this you do not help," he wrote, "you fail me precisely in the point for which I sought your assistance." The tone was somewhat tart, doubtless because Lincoln was irked at having to ask for what should have been forthcoming as a matter of course, and he added: "Your military skill is useless to me, if you will not do this."

The letter was forwarded through Stanton, who gave it to Halleck that same morning at the reception. "Old Brains," as he was called, was taken aback. Twice already in this war he had ventured into the field —one occasion was the inchworm advance on Corinth, back in May, when all he got for his pains was an empty town, plus the guffaws that went with being hoodwinked; the other was his trip to see McClellan down on the York-James peninsula, shortly after his arrival East in late July, when he ordered the withdrawal that had permitted Lee to concentrate against Pope with such disastrous results on the plains of Manassas —and he was having no more of such exposure to the jangle of alarums and excursions. He prized the sweatless quiet of his office, where he could scratch his elbows in seclusion and ponder the imponderables of war. Lincoln's letter was a wrench, not so much because of what it said— which was, after all, little more than a definition of Halleck's duties— but because of the way it said it. The fact that his chief had thought it necessary to put the thing on record, in black and white, instead of making the suggestion verbally, which would have left no blot, seemed to him to indicate a lack of confidence. His reaction was immediate and decisive. As soon as the reception was over he went to his office, wrote out his resignation, and sent it at once to the Secretary of War.

Lincoln heard of this development from Stanton late that afternoon, following the signing of the Emancipation Proclamation. Saddened though he was by the general's reaction, which deprived him, as he said, of the professional advice he badly needed at this juncture, he still did not want to lose the services of Old Brains, such as they were. To mollify the offended man he recalled the letter that same day and put it away in his files with the indorsement: "Withdrawn, because considered harsh by General Halleck." He was pleased when the general then agreed to remain at his post, even though he amounted, as Lincoln subsequently remarked, to "little more . . . than a first-rate clerk." The fact was, in spite of his objection to what he called "Halleck's habitual attitude of demur," he valued his opinions highly, especially those on theoretical or procedural matters. "He is a military man, has had a military education. I brought him here to give me military advice." So Lincoln defended him, and added: "However you may doubt or disagree [with] Halleck, he is very apt to be right in the end." Then too, since he knew something of the unfortunate general's sufferings from hemorrhoids, which made him gruff as a sore-tailed bear and caused him to be avoided by all who could possibly stay beyond his reach, Lincoln's sympathy was aroused. Once when he was asked why he did not get rid of so unpleasant a creature, he replied: "Well, the fact is the man has no friends. [He] should be taken care of."

All in all, it had been a wearing day, and as Lincoln went to bed that night (having attended to several other less important matters, such as the complaint made to him by "an old lady of genteel appearance" that, despite previous assurances to the contrary, her boarding house near the corner of Tenth and E Streets was about to be commandeered by the War Department; "I know nothing about it myself," he wrote Stanton, "but promised to bring it to your notice") he might well have slept the sleep of nervous exhaustion: unless, that is, he was kept awake by an aching right hand, which had been squeezed and pumped by more than a thousand people in the course of this busy New Year's, or by the knowledge that from now on — or at any rate until he found the man who, as he said, could "face the arithmetic"— he would have to continue to act as his own general-in-chief, as in fact he had been doing all along, leaving the West Pointer who occupied the post at present to act as little more than a clerk, albeit a first-rate one.

In the days that followed hard on this, the one touch of relief in a prevailing military gloom was the news that Bragg had retreated from Stones River and that Rosecrans had taken Murfreesboro. Lincoln would have preferred a bolder pursuit, but he was grateful all the same for what he got. "I can never forget, while I remember anything," he told Rosecrans some months later, looking back, "that at about the end of last year, and beginning of this, you gave us a hard-earned victory which, had there been a defeat instead, the nation could scarcely have lived over." The law of diminishing utility obtained here in reverse; by contrast, this one glimmer swelled to bonfire proportions. All else was blackness — even afloat, where up to now the salt-water navy (so long at least as it had kept to its proper medium and stayed out of the muddy Mississippi) had suffered not a single major check in all the more than twenty months since the opening shots were fired at Sumter. Now suddenly all the news was bad and the checks frequent: not only at Galveston, where Magruder's cotton-clads had wrecked and panicked the Union warships, driving them from the bay, but also at other points along and off the rebel shore, before and after that disaster.

The first of these several naval wounds was self-inflicted, so to speak, or at any rate was not the result of enemy action. This did not make it any less painful or sad, however, for though the loss amounted to only one ship, that one was the most famous in the navy. Under tow off stormy Hatteras, with waves breaking over her deck and starting the oakum from her turret seam, the little ironclad *Monitor* — David to the *Merrimac*'s Goliath in Hampton Roads almost ten months ago — foundered and went to the bottom in the first hour of the last day of the year, taking four of her officers and a dozen of her crew down with her. This was hard news for the North, and close on its heels came word of what happened in Galveston harbor the following day. By way of reaction, the squadron commander at Pensacola ordered the 24-gun screw steamer *Brooklyn* and six gunboats to haul off from the blockade of Mobile and proceed at once to Texas to retrieve the situation. They arrived on January 8, but found there was little they could do except resume the blockade outside the harbor and engage in long-range shelling of the island town, now fast in rebel hands. They kept this up for three days, with little or no profit, until on January 11 they were handed another jolt.

About an hour before sundown the *Brooklyn*'s lookout spotted a bark-rigged vessel, apparently a merchantman, approaching from the south. When she saw the blockaders she halted as if surprised, and the Union flag officer, finding her manner suspicious, ordered the 10-gun sidewheel steamer *Hatteras* to heave her to for investigation of her papers. As the gunboat approached, she drew off and the chase began. It was a strange business. She ran awkwardly, despite the trimness of her lines, and though she managed to maintain her distance, on through twilight into a moonless darkness relieved only by the stars, the blockader had no difficulty in keeping her within sight. At last she hove to, as if exhausted, her sails furled. The *Hatteras* closed to within a hundred yards, stopped dead, and put a boat out. Before the boarding party reached her, however, a loud clear voice identified the vessel: "This is the Confederate States steamer *Alabama;* FIRE!" and a broadside lurched her sideways in the water, striking the *Hatteras* hard amidships so that she too recoiled, as if in horror. Ten guns to eight, the Federal outweighed her adversary by one hundred tons, but the advantage of surprise was decisive. Though she promptly returned the fire, the fight was brief. Within thirteen minutes, her walking beam shot away and her magazine flooded, she hoisted the signal for surrender.

"Have you struck?"

"I have."

"Cease fire! Cease fire!"

Within another six minutes she was on the bottom, thirty-fifth on the list of vessels taken, sunk, or ransomed by Captain Raphael Semmes, who would add another thirty-six to the list before the year was out.

He had read in captured Boston newspapers that the 30,000-man expedition under Banks was scheduled to rendezvous off Galveston on January 10 for the conquest of Texas, and he had shown up the following day, intending to get among the transports under cover of darkness, just outside the bar, and sink them left and right. When he saw the gunboats shelling the town, however, he knew it had been retaken, and he seized the opportunity to realize his life's ambition to stage a hand-to-hand fight with an enemy warship, provided he could lure one into pursuit and single combat: which he had done, fluttering just beyond her reach like a wounded bird until, having her altogether to himself, he turned and pounced. He was proud of the outcome of this "first yardarm engagement between steamers at sea," but just now his problem was to get away before his victim's friends, warned of the hoax by the flash and roar of guns, came up to avenge her. Pausing long enough to pick up the 118 survivors — about as many as he had in his whole crew, whose only casualty was a carpenter's mate with a cheek wound — he doused his lights and made off through the night. The *Brooklyn* and the other gunboats, arriving shortly thereafter, saw no sign of the *Hatteras* until dawn showed bits of her wreckage tossed about by the waves. By that time the *Alabama* was a hundred miles away, running hard for Jamaica, where Semmes and his crew — that "precious set of rascals," as he called them, being known in turn as "Old Beeswax" because of the needle-sharp tips to his long black mustache — would parole their captives and celebrate their exploit. Chagrined, the Union skippers turned back to resume their fruitless shelling of the island, bitterly conscious of the fact that instead of redeeming the late Galveston disaster, as they had intended, they had enlarged it.

Word of this no sooner reached Washington than it was followed, four days later, by news that was potentially even worse. At Mobile, where the departure of the *Brooklyn* and her consorts had weakened the cordon drawn across the entrance to the bay, the other famous Confederate raider *Florida* had been bottled up since early September, when she slipped in through the blockade with her crew and captain, Commander John N. Maffitt, down with yellow fever. By now they were very much up and about, however: as they proved on the night of January 15, when they steered the rebel cruiser squarely between two of the largest and fastest ships in the blockade squadron and made unscathed for the open sea, leaving her frantic pursuers far behind. Within ten days she had captured and sunk three U.S. merchantmen, the first of more then twenty she would take before midsummer, in happy rivalry with her younger sister the *Alabama*. Secretary Welles had been so furious over her penetration of the cordon, four months back, that he had summarily dismissed the squadron commander from the navy, despite the fact that he was a nephew of Commodore Edward Preble of *Constitution* fame; but this repetition of the exploit, outward bound, was seen by some as a reflection on the Secretary himself and a substantiation of the protest a prominent New Yorker had made to Lincoln, on the occasion of the Connecticut journalist's appointment, that if he would "select an attractive figurehead, to be adorned with an elaborate wig and luxuriant whiskers, and transfer it from the prow of a ship to the entrance of the Navy Department, it would in my opinion be quite as serviceable . . . and less expensive."

Nor was this by any means the last bad news to reach the Department from down on the Gulf before the month was out. On January 21, at the end of the week that had opened with the *Florida*'s escape, John Magruder staged in Texas — apparently, like Browning's thrush, lest it be thought that the first had been no more than a fine careless rapture — a re-enactment of the previous descent on the Union flotilla in Galveston harbor. This time the scene was Sabine Pass, eighty miles to the east, and once more two cotton-clad steamboats were employed, with like results. The *Morning Light*, a sloop of war, and the schooner *Velocity*, finding themselves unable to maneuver in all the confusion, struck their flags and surrendered 11 guns and more than a hundred seamen to the jubilant Confederates who had come booming down the pass with a rattle of small arms and a caterwaul of high-pitched rebel yells. Next day the blockade was re-established by gunboats sent over from the flotilla cruising off Galveston, but there was little satisfaction in the fact, considering the increase of tension in the wardrooms and on lookout stations. However, a lull now followed, almost as if the crowing rebels were giving the bluejackets time to digest the three bitter pills administered in the course of the past three weeks.

For Lincoln there was no such lull, nor did there seem likely to be one so long as the present commander of the Army of the Potomac remained at his post. He had chosen Burnside primarily as a man of action, and however far the ruff-whiskered general had fallen short of other expectations, from the day of his appointment he had never done less than his fervent best to measure up to this one. The Fredericksburg fight, pressed despite a snarl-up of preparatory matters which had turned it into something quite different from what had been intended at the outset, was an instance of that determination to be up and doing, and Lincoln was in constant trepidation that a similar sequence of snarl-ups — the canceled year-end maneuver, for example — presaged a similar disaster. The signs were unmistakably there.

Four days after the New Year's conference Burnside informed the President that he still intended to attempt another Rappahannock crossing, and had in fact alerted his engineers, although his generals practically unanimously remained opposed to the movement. Inclosed with the note was his resignation; Lincoln could either sustain him or let him return to civilian life. Another letter went to Halleck this same day. "I do not ask you to assume any responsibility in reference to the mode or place of crossing," Burnside wrote, "but it seems to me that, in making so hazardous a movement, I should receive some general directions from you as to the advisability of crossing at some point, as you are necessarily well informed of the effect at this time upon other parts of the army of a success or a repulse." However, this attempt to wring a definite personal commitment from the general-in-chief was no more productive than Lincoln's had been. Halleck — described by a correspondent as resembling "an oleaginous Methodist parson in regimentals," with a "large, tabular, Teutonic" face — replied on January 7, administering an elementary textbook strategy lecture. He had always been in favor of an advance, he said, but he cautioned Burnside to "effect a crossing in a position where we can meet the enemy on favorable or even equal terms. . . . If the enemy should concentrate his forces at the place you have selected for a crossing, make it a feint and try another place. Again, the circumstances at the time may be such as to render an attempt to cross the entire army not advisable. In that case theory suggests that, while the enemy concentrates at that point, advantages can be gained by crossing smaller forces at other points, to cut off his lines, destroy his communication, and capture his rear guards, outposts, &c. The great object is . . . to injure him all you can with the least injury to yourself. . . . As you yourself admit, it devolves upon you to decide upon the time, place, and character of the crossing which you may attempt. I can only advise that an attempt be made, and as early as possible. Very respectfully, your obedient servant, H. W. Halleck, General-in-Chief."

Burnside had asked for "general directions." What he got was very general advice. Tacked onto it, however, was a presidential indorsement in which, after urging him to "be cautious, and do not understand that the Government or the country is driving you," Lincoln added: "I do not yet see how I could profit by changing the command of the Army of the Potomac, and if I did, I should not do it by accepting the resignation of your commission." The "yet" might well have given Burnside pause, but at any rate he had a sort of left-handed reply to his ultimatum demanding that the President either fire or sustain him. He prepared therefore to go ahead with his plan for an upstream crossing, beyond Lee's left, and a southward march to some rearward point athwart the Confederate lines of supply and communication. This time he intended to guard against failure by feeling his way carefully beforehand. After originally selecting United States Ford as the bridgehead, a dozen miles above Fredericksburg, he rejected it when a cavalry reconnaissance showed the position well covered by Confederate guns, and selected instead Banks Ford, which was not only less heavily protected but was also less than half as far away. By January 19 his preparations were complete. Next morning his soldiers assembled under full packs for the march, stood there while a general order was read to them, and set out with its spirited phrases ringing in their ears: "The commanding general announces to the Army of the Potomac that they are about to meet the enemy once more. . . . The auspicious moment seems to have arrived to strike a great and mortal blow to the rebellion, and to gain that decisive victory which is due to the country."

It took several hours for so many men to clear their camps, but once this had been done the march went well — indeed, auspiciously — until midafternoon, when a slow drizzle began. For a time it seemed no more than a passing shower, but the sun went down behind a steely curtain of true rain, which was pattering steadily by nightfall. All night it fell; by morning it was drumming without letup. Looking out from their sodden bivouacs, in which they could find not even enough dry twigs for boiling coffee, the soldiers could hardly recognize yesterday's Virginia. "The whole country was an ocean of mud," one wrote. "The roads were rivers of deep mire, and the heavy rain had made the ground a vast mortar bed." Presently, as the troops fell in coffeeless to resume the march in a downpour that showed no sign of slacking, broad-tired wagons loaded with big pontoons (despite all Burnside's precautions against snarl-ups, the pontoniers had been late in getting the word) churned the roads to near-impassability. Their six-mule teams were doubled and even tripled, but to small avail. Then long ropes were attached to the cumbersome things, affording hand-holds for as many as 150 men at a time, but this still did no real good according to a correspondent who watched them strain and fail: "They would flounder through the mire for a few feet — the gang of Lilliputians with their huge-ribbed Gulliver — and then give up breathlessly." Guns were even more perverse. Whole regiments pulled them along with the help of prolonges, leaving deep troughs in the roadbed to mark their progress, but if they stopped for a breather, without first putting brush or logs under the axle, the gun would begin to sink and, what was worse, would keep on sinking until only its muzzle showed, and the men would have to dig it out with shovels. "One might fancy that some new geologic cataclysm had overtaken the world," a reporter declared, surveying the desolation, "and that he saw around him the elemental wrecks left by another Deluge." When Burnside himself, trailing a gaudy kite-tail of staff officers, came riding through this waste of mired confusion, one irreverent teamster whose mules and wagon were stalled like all the rest called out to him across the sea of mud: "General, the auspicious moment has arrived!"

He was undaunted, even in the face of this. Though the rain was still coming down steadily, without a suggestion of a pause, and though most of his soldiers were thinking, as one recalled, that "it was no longer a question of how to go forward, but how to get back," Burnside no more had it in mind to quit now than he had had six weeks ago, when he had kept throwing some of these same men against the fuming base of Marye's Heights. Today was finished but there was still tomorrow, and he gave orders that the march would be resumed at dawn. However, in an attempt to raise the dejected spirits of the troops, he directed that a ration of whiskey be issued to all ranks. Somehow the barrels were brought up in the night and the distribution made next morning. The result, in several cases — for the officers poured liberally and the stuff went into empty stomachs — was spectacular. For example, rival regiments from Pennsylvania and Massachusetts promptly decided the time had come for them to settle a long-term feud, and when a Maine outfit stepped in to try and stop the scuffle, the result was the biggest three-sided fist fight in the history of the world. Meanwhile, from grandstand seats on the crests of hills across the way, the rebels were enjoying all of this enormously. Pickets jeered from the south bank of the Rappahannock, and one butternut cluster went so far as to hold up a crudely lettered placard: THIS WAY TO RICHMOND, underlined with an arrow pointing in the opposite direction. Finally, about noon, even Burnside saw the hopelessness of the situation. He gave orders and the long, bedraggled files of men faced painfully about. The Mud March — so called in the official records — was over.

It was over, that is for most of them, except for the getting back to camp and the consequences. For some, though, it was over then and there; they kept slogging northward, right on out of the war. Desertion reached an all-time high. Sick lists had never been so long. Morale hit an all-time low. "I never knew so much discontent in the army before," an enlisted diarist wrote. "A great many say that they 'don't care whether school keeps or not,' for they think there is a destructive fate hovering over our army." This reaction was by no means limited to the ranks, and what was more the men in higher positions were specific in their placement of the blame. "I came to the conclusion that Burnside was fast losing his mind," Franklin was presently saying, and Hooker was even more emphatic in the expression of his views. Without limiting his criticism to the luckless army commander, whom he considered merely inept, he told a newsman that the President was an imbecile, not only for keeping Burnside on but also in his own right, and that the administration itself was "all played out." What the country needed, Fighting Joe declared, and the sooner the better, too, was a dictator. ...Much of this reached army headquarters in one form or another, and Burnside's thin-stretched patience finally snapped under the double burden of abuse and ridicule. Early next evening, January 23, while his troops were still straggling forlornly back to their camps, he wired Lincoln: "I have prepared some very important orders, and I want to see you before issuing them. Can I see you alone if I am at the White House after midnight?"

In mud and fog and darkness he left headquarters about 9 o'clock in an ambulance, lost the road, found it, then lost it again, bumping into dead mules, stalled caissons, and other derelicts of the late lamented march. Finally, near midnight, he arrived at the Falmouth railhead, two miles from his starting point, only to learn that the special locomotive he had ordered held had given him up and chuffed away on other business. He took a lantern and set out down the track to meet it coming back, flagged and boarded it, and at last got onto a steamer at Aquia Landing. It was midmorning before he was with Lincoln at the White House, but the orders he brought for his perusal were no less startling for having been delayed. What Burnside was suggesting — in fact *ordering*, "subject to the approval of the President" — was the immediate dismissal of four officers from the service and the relief of six from further duty with the Army of the Potomac. The first group was headed by Joe Hooker, who was referred to as "a man unfit to hold an important commission during a crisis like the present, when so much patience, charity, confidence, consideration, and patriotism are due from every soldier in the field." Next came Brigadier General W.T.H. Brooks, a division commander accused of "using language tending to demoralize his command." The other two, lumped together in one paragraph, were Newton and Cochrane, whose names Burnside had learned simply by checking the morning reports to see what general officers had been on pass at the time of their late-December conference with Lincoln. These four were to be cashiered. The six who were to be relieved were two major generals — Franklin and W. F. Smith, Newton's and Cochrane's corps commander — three brigadiers (including, by some strange oversight, Cochrane, who supposedly had just been cashiered) and one lieutenant colonel, a lowly assistant adjutant who was apparently to be struck by an incidental pellet from the blast that was to bring down all those other, larger birds.

Burnside left the order with the startled President, telling him plainly to make a choice between approving it or accepting its author's resignation from command of an army that included such a set of villains. The order was dated the 23d, a Friday. Lincoln took what was left of Saturday to think the matter over. Then on Sunday, January 25, the ruff-whiskered general got his answer in the form of a general order of Lincoln's own, directing: 1) that Burnside be relieved of command, upon his own request; 2) that Sumner be relieved, also upon his own request; 3) that Franklin be relieved, period; and 4) "that Maj. Gen. J. Hooker be assigned to the command of the Army of the Potomac."

This last was a hard thing for the departing commander to accept. He had planned to blow up Hooker, but instead he had blown himself up, and Hooker into his place. It was hard, too, for Sumner and for Franklin; the fact that both were the new commander's seniors necessitated their transfer after long association with the eastern army. Lincoln did not so much regret having to sidetrack Franklin, whose lack of aggressiveness at South Mountain and Fredericksburg was notorious, but he was sorry to have to offend the superannuated Sumner, who had saved the day at Fair Oaks and fought well on every field until his soul was sickened by the slaughter at Antietam. Nor had he hurt without regret the normally good-natured Burnside, whose forthright honesty in admission of faults and acceptance of blame was so different from what was ordinarily encountered. However, what there had been of hesitation was mainly based on what Lincoln knew of Fighting Joe himself, who was next in line for the assignment. He had heard from others beside Burnside of Hooker's infidelity to his chief, and also of his excoriation of the Washington authorities. In fact, when the *Times* reporter who had talked recently with Hooker came to Lincoln on this Sunday and told him of what the general had said about the administration's shortcomings and the need for a dictator, Lincoln showed no trace of surprise. "That is all true; Hooker does talk badly," he admitted. But he decided, all the same, that Hooker was what the army and the country needed in the present crisis — a fighter who, unlike Burnside, had self-confidence and a reputation for canniness. "Now there is Joe Hooker," Lincoln had remarked a short time back. "He can fight. I think that is pretty well established."

And so it was. Without consulting Halleck or Stanton or anyone else, and despite the admitted risk to the national cause and the incidental injury to Burnside and Sumner, he made his choice and acted on it. However, before the new commander had been two days at his post, Lincoln sent for him and handed him a letter which was calculated to let him know how much he knew about him, as well as to advise him of what was now expected:

General:
  I have placed you at the head of the Army of the Potomac. Of course I have done this upon what appear to me to be sufficient reasons, and yet I think it best for you to know that there are some things in regard to which I am not quite satisfied with you. I believe you to be a brave and a skillful soldier, which of course I like. I also believe you do not mix politics with your profession, in which you are right. You have confidence in yourself, which is a valuable if not an indispensable quality. You are ambitious, which, within reasonable bounds, does good rather than harm; but I think that during General Burnside's command of the army you have taken counsel of your ambition and thwarted him as much as you could, in which you did a great wrong to the country and to a most meritorious and honorable brother officer. I have heard, in such way as to believe it, of your recently saying that both the army and the government needed a dictator. Of course it was not for this, but in spite of it, that I have given you the command. Only those generals who gain successes can set up dictators. What I now ask of you is military success, and I will risk the dictatorship. The government will support you to the utmost of its ability, which is neither more nor less than it has done and will do for all commanders. I much fear that the spirit which you have aided to infuse into the army, of criticising their commander and withhold-

ing confidence from him, will now turn upon you. I shall assist you
as far as I can to put it down. Neither you nor Napoleon, if he were
alive again, could get any good out of an army while such a spirit
prevails in it.

And now, beware of rashness. Beware of rashness, but with energy
and sleepless vigilance go forward and give us victories.

Yours very truly
A. LINCOLN

✗ 2 ✗

McClernand, conferring with Sherman at Milliken's Bend on the day
after his arrival from upriver — it was January 3; the two were aboard
the former Illinois politician's headquarters boat, the *Tigress,* tied up to
bank twenty-odd miles above Vicksburg — did not blame the red-
haired Ohioan for the repulse suffered earlier that week at Chickasaw
Bluffs; Sherman, he said in a letter to Stanton that same day, had "probably done all in the present case anyone could have done." The fault
was Grant's, and Grant's alone. Grant had designed the operation and
then, taking off half-cocked in his eagerness for glory that was right-
fully another's, had failed to co-operate as promised, leaving Sherman to
hold the bag and do the bleeding. So McClernand said, considerably em-
bittered by the knowledge that a good part of the nearly two thousand
casualties lost up the Yazoo were recruits he had been sending down
from Cairo for the past two months, only to have them snatched from
under him while his back was turned. "I believe I am superseded.
Please advise me," he had wired Lincoln as soon as he got word of
what was afoot. But permission to go downriver had not come in time
for him to circumvent the circumvention; the fighting was over before
he got there. He took what consolation he could from having been
spared a share in a fiasco. At least he was with his men again — what
was left of them, at any rate — and ready to take over. "Soon as I shall
have verified the condition of the army," he told Stanton, "I will assume
command of it."

He did so the following day. Christening his new command "The
Army of the Mississippi" in nominal expression of his intentions, or at
any rate his hopes, he divided it into two corps of two divisions each,
the first under George Morgan and the second under Sherman —
which, incidentally, was something of a bitter pill for the latter to swal-
low, since he believed a large share of the blame for the recent failure up
the Yazoo rested with Morgan, who had promised that in ten minutes
he would "be on those hills," but who apparently had forgot to wind
his watch. However that might be, McClernand now had what he had
been wanting all along: the chance to prove his ingenuity and dem-
onstrate his mettle in independent style. His eyes brightened with an-

ticipation of triumph as he spoke of "opening the navigation of the Mississippi," of "cutting my way to the sea," and so forth. For all the expansiveness of his mood, however, the terms in which he expressed it were more general than specific; or, as Sherman later said, "the *modus operandi* was not so clear."

In this connection — being anxious, moreover, to balance his re-cent defeat with a success — the Ohioan had a suggestion. During the Chickasaw Bluffs expedition the packet *Blue Wing,* coming south out of Memphis with a cargo of mail and ammunition, had been captured by a Confederate gunboat that swooped down on her near the mouth of the Arkansas and carried her forty miles up that river to Arkansas Post, an outpost established by the French away back in 1685, where the reb-els had constructed an inclosed work they called Fort Hindman, gar-risoned by about 5000 men. So long as this threat to the main Federal supply line existed, Sherman said, operations against Vicksburg would be subject to such harassment, and it was his belief that, by way of pre-amble to McClernand's larger plans — whatever they were, precisely — he ought to go up the Arkansas and abolish the threat by "thrashing out Fort Hindman."

McClernand was not so sure. He had suffered no defeat that needed canceling, and what was more he had larger things in mind than the capture of an obscure and isolated post. However, he agreed to go with Sherman for a discussion of the project with Porter, whose co-operation would be required. They steamed downriver and found the admiral aboard his headquarters boat, the *Black Hawk,* anchored in the mouth of the Yazoo. It was late, near midnight; Porter received them in his nightshirt. He too was not so sure at first. He was short of coal, he said, and the ironclads, which would be needed to reduce the fort, could not burn wood. Presently, though, as Sherman continued to press his suit, asking at least for the loan of a couple of gunboats, which he offered to tow up the river and thus save coal, Porter — perhaps re-flecting that he had on his record that same blot which a victory would erase — not only agreed to give the landsmen naval support; "Suppose I go along myself?" he added. Suddenly, on second thought, McClern-and was convinced: so much so, indeed, that instead of merely sending Sherman to do the job with half the troops, as Sherman had expected, he decided it was worth the undivided attention of the whole army and its commander, whose record, if blotless, was also blank. With no minus to cancel, this plus would stand alone, auspicious, and make a good beginning as he stepped off on the road that led to glory and the White House.

He took three days to get ready, then (but not until then) sent a message by way of Memphis to notify Grant that he was off — one of his purposes being, as he said, "the counteraction of the moral effect of the failure of the attack near Vicksburg and the reinspiration of the forces repulsed by making them the champions of new, important, and successful enterprises." He left Milliken's Bend that same day, January 8, his 30,000 soldiers still aboard their fifty transports, accompanied by 13 rams and gunboats, three of which were ironclads and packed his Sunday punch. By way of deception the flotilla steamed past the mouth of the Arkansas, then into the White, from which a cutoff led back into the bypassed river. Late the following afternoon the troops began debarking three miles below Fort Hindman, a square bastioned work set on high ground at the head of a horseshoe bend, whose dozen guns included three 9-inch Columbiads, one to each riverward casemate, and a hard-hitting 8-inch rifle. A good portion of the defending butternut infantry, supported by six light pieces of field artillery, occupied a line of rifle-pits a mile and a half below the fort, but these were quickly driven out when the gunboats forged ahead and took them under fire from the flank. Late the following afternoon, when the debarkation had been completed and the four divisions were maneuvering for positions from which to launch an assault, the ironclads took the lead. The *Louisville*, the *De Kalb*, and the *Cincinnati* advanced in line abreast to within four hundred yards of the fort, pressing the attack bows on, one to each casemate, while the thinner-skinned vessels followed close behind to throw in shrapnel and light rifled shell. It was hot work for a time as the defenders stood to their guns, firing with precision; the *Cincinnati*, for example, took eight hits from 9-inch shells on her pilot house alone, though Porter reported proudly that they "glanced off like peas against glass"; the only naval casualties were suffered from unlucky shots that came in through the ports. When the admiral broke off the fight because of darkness, the fort was silent, apparently overwhelmed. But when Sherman, reconnoitering by moonlight, drew close to the enemy outposts he could hear the Confederates at work with spades and axes, drawing a new line under cover of their heavy guns and preparing to continue to resist despite the long numerical odds. Crouched behind a stump in the predawn darkness of January 11 he heard a rebel bugler sound what he later called "as pretty a reveille as I ever listened to."

Shortly before noon he sent word that he was ready. His corps was on the right, Morgan's on the left; both faced the newly drawn enemy line which extended across the rear of the fort, from the river to an impassable swamp one mile west. McClernand, having established a command post in the woods and sent a lookout up a tree to observe and report the progress of events, passed the word to Porter, who ordered the ironclads forward at 1.30 to renew yesterday's attack. Sherman heard the clear ring of the naval guns, the fire increasing in volume and rapidity as the range was closed. Then he and Morgan went forward, the troops advancing by rushes across the open fields, "once or twice falling to the ground," as Sherman said, "for a sort of rest or pause." As they approached the fort they saw above its parapet the pennants of the ironclads, which had smothered the heavy guns by now and were giving the place a close-up pounding. Simultaneously, white flags began to break out all along the rebel line. "Cease firing! Cease firing!" Sherman cried, and rode forward to receive the fort's surrender.

But that was not to be: not just yet, at any rate, and not to Sherman. Colonel John Dunnington, the fort's commander, a former U.S. naval officer, insisted on surrendering to Porter, and Brigadier General Thomas J. Churchill, commander of the field force, did not want to surrender at all. As Sherman approached, Churchill was arguing with his subordinates, wanting to know by whose authority the white flags had been shown. (He had received an order from Little Rock the night before, while there was still a chance to get away, "to hold out till help arrives or until all dead" — which Holmes later explained with the comment: "It never occurred to me when the order was issued that such an overpowering command would be devoted to an end so trivial.") One brigade commander, Colonel James Deshler of Alabama, a fiery West Pointer in his late twenties — "small but very handsome," Sherman called him — did not want to stop fighting even now, with the Yankees already inside his works. When Sherman, wishing as he said "to soften the blow of defeat," remarked in a friendly way that he knew a family of Deshlers in his home state and wondered if they were relations, the Alabamian hotly disclaimed kinship with anyone north of the Ohio River; whereupon the red-headed general changed his tone and, as he later wrote, "gave him a piece of my mind that he did not relish." However, all this was rather beside the point. The fighting was over and the butternut troops stacked arms. The Federals had suffered 31 navy and 1032 army casualties, for a total of 140 killed and 923 wounded. The Confederates, on the other hand, had had only 109 men hit; but that left 4791 to be taken captive, including a regiment that marched in from Pine Bluff during the surrender negotiations.

McClernand, who had got back aboard the *Tigress* and come forward, was tremendously set up. "Glorious! Glorious!" he kept exclaiming. "My star is ever in the ascendant." He could scarcely contain himself. "I had a man up a tree," he said. "I'll make a splendid report!"

Grant by now was in Memphis. He had arrived the day before, riding in ahead of the main body, which was still on the way under McPherson, near the end of its long retrograde movement from Coffeeville, northward through the scorched wreckage of Holly Springs, then westward by way of Grand Junction and LaGrange. Having heard no word from Sherman, he knew nothing of his friend's defeat downriver — optimistic as always, he was even inclined to credit rumors that the Vicksburg defenses had crumbled under assault from the Yazoo —

until the evening of his arrival, when he received McClernand's letter from Milliken's Bend informing him of the need for "reinspiration of the forces repulsed."

This was something of a backhand slap, at least by implication — McClernand seemed to be saying that he would set right what Grant had bungled — but what disturbed him most was the Illinois general's expressed intention to withdraw upriver for what he called "new, important, and successful enterprises." For one thing, if Banks was on the way up from New Orleans in accordance with the instructions for a combined assault on Vicksburg, it would leave him unsupported when he got there. For another, any division of effort was wrong as long as the true objective remained unaccomplished, and Grant said so in no uncertain terms next morning when he replied to McClernand's letter: "I do not approve of your move on the Post of Arkansas while the other is in abeyance. It will lead to the loss of men without a result. . . . It might answer for some of the purposes you suggest, but certainly not as a military movement looking to the accomplishment of the one great result, the capture of Vicksburg. Unless you are acting under authority not derived from me, keep your command where it can soonest be assembled for the renewal of the attack on Vicksburg. . . . From the best information I have, Milliken's Bend is the proper place for you to be, and unless there is some great reason of which I am not advised you will immediately proceed to that point and await the arrival of reinforcements and General Banks' expedition, keeping me fully advised of your movements."

He expressed his opinion more briefly in a telegram sent to Halleck that afternoon: "General McClernand has fallen back to White River, and gone on a wild-goose chase to the Post of Arkansas. I am ready to reinforce, but must await further information before knowing what to do." The general-in-chief replied promptly the following morning, January 12: "You are hereby authorized to relieve General McClernand from command of the expedition against Vicksburg, giving it to the next in rank or taking it yourself."

Grant now had what he wanted. Formerly he had moved with caution in the prosecution of his private war, by no means sure that in wrecking McClernand he would not be calling down the thunder on his own head; but not now. Halleck almost certainly would have discussed so important a matter with Lincoln before adding this ultimate weapon to Grant's arsenal and assuring him that there would be no restrictions from above as to its use. In short, Grant could proceed without fear of retaliation except from the victim himself, whom he outranked. However, two pieces of information that came to hand within the next twenty-four hours forestalled delivery of the blow. First, he learned that Port Hudson was a more formidable obstacle than he had formerly supposed, which meant that it was unlikely that Banks's upriver thrust would reach Vicksburg at any early date. And, second, he received next day from McClernand himself the "splendid report" announcing the fall of Arkansas Post and the capture of "a large number of prisoners, variously estimated at from 7000 to 10,000, together with all [their] stores, animals, and munitions of war." Not only was the urgency for a hookup with Banks removed, but to proceed against McClernand now would be to attack a public hero in his first full flush of victory; besides which, Grant had also learned that the inception of what he had called the "wild-goose chase" had been upon the advice of his friend Sherman, and this put a different complexion on his judgment as to the military soundness of the expedition. All that remained was to play the old army game — which Grant well knew how to do, having had it played against him with such success, nine years ago in California, that he had been nudged completely out of the service. When the time came for pouncing he would pounce, but not before. Meanwhile he would wait, watching and building up his case as he did so.

This did not mean that he intended to sit idly by while McClernand continued to gather present glory; not by a long shot. Four days later, January 17 — McClernand having returned as ordered to the Mississippi, awaiting further instructions at Napoleon, just below the mouth of the Arkansas — Grant got aboard a steamboat headed south from the Memphis wharf. Before leaving he wired McPherson, who had called a halt at LaGrange to rest his troops near the end of their long retreat from Coffeeville: "It is my present intention to command the expedition down the river in person."

★　★　★

Banks was going to be a lot longer in reaching Vicksburg than Grant knew, and more was going to detain him than the guns that bristled atop the bluff at Port Hudson. After a sobering look at this bastion he decided that his proper course of action, before attempting a reduction of that place or a sprint past its frowning batteries, would be a move up the opposite bank of the big river, clearing out the various nests of rebels who otherwise would interfere with his progress by harassing his flank as he moved upstream. Brigadier General Godfrey Weitzel, a twenty-eight-year-old West Pointer who already had been stationed in that direction by Ben Butler, was reinforced by troops from the New Orleans and Baton Rouge garrisons and told to make the region west of those two cities secure from molestation. He built a stout defensive work at Donaldsonville, commanding the head of Bayou La Fourche, and threw up intrenchments at Brashear City, blocking the approach from Berwick Bay. Then, crossing the bay with his mobile force on January 13, he entered and began to ascend the Teche, accompanied by three gunboats. This brought him into sudden contact next morning with Richard Taylor, who fought briefly and fell back,

sinking the armed steamer *Cotton* athwart the bayou as he did so, cork-
ing it against farther penetration. Weitzel, who had lost 33 killed and
wounded, including one of the navy skippers picked off by a sniper, reported proudly as he withdrew: "The Confederate States gunboat
Cotton is one of the things that were. . . . My men behaved magnifi-
cently. I am recrossing the bay."

As a successful operation — the first of what he intended would
be many — this was unquestionably gratifying to Banks, who made the
most of it in reporting the action to Washington as a follow-up to the
bloodless reoccupation of the Louisiana capital. Yet even as he tendered
his thanks to Weitzel for "the skillful manner in which he has performed
the task confided to him," he could also see much that was foreboding
in this small-scale expedition up the Teche. For one thing, the rebels
were very much there, though in what numbers he did not know, and
for another they would fight, but only as it suited them, choosing the
time and place that gave them the best advantage, fading back into the
rank undergrowth quite as mysteriously as they had appeared, and then
moving forward again as the bluecoats withdrew from what Taylor
himself, who knew all its crooks and byways, called "a region of lakes,
bayous, jungle, and bog." How long it might take to clear such an army
of phantoms from the district, or whether indeed it could ever be done,
Banks could not tell. By mid-January, however, he had decided that it
would have to be done. His expectations, described in mid-December
as "most sanguine," were tempered now by prudence and better acquaintance with the peculiar factors involved. He perceived that they
would have to be refashioned to conform to a different schedule before he attempted the reduction of Port Hudson and the eventual link-up
with Grant in front of Vicksburg, all those devious hundreds of miles up
the tawny Mississippi.

In Northwest Arkansas and South Missouri things were not going
much better for John Schofield, who had risen from a sickbed to resume
command of his army on the morrow of Prairie Grove. They could
in fact be said to be going a good deal worse, so far at least as personal
vexation was concerned. He had won a battle (or anyhow Blunt and
Herron had, with the result that they were about to be promoted over
his head) and had followed it up with a lunge at Van Buren, resulting
in the destruction of Hindman's stores, before withdrawing to Fayetteville; but he had no sooner regained the presumed security of this pro-
Union district, where he expected to enjoy in comparative relaxation his
belated but welcome promotion to major general, than he was distracted
by a series of explosions in his rear. First, Hindman unleashed his cavalry
under Brigadier General John S. Marmaduke, a Missouri-born West
Pointer, for an all-out raid on the main Federal supply base at Springfield, a hundred miles north of the point where Schofield was in the

process of drawing his lines facing south. On New Year's Eve Marmaduke left Lewisburg, on the north bank of the Arkansas River midway across the state, and reached his objective one week later at the head of 2300 horsemen, many of them picked up along the way and added to the original brigade of veterans under Colonel J. O. Shelby, who had led them on every field since Wilson's Creek. Attacking on January 8 the raiders burned the Springfield depot of supplies and withdrew eastward 45 miles to strike at Hartville on the 11th, with similar results after savage fighting, then turned south through a gale of sleet and snow, gobbling up enemy detachments as they went, and recrossed the White River at Batesville on January 25.

Casualties in the two main fights had been about 250 on each side, in addition to which Marmaduke not only had captured and paroled more than 300 of the enemy in the course of the raid, for the most part turning them loose in bitter weather without their outer garments — "In winter," one observer remarked, "the overcoat-bearing Federal was esteemed especially for his pelt" — but also had destroyed vital reserve supplies and refitted his troopers with arms and equipment greatly superior to the ones they had carried northward. All this came out of Schofield's pocket, so to speak, but that was by no means the most painful aftereffect of the operation. Major General Samuel Curtis, promoted to command of the department as a result of his Pea Ridge victory back in March, took alarm and ordered the Army of the Frontier withdrawn from Fayetteville to protect the penetrated region across the state line in its rear, abolishing at a stroke the hard-won gains of Prairie Grove. Schofield protested, to no avail; Missouri soon had greater need than ever for on-the-spot protection, Marmaduke's excursion having served to bring the guerillas out of hiding and onto the highways, along which new recruits hastened to join the bands reassembling under such leaders as George Todd, David Pool, William C. Anderson, called "Bloody Bill," and William C. Quantrill. Enrolling was a simple process. All a recruit had to do was answer "Yes" to the question: "Will you follow orders, be true to your fellows, and kill all those who serve and support the Union?"

In the wake of this sudden activity, in effect not unlike the upsetting of a beehive, came violent dissension in the ranks of the Union leaders. Curtis, a former Iowa Republican congressman and abolitionist, represented the radical faction, while Schofield, with the support of Governor Hamilton R. Gamble, became the champion of conservative views. Militarily, as well, the two generals were divergent in opinion. Curtis wanted to hold all available troops within the borders of the state in order to use them in putting down troublemakers of all sorts, armed or unarmed; Schofield on the other hand believed in taking the offensive against the Confederates to his front in Arkansas. At length, as the situation grew more tense between the two, Lincoln was appealed to as arbitrator. He backed the department commander, ordering Schofield east of the Mississippi and leaving the hero of Pea Ridge in full control. However, the storm of protest which followed this decision gave promise of greater trouble than ever, and caused him to seek a different solution. Transferring Curtis out to Kansas, where his political views would be more in accord with those of the majority of the people, Lincoln appointed as the new commander of the Department of Missouri old Edwin V. Sumner, lately relieved of duty with the Army of the Potomac. But this did not work either; Sumner died en route. . . . It was March 21. Breaking his journey at Syracuse, New York, the old soldier lay in a coma, as if in belated reaction to the horror of Antietam, where he had begun to lose the grip that had been strong enough to save the day at Fair Oaks. "The Second Corps never lost a flag or a cannon!" he suddenly cried out. When his aide came over he opened his eyes. "That is true; never lost one," he said weakly. At sixty-six he was nearing the end of forty-four years of army service, and except for his long sharp nose he resembled a death's-head. The aide raised him to a more comfortable position on the bed and poured him a glass of wine, prescribed by the doctor to keep up his strength. Sumner took a sip, saying across the rim of the glass by way of a toast: "God save my country, the United States of America," then dropped the glass and died. . . . Lincoln, receiving the news of Sumner's death, decided that Schofield was probably the best man to take charge in Missouri after all. In reassigning him to duty there, however, he thought it proper to give him some advice on how to proceed among people who were engaged in what he called "a pestilent factional quarrel among themselves." It was, he said in the accents of Polonius, "a difficult role, and so much greater will be the honor if you perform it well. If both factions, or neither, shall abuse you, you will probably be about right. Beware of being assailed by one and praised by the other."

The trouble with this, as advice, was that it was the counsel of perfection, since the only way a man could avoid factions, being championed on the one hand and excoriated on the other, was to stay out of Missouri in the first place. Schofield, a rather plump New York West Pointer who wore a long thin growth of curly whiskers in partial compensation for the fact that he was already balding at the age of thirty-two, was quite aware of this, of course, but promised to do his best in that regard. At the same time, however — it was late spring by then, well up in May — he had to forgo his plans for an offensive into Arkansas, not only because of guerilla troubles within his department (they continued to grow worse as time went by, until at last they exceeded in horror the wildest nightmares Curtis or anyone else, except possibly Bill Anderson and Quantrill — not to mention old John Brown — had ever had) but also because he lacked the troops, Missouri having become in effect a recruiting ground for the support of operations far down the big river that laved its eastern flank. Schofield could only give what he had promised, his best, and if this was not a great deal, under the nearly impossible circumstances it was enough.

He could take consolation, however, in the fact that the Confederates to the south were quite as bedeviled as he himself was, though in a different way: with the result that throughout this unhappy season, when so much of military importance was moving inexorably toward a climax on the east flank of the theater, they were no more able to assume the offensive than Schofield was. Not only were they suffering from an even more acute shortage of troops, but a sequence of rapid-fire shifts in command, beginning at the very top, quite paralyzed whatever movements they might otherwise have undertaken.

Not that the shifts were avoidable. It had in fact already become apparent that Holmes had been given a good deal more than he could handle. In mid-January, a week after his return to Richmond from his western journey, Davis sent for Kirby Smith, whom he admired, and assigned him to command the newly created Department of West Louisiana and Texas, intending in this way to relieve Holmes of the task of co-ordinating the efforts of Taylor and Magruder. "Am I thus to be sent into exile?" Smith asked wistfully. Not yet thirty-nine, he ranked second among the nation's seven lieutenant generals, and Lee himself had lately said that he would be pleased to have him as a corps commander, alongside Longstreet and Jackson. Davis explained that the assignment, far from amounting to exile, was as important as any in the whole Confederacy, since his main duty "would be directed to aiding in the defense of the Lower Mississippi and keeping that great artery of the West effectually closed to Northern occupation or trade." Acquiescing, Smith set out in early February, only to learn en route that his command had been enlarged to include the entire Transmississippi. In the light of this he arranged with Pemberton for the transfer of Major General Sterling Price, who was much admired in the Far West and had formerly been governor of Missouri, the scene of his early victories at Wilson's Creek and Lexington. It was hoped that Price would repeat them presently, although a sadly large proportion of the men with whom he had won them were buried now in shallow graves around Corinth and Iuka, and the survivors, few as they were in number, were too badly needed around Vicksburg to be allowed to recross the river. How he would replace them Smith did not know, for the region had been stripped of troops, first by Van Dorn, who had brought them east after his defeat at Elkhorn Tavern, and then by Hindman, who, by stringent enforcement of the conscription laws, had raised the army which he had taken across the Boston Mountains and then returned with no more than a comparative handful. Smith soon found his worst fears confirmed. "The male population remaining are old men, or have furnished substitutes," he reported, "are lukewarm, or are wrapped up in speculation and money-making."

Crossing at Port Hudson, he ascended Red River in a steamboat Richard Taylor had waiting for him by prearrangement, and on March 7 at Alexandria, Louisiana, he assumed command of all troops west of the Mississippi. What he encountered first-off gave his Regular Army nature quite a shock. "There was no general system, no common head," he later reported; "each district was acting independently." It was necessary, he said, to "begin *de novo* in any attempt at a general systematizing and development of the department resources." Accordingly he set out at once on a preliminary tour of inspection, which only served to increase his first dismay. Conferring with Holmes at Little Rock — the North Carolinian now had charge of the subdepartment including Arkansas, Missouri, and Indian Territory — he found him anxiously awaiting the arrival of Price to command the army remnant left by Hindman, who had resigned in a huff at having been superseded by Holmes on the occasion of that officer's step-down from command of the whole theater. Price arrived before the end of the month, yet there was little he could do until he got his men in condition to fight, which obviously would not be soon. Smith meantime established his headquarters at Shreveport. He considered it "a miserable place with a miserable population," but it had the virtue of central location, at the head of navigation of Red River and on the direct route between Texas and Richmond. Here he set to work, laying the groundwork for organization of the enormous region which in time would be known as Kirby-Smithdom. He worked long hours and did not spare himself or his subordinates; but spring had come, and so had Banks and Grant, before his command — which included, in all, about 30,000 soldiers between the Mississippi and the Rio Grande, fewer even than Bragg had in the Duck River Valley or Pemberton had at Vicksburg and Port Hudson — was in any condition to offer them anything more than a token resistance.

★ ★ ★

After an all-night boat ride down the Mississippi, from Memphis past the mouth of the Arkansas, Grant reached Napoleon on January 18 to find McClernand, Porter, and Sherman awaiting his arrival with mixed emotions — mixed, that is, so far as McClernand's were concerned; Porter and Sherman were united, if by nothing more than a mutual and intense dislike of the congressman-turned-commander. To them, Grant came as something of a savior, since he outranked the object of their scorn. To McClernand, on the other hand, he seemed nothing of the sort; McClernand plainly suspected another attempt to steal his thunder, if not his army. He had enlarged his Arkansas Post exploit by sending a pair of gunboats up White River to drive the rebels from St Charles and wreck their installations at De Valls Bluff, terminus of the railroad running east from Little Rock toward Memphis. It was smartly done, accomplishing at the latter place the destruction of the depot and some rolling stock, as well as the capture of two 8-inch guns which the flustered garrison was trying to load aboard the cars for a getaway west. Still at Fort Hindman while this was in progress, McClernand received Grant's curt and critical letter ordering him back to the Mississippi at once, and he bucked it along to Lincoln with a covering letter of his own.

"I believe my success here is gall and wormwood to the clique of West Pointers who have been persecuting me for months," he wrote, imploring his friend and fellow-townsman not to "let me be clandestinely destroyed, or, what is worse, dishonored, without a hearing." He asked, "How can General Grant at a distance of 400 miles intelligently command the army with me?" and answered his own question without a pause: "He cannot do it. It should be made an independent command, as both you and the Secretary of War, as I believe, originally intended."

Grant was about to get in some licks of his own in this regard, if not through out-of-channels access to Lincoln — whom he had not only never met, but had never even seen, despite the fact that both had gone to war from Illinois — then at any rate through Halleck, which was the next-best thing. For the present he merely conferred with the three officers, collectively and singly, and ordered the return of the whole expedition to Milliken's Bend for a renewal of the drive on Vicksburg by the direct route. By now, however, as a result of his talk with these men who had been there, he was beginning to see that the only successful approach, after all, might have to be roundabout. "What may be necessary to reduce the place I do not yet know," he wired the general-in-chief, "but since the late rains [I] think our troops must get below the city to be used effectually."

He spent the night ashore at Napoleon, whose partial destruction by incendiaries the day before caused Sherman to declare that he was "free to admit we all deserve to be killed unless we can produce a state of discipline when such disgraceful acts cannot be committed unpunished." One solution, he decided, would be "to assess the damages upon the whole army, officers included," but no such drastic remedy was adopted. The following morning Grant saw the transports and their escort vessels steam away south, in accordance with his orders, and returned that evening to Memphis. Next day, January 20, he sent Halleck a long dispatch explaining the tactical situation as he saw it and announcing that, by way of a start, he intended to try his hand at redigging the canal across the base of the hairpin bend in front of Vicksburg, abandoned the previous summer by Butler's men when the two Union fleets were sundered and repulsed by the rebel warship *Arkansas*, now fortunately at the bottom of the river. Grant suggested that, in view of the importance of the campaign he was about to undertake, it would be wise to combine the four western departments, now under Banks, Curtis, Rosecrans, and himself, under a single over-all commander in order to assure co-operation. "As I am the senior department commander in the West," he wrote — apparently unaware that Banks was nine months his senior and in point of fact had been a major general before Grant himself was even a brigadier — "I will state that I have no desire whatever for such combined command, but would prefer the command I now have to any other than can be given." From which disclaimer he passed at once to the subject of John McClernand: "I regard it as my duty to state that I found there was not sufficient confidence felt in General Mc-Clernand as a commander, either by the Army or Navy, to insure him success. Of course, all would co-operate to the best of their ability, but still with a distrust. This is a matter I made no inquiries about, but it was thrust upon me." (As a later observer pointed out, there was "a touch of artfulness" in this; Grant "elevated Sherman and Porter to speak for entire branches of the service, then sought audiences with them so that the issue might be forced upon him!") However, he continued, "as it is my intention to command in person, unless otherwise directed, there is no special necessity of mentioning this matter; but I want you to know that others besides myself agree in the necessity of the course I had already determined upon pursuing."

His belief that Old Brains was on his side was strengthened the following day by a quick reply to his suggestion that "both banks of the Mississippi should be under one command, at least during the present operations." "The President has directed that so much of Arkansas as you may desire to control be temporarily attached to your department," Halleck wired. "This will give you control of both banks of the river." Pleased to learn of Lincoln's support, even at second hand, Grant kept busy with administrative and logistical matters preparatory to his departure from Memphis at the earliest possible date. McPherson was marching in from LaGrange with two divisions to accompany him down-river; these 14,979, added to the 32,015 already there, would give him an "aggregate present" of 46,994 in the vicinity of Vicksburg, with more to follow, not only from his own Department of the Tennessee, which included a grand total of 93,816 of all arms, but also from the Department of Missouri, now under Curtis and later under Schofield. On January 25 he received further evidence of Lincoln's interest in the campaign for control of the Lower Mississippi, whose whimsical habit of carving itself new channels the Chief Executive knew from having made two flatboat voyages down it to New Orleans as a youth. "Direct your attention particularly to the canal proposed across the point," Halleck urged. "The President attaches much importance to this."

Grant himself was about ready to embark by now, wiring the general-in-chief this same day: "I leave for the fleet . . . tomorrow." Last-minute details held him up an extra day, but on the 27th he was off. "The work of reducing Vicksburg will take time and men," he had told Halleck the week before, "but can be accomplished."

Sherman was already hard at work on the project which had drawn Lincoln's particular attention, and with his present arduous endeavor — in effect a gigantic wrestling match with Mother Nature herself, or at any rate with her son the Father of Waters — added to his previous bloody experience up the Yazoo, he could testify as to the validity of Grant's long-range observation that the conquest of Vicksburg would "take time and men." In fact, he was inclined to think it might require so much of both commodities as to prove impossible. Both were expendable in the ordinary sense, but after all there were limits. He was discouraged, he wrote his senator brother John this week, by the lack of substantial progress by Union arms, East and West, and by the unexpected resilience of the Confederates, civilian as well as military: "Two years have passed and the rebel flag still haunts our nation's capital. Our armies enter the best rebel territory and the wave closes in behind. The utmost we can claim is that our enemy respects our power to do them physical harm more than they did at first; but as to loving us any more, it were idle even to claim it. . . . I still see no end," he added, "or even the beginning of the end."

Perhaps the senseless burning of Napoleon the week before was on his mind or conscience, but the truth was he had enough on his hands to distress him here and now. The rain continued to come down hard — even harder, perhaps, than it was falling along the Rappahannock, where Burnside's Mud March was coming to its sticky close and the soldiers were composing a parody of a bedtime prayer:

> *Now I lay me down to sleep*
> *In mud that's many fathoms deep.*
> *If I'm not here when you awake*
> *Just hunt me up with an oyster rake*

— with the result that Sherman's men, in addition to having to widen and deepen the old canal, which was little more than a narrow ditch across the base of the low-lying tongue of land, had to work day and night at throwing up a levee along its right flank in order not to be washed away by water from the flooded bayous in their rear. Besides, even if the river could be persuaded to scour out a new channel along this line and thus "leave Vicksburg out in the cold," as Sherman said, it would be no great gain so far as he could see. The Confederates would merely shift their guns southward along the bluff to command the river at and below the outlet, leaving the shovel-weary Federals no better off than before. So he told his brother. And Porter, watching his red-haired friend slosh around in the mud and lose his temper a dozen times a day — "half sailor, half soldier, with a touch of the snapping turtle," he called him — once more found it necessary to bolster Sherman's spirits with hot rum and rollicking words. "If this rain lasts much longer we will not need a canal," he ended a note to the unhappy general on January 27. "I think the whole point will disappear, troops and all, in which case the gunboats will have the field to themselves."

Next day, however, Grant arrived, and Porter, reporting the fact to Welles, could say: "I hope for a better state of things."

❊ 3 ❊

The word *shoddy* was comparatively new, having originated during the present century in Yorkshire, where it was used in reference to almost worthless quarry stone or nearly unburnable coal. Crossing the ocean to America it took on other meanings, at first being used specifically to designate an inferior woolen yarn made from fibers taken from worn-out fabrics and reprocessed, then later as the name for the resultant cloth itself. "Poor sleazy stuff," one of Horace Greeley's *Tribune* reporters called it, "woven open enough for sieves, and then filled with shearmen's dust," while *Harper's Weekly* used even harsher words in referring to it as "a villainous compound, the refuse and sweepings of the shop, pounded, rolled, glued, and smoothed to the external form and gloss of cloth, but no more like the genuine article than the shadow is to the substance." Thoroughly indignant, the magazine went on to tell how "soldiers, on the first day's march or in the earliest storm, found their clothes, overcoats, and blankets scattering to the wind in rags or dissolving into their primitive elements of dust under the pelting rain."

It followed that the merchants and manufacturers who supplied the government with such cloth became suddenly and fantastically rich in the course of their scramble for contracts alongside others of their kind, the purveyors of tainted beef and weevily grain, the sellers of cardboard haversacks and leaky tents. No one was really discomforted by all this — so far, at least, as they could see — except the soldiers, the Union volunteers whose sufferings under bungling leaders in battles such as Fredericksburg and Chickasaw Bluffs were of a nature that made their flop-soled shoes and tattered garments seem relatively unimportant, and the Confederate jackals who stripped the blue-clad corpses after the inevitable retreat. If the generals were unashamed, were hailed in fact as heroes after such fiascos, why should anyone else have pangs of conscience? The contractors asked that, meanwhile raking in profits that were as long as they were quick. The only drawback was the money itself, which was in some ways no more real than the sleazy cloth or the imitation leather, being itself the shadow of what had formerly been substance. With prosperity in full swing and gold rising steadily, paper money declined from day to day, sometimes taking sickening drops as it passed from hand to hand. All it seemed good for was spending, and they spent it. Spending, they rose swiftly in the social scale, creating in the process a society which drew upon itself the word that formerly had been used to describe the goods they bartered — "shoddy" — and upon their heads the scorn of those who had made their money earlier and resented the fact that it was being debased. One such was Amos Lawrence, a millionaire Boston merchant. "Cheap money makes specu- lation, rising prices, and rapid fortunes," Lawrence declared, "but it will not make patriots." He wanted hard times back again. Closed fac- tories would turn men's minds away from gain; then and only then could the war be won. So he believed. "We must have Sunday all over the land," he said, "instead of feasting and gambling."

For the present, though, all that was Sunday about the leaders of the trend which he deplored was their clothes. They wore on week- days now the suits they once had reserved for wear to church, and as they prospered they bought others, fine broadcloth with nothing shoddy about them except possibly what they inclosed. So garbed, and still with money to burn before it declined still further, the feasters and gamblers acquired new habits and pretensions, with the result that the disparaging word was attached by the New York *World* not only to the new society, but also to the age in which it flourished:

> The lavish profusion in which the old southern cotton aristocracy used to indulge is completely eclipsed by the dash, parade, and mag- nificence of the new northern shoddy aristocracy of this period. Ideas of cheapness and economy are thrown to the winds. The individual who makes the most money — no matter how — and spends the most money — no matter for what — is considered the greatest man. To be extravagant is to be fashionable. These facts sufficiently account for the immense and brilliant audiences at the opera and the theatres, and until the final crash comes such audiences undoubtedly will con- tinue. The world has seen its iron age, its silver age, its golden age, and its brazen age. This is the age of shoddy.
>
> The new brown-stone palaces on Fifth Avenue, the new equipages at the Park, the new diamonds which dazzle unaccustomed eyes, the new silks and satins which rustle overloudly, as if to demand atten- tion, the new people who live in the palaces, and ride in the carriages, and wear the diamonds and silks — all are shoddy.... They set or follow the shoddy fashions, and fondly imagine themselves à la mode de Paris, when they are only à la mode de shoddy. They are shoddy brokers on Wall Street, or shoddy manufacturers of shoddy goods, or shoddy contractors for shoddy articles for a shoddy government. Six days in the week they are shoddy business men. On the seventh day they are shoddy Christians.

Nor were journalists and previously wealthy men the only ones to express a growing indignation. Wages had not risen in step with the rising cost of food and rent and other necessities of life, and this had brought on a growth of the trade-union movement, with mass meetings held in cities throughout the North to protest the unequal distribution of advantages and hardships. (Karl Marx was even now at work on *Das Kapital* in London's British Museum, having issued with Friedrich Engels *The Communist Manifesto* fifteen years ago, and Lincoln himself had said in his first December message to Congress: "Labor is prior to, and independent of, capital. Capital is only the fruit of labor, and could never have existed if labor had not first existed. Labor is the superior of capital, and deserves much the higher consideration.") One such meeting, held about this time at Cooper Union, filled the building to capacity while hundreds of people waited outside for word to be passed of what was being said within by delegates on the rostrum; whatever it was was being received with cheers and loud applause, along with a sprinkling of hisses and vehement boos. A representative of the hatters, one McDonough Bucklin, believed that the war was being used by the rich as an excuse for increased exploitation of the poor. As Bucklin put it, "The machinery is forging fetters to bind you in perpetual bondage. It gives you a distracted country with men crying out loud and strong for the Union. Union with them means no more nor less than that they want the war prolonged that they may get the whole of the capital of the country into their breeches pocket and let it out at a percentage that will rivet the chain about your neck." It was the old story: "Every day the rich are getting richer, the poor poorer." Apparently at this point Bucklin got carried away, for a *World* reporter noted that "the speaker made some concluding remarks strongly tainted with communism, which did not meet with general approval."

And yet, for all the offense to the sensibilities of the Boston millionaire, who had made his pile in a different time, as well as to those of the New York journalist, whose indignation was one of the tools he used in earning a living, and the labor delegate, who after all was mainly concerned with the fact that he and his hatters were not getting what he considered a large fair slice of the general pie, much of the undoubted ugliness of the era — the Age of Shoddy, if you will — was little more than the manifest awkwardness of national adolescence, a reaction to growing pains. Unquestionably the growth was there, and unquestionably, too — despite the prevalent gaucherie, the scarcity of grace and graciousness, the apparent concern with money and money alone, getting and spending — much of the growth was solid and even permanent. The signs were at hand for everyone to read. "Old King Cotton's dead and buried; brave young Corn is king," was the refrain of a popular song written to celebrate the bumper grain crops being gathered every fall, of which the ample surpluses were shipped to Europe, where a coincidental succession of drouths — as if the guns booming and growling beyond the Atlantic had drawn the rain clouds, magnet-like, and then discharged them empty — resulted in poor harvests which otherwise would have signaled the return of Old World famine. More than five million quarters of wheat and flour were exported to England in 1862, whereas the total in 1859 had been less than a hundred thousand. In the course of the conflict the annual pork pack nearly doubled in the northern states, and the wool clip more than tripled. Meanwhile, industry not only kept pace with agriculture, it outran it. In Philadelphia alone, 180 new factories were established between 1862 and 1864 to accommodate labor-saving devices which had been invented on the eve of war but which now came into their own in response to the accelerated demands of the boom economy of wartime: the Howe sewing machine, for example, which revolutionized the garment industry, and the Gordon McKay machine for stitching bootsoles to uppers, producing one hundred pairs of shoes in the time previously required to finish a single pair by hand. All those humming wheels and clamorous drive-shafts needed oil; and got it, too, despite the fact that no such amounts as were now required had even existed before, so far at least as men had suspected a short while back; for within that same brief three-year span the production of petroleum, discovered in Pennsylvania less than two years before Sumter, increased from 84,000 to 128,000,000 gallons. The North was fighting the South with one hand and getting rich with the other behind its back, though which was left and which was right was hard to say. In any case, with such profits and progress involved, who could oppose the trend except a comparative handful of men and women, maimed or widowed or otherwise made squeamish, if not downright unpatriotic, by hard luck or oversubscription to Christian ethics?

A change was coming upon the land, and upon the land's inhabitants; nor was the change merely a dollars-and-cents affair, as likely to pass as to last. Legislation which had long hung fire because of peacetime caution and restraints imposed by jealous Southerners, now departed, came out of the congressional machine about as fast as proponents could feed bills into the hopper. Kansas had become a state and Colorado, Dakota, and Nevada were organized as Territories before the war was one year old, with the result that no part of the national area remained beyond the scope of the national law. Wherever a man went now the law went with him, at least in theory, and this also had its effect. Helping to make room on the eastern seaboard for the nearly 800,000 immigrants who arrived in the course of the conflict — especially from Ireland and Germany, where recruiting agents were hard at work, helping certain northern states to fill their quotas — no less than 300,000 people crossed the prairies, headed west for Pike's Peak or California, Oregon or the new Territories, some in search of gold as in the days of '49 and others to farm the cornlands made available under the Homestead Act of 1862, whereby a settler could stake off a claim to a quarter-section of public land and, upon payment of a nominal fee, call those 160 acres his own; 15,000 such homesteads were settled thus in the course of the war, mostly in Minnesota, amounting in all to some 2,500,-ooo acres. In this way the development of the Far West continued, despite the distraction southward, while back East the cities grew in wealth and population, despite the double drain in both directions. Nor were the cultural pursuits neglected, and these included more than attendance of the opera as a chance to show off the silks and satins whose rustling had disturbed the *World* reporter. Not only did university enrollments not decline much below what could be accounted for by the departure of southern students, but while the older schools were expanding their facilities with the aid of numerous wartime bequests, fifteen new institutions of higher learning were founded, including Cornell and Swarthmore, Vassar and the Massachusetts Institute of Technology. Campus life was not greatly different as a whole, once the undergraduates and professors grew accustomed to the fact that armies were locked in battle from time to time at various distances off beyond the southern horizon. Interrupted in 1861, for example, the Harvard-Yale boat races were resumed three years later in the midst of the bloodiest season of the war, and not a member of either crew volunteered for service in the army or the navy.

The draft, passed in early January as if in solution of the problem of Fredericksburg losses, hardly affected anyone not willing to be affected or else so miserably poor in these high times as not to be able to scrape up the $300 exemption fee as often as his name or number came up at the periodic drawings, in which case it might be said that he was about as well off in the army as out of it, except for the added discomfort of being drilled and possibly shot at. Large numbers of men from the upper classes, whether recently arrived at that level or established there of old, went to the expense of hiring substitutes (usually immigrants who were brought over by companies newly formed to supply the demand, trafficking thus in flesh to an extent unknown since the stoppage of the slave trade, and who were glad of the chance to earn a nest egg, which included the money they got from the men whose substitutes they were, plus the bounty paid by that particular state to volunteers — minus, of course, the fee that went to the company agent who had got them this opportunity in the first place) not only because it meant that the substitute-hirer was done with the problem of the draft for the duration, but also because it was considered more patriotic. All the same, the parody *We Are Coming, Father Abraham, Three Hundred Dollars More* was greeted with laughter wherever it was heard; for there was no stigma attached to the man who stayed out of combat, however he went about it short of actual dodging or desertion.

"In the vast new army of 300,000 which Mr Lincoln has ordered to be raised," one editor wrote, marveling at this gap disclosed in the new prosperity, "there will not be *one* man able to pay $300. Not one! Think of that!"

Washington itself was riding the crest of the wave thrown up by the boom, its ante-bellum population of 60,000 having nearly quadrupled under pressure from the throng of men and women rushing in to fill the partial vacuum created by the departure of the Southerners who formerly had set the social tone. Here the growing pains were the worst of all, according to Lincoln's young secretary John Hay, who wrote: "This miserable sprawling village imagines itself a city because it is wicked, as a boy thinks he is a man when he smokes and swears." In this instance Hay was offended because he and the President, riding back from the Soldiers Home after an interesting talk on philology — for which, he said, Lincoln had "a little indulged inclination" — encountered "a party of drunken gamblers and harlots returning in the twilight from [*erased*]." The fact was, the carousers might have been returning from almost any quarter of the city; for the provost marshal, while unable to give even a rough estimate of the number of houses of prostitution doing business here beside the Potomac, reported 163 gambling establishments in full swing, including one in which a congressman had lately achieved fame by breaking the bank in a single night and leaving with $100,000 bulging his pockets. It was a clutch-and-grab society now, with a clutch-and-grab way of doing business, whether its own or the government's, though it still affected a free and easy manner out of office hours. Nathaniel Hawthorne, in town for a look-round, found that the nation's pulse could be taken better at Willard's Hotel, especially in the bar, than at either the Capitol or the White House. "Everybody may be seen there," he declared. "You exchange nods with governors of sovereign states; you elbow illustrious men, and tread on the toes of generals; you hear statesmen and orators speaking in their familiar tones. You are mixed up with office-seekers, wire pullers, inventors, artists, poets, editors, army correspondents, attachés of foreign journals, long-winded talkers, clerks, diplomats, mail contractors, railway directors, until your own identity is lost among them. You adopt the universal habit of the place, and call for a mint julep, a whiskey skin, a gin cocktail, a brandy smash, or a glass of pure Old Rye; at any hour all these drinks are in request."

Not that there were no evidences of war aside from the uniforms, which were everywhere, and the personal experience of wounds or bereavement. There were indeed. War was the central fact around which life in Washington revolved, and what was more there were constant reminders that war was closely involved with death in its more unattractive forms. Although men with wrecked faces and empty sleeves or trouser-legs no longer drew the attention they once had drawn, other signs were not so easily ignored. Under huge transparencies boasting their skill at embalming, undertakers would buttonhole you on the street and urgently guarantee that, after receiving payment in advance, they would bring you back from the place where you caught the bullet "as lifelike as if you were asleep," the price being scaled in accordance with your preference for rosewood, pine, or something in between. One section of the city ticked like an oversized clock as the coffinmakers plied their hammers, stocking their shops against the day of battle, the news of which would empty their storerooms overnight and step up the tempo of their hammers in response to the law of supply and demand, as if time itself were hurrying to keep pace with the rush of events. In the small hours of the night, when this cacophonous ticking was stilled, men might toss sleepless on their beds, with dread like a presence in the room and sweat breaking out on the palms and foreheads even of those who knew the horror only by hearsay; but the outward show, by daylight or lamplight, was garish. Pennsylvania Avenue was crowded diurnally, to and beyond its margins of alternate dust and mud, and the plumes and sashes of the blue-clad officers, setting off the occasional gaudy splash of a Zouave, gave it the look of a carnival midway. This impression was heightened by the hawkers of roasted chestnuts and rock candy, and the women also did their part, contributing to the over-all effect the variegated dresses and tall hats that had come into fashion lately, the latter burdened about their incongruously narrow brims "with over-hanging balconies of flowers."

A future historian described them so, finding also in the course of her researches that the ladies "were wearing much red that season." Magenta and Solferino were two of the shades; "warm, bright, amusing names," she called them, derived from far-off battlefields "where alien men had died for some vague cause." Search as she might, however, she could find no shade of red identified with Chickasaw Bluffs, and it was her opinion that the flightiest trollop on the Avenue would have shrunk from wearing a scarlet dress that took its name from Fredericksburg.

★ ★ ★

Across the Atlantic, unfortunately for Confederate hopes of official acceptance into the family of nations, the Schleswig-Holstein problem, unrest in Poland, and the rivalry of Austria and Prussia gave the ministries of Europe a great deal more to think about than the intricacies of what was called "the American question." Aware that any disturbance of the precarious balance of power might be the signal for a general conflagration, they recalled Voltaire's comment that a torch lighted in 1756 in the forests of the new world had promptly wrapped the old world in flames. Russia, by coincidence having emancipated her serfs in the same year the western conflict began, was pro-Union from the start, while France remained in general sympathetic to the South; but neither could act without England, and England could not or would not intervene, being herself divided on the matter. The result, aside from occasional fumbling and inopportune attempts at mediation — mostly on the part of Napoleon III, who had needs and ambitions private and particular to himself — was that Europe, in effect, maintained a hands-off policy with regard to the blood now being shed beyond the ocean.

The double repulse, at Sharpsburg and Perryville, of the one Confederate attempt (so far) to conquer a peace by invasion of the North did not mean to Lord Palmerston and his ministers that the South would necessarily lose the war; far from it. But it did convince these gentlemen that the time was by no means ripe for intervention, as they had recently supposed, and was the basis for their mid-November rejection of a proposal by Napoleon that England, France, and Russia join in urging a North-South armistice, accompanied by a six-month lifting of the blockade. The result, if they had agreed — as they had been warned in no uncertain terms by Seward in private conversations with British representatives overseas — would have been an immediate diplomatic rupture, if not an outright declaration of war: in which connection the London *Times* remarked that "it would be cheaper to keep all Lancashire in turtle and venison than to plunge into a desperate war with the Northern States of America, even with all Europe at our back." No one knew better than Palmerston the calamity that might ensue, for he had been Minister at War from 1812 to 1815, during which period Yankee privateers had sunk about 2500 English ships, almost the entire marine. At that rate, with all those international tigers crouched for a leap in case the head tiger suffered some crippling injury, England not only could not afford to risk the loss of a sideline war; she could not even afford to win one.

Besides, desirable though it was that the flow of American cotton to British spindles be resumed — of 534,000 operatives, less than a quarter were working full time and more than half were out of work entirely; including their dependents, and those of other workers who lost their jobs in ancillary industries, approximately two million people were without means of self-support as a result of the cotton famine — the over-all economic picture was far from gloomy. In addition to the obvious example of the munitions manufacturers, who were profiting handsomely from the quarrel across the way, the linen and woolen industries had gained an appreciable part of what the cotton industry had lost, and the British merchant marine, whose principal rival for world trade was being chased from the high seas by rebel cruisers, was prospering as never before, augmented by more than seven hundred American vessels which transferred to the Union Jack in an attempt to avoid capture or destruction. And though there were those who favored intervention on the side of the South as a means of disposing permanently of a growing competitor, if by no other way then by assisting him to cut himself in two — the poet Matthew Arnold took this line of reason even further, speaking of the need "to prevent the English people from becoming, with the growth of democracy, *Americanized*" — the majority, even among the hard-pressed cotton operatives, did not. The Emancipation Proclamation saw to that, and Lincoln, having won what he first had feared was a gamble, was quick to press the advantage he had gained. When the workingmen of Manchester, the city hardest hit by the cotton famine, sent him an address approved at a meeting held on New Year's Eve, announcing their support of the North in its efforts to "strike off the fetters of the slave," Lincoln replied promptly in mid-January, pulling out all the stops in his conclusion: "I know and deeply deplore the sufferings which the workingmen at Manchester and in all Europe are called upon to endure in this crisis. . . . Under these circumstances, I cannot but regard your decisive utterance upon the question as an instance of sublime Christian heroism which has not been surpassed in any age or in any country. It is, indeed, an energetic and reinspiring assurance of the inherent power of truth and of the ultimate and universal triumph of justice, humanity, and freedom. I do not doubt that the sentiments you have expressed will be sustained by your great nation, and, on the other hand, I have no hesitation in assuring you that they will excite admiration, esteem, and the most reciprocal feelings of friendship among the American people. I hail this interchange of sentiment, therefore, as an augury that whatever else may happen, whatever misfortune may befall your country or my own, the peace and friendship which now exist between the two nations will be, as it shall be my desire to make them, perpetual."

Palmerston could have made little headway against the current of this rhetoric, even if he had so desired. In point of fact he did not try. Having resisted up to now the efforts of Confederate envoys to rush him off his feet — which they had done their best to do, knowing that it was their best chance to secure European intervention: aside, that is, from such happy accidents as the *Trent* affair, which unfortunately after a great deal of furor had come to nothing — he would have little trouble in keeping his balance from now on. Napoleon, across the Channel, was another matter. Practically without popular objection to restrain him, he continued to work in favor of those interests which, as he saw them, coincided with his own. Through the prominent Paris banking firm, Erlanger et Cie — whose president's son had lately married Matilda Slidell, daughter of the Confederate commissioner — a multi-million-dollar loan to the struggling young nation across the Atlantic was arranged, not in answer to any plea for financial assistance (it had not occurred to the Southerners, including John Slidell, despite the recent matrimonial connection, that asking would result in anything more than a Gallic shrug of regret) but purely as a gesture of good will. So the firm's representatives said as they broached the subject to Secretary of State Judah P. Benjamin in Richmond, having crossed the ocean for that purpose. However, being bankers — and what is more, French bankers — they added that they saw no harm in combining the good-will gesture with the chance to turn a profit, not only for the prospective buyers of the bonds that would be issued, but also for Erlanger et Cie. Then came the explanation, which showed that the transaction, though ostensibly a loan, was in fact little more than a scheme for large-scale speculation in cotton. Each 8% bond, which the firm would obtain at 70 for sale at approximately 100, was to be made exchangeable at face value, not later than six months after the end of the war, for New Orleans middling cotton at 12¢ a pound. There was the catch; for cotton was worth twice that much already, and was still rising. Benjamin, who was quite as sharp as the visiting bankers or their chief — Erlanger was a Jew and so was he; Erlanger was a French-man and so was he, after a manner of speaking, being Creole by adoption — saw through the scheme at once, as indeed anyone but a blind man would have done; but he also saw its propaganda value, which amounted at least to financial recognition of the Confederacy as a member of the family of nations. After certain adjustments on which he insisted, though not without exposing himself to charges of ingratitude for having looked a gift horse in the mouth — the original offer of $25,000,000 was scaled down to $15,000,000 and the interest rate to 7%, while the price at which the firm was to secure the bonds was raised to 77 — the deal was closed.

That was in late January, and at first all went well. Issued in early March at 90 — which gave Erlanger a spread of 13 points, plus a 5% commission on all sales — the bonds were enthusiastically oversubscribed and quickly arose to 95½. But that was the peak. Before the month was out they began to fall, and they kept falling, partly because of the influence of U.S. foreign agents who, basing their charge on the fact that Jefferson Davis himself had been a prewar advocate of the repudiation of Mississippi state bonds, predicted vociferously that the Southerners, if by some outside chance they won the war, would celebrate their victory by repudiating their debts. This had its effect. As the price declined, the alarmed Parisian bankers brought pressure on James M. Mason, the Confederate commissioner in London, to bull the market by using the receipts of the first installment for the purchase of his government's own bonds. Reluctantly, with the agreement of Slidell, he consented and, before he was through, put $6,000,000 into the attempt. But even this caused no more than a hesitation. When the artificial respiration stopped, the decline resumed, eventually pausing of its own accord at a depth of 36 before the bonds went off the board entirely. By that time, however, Erlanger et Cie was well in the clear, with a profit of about $2,500,000: which was more than the Confederacy obtained in all from a bond issue for which it had pledged six times that amount in capital and 7% in interest. The real losers, though, were the individual purchasers, mostly British admirers of the Confederacy, who left to their descendants the worthless scroll-worked souvenirs of a curious chapter in international finance.

As a fund-raising device the experiment was nearly a total failure — for the Confederates, that is, if not for the French bankers — but it did provide an additional incentive for Napoleon, who had taken considerable interest in the transaction, to hope for a southern victory. On February 3, after the bond issue had been authorized but before it had begun, the Emperor had his minister at Washington, Henri Mercier by name, present an offer of mediation, suggesting that representatives of the North and South meet on neutral soil for a discussion of terms of peace. The reaction to this was immediate and negative, at least on the part of the North. Seward replied that the Federal government had not the slightest notion of abandoning its efforts to save the Union, and certainly not by any such relinquishment of authority as the French proposal seemed to imply. This was seconded emphatically by Congress on March 3, when both houses issued a joint resolution denouncing mediation as "foreign interference" and reaffirming their "unalterable purpose" to suppress a rebellion which had for its object the tearing of the fabric of the finest government the world had ever known. In short, all that came of this latest effort by Napoleon to befriend the South was a further reduction of his possible influence. And Palmerston, watching the outcome from across the Channel, was more than ever convinced that no good could proceed from any such machinations. Dependent as his people were on U.S. grain to keep them from starvation, with Canada liable to seizure as a hostage to fortune and the British merchant marine exposed to being crippled if not destroyed, it seemed to him little short of madness to step into an argument which was after all a family affair. "Those who in quarrels interpose, Are apt to get a bloody nose," he intoned, falling back on doggerel to express his fears.

A. Dudley Mann, third in the trio of Confederate commissioners in Europe, had opened the year by complaining to his government that "the conduct of [England and France] toward us has been extremely shabby" and deploring their lack of spirit in the face of "the arrogant pretensions of the insolent Washington concern." Now in mid-March, as the third spring of the war began its green advance across the embattled South, all those thousands of miles away, Slidell in Paris was becoming increasingly impatient with Napoleon, whose avowed good will and favors never seemed to lead to anything valid or substantial, and Mason in London was lamenting bitterly that he had "no intercourse, unofficial or otherwise, with any member of the [British] Government." It was his private opinion, expressed frequently to Benjamin these days, that instead of continuing to put up with snubs and rebuffs, he would do better to come home.

★ ★ ★

If he had come home to Virginia now — as he did not; not yet — he would have done well to brace himself for the shock of finding it considerably altered from what it had been when he left it, a year and a half ago, to begin his aborted voyage on the *Trent*. That was perhaps the greatest paradox of all: that the Confederacy, in launching a revolution against change, should experience under pressure of the war which then ensued an even greater transformation, at any rate of the manner in which its citizens pursued their daily rounds, than did the nation it accused of trying to foist upon it an unwanted metamorphosis, not only of its cherished institutions, but also of its very way of life.

That way of life was going fast, and some there were, particularly among those who could remember a time when a society was judged in accordance with its sense of leisure, who affirmed that it was gone already. Nowhere was the change more obvious than in Richmond. Though the city was no longer even semi-beleaguered, as it had been in the time of McClellan, the outer fortifications had been lengthened and strengthened to such an extent that wags were saying, "They ought to be called fiftyfications now." Within that earthwork girdle, where home-guard clerks from government offices walked their appointed posts in their off hours, an ante-bellum population of less than 40,000 had mushroomed to an estimated 140,000, exclusive of the Union captives and Confederate wounded who jammed the old tobacco warehouses converted to prisons and hospitals. Yet the discomfort to which the older residents objected was not so much the result of the quantity of these late arrivers as it was of their quality, so to speak, or lack of it. "Virginians regarded the newcomers much as Romans would regard the First Families of the Visigoths," a diarist wrote. In truth, they had provocation far beyond the normal offense to their normal snobbery. Tenderloin districts such as Locust Alley, where painted women helped furloughed men forget the rigors of the field, and Johnny Worsham's gambling hell, directly across from the State House itself, had given the Old Dominion capital a reputation for being "the most corrupt and licentious city south of the Potomac." A Charlestonian administered the unkindest cut, however, by writing home that he had come to Richmond and found an entirely new city erected "after the model of Sodom and New York." According to another observer, an Englishman with a sharper ear for slang and a greater capacity for shock, the formerly decorous streets were crowded now with types quaintly designated as pug-uglies, dead rabbits, shoulder-hitters, "and a hundred other classes of villains for whom the hangman has sighed for many a long year."

Richmond saw and duly shuddered; but there was grimmer cause for shuddering than the wrench given its sense of propriety by the whores and gamblers who had taken up residence within its gates. As new-mounded graves spread over hillsides where none had been before, the population of the dead kept pace with the fast-growing population of the living. Though the Confederates in general lost fewer men in battle than their opponents, the fact that they had fewer to lose gave the casualty lists a greater impact, and it was remarked that "funerals were so many, even the funerals of friends, that none could be more than sparsely attended." Even more pitiful were the dying; Richmonders had come to know what one of them called "the peculiar chant of pain" that went up from a line of springless wagons hauling wounded over a rutted road or a cobbled street. You saw the maimed wherever you looked. For the city's hospitals — including the one on Chimborazo Heights, which had 150 buildings and was said to be the largest in the world — were so congested during periods immediately following battles that men who had lost an arm three days before had to be turned out, white-faced and trembling from shock and loss of blood, to make room for others in more urgent need of medical attention. It was up to the people to take them into their houses for warmth and food, and this they did, though only by the hardest, for both were dear and getting further beyond their means with every day that passed.

A gold dollar now was worth four in Confederate money, and even a despised $1 Yankee greenback brought $2.50 in a swap. Of coined money there was none, and in fact there had never been any, except for four half-dollars struck in the New Orleans mint before the fall of that city caused the government to abandon its plans for coinage. Congress's first solution to the small-change problem had been to make U.S. silver coins legal tender up to $10, along with English sovereigns, French napoleons, and Spanish and Mexican doubloons, but presently a flood of paper money was released upon the country, bills of smaller denominations being known as "shinplasters" because a soldier once had used a fistful to cover a tibia wound. Sometimes, as depreciation continued, that seemed about all they were good for. A War Department official, comparing current with prewar household expenses — flour, then $7, now $28 a barrel; bacon, then 20¢, now $1.25 a pound; firewood, then $3 or $4, now $15 a cord — found, as many others were finding, that he could not make ends meet; "My salary of $3000 will go about as far as $700 would in 1860." Wool and salt, drugs and medicines, nails and needles were scarcely to be had at any price, though the last were often salvaged from sewing kits found in the pockets of dead Federals. Dress muslin was $6 to $8 a yard, calico $1.75, coal $14 a cartload, and dinner in a first-class hotel ran as high as $25 a plate. In addition to genuine shortages, others were artificial, the result of transportation problems. Items that were plenteous in one part of the country might be as rare as hen's teeth in another. Peaches selling for 25¢ a dozen in Charleston, for instance, cost ten, fifteen, even twenty cents apiece in Richmond nowadays. For men perhaps the worst shock was the rising price of whiskey. As low as 25¢ a gallon in 1861, inferior stuff known variously as bust-head, red-eye, and tangle-foot now sold for as high as $35 a gallon. For women, on the other hand, the main source of incidental distress was clothes, the lack of new ones and the unsuitability of old ones through wear-and-tear and changing styles, although the latter were of necessity kept to a minimum. "Do you realize the fact that we shall soon be without a stitch of clothes?" a young woman wrote to a friend in early January. "There is not a bonnet for sale in Richmond. Some of the girls smuggle them, which I for one consider in the worst possible taste." Apparently ashamed to have let her mind turn in this direction at this time, she hastened to apologize for her flightiness, only to fall into fresh despair. "It seems rather volatile to discuss such things while our dear country is in such peril. Heaven knows I would costume myself in coffee-bags if that would help, but having no coffee, where would I get the bags?"

One provident source of amusement and delivery from care was the theater, which was popular as never before, though it did not escape the censure of the more respectable. "The thing took well, and money flowed into the treasury," a manager afterwards recalled, "but often had I cause to upbraid myself for having fallen so low in my own estimation, for I had always considered myself a gentleman, and I found that in taking control of this theatre and its vagabond company I had forfeited my claim to a respectable stand in the ranks of Society." A prominent Baptist preacher's complaint from his pulpit that "twenty *gentlemen* for the chorus and the ballet" might be more useful to their country in the army, where they could do more than "mimic fighting on the stage," met with the approval of his congregation; but the S.R.O. signs continued to go up nightly beside the ticket windows. When the Richmond Theatre burned soon after New Year's, an entirely new building was promptly raised on the old foundations. Opening night was greeted with an "Inaugural Poem" by Henry Timrod, concluding:

> Bid Liberty rejoice! Aye, though its day
> Be far or near, these clouds shall yet be red
> With the large promise of the coming ray.
> Meanwhile, with that calm courage which can smile
> Amid the terrors of the wildest fray
> Let us among the charms of Art awhile
>   Fleet the deep gloom away;
> Nor yet forget that on each hand and head
> Rest the dear rights for which we fight and pray.

If the production itself — Shakespeare's *As You Like It*; "but not as *we* like it," one critic unkindly remarked — left much to be desired in the way of professional excellence, Richmonders were glad to have found release "among the charms," and even the disgruntled reviewer was pleased to note "that the audience evinced a disposition at once to stop all rowdyism." For example, when the callboy came out from behind the curtain to fasten down the carpet, certain ill-bred persons began to yell, "Soup! Soup!" but were promptly shushed by those around them.

An even better show, according to some, was presented at the Capitol whenever Congress was in session, though unfortunately — or fortunately, depending on the point of view — these theatricals were in general unavailable to the public, being conducted behind closed doors. It was not so much what occurred in the regular course of business that was lively or amusing (for, as was usual with such bodies, there was a good deal more discussion of what to do than there was of doing. One member interrupted a long debate as to a proper time for adjournment by remarking, "If the House would adjourn and not meet any more, it would benefit the country." Others outside the legislative assembly agreed, including a Deep South editor who, learning that Congress had spent the past year trying without success to agree on a device for the national seal, suggested "A terrapin *passant*," with the motto "Never in haste"); it was what happened beside the point, so to speak, that provided the excitement. In early February the Alabama fire-eater William L. Yancey, opposing the creation of a Confederate Supreme Court — which, incidentally, never came into being because of States Rights obstructionists — so infuriated Benjamin H. Hill of Georgia, a moderate, that he threw a cutglass inkstand at the speaker and cut his cheek to the bone. As Yancey, spattered with blood and ink, started for him across the intervening desks, Hill followed up with a second shot, this time a heavy tumbler, which missed, and the sergeant-at-arms had to place both men in restraint and remove them from the chamber. Less fortunate was the chief clerk, shot to death on Capitol Square two months later by the journal clerk, who was angry at having been accused of slipshod work by his superior. The killer was sentenced to eighteen years in the penitentiary, but nothing at all was done to a woman who appeared one day on the floor of the House and proceeded to cowhide a Missouri congressman. She too was a government clerk, but it developed that her wrath had been aroused by information that Congress, in connection with enforcement of the Conscription Act, was about to require all clerks to divulge their ages. Deciding that the woman was demented, the House voted its confidence in the unlucky Missourian, who apparently had been selected at random. No such vote was ever given Jefferson Davis's old Mississippi stump opponent Henry S. Foote, who worked hard to deserve the reputation of being the stormiest man in Congress. He fought with his fists, in and out of the chamber, and was always ready to fall back on dueling pistols, with which he had had considerable experience. An altercation with an expatriate Irishman and a Tennessee colleague, who struck Foote over the head with an umbrella and then dodged nimbly to keep from being shot, caused all three to be brought into the Mayor's Court and placed under a peace bond. Another three-sided argument occurred in the course of a congressional hearing in which a Commissary Department witness was so badgered by Foote that the two came to blows. Foote tore off his adversary's shirt bosom, and when Commissary General Lucius B. Northrop came to the witness's assistance Foote knocked him into a corner. According to some who despised Colonel Northrop, asserting that he was attempting to convert the southern armies to vegetarianism, this was Foote's one real contribution to the Confederate war effort. But he was by no means through providing excitement. In the course of a speech by E. S. Dargan of Alabama, Foote broke in to call him a "damned rascal," which so infuriated the elderly congressman that he went for the Mississippian with a knife. Foote avoided the lunge, and then — Dargan by now had been disarmed and lay pinned to the floor by colleagues — stepped back within range and, striking an attitude not unworthy of Edwin Booth, whose work he much admired, hissed at the prostrate Alabamian: "I defy the steel of the assassin!"

All this was part and parcel of the revolution-in-progress, and if much of it was scandalous and distasteful, most Confederates could take that too in stride, along with spiraling prices and increasing scarcities. A native inclination toward light-heartedness served them well in times of strain. What the newcomers to Richmond lacked in tone they more than made up for in gaiety. Practically nothing was exempt from being laughed at nowadays, not even the sacred escutcheon of Virginia, whose motto *Sic semper tyrannis,* engraved below the figure of Liberty treading down Britannia, was freely rendered as "Take your foot off my neck!" Officers and men on leave and furlough from the Rappahannock line opened Volume I, "Fantine," of Victor Hugo's *Les Misérables,* which had come out in France the year before, and professed surprise at finding that it was not about themselves, "Lee's Miserables, Faintin'." One whose spirits never seemed to falter was Judah Benjamin, who remarked in this connection that it was "wrong and useless to disturb oneself and thus weaken one's energy to bear what was foreordained." This hedonistic fatalist went his way, invariably smiling, whether in attendance at government councils or at Johnny Worsham's green baize tables across the way. He once assured Varina Davis that with a glass of McHenry sherry, of which she had a small supply, and beaten biscuits made of flour from Crenshaw Mills, spread with a paste made of English walnuts from a tree on the White House grounds, "a man's patriotism became rampant." She found him amusing, an ornament to her receptions, and an excellent antidote to the FFV's who currently were condemning her as "disloyal to the South" because of a rumor that she had employed a white nurse for her baby.

The easy laughter was infectious, though some could hear it for what it was, part of an outward pose assumed at times to hide or hold back tears. What was happening behind the mask — not only Benjamin's, but the public's at large — no one could say for certain. Presently, however, there were signs that the mask was beginning to crack, or at any rate slip, and thus disclose what it had been designed to cover. When the President proclaimed March 5 another "day of fasting and prayer," this too was not exempt from unregenerate laughter; "Fasting in the midst of famine!" some remarked sardonically. Then, just short of one month later, on Holy Thursday — Easter came on April 5, a week before the second anniversary of Sumter — a demonstration staged on the streets of the capital itself gave the authorities cause to question whether all was as well concerning public morale here in the East as they had supposed, especially among those citizens who could not enjoy the relaxations afforded by such places as Johnny Worsham's, where a lavish buffet was maintained for the refreshment of patrons at all hours. The Holy Thursday demonstration, at least at the start, was concerned with more basic matters: being known, then and thereafter, as the Bread Riot.

Apparently it began at the Oregon Hill Baptist church, where Mary Jackson, a huckster with "straight, strong features and a vixenish eye," harangued a group of women who had gathered to protest the rising cost of food. Adjourning to Capitol Square they came under the leadership of a butcher's Amazonian assistant, Minerva Meredith by name. Six feet tall and further distinguished by a long white feather that stood up from her hat and quivered angrily as she tossed her head, she proposed that they move on the shops to demand goods at government prices and to take them by force if this was refused. As she spoke she took from under her apron, by way of emphasis, a Navy revolver and a Bowie knife. Brandishing these she set out for the business section at the head of a mob which quickly swelled to about three hundred persons, including the children some of the women had in tow. "Bread! Bread!" they shouted as they marched. Governor John Letcher, who had watched from his office as the demonstration got under way, had the mayor read the Riot Act to them, but they hooted and surged on past him, smashing plate-glass windows in their anger and haste to get at the goods in the shops on Main and Cary. It was obvious that they were after more than food, for they emerged with armloads of shoes and clothes, utensils and even jewelry, which some began to pile in to handcarts they had thought to bring along. Governor Letcher sent for a company of militia and threatened to fire on the looters when it arrived, but the women sneered at him, as they had done at the mayor, and went on with their vandalism. Just then, however, those on the outer fringes of the mob saw a tall thin man dressed in gray homespun climb onto a loaded dray and begin to address them sternly. They could not hear what he was saying, but they saw him do a strange thing. He took money from his pockets and tossed it in their direction. Whereupon they fell silent and his voice came through: "You say you are hungry and have no money. Here is all I have. It is not much, but take it." His pockets empty of all but his watch, he took that out too, but instead of throwing it at them, as he had done the money, he stood with it open in his hand, glancing sidelong at the militia company which had just arrived. "We do not desire to injure anyone," he said in a voice that rang clear above the murmur of the crowd, "but this lawlessness must stop. I will give you five minutes to disperse. Otherwise you will be fired on."

Recognizing the President — and knowing, moreover, that he was not given to issuing idle threats — the mob began to disperse, first slowly, then rapidly as the deadline approached. By the time the five minutes were up, there was no one left for the soldiers to fire at. Davis put his watch back in his pocket, climbed down off the dray, and returned to his office. Outwardly calm, inwardly he was so concerned that he did something he had never done before. He made a special appeal to the Richmond press, requesting that it "avoid all reference directly or indirectly to the affair," and ordered the telegraph company to "permit nothing relative to the unfortunate disturbance . . . to be sent over the telegraph lines in any direction for any purpose." He feared the reaction abroad, as well as in other parts of the South, if it became known that the streets of the Confederate capital had been the scene of a riot that had as its cause, if only by pretense, a shortage of food. Two days later, however, the *Enquirer* broke the story by way of refuting defeatist rumors that were beginning to be spread. Identifying the rioters as "a handful of prostitutes, professional thieves, Irish and Yankee hags, gallows birds from all lands but our own," the paper denounced them for having broken into "half a dozen shoe stores, hat stores and tobacco houses and robbed them of everything but bread, which was just the thing they wanted least."

This one attempt at suggesting censorship was as useless as it was ineffective: Richmond was by no means the only place where such disturbances occurred in the course of Holy Week. Simultaneously in Atlanta a group of about fifteen well-dressed women entered a store on Whitehall Street and asked the price of bacon. $1.10 a pound, they were told: whereupon their man-tall leader, a shoemaker's wife "on whose countenance rested care and determination," produced a revolver with which she covered the grocer while her companions snatched what they wanted from the shelves, paying their own price or nothing. From there they proceeded to other shops along the street, repeating the performance until their market baskets were full, and then went home. A similar raid was staged at about the same time in Mobile, as well as in other towns and cities throughout the South. Presently countrywomen took their cue from their urban sisters. North Carolina experienced practically an epidemic of demonstrations by irate housewives. Near Lafayette, Alabama, a dozen such — armed, according to one correspondent, with "guns, pistols, knives, and tongues" — attacked a rural mill and seized a supply of flour, while a dozen more came down out of the hills around Abingdon, Virginia, and cowered merchants into handing over cotton yarn and cloth; wagon trains were stopped at gunpoint and robbed of corn near Thomasville and Marietta, Georgia. All these were but a few among the many, and there were those who saw in this ubiquitous manifestation of discontent the first crack in the newly constructed edifice of government. If the Confederacy could not be defeated from without, then it might be abolished from within; for the protests were not so much against shortages, which were by no means chronic at this stage, as they were against the inefficiency which resulted in spiraling prices. These observers saw the demonstrations, in fact — despite the recent successes of southern arms, both East and West — as symptoms of war weariness, the one national ailment which could lead to nothing but defeat. The new government could survive, and indeed had survived already, an assortment of calamities; but that did not and could not include the loss of the will to fight, either by the soldiers in its armies or by the people on its home front.

No one saw the danger more clearly than the man whose principal task — aside, that is, from his duties as Commander in Chief, which now as always he placed first — was to do all he could to avert it. Recently he had undertaken a 2500-mile year-end journey to investigate and shore up crumbling morale, with such apparent success that on his return he could report to Congress, convening in Richmond for its third session on January 12, that the state of the nation, in its civil as well as in its military aspect, "affords ample cause for congratulation and demands the most fervent expression of our thankfulness to the Almighty Father, who has blessed our cause. We are justified in asserting, with a pride surely not unbecoming, that these Confederate States have added another to the lessons taught by history for the instruction of man; that they have afforded another example of the impossibility of subjugating a people determined to be free, and have demonstrated that no superiority of numbers or available resources can overcome the resistance offered by such valor in combat, such constancy under suffering, and such cheerful endurance of privation as have been conspicuously displayed by this people in the defense of their rights and liberties." Moreover, he added, flushed by the confidence his words had generated: "By resolute perseverance in the path we have hitherto pursued, by vigorous efforts in the development of all our resources for defense, and by the continued exhibition of the same unfaltering courage in our soldiers and able conduct in their leaders as have distinguished the past, we have every reason to expect that this will be the closing year of the war."

Since then, despite continued successful resistance by the armies in the field, symptoms of unrest among civilians had culminated in the rash of so-called Bread Riots, the largest of which had occurred in the capital itself and had been broken up only by the personal intervention of the Chief Executive. Two days later — on April 10, just short of three months since his confident prediction of an early end to the conflict — Davis issued, in response to a congressional resolution passed the week before, a proclamation "To the People of the Confederate States." Observing that "a strong impression prevails throughout the country that the war . . . may terminate during the present year," Congress urged the people not to be taken in by such false hopes, but rather to "look to prolonged war as the only condition proffered by the enemy short of subjugation." The presidential proclamation, issued broadcast across the land, afforded the people the unusual opportunity of seeing their President eat his words, not only by revoking his previous prediction, but by substituting another which clearly implied that what lay ahead was a longer and harder war than ever.

Though "fully concurring in the views thus expressed by Congress," he began with the same boldness of assertion as before. "We have reached the close of the second year of the war, and may point with just pride to the history of our young Confederacy. Alone, unaided, we have met and overthrown the most formidable combination of naval and military armaments that the lust of conquest ever gathered together for the subjugation of a free people. . . . The contrast between our past and present condition is well calculated to inspire full confidence in the triumph of our arms. At no previous period of the war have our forces been so numerous, so well organized, and so thoroughly disciplined, armed, and equipped as at present." Then he passed to darker matters. "We must not forget, however, that the war is not yet ended, and that we are still confronted by powerful armies and threatened by numerous fleets. . . . Your country, therefore, appeals to you to lay aside all thoughts of gain, and to devote yourselves to securing your liberties, without which those gains would be valueless. . . . Let fields be devoted exclusively to the production of corn, oats, beans, peas, potatoes, and other food for man and beast; let corn be sown broadcast for fodder in immediate proximity to railroads, rivers, and canals, and let all your efforts be directed to the prompt supply of these articles in the districts where our armies are operating. . . . Entertaining no fear that you will either misconstrue the motives of this address or fail to respond to the call of patriotism, I have placed the facts fully and frankly before you. Let us all unite in the performance of our duty, each in his own sphere, and with concerted, persistent, and well-directed effort . . . we shall maintain the sovereignty and independence of these Confederate

States, and transmit to our posterity the heritage bequeathed to us by our fathers."

As usual, the people responded well for the most part to a clear statement of necessity. But there were those who reacted otherwise. The Georgia fire-eater Robert Toombs, for example, who had left the cabinet to join the army on the day of First Manassas and then had left the army to re-enter politics after his one big day at Sharpsburg, petulantly announced that he was increasing his plantation's cotton acreage. Nor were opposition editors inclined to neglect the opportunity to launch the verbal barbs they had been sharpening through months of increasing dissatisfaction. "Mr Davis is troubled by blindness," the Mobile *Tribune* told its subscribers, "is very dyspeptic and splenetic, and as prejudiced and stubborn as a man can well be, and not be well."

Thus did the Confederacy enter upon its third year of war.

✶ 4 ✶

Disenchantment was mainly limited to civilians, but it was by no means limited to the sphere of civilian activities. Illogically or not — that is, despite the lopsided triumphs at Fredericksburg and Chickasaw Bluffs, the flood-reversing coups at Holly Springs and Galveston, the brilliant cavalry forays into Kentucky and West Tennessee, and the absence of anything resembling a clear-cut defeat east of the Mississippi — there was a growing impression that victory, on field after field, brought little more than temporary joy, which soon gave way to sobering realizations. The public's reaction was not unlike that of a boxer who delivers his best punch, square on the button, then sees his opponent merely blink and shake his head and bore back in. People began to suspect that if the North could survive Fredericksburg and the Mud March, Chickasaw Bluffs and the loss of the *Cairo* to a demijohn of powder, it might well be able to survive almost anything the South seemed able to inflict. A whole season of victories apparently had done nothing to bring peace and independence so much as one day closer. Howell Cobb of Georgia could say, not altogether in jest, "Only two things stand in the way of an amicable settlement of the whole difficulty: the Landing of the Pilgrims and Original Sin," while the Richmond *Examiner* could simultaneously call attention to the chilling fact that, aside from Sumter, "[Lincoln's] pledge once deemed foolish by the South, that he would 'hold, occupy, and possess' all the forts belonging to the United States Government, has been redeemed almost to the letter."

Fredericksburg had been hailed at the outset as the turning point of the war. Presently, however, as Lee and his army failed to find a way to follow it up, the triumph paled to something of a disappointment. In time, paradoxically, the more perceptive began to see that it had indeed been a turning point, though in a sense quite different from the one origi-nally implied; for no battle East or West, whether a victory or a defeat, showed more plainly the essential toughness of the blue-clad fighting man than this in which, judging by a comparison of the casualties in-flicted and received, he suffered the worst of his several large-scale drub-bings. But this was an insight that came gradually and only to those who were not only able but also willing to perceive it. Murfreesboro was more immediately disappointing in respect to Confederate expectations, and no such insight was required. Here the contrast between claims and accomplishments was as stark as it was sudden. First it was seen to be a much less brilliant victory than the southern commander had announced before his guns had hushed their growling. Then it was seen to be scarcely a victory at all. It was seen, in fact, to have several of the aspects of a typical defeat: not the least of which was the undeniable validity of the Federal claim to control of the field when the smoke had cleared. "So far the news has come in what may be called the classical style of the Southwest," the *Examiner* observed caustically near the end of the first week in January, having belatedly learned of Bragg's withdrawal. "When the Southern army fights a battle, we first hear that it has gained one of the most stupendous victories on record; that regiments from Mis-sissippi, Texas, Louisiana, Arkansas, &c. have exhibited an irresistible and superhuman valor unknown in history this side of Sparta and Rome. As for their generals, they usually get all their clothes shot off, and replace them with a suit of glory. The enemy, of course, is simply annihilated. Next day more dispatches come, still very good, but not quite as good as the first. The telegrams of the third day are invariably such as make a mist, a muddle, and a fog of the whole affair."

No mist, muddle, or fog could hide Bragg from the ire aroused when the public learned the premature and insubstantial basis for his wire announcing that God had granted him and them a Happy New Year. What saved him from the immediate consequences of their anger was his adversary Rosecrans, who, despite his recent promise to "press [the reb-els] to the wall," not only refused to follow up the victory he claimed, but resisted with all his strength — as he had done through the months preceding the march out of Nashville, pleading the need to lay in "a cou-ple of millions of rations"— the efforts by his superiors to prod him into motion. Crittenden, who had commanded the unassailed left wing throughout the first day's fight and then repulsed his fellow-Kentuckian Breckinridge on the second, stated the case as it appeared to many in the Union ranks: "The battle was fought for the possession of Middle Ten-nessee. We went down to drive the Confederates out of Murfreesboro, and we drove them out. They went off a few miles and camped again. And we, although we were the victors, virtually went into hospital for six months before we could march after them again." He added, by way of developing a theory: "As in most of our battles, very meager fruits resulted to either side from such partial victories as were for the most part won. Yet it was a triumph. It showed that in the long run the big purse and the big battalions — both on our side — must win; and it proved that there were no better soldiers than ours."

Rosecrans disagreed with much of this critique, particularly the remark that the army had gone "into hospital," but he not only subscribed to Crittenden's opinion about the big purse and the big battalions, he also took it a step further by insisting that the last ounce be wrung from the advantage. What good were riches, he seemed to be asking, unless they were at hand? When he swung the purse he wanted it to be heavy. "I believe the most fatal errors of this war have begun in an impatient desire of success, that would not take time to get ready," he protested in mid-February, by way of reply to Halleck's continuous urging. So the general-in-chief changed his tack. "There is a vacant major generalcy in the Regular Army," he wired on March 1, "and I am authorized to say that it will be given to the general in the field who first wins an important and decisive victory." The implication was that Rosecrans had better get to Chattanooga before Grant got to Vicksburg; but Old Rosy did not react at all in the way that had been intended. "As an officer and a citizen, I feel degraded to see such auctioneering of honor," he replied. "Have we a general who would fight for his own personal benefit, when he would not for honor and the country? He would come by his commission basely in that case, and deserve to be despised by men of honor." Halleck in turn resented this show of righteous indignation, and said so, which only served to increase their differences. Rosecrans was convinced by now that all of Washington was against him: especially Stanton, who had promised, in the first flush of excitement over the news of a hard-fought triumph, to withhold "nothing . . . within my power to grant," but who lately had bridled at filling the balky commander's many requisitions and requests, including one that his latest promotion be predated so as to give him rank over Grant and all the other western generals. Finally he protested to the President himself, who gave him little satisfaction beyond assurances of admiration. "I know not a single enemy of yours here," Lincoln wrote, and added: "Truth to speak, I do not appreciate this matter of rank on paper as you officers do. The world will not forget that you fought the battle of Stones River, and it will never care a fig whether you rank Gen. Grant on paper, or he so ranks you."

By then it was mid-March. The bloody contest, ten weeks back, had done much to increase Old Rosy's appreciation of the dangers involved in challenging the rebs on their own ground. The rest of March went by, and all of April. Still he would not budge. May followed. Still he would not move until he was good and ready, down to the final nail in the final horseshoe. As June came on, approaching the end of the six-month term which Crittenden said the army spent "in hospital," Rosecrans made a virtue of his immobility, claiming that by refraining from driving Bragg southward he was preventing him from co-operating with Pemberton against Grant. Besides, he added, he had held a council of war at which it had been decided to "observe a great military maxim, not to risk two great and decisive battles at the same time." He thought it best to wait till Vicksburg fell or Grant abandoned the effort to take it, whereupon he himself would advance against Bragg and Chattanooga. Halleck by now was fairly frantic. A master of maxims, he fired one back at Rosecrans: "Councils of war never fight." But this had no more effect than the earlier proddings had done; Old Rosy stayed exactly where he was. If Bragg would only leave him alone, he would gladly return the favor, at any rate until he was good and ready to advance. Just when that would be he would not say.

He might have taken some measure of consolation, amid the prod-dings, from the fact that his opponent's troubles quite overmatched his own. The difference was that Rosecrans' woes came mainly from above, whereas Bragg's came mainly from below. As a result, the latter were not only more widely spread, they were also frequently sharper barbed. His harsh discipline in camp, unbalanced by conspicuous victories in the field, and his reputation as a commander who invariably retreated after battle, whether his troops won or lost, had resulted in bitter censure from all sides, civil as well as military, in and out of the newspapers. Rid-ing one day near his Tullahoma headquarters, soon after his withdrawal behind Duck River, he encountered a man wearing butternut garb and requested information about the roads. When this had been given, the general thanked him and, unable to tell from his clothes whether the man was a soldier or a civilian — the kindest thing that could be said about dress in the Army of Tennessee was that it was informal — asked if he belonged to Bragg's army. "Bragg's army?" the countryman replied, scowling at the grim-faced man on horseback. "Bragg's got no army. He shot half of them himself, up in Kentucky, and the other half got killed at Murfreesboro."

Bragg laughed and rode on, curbing for once his terrible temper. But the experience rankled under pressure of newspaper criticisms leveled at him while his troops were getting settled along their new defensive line: particularly the charge, widely printed and reprinted, that he had pulled out of Murfreesboro against the advice of his lieutenants. This was patently untrue, as he could prove by the note from Cheatham and With-ers, urging immediate retreat, which he had rejected, at least at first, despite Polk's indorsement of their plea. Accordingly, he decided to make an issue of it, addressing on January 11 a letter to his chief subordi-nates. "It becomes necessary for me to save my fair name," he wrote, and "stop the deluge of abuse which [threatens to] destroy my usefulness and demoralize this army." He asked them to acquit him of the fabrication that he had gone against their wishes in ordering a retreat, which in point of fact "was resisted by me for some time after [it was] advised by my corps and division commanders. . . . Unanimous as you were in council in verbally advising a retrograde movement," he added, "I cannot doubt that you will cheerfully attest the same in writing." So far, he was on safe ground. Unwilling to let it go at that, however, he closed with something of a flourish: "I desire that you will consult your subordinate commanders and be candid with me. . . . I shall retire without a regret if I find I have lost the good opinion of my generals, upon whom I have ever relied as upon a foundation of rock."

This last was what opened the floodgates. Though none could fail to exonerate him from the specific charge that he had originated the notion of retreat, his closing statement that he would retire if he found that he had lost their good opinion presented the generals with a once-in-a-lifetime opportunity, which they did not neglect. Hardee, after pointing out that neither he nor his division commanders had proposed a withdrawal, though they had made no objection once the decision had been announced, replied that he had consulted his subordinates, as requested, and found them "unanimous in the opinion that a change in the command of this army is necessary. In this opinion I concur." He had "the highest regard for the purity of your motives, your energy, and your personal character," he told Bragg, but he was "convinced, as you must feel, that the peril of the country is superior to all personal considerations." His lieutenants replied in a similar vein. "I have consulted with my brigade commanders," Cleburne wrote, "and they unite with me in personal regard for yourself . . . but at the same time they see, with regret, and it has also met my observation, that you do not possess the confidence of the army in other respects in that degree necessary to secure success." Breckinridge was as forthright, and what was more — the officers and men of his division having found Bragg's report of the recent battle so disparaging to themselves and their dead comrades that they had urged their chief to challenge him to a duel — took perhaps the greatest satisfaction of all in seizing the present chance to sit in judgment. "Acting with the candor which you invoke," the former Vice President replied, "[my brigade commanders] request me to say that, in their opinion, the conduct of the military operations in front of Murfreesboro made it necessary for our army to retire." Lest the irony of this be lost, he passed at once to a summation. "They also request me to say that while they entertain the highest respect for your patriotism, it is their opinion that you do not possess the confidence of the army to an extent which will enable you to be useful as its commander. In this opinion I feel bound to state that I concur."

Polk was away on leave at the time, visiting his refugee family in North Carolina, and in his absence Cheatham and Withers merely replied with an acknowledgment that they had made the original suggestion to withdraw. When the bishop returned at the end of the month he found the army a-buzz with talk of this latest development. Since there was some difference of opinion as to whether Bragg had really intended to call down all this thunder on his head, Polk wrote to ask whether his chief had meant for him to answer both questions — 1) as to who was responsible for bringing up the subject of retreat, and 2) as to whether the army commander had lost the confidence of his subordinates — or only the first. Bragg by now had had quite enough "candid" responses to the second question, and stated that he had only wanted to get an opinion on the inception of the retreat; "The paragraph relating to my supercedure was only an expression of the feeling with which I should receive your replies." In that case, Polk responded, he believed the original battlefield note would suffice as a documentary answer. He was content to let the matter drop. But learning presently that Hardee and his officers felt that he had dodged the issue, thereby leaving them in the position of insubordinate malcontents, he decided to write directly to his friend the President, attaching the rather voluminous correspondence he had had with Bragg. "I feel it my duty to say to you," he told Davis, "that had I and my division commanders been asked to answer, our replies would have coincided with those of the officers of the other corps. . . . My opinion is he had better be transferred." The best place for him, Polk believed, was Richmond, where "his capacity for organization and discipline, which has not been equaled among us, could be used by you at headquarters with infinite advantage to the whole army. I think, too," he added, "that the best thing to be done in supplying his place would be to give his command to General Joseph E. Johnston. He will cure all discontent and inspire the army with new life and confidence. He is here on the spot, and I am sure will be content to take it."

Davis was quite aware that Johnston was at Tullahoma, having ordered him there two weeks ago, when Bragg's circular, together with the replies of Hardee and his lieutenants, first landed on the presidential desk. "Why General Bragg should have selected that tribunal, and have invited its judgment upon him, is to me unexplained; it manifests, however, a condition of things which seems to me to require your presence." So Davis wrote Johnston, who was engaged at the time in an inspection of the Mobile defenses, instructing him to proceed at once to Bragg's headquarters and determine "whether he had so far lost the confidence of the army as to impair his usefulness in his present position. . . . You will, I trust, be able, by conversation with General Bragg and others of his command, to decide what the best interests of the service require, and to give me the advice which I need at this juncture. As that army is part of your command," the President added, knowing the Virginian's meticulosity in such matters, "no order will be necessary to give you authority there, as, whether present or absent, you have a right to direct its operations and do whatever else belongs to the general commanding."

However, Johnston's squeamishness went further than Davis reckoned. He found much that was improper in the conduct of an inquiry which might result in the displacement of the officer under investigation by the one who was doing the investigating. Besides, he had a high regard for the grim-faced North Carolinian's abilities. "Bragg has done wonders, I think," he wrote privately. "No body of troops has done more in proportion to numbers in the same time." Accordingly on February 3, ten days after his arrival, although "incessant rain has permitted me to see but a fourth of the troops as yet," he reported them "in high spirits, and as ready as ever for fight." He found his confidence in Bragg not only unshaken but "confirmed by his recent operations, which, in my opinion, evince great vigor and skill." In short: "It would be very unfortunate to remove him at this juncture, when he has just earned, if not won, the gratitude of the country." He would report more fully, Johnston said, when he had completed his inspection. Meanwhile, "I respectfully suggest that, should it appear to you necessary to remove General Bragg, no one in this army or engaged in this investigation ought to be his successor." Nine days later, his final report buttressed his first impression. He had found the men "well clothed, healthy, and in good spirits," which gave "positive evidence of General Bragg's capacity to command. . . . To me it seems that the operations of this army in Middle Tennessee have been conducted admirably. I can find no record of more effective fighting in modern battles than that of this army in December, evincing great skill in the commander and courage in the troops." He had heard, he said in closing, that Polk and Hardee had advised their present chief's removal and his own appointment to the command; but "I am sure that you will agree with me that the part I have borne in this investigation would render it inconsistent with my personal honor to occupy that position. . . . General Bragg should not be removed."

With that, he left for Chattanooga. Davis replied that he was "truly gratified at the language of commendation which you employ in relation to General Bragg," but he considered it "scarcely possible," in the light of Polk's and Hardee's formal disapproval, "for [Bragg] to possess the requisite confidence of the troops." He still thought Johnston should take over, and he could not see that this involved any breach of military etiquette. Johnston was already in command, by rank and title, whenever he was on the scene; "The removal of General Bragg would only affect you so far as it deprived you of his services." However, Davis assured him, "You shall not be urged by me to any course which would wound your sensibility of views of professional propriety." In early March, Johnston having made no reply to this, the Secretary of War added his pleas to those of the Commander in Chief. It was his opinion that Bragg should be "recalled altogether," but if Johnston's conscience would not permit this, then he suggested that he keep him at hand, "as an organizer and disciplinarian," in the post of assistant commander. "Let me urge you, my dear general," Seddon wrote, "to think well, in view of all the great interests to our beloved South . . . and, if possible, make the sacrifice of your honorable delicacy to the importance of the occasion and the greatness of our cause." When Johnston still did not reply — he was back in Mobile by now, though Davis and Seddon supposed he was still in Chattanooga — the matter was taken out of his hands by a wire from Richmond, which reached him on March 12: "Order General Bragg to report to the War Department here for conference. Assume yourself direct charge of the army in Middle Tennessee."

Perhaps Davis and Seddon had decided that what Johnston had been wanting all along, and even hinting at, was for them to *order* him to the post in spite of his objections; that way, the conditions of honor would be met, since he would have done all he could to avoid the outcome. If so, they were wrong. Johnston really did not want the command. The fact was, he did not want the larger one he had already — his duties, he said disparagingly, were those of an "inspector general"— despite the President's and the Secretary's insistence that it was the most important post in the Confederacy. If that was the case, Lee should have it as a reward for his recent accomplishments; then "with great propriety," Johnston wrote in confidence to a friend, he himself could return to his native Virginia and resume command of the army he had lost at Seven Pines, "where the Yankee bullets found me." Now it looked as if that hope was going up in smoke. He was ordered to Middle Tennessee, with no alternative to compliance except submission of his resignation.

So it seemed. When he returned to Tullahoma on March 19, however, he found a way — still on grounds of sparing offense to what Seddon had called his "honorable delicacy"— at least to delay what he had sought all this time to avoid. Bragg's wife was down with typhoid, despaired of by the doctors, and her husband had given over his official duties in order to be at her bedside round the clock. It was therefore no more than normal courtesy, under the circumstances, for Johnston to carry out that portion of the orders which required him to take command of the army; but as for increasing the distracted general's present woes by instructing him to report at once to Richmond, that was manifestly impossible, Johnston wired the authorities, "on account of Mrs Bragg's critical condition." Besides, he added, the country was "becoming practicable" now that the rains had slacked and the roads were drying; "Should the enemy advance, General Bragg will be indispensable here." Apparently he intended to take the Secretary's earlier suggestion that he keep the unpopular general at hand as his assistant. But presently even this went by the board. By the time Mrs Bragg had recovered sufficiently from her illness to permit her husband's return to active duty, Johnston himself was bedridden, suffering from a debility brought on by a flare-up of his wounds. "General Bragg is therefore necessary here," he notified Richmond on April 10. "If conference with him is still desirable, might not a confidential officer visit him, for the purpose, in Tullahoma?"

★ ★ ★

That was that; Bragg remained at his post by default, so to speak. Meanwhile — principally by courtesy of Rosecrans, who, though the methods employed to avoid compliance were quite different in each case, would no more be budged by his superiors than Johnston would be influenced by his — the Army of Tennessee enjoyed, throughout the opening half of the year, the longest period of inaction afforded any considerable body of Confederates in the whole course of the war. Polk's corps was on the left at Shelbyville, Hardee's on the right at Wartrace, with cavalry extending the long defensive line westward to Columbia and eastward to McMinnville, seventy air-line miles apart. Breastworks protected by abatis were thrown up along the critical center, and behind them, once the countryside emerged from the quagmires created by the late winter and early spring rains — which had afforded one self-styled etymologist the opportunity to remark that the name of the little railroad town where Bragg had his headquarters was derived from the conjunction of two Greek words: *tulla*, meaning "mud," and *homa*, meaning "more mud" — the infantry enjoyed the foison of the lush Duck River Valley and indulged in such diversions as attending church services and revival meetings (Bragg set an example here by allowing himself to be baptized in an impressive ceremony) or chuck-a-luck games and cockfights, depending on individual inclinations. The army's effective strength had risen by now to almost 50,000 of all arms, including better than 15,000 cavalry, who passed the time in a quite different manner by probing at Rosecrans' flanks and rear and harassing his front.

Joe Wheeler got things off to a rousing start on January 13 with a strike at Harpeth Shoals, midway between Nashville and Clarksville, where he captured or sank four loaded packets and one lightly armored gunboat, taking them under fire from the bank, and thus effectively suspended the flow of goods up the Cumberland River, the main Federal supply line. But this accomplishment was more than offset, another fifty miles downstream, by the repulse he suffered on February 3 when he launched an ill-conceived and poorly co-ordinated assault on an outnumbered but stout blue garrison at Dover, two weeks short of the anniversary of the fall of adjacent Fort Donelson to Grant. Bedford Forrest, who had not only lost some of his best men but had also had two fine horses shot from under him in the course of attacks which he had advised against making in the first place, was so incensed by Wheeler's handling of the affair that he bluntly told the young commander that he would resign from the army before he would fight again under his direction. The discouraged graybacks limped back to Columbia, the western tip of Bragg's long crescent. Meanwhile, far out the opposite horn, Morgan was doing no better, if indeed as well. With two of his regiments de-

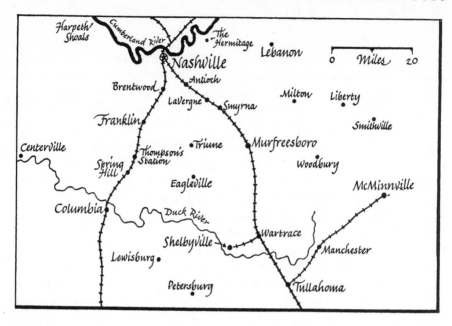

tached to stir up excitement in Kentucky, he too suffered a bloody repulse at the hands of an inferior force on March 20 at Milton, fifteen
miles northeast of Murfreesboro, and still another, two weeks later, at
nearby Liberty, which resulted in his being driven in some confusion back
on his base at McMinnville. Perhaps the best that could be said for all
these various affairs, at any rate from the Confederate point of view, was
that they all occurred within the Union lines and therefore served, victories and defeats alike, to keep Rosecrans off balance by increasing his native caution and apprehensiveness. "Their numerous cavalry goads and
worries me," he had informed Washington at the outset, "but I will try
to be equal to them."

This was going to be more difficult than he knew. Even as he
wrote, Earl Van Dorn, the South's ranking major general — ordered
north by Johnston over Pemberton's frantic protest at thus being practically stripped of cavalry despite the skill he recently had shown in handling that arm — was on the way from Mississippi with two divisions of
horsemen, all thirsty for more of the glory they lately had tasted when
they threw a whole Yankee army into retreat from Holly Springs. In
this respect, their leader was the thirstiest man among them. After the
Transmississippi disasters and the Corinth fiasco, which had resulted,
amid wholesale condemnation, in his being superseded as commander of
his home state forces, his bad luck had suddenly turned good, and he was
eager to take further advantage of the switch. Presently, soon after his
arrival on February 22 at Columbia, where he assumed responsibility for
protecting the left horn of Bragg's crescent while Wheeler protected the
right, Rosecrans gave the diminutive Mississippian just the chance he had
been seeking ever since his return to his first love, cavalry. The Federal

plan was for a convergence of two infantry columns, one out of Murfreesboro under Phil Sheridan, the other out of Franklin, directly south of Nashville, under Colonel John Coburn; they would unite at Spring Hill, a dozen miles north of Columbia, then move together against that place, foraging as they went. Coburn set out on March 4, with just under 3000 of all arms. Van Dorn was waiting for him next morning at Thompson's Station, just above the intended point of convergence, with twice as many men — including Forrest, who had been transferred in consideration of his vow to serve no more under Wheeler. The result was a sudden and stunning victory, cinched by Forrest, who came in on the flank and rear while Van Dorn maintained pressure against the front, and a bag of 1221 prisoners, including Coburn, whose artillery and cavalry, along with one of his infantry regiments assigned to guard the forage train, had fled at the first detection of the odds. His thirst unslaked, Van Dorn sent his captives south and turned east to tackle Sheridan, intending thus to sweep the board of all available opponents, but found that the other column had taken warning from the boom of guns and pulled back out of danger.

Rosecrans too had taken alarm, and though his present-for-duty strength now stood at 80,124, as compared to Bragg's 49,068, he began to suspect that he was outnumbered. "I am not, as you know, an alarmist," he wired Halleck on the day after Coburn's defeat, "but I do not think it will do to risk as we did before." He reinforced the threatened quarter, causing the rebel horsemen to pull back. But when the blue tide once more receded, Van Dorn returned again, cutting and slashing, left and right, and playing all the while on Rosecrans' fears. On March 24, having leapfrogged his headquarters to Spring Hill, he sent Forrest against Brentwood (ten miles north of Federal-held Franklin) where a garrison of about 800 Wisconsin and Michigan infantry protected army stores and a stockaded railroad bridge across the Little Harpeth River. Forrest appeared before the place next morning, demanding an unconditional surrender. "Come and take us," Colonel Edward Bloodgood replied stoutly, until he saw the graybacks preparing to do just that: whereupon he changed his mind and hauled down his flag. Setting fire to the stockade and packing the stores for removal along with his captives, Forrest sent one regiment up the Nashville pike to spread the scare in that direction — which it did, penetrating the southern environs of the city and riding within plain sight of the capitol tower — while the main body, after pausing to fight a confused rear-guard action provoked by a blue column that moved up from Franklin, made its getaway eastward before turning south to safety. In a general order issued on the last day of the month, Bragg expressed the "pride and gratification" he felt as a result of the "two brilliant and successful affairs recently achieved by the forces of the cavalry of Major General Van Dorn."

Unwilling to rest on his laurels now that fortune's smile was broadening still further, Van Dorn moved on April 10 against Franklin itself. A forced reconnaissance, he called it afterwards, though the defenders insisted that it had been an all-out attempt to take the place by storm. In support of the former contention was the fact that casualties were fewer than a hundred on each side; anyhow, he disengaged and withdrew when he found that the Union commander, Major General Gordon Granger, had been reinforced to a strength of about 8000. Back at Spring Hill, he continued to design projects for the discomfiture of the enemy, assisting Bragg to hold onto the fruitful region despite the odds which favored a Federal advance. On through April he labored, and into May, though apparently not so exclusively as to require him to abandon other pursuits; for at 10 o'clock on the morning of May 7, Dr George B. Peters, a local citizen, walked into headquarters, where Van Dorn was hard at work at his desk, and shot him in the back of the head with a pistol. He died about 2 o'clock that afternoon, by which time the assassin was safe within the Union lines, having ridden off in the buggy he had left parked outside while he stepped indoors to carry out his project. The accepted explanation was that the doctor had chosen this emphatic means to protest the general's attention to his young wife, though there were some who claimed that he had done the shooting for political reasons. At any rate, that was the end of the saga of Buck Van Dorn. Fortune's smile had turned out fickle after all, and they buried him in Columbia next day.

Wheeler had got back in stride by then with a double blow at Rosecrans' rail supply lines on April 10, the day Van Dorn tested the Franklin defenses and found them strong. The first was scored northeast of Nashville, beyond Andrew Jackson's Hermitage, by secretly posting guns along the near bank of a bend that took the Cumberland River within 500-yard range of the Louisville & Nashville tracks. After a wait of two hours, Wheeler reported, "a very large locomotive came in view, drawing eighteen cars loaded with horses and other stock." Though the target was moving his marksmanship was excellent, according to a Federal brigadier. "The first shot knocked off the dome of the locomotive, the next went through the boiler, one shot broke out a spoke in one of the driving-wheels." When the engine stalled in a cloud of steam, the gunners continued to pump shells into the cars, scattering bluecoats, horses, and cattle in all directions. Meanwhile, on the Nashville & Chattanooga side of the Tennessee capital, another group of Wheeler's men rode into Antioch, where they ambushed and derailed a train by spreading the tracks and took from the wreckage about seventy Union captives — including twenty officers, three of whom were members of Rosecrans' staff — along with some forty Confederates en route to Ohio prison camps, $30,000 in greenbacks, and a large mail containing much useful information. Loaded with booty, the raiders got away eastward to join their friends, who by now had ridden back past the Hermitage after their shooting-gallery fun on the Cumberland. Wheeler's total cost for both accomplishments was one man wounded.

He was cheered all round and greeted with smiles on his return, for both actions had a somewhat comic tinge. But the loudest cheers and the broadest smiles were reserved for Bedford Forrest, who began to win his *nom de guerre* "the Wizard of the Saddle" with an exploit which took him, through the closing days of April and the opening days of May, into parts of three states and across the northern width of Alabama. He was drawn in that direction by a Federal project which got under way, by coincidence on that same April 10, with the embarkation at Nashville of an expedition designed to sever Bragg's main supply line, the Western & Atlantic Railroad, between Atlanta and Chattanooga. This had been attempted once before, a year ago this week, but had resulted in the Great Locomotive Chase and the capture of the twenty-two spies who tried it. The new plan, while perhaps equally daring, was of a quite different nature. Taking a page from the book the rebel cavalry fought by — particularly John Morgan and Forrest himself — Colonel Abel D. Streight, New-York-born commander of a regiment of Hoosier infantry, proposed to Rosecrans that a large body of men, say 2000, be mounted for a quick but powerful thrust, into and out of the South's vitals. Rosecrans, who so often had been on the receiving end of this kind of thing, was delighted at the prospect of turning the tables, and his delight increased when Streight removed his final objection by agreeing to mount the men on mules instead of horses, of which there was a shortage; mules, he said, were not only more sure-footed, they were also more intelligent. (Which was true, so far as it went, though that was by no means all of the story. Mules had other, less admirable qualities: as he would presently discover.) At any rate, Rosecrans gave his approval to the project, designated Streight as commander, and assigned him three more regiments of Ohio, Indiana, and Illinois infantry, together with two companies of North Alabama Unionists — a breed of men who were known to their late compatriots as "homemade Yankees," but who were expected to prove invaluable as guides through a region unfamiliar to everyone else in the flying column — and a requisition for some nine hundred quartermaster mules. This would mount only about half of the troops, but Rosecrans explained that the rest could secure animals by commandeering them from rebel sympathizers while on the way to their starting point in the northeast corner of Mississippi.

So Streight got his men and mules aboard the transports and steamed next morning down the Cumberland to unload at Palmyra, on the left bank just around the bend from Clarksville, for a stock-gathering march to Fort Henry, where they again met the transports for the long ride south up the Tennessee to Eastport, Mississippi. That was the true starting point, tactically speaking, but Streight — a broad-chested man of soldierly appearance, just past forty, with a tall forehead, light-colored eyes, a fleshy, powerful-looking nose, and a dark, well-trimmed beard framing a wide, determined mouth exposed below a clean-shaven upper lip — had already encountered complications well outside the original margin he had allowed for error. For one thing, after waiting to pick up rations and forage on the Ohio, the navy did not turn up at Fort Henry on time, with the result that he did not reach Eastport until April 19, three days behind schedule. For another, a delayed check disclosed that a large proportion of the quartermaster mules were sadly afflicted with distemper, while many others were unbroken colts, not over two years old. This last exposed a further drawback; for he found that his converted infantrymen, as one of them remarked, "were at first very easily dismounted, frequently in a most undignified and unceremonious manner." Practice might improve the men's equestrian skill, but the mules were going to remain a problem. About five hundred had been commandeered on the course of the overland march, which more than made up for the hundred-odd who died of sickness and exhaustion while en route; but this gain was canceled on the evening of his arrival at Eastport. Returning to headquarters about midnight from a conference with Brigadier General Grenville M. Dodge, who had brought a 7500-man column over from Corinth to serve as a screen for the raiders' departure, he learned that some four hundred of the creatures — naturally the most intelligent of the lot — had escaped from their crudely built corrals and now were scattered about the countryside, disrupting the stillness of the night and mocking his woes with brays that had the sound of fiendish laughter. Two more days were spent here in rounding them up; half of them, that is, for the rest were never recovered. However, Dodge made up the difference with animals out of his pack train, and Streight at last got started in earnest, moving eastward across Bear Creek on the morning of April 22.

Five days behind schedule, but still protected from inquisitive eyes by the screen Dodge's troops had drawn along the south bank of the Tennessee River, he reached Tuscumbia late on the 24th and called a final two-day rest halt before resuming the march at 11 p.m. of the 26th, his force reduced to 1500 by a rigid inspection in which the surgeons culled such men as they judged unfit for the rigorous work ahead. All next day, and the next, as the column moved south to Russellville, then eastward to Mount Hope, rain and mud held its progress to a crawl and 300 of the fledgling troopers were reconverted to infantry because their mounts were too weak to carry anything heavier than a saddle. On the 29th, however, the sun broke through, giving "strong hopes of better times," as Streight declared in his last rearward message, and he began to pick up speed, along with replacements for his ailing mules. Thirty-five miles he made that day, clearing Moulton to make camp that night at the western foot of Day's Gap, a narrow defile piercing a lofty ridge that signaled the advent of the Appalachians. At this point, with the tactically dangerous flatlands left behind, he was about halfway to his first objective: Rome, Georgia, where the Confederacy had a cannon foundry and machine shops for the Western & Atlantic, whose main line was barely a half-day's ride beyond. Starting early next morning, the last day of April, Streight rode at the head of the column toiling upward through the gap. "The sun shone out bright and beautiful as spring day's sun ever beamed," his adjutant later recalled, "and from the smouldering camp-fires of the previous night the mild blue smoke ascended in graceful curves and mingled with the gray mist slumbering on the mountain tops above." There was in fact much that was dreamlike and idyllic about the scene —"well calculated to inspire and refresh the minds of our weary soldiers," the admiring lieutenant phrased it — until suddenly, without previous intimation of a transition, as Streight and the forward elements of the column neared the crest, the dream shifted kaleidoscopically into nightmare. From downhill, in the direction of last night's camp, the deep-voiced booms of guns, mixed in with the tearing rattle of musketry, abruptly informed him that he was under attack.

It was Forrest. A week ago today — the day after Streight left Eastport — he had received at Spring Hill, Tennessee, orders from Bragg to proceed south to the Florence-Tuscumbia region and assist the inadequate local defense units to oppose the force moving eastward under Dodge. He left next morning, April 24, and thirty-six hours later had his 1577-man brigade at Brown's Ferry, Alabama, ninety miles away. Leaving one of his three regiments to guard the north bank of the Tennessee in case Dodge decided to strike in that direction, he ferried the others across on the 26th and moved west through Courtland to Town Creek, which he reached in time to challenge a Federal crossing. The long-range skirmish continued until dusk of the following day, when Forrest received word from a scout that a mounted column estimated at 2000 men had left Mount Hope that morning, headed east. This was the first he had heard of Streight's existence, but he decided at once that this was the major threat, not the larger force immediately to his front. Accordingly, leaving Dodge to the local defenders and the regiment already posted beyond the river, he took off southward at dawn of the 29th for Moulton, which Streight had cleared six hours before. At midnight, having covered fifty miles of road with just over a thousand horsemen and eight guns, he went into bivouac, four miles short of Streight's camp at Day's Gap, in order to give his saddle-weary troopers some rest for tomorrow, and soon after sunrise was banging away at the Federal rear.

In the course of the three-day running fight which followed, the pursued had certain definite advantages. The first was a superiority of numbers, although Streight's enjoyment of this was considerably diminished by the fact that he did not know·he had it. All the same, the numerical odds were with him, three to two, whether he knew it or not, and what was more they grew as he moved eastward past well-stocked farms untouched by war till now. When his mules gave out, as they frequently did, he could remount his men by seizing others; whereas for Forrest, coming along in the raiders' clean-swept wake, a broken-down horse meant a lost rider. Another tactical advantage accruing to the blue commander was that whenever he chose to make a stand he could not only select the terrain best suited for defensive fighting, he could also lay small-scale ambushes by which a rear-guard handful could shock the pursuers with surprise fire, forcing them to halt and deploy, then hurry ahead to rejoin the main body before the attack was delivered. Streight was altogether aware of this advantage, and used it first within three miles of the point where he heard the opening boom of guns. Selecting a position along a wooded ridge, with a boggy creek protecting his left and a steep ravine his right, he sent back word for the rear-guard Alabama Unionists, still skirmishing in Day's Gap, to retreat on the run through the newly drawn line and thus draw the graybacks into ambush. It worked to perfection. As the pursuers rode fast to overtake the home-made Yankees, the waiting bluecoats rose from the underbrush and shattered the head of the column with massed volleys. When reinforcements came up to repeat the attempt, this time advancing a section of artillery to counterbalance the two 12-pounder mountain howitzers firing rapidly from the ridge, the defenders followed up a second repulse with a counterattack and captured both of the guns, then drew off, leaving the rebels rocked back on their heels.

Forrest was thrown into a towering rage by the loss of his guns and the fact that the raiders had won first honors and drawn first blood — including that of his brother, Captain William Forrest, who had led his company of scouts in the charge and had been unhorsed by a bullet that broke his thigh — but by the time he got his troopers back into line for a third attack, the bluecoats had pulled out. He pushed on, closing again on their rear at Crooked Creek, where Streight again formed line of battle, six miles beyond the first. Here, from about an hour before dark until 10 o'clock that night, the two forces engaged in a fire fight. Determined to give the raiders no rest, Forrest kept forcing the issue by moonlight, and his orders, though brief, were conclusive: "Shoot at everything blue and keep up the scare." Finally, with one flank about to crumple, Streight "resumed the march," leaving the two captured guns behind him, spiked. At midnight, then again two hours later, he laid ambushes, but Forrest kept crowding him and did not call a halt till daylight, when he paused long enough to water and feed the horses and give the weaker ones an opportunity to catch up. Streight meanwhile pushed on to the outskirts of Blountsville, which he reached about midmorning of May Day, having covered forty-three miles over mountain roads since the skirmishing began soon after sunrise yesterday. However, before his men could finish feeding their weary mounts, Forrest once more was driving in the pickets, and the two commands went through the town in a whirl of dust and gunsmoke, shooting at one another over the ears of their horses or the cruppers of their mules.

So it went, all that day and the next, eastward another fifty miles, then northeastward along the near bank of the Coosa River, with Streight making stands behind the east fork of the Black Warrior River and Big Will's Creek, laying ambushes in the heavily wooded valley off the southern end of Lookout Mountain, and burning the only bridge across Black Creek, just short of Gadsden. Forrest kept the pressure on, however. He got over the last-named obstacle by using a ford that was shown him, under fire from the opposite bank, by a sixteen-year-old farm girl, Emma Sanson — in appreciation of whose courage he took time and pains to leave an autograph note of thanks:

> *Hed Quaters in Sadle*
> *May 2 1863*
> *My highest regardes to miss Ema Sanson for hir Gallant con-*
> *duct while my posse was skirmishing with the Federals across*
> *Black Creek near Gadesden Allabama.*
> *N. B. Forrest*
> *Brig Genl Comding N. Ala —*

and pressed on after the blue raiders, engaging them in another running fight through Gadsden and beyond, where they soon were forced to make another stand. He had the advantage of singleness of purpose, plus the chance to give his men a breather when he chose, pursuing as it were in shifts, some resting while others kept up the chase; whereas Streight not only had to keep fending off the myriad and apparently inexhaustible graybacks hot on his trail — a profitless business at best — but also had to keep pushing on toward the accomplishment of his mission in North Georgia. After nearly three days of riding and fighting, and two nights without rest, his men were falling asleep on muleback and even in line of battle whenever he called a halt to lay another ambush or defend another opportune position, and now that his pursuers had avoided delay at Black Creek, thanks to Emma Sanson, he faced another sleepless night. "It now became evident to me," he later reported, "that our only hope was in crossing the river at Rome and destroying the bridge, which would delay Forrest a day or two and give us time to collect horses and mules and allow the command a little time to sleep, without which it was impossible to proceed."

Accordingly, when he reached Turkeytown, eight miles beyond Gadsden, he selected two hundred of the best-mounted men and sent them ahead to seize the bridge across the Oostanaula River at Rome and hold it until the main body came up. At sunset, four miles farther along, he formed again for battle "as it was impossible to continue the march through the night without feeding and resting." In the course of the preliminary skirmish, however, he discovered that much of the men's

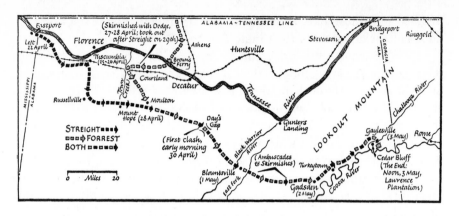

ammunition had been ruined by dampness and abrasion. Instead of risk-
ing another general engagement under these circumstances, he decided
to disengage — "unobserved, if possible" — and lay another ambush in
a thicket half a mile ahead. When Forrest detected the ruse and began to
move out on the flank, Streight had to pull back and make a run for it in
the dusk, beginning another horrendous night march with men who
by now had the look of somnambulists and mules that were "jaded,
tender-footed, and worn out." But the worst development, so far, was
encountered when they reached the Cedar Bluff ferry across the Chattooga River, just above its confluence with the Coosa. The 200-man
detail had passed this way a short while back, headed for Rome, but had
neglected to post a guard: with the result that some citizens had spirited
the ferryboat away, leaving Streight with the sort of problem he had
been leaving Forrest all along.

Yet he was nothing if not persevering. Turning left, he plodded
wearily through the darkness along the west bank of the Chattooga,
intent on reaching a bridge near Gaylesville, half a dozen miles upstream. Whereupon — while Forrest was giving his troopers a few hours'
sleep: all but one squadron, which he instructed to stay on the trail of
the raiders and "devil them all night" — Streight and his muleback
soldiers entered the worst of their several Deep South nightmares.
The way led through extensive "choppings" where the timber had been
cut and burned to furnish charcoal for nearby Round Mountain Furnace,
which in turn supplied the Rome foundry with pig iron. Though the
raiders succeeded in wrecking part of the smelting plant — the one substantial blow they struck in the course of their long ride across Alabama — they paid a high price in the extra miles they covered in order to bring it within reach. Lost in a maze of wagon trails, segments of
the blue column were scattered about the choppings until daylight
showed them the way back to the river and then to the bridge, which
they crossed and burned in their wake. Wobbly with fatigue, animals
and men alike, they staggered along the opposite bank, again to the

vicinity of Cedar Bluff, then turned eastward five more miles to the Lawrence plantation, which they reached about 9 a.m. The Georgia line was only five miles ahead, with Rome barely another fifteen miles beyond, but Streight had no choice except to drop from exhaustion or halt for rest and food. He had no sooner begun the distribution of rations, however, than the graybacks once more were driving in his pickets.

Forrest had swum the Chattooga at sunup, using long ropes to drag two of his guns across, submerged on the sandy bottom. Down to six hundred men by now, he was outnumbered worse than two to one and knew it, even if Streight did not. All along he had had to avoid the obvious maneuver of circling the flank of the blue column in order to block its path; for in that case, goaded by desperation, the Federals might have run right over him, swamping his line with the sheer weight of numbers. Even now, in fact, though his troopers were considerably refreshed by the sleep they had enjoyed while the bluecoats were stumbling around in the choppings south of Gaylesville, he preferred not to risk a pitched battle if he could accomplish his purpose otherwise. So he did as he had done before, in similar circumstances: sent forward, under a flag of truce, an officer with a note demanding immediate surrender "to stop the further and useless effusion of blood."

Streight, who had had to wake his men to put them into line of battle — where they promptly fell asleep again, with bullets whistling overhead — replied that he was by no means ready to give up, but that, sharing Forrest's humane views as to unnecessary bloodshed, he was willing to parley. He insisted further, when the guns fell silent and the two commanders met between the lines, that he would not even consider laying down his arms unless his opponent would prove that he had an overwhelming superiority of numbers. Forrest declined to show his hand in any such manner; but all the while, acting under previous instructions, the officer in charge of the section of artillery kept bringing his two guns over a distant rise in the road, then back under cover and over the rise again, producing for the benefit of Streight, who had been placed so as to watch all this over Forrest's shoulder, the appearance of a stream of guns arriving at intervals to bolster the rebel line. "Name of God!" Streight cried at last. "How many guns have you got? There's fifteen I've counted already." Forrest looked around casually. "I reckon that's all that has kept up," he said. So Streight went back to his own lines for a conference with his regimental commanders, most of whom, as he later reported, "had already expressed the opinion that, unless we could reach Rome and cross the river before the enemy came up with us again, we should be compelled to surrender." At this juncture, a messenger arrived from the 200-man detail sent ahead the night before and reported that the bridge across the Oostanaula was strongly held by rebel troops in Rome. That did it; Streight returned and announced his willingness to surrender. Forrest replied, "Stack your arms right along there, Colonel, and march your men away down that hollow."

The total bag, including the 200-man detail picked up on the way into Rome that same Sunday afternoon as it returned from its fruitless mission, was 1466 bluecoats, and though they had been feared as would-be conquerors — a fear which had thrown the Rome citizenry into such a panic of feverish activity that the Federal scouts, observing from across the Oostanaula, had mistaken the milling for preparedness — they were welcomed and fed generously as captives. Forrest's own entrance was the occasion for the presentation of a horseshoe wreath of flowers, hailing him as the town's deliverer, and a fine saddle horse, which helped to make up for the two that had been shot from under him in the course of the long chase. Then began a famous celebration, attended by what one matron called "just a regular wholesale cooking of hams and shoulders and all sorts of provisions" to relieve the hunger pangs of the gray heroes. Nor were the prisoners excluded from this bounty; "We were quite willing to feed the Yankees when they had no guns," she added. But the Roman holiday was cut short on the night of May 5 by the arrival of word that another column of blue raiders had left Tuscumbia that afternoon, headed southeast for Jasper and possibly Montgomery. Forrest and his men were back in the saddle next morning. Riding once more through Gadsden the following day, they learned that the rumor was groundless, Dodge having returned to Corinth; so they swung north, recovering the third regiment en route, to resume their accustomed work in Tennessee. On May 10, however — another Sunday — Forrest was handed orders from Bragg, instructing him to have his brigade continue its present march but for him to report in person to army headquarters, where he would receive, along with a recommendation for promotion to major general, appointment to the command Van Dorn had vacated three days ago, when he came under the Spring Hill doctor's pistol.

✘ 5 ✘

Along toward sunset of January 28, completing a 400-mile overnight trip from Memphis down the swollen, tawny, mile-wide Mississippi, a stern-wheel packet warped in for a west-bank landing at Young's Point, just opposite the base of the long hairpin bend in front of Vicksburg and within half a dozen air-line miles of the guns emplaced along the lip of the tall clay bluff the city stood on. First off the steamboat, once the deck hands had swung out the stageplank, was a slight man, rather stooped, five feet eight inches in height and weighing less than a hundred and forty pounds, who walked with a peculiar gait, shoulders hunched "a little forward of the perpendicular," as one observer re-marked, so that each step seemed to arrest him momentarily in the act of pitching on his face. He had on a plain blue suit and what the same reporter called "an indifferently good 'Kossuth' hat, with the top bat-tered in close to his head." Forty years old, he looked considerably older, partly because of the crow's-feet crinkling the outer corners of his eyes — the result of intense concentration, according to some, while others identified them as whiskey lines, plainly confirming rumors of over-indulgence and refuting the protestations of friends that he never touched the stuff — but mainly because of the full, barely grizzled, light brown beard, close-cropped to emphasize the jut of a square jaw and expose a mouth described as being "of the letterbox shape," clamped firmly shut below a nose that surprised by contrast, being delicately chiseled, and blue-gray eyes that gave the face a somewhat out-of-balance look because one was set a trifle lower than the other. Wearing neither sword nor sash, and indeed no trappings of rank at all, except for the twin-starred straps of a major general tacked to the weathered shoulders of his coat, he was reading a newspaper as he came down the plank to the Louisiana shore, and he chewed the unlighted stump of a cigar, which not only seemed habitual but also appeared to be a more congruous facial appendage than the surprisingly aquiline nose.

"There's General Grant," an Illinois soldier told a comrade as they stood watching this unceremonious arrival.

"I guess not," the other replied, shaking his head. "That fellow don't look like he has the ability to command a regiment, much less an army."

It was not so much that Grant was unexpected; he had a habit of turning up unannounced at almost any time and place within the limits of his large department. The trouble was that he bore such faint re-semblance to his photographs, which had been distributed widely ever since Donelson and which, according to an acquaintance, made him look like a "burly beef-contractor." In person he resembled at best a badly printed copy of one of those photos, with the burliness left out. Con-versely, the lines of worry — if his friends were right and that was what they were — were more pronounced, as was perhaps only natural when he had more to fret about than the discomfort of holding still for a camera. Just now, for instance, there was John McClernand, who per-sisted in considering the river force a separate command and continued to issue general orders under the heading, "Headquarters, Army of the Mississippi." Before Grant had been downriver two days he received a letter from McClernand, noting "that orders are being issued directly from your headquarters directly to army corps commanders, and not through me." This could only result in "dangerous confusion," McCler-nand protested, "as I am invested, by order of the Secretary of War, in-dorsed by the President, and by order of the President communicated to

you by the General-in-Chief, with the command of all the forces operating on the Mississippi River. . . . If different views are entertained by
you, then the question should be immediately referred to Washington,
and one or the other, or both of us, relieved. One thing is certain; two
generals cannot command this army, issuing independent and direct orders to subordinate officers, and the public service be promoted."

Grant agreed at least with the final sentence — which he later
paraphrased and sharpened into a maxim: "Two commanders on the
same field are always one too many" — but he found the letter as a whole
"more in the nature of a reprimand than a protest." The fact was, it approached outright insubordination, although not quite close enough to
afford occasion for the pounce Grant was crouched for. "I overlooked
it, as I believed, for the good of the service," he subsequently wrote. By
way of reply, instead of direct reproof, he issued orders announcing that
he was assuming personal command of the river expedition and instructing all corps commanders, including McClernand, to report henceforth
directly to him; McClernand's corps, he added by way of a stinger,
would garrison Helena and other west-bank points well upriver. Outraged at being the apparent victim of a squeeze play, the former congressman responded by asking whether, "having projected the Mississippi
River expedition, and having been by a series of orders assigned to the
command of it," he was thus to be "entirely withdrawn from it." Grant
replied to the effect that he would do as he saw fit, since "as yet I have
seen no order to prevent my taking command in the field." McClernand
acquiesced, as he said, "for the purpose of avoiding a conflict of authority
in the presence of the enemy," but requested that the entire matter be
referred to their superiors in Washington, "not only in respect for the
President and Secretary, under whose authority I claim the right to
command the expedition, but in justice to myself as its author and actual
promoter." Grant accordingly forwarded the correspondence to Halleck, saying that he had assumed command only because he lacked confidence in McClernand. "I respectfully submit the whole matter to the
General-in-Chief and the President," he ended his indorsement. "Whatever the decision made by them, I will cheerfully submit to and give a
hearty support."

In bucking all this up to the top echelon Grant was on even safer
ground than he supposed. Just last week McClernand had received, in
reply to a private letter to Lincoln charging Halleck "with wilful contempt of superior authority" because of his so-far "interference" in the
matter, "and with incompetency for the extraordinary and vital func-
tions with which he is charged," a note in which the President told him
plainly: "I have too many *family* controversies (so to speak) already on
my hands to voluntarily, or so long as I can avoid it, take up another.
You are now doing well — well for the country, and well for yourself
— much better than you could possibly be if engaged in open war with

General Halleck. Allow me to beg that for your sake, for my sake, and for the country's sake, you give your whole attention to the better work." So it was: McClernand already had his answer before he filed his latest appeal. Lincoln would not interfere. The army was Grant's, and would remain Grant's, to do with as he saw fit in accomplishing what Lincoln called "the better work."

His problem was how best to go about it. Now that he had inspected at first hand the obstacles to success in this swampy region, much of which was at present under water and would continue to be so for months to come, he could see that the wisest procedure, from a strategic point of view, "would have been to go back to Memphis, establish that as a base of supplies, fortify it so that the storehouses could be held by a small garrison, and move from there along the line of the [Mississippi & Tennessee] railroad, repairing as we advanced to the Yalobusha," from which point he would have what he now so gravely lacked: a straight, high-ground shot at the city on the rebel bluff. So he wrote, years later, having gained the advantage of hindsight. For the present, however, he saw certain drawbacks to the retrograde movement, which in his judgment far outweighed the strictly tactical advantages. For one thing, the November elections had gone against the party that stood for all-out prosecution of the war, and this had turned out to be a warning of future trouble, with the croakers finding encouragement in the reverse. There was the question of morale, not only in the army itself, but also on the home front, where even a temporary withdrawal would be considered an admission that Vicksburg was too tough a nut to crack. At this critical juncture, both temporal and political, with voluntary enlistment practically at a standstill throughout much of the North and the new conscription laws already meeting sporadic opposition, such a discouragement might well prove fatal to the cause. "It was my judgment at the time," Grant subsequently wrote, "that to make a backward movement as long as that from Vicksburg to Memphis, would be interpreted, by many of those yet full of hope for the preservation of the Union, as a defeat, and that the draft would be resisted, desertions ensue, and the power to capture and punish deserters lost. There was nothing left to be done but to *go forward to a decisive victory*. This was in my mind from the moment I took command in person at Young's Point."

In his own mind at least that much was settled. He would stay. But this decision only brought him face to face with the basic problem, as he put it, of how "to secure a footing upon dry ground on the east side of the river, from which the troops could operate against Vicksburg ... without an apparent retreat." Aside from a frontal assault, either against the bluff itself or against the heights flanking it on the north — which Sherman, even if he had done nothing more last month, had proved would not only be costly in the extreme but would also be fruitless, and which Grant said "was never contemplated; certainly not by me" — the choice lay between whether to cross upstream or down, above or below the rebel bastion. One seemed about as impossible as the other. Above, the swampy, fifty-mile-wide delta lay in his path, practically roadless and altogether malarial. Even if he were able to slog his foot soldiers across it, which was doubtful, it was worse than doubtful whether he would be able to establish and maintain a vital supply line by that route. On the other hand, to attempt a crossing below the city seemed even more suicidal, since this would involve a run past frowning batteries, not only at Vicksburg itself, but also at Warrenton and Grand Gulf, respectively seven and thirty-five miles downriver. Armored gunboats — as Farragut had demonstrated twice the year before, first up, then down, with his heavily gunned salt-water fleet — might run this fiery gauntlet, taking their losses as they went, but brittle-skinned transports and supply boats would be quite another matter, considering the likelihood of their being reduced to kindling in short order, with much attendant loss of life and goods. . . . In short, the choice seemed to lie between two impossibilities, flanking a third which had been rejected before it was even considered.

Two clear advantages Grant had, however, by way of helping to offset the gloom, and both afforded him comfort under the strain. One was the unflinching support of his superiors; the other was an ample supply of troops, either downstream with him or else on call above. "The eyes and hopes of the whole country are now directed to your army," Halleck presently would tell him. "In my opinion, the opening of the Mississippi River will be to us of more advantage than the capture of forty Richmonds. We shall omit nothing which we can do to assist you." Already, before Grant left Memphis, Old Brains had urged him: "Take everything you can dispense with in Tennessee and [North] Mississippi. We must not fail in this if within human power to accomplish it." His total effective strength within his department, as of late January, was approximately 103,000 officers and men, and of these, as a result of abandoning railroads and other important rear-area installations, Grant had been able to earmark just over half for the downriver expedition: 32,000 in the two corps under McClernand and Sherman, already at hand, and 15,000 in McPherson's corps, filing aboard transports southbound from Memphis even now. In addition to these 47,000 — the official total, "present for duty, equipped," was 46,994 — another 15,000 were standing by under Hurlbut, who commanded the fourth corps, ready to follow McPherson as soon as they got the word. Just now, though, there not only was no need for them; there actually was no room. Because of the high water and the incessant rain overflowing the bayous, there was no place to camp on the low-lying west bank except upon the levee, with the result that the army was strung out along it for more than fifty miles, north and south, under conditions that were anything but healthy.

As morale declined, the sick-lists lengthened; desertions were up; funerals were frequent. "Go any day down the levee," one recruit wrote home, "and you could see a squad or two of soldiers burying a companion, until the levee was nearly full of graves and the hospitals still full of sick. And those that were not down sick were not well by a considerable." Pneumonia was the chief killer, with smallpox a close second. Some regiments soon had more men down than up. The food was bad. Paymasters did not venture south of Helena, which increased the disaffection, and the rumor mills were grinding as never before. When the mails were held up, as they frequently were, it was reported from camp to camp, like a spark moving along a fifty-mile train of powder, that the war was over but that the news was being kept from the troops "for fear we could not be held in subjection if we knew the state of affairs." They took out at least a share of their resentment on such rebel property as came within their reach. "Farms disappear, houses are burned and plundered, and every living animal killed and eaten," Sherman informed his senator brother. "General officers make feeble efforts to stay the disorder, but it is idle." Then when the mail came through at last they could read in anti-administration newspapers of the instability and incompetence of the West Pointers responsible for their welfare, including Sherman — "He hates reporters, foams at the mouth when he sees them, snaps at them; sure symptoms of a deep-seated mania" — and the army commander himself: "The confidence of the army is greatly shaken in General Grant, who hitherto undoubtedly depended more upon good fortune than upon military ability for success."

The wet season would continue for months, during which all these problems would be with him. As Grant said in retrospect, "There seemed to be no possibility of a land movement before the end of March or later." Yet "it would not do to lie idle all this time. The effect would be demoralizing to the troops and injurious to their health. Friends in the North would have grown more and more insolent in their gibes and denunciations of the cause and those engaged in it." So he launched (or rather, continued) what he called "a series of experiments," designed not only "to consume time," but also to serve the triple purpose of diverting "the attention of the enemy, of my troops, and of the public generally." Two failures were already behind him in his campaign against Vicksburg: the advance down the Mississippi Central and the assault on the Chickasaw Bluffs, both of which had ended in retreat. Now there followed five more failures, bringing the total to seven. Looking back on them later he was to say — quite untruthfully, as the record would show — that he had "never felt great confidence that any of the experiments resorted to would prove successful," though he had always been "prepared to take advantage of them in case they did."

The third of these seven "experiments" — the attempt, by means of a canal across the base of the tongue of land in front of Vicksburg, to divert the channel of the river and thus permit the column of warships, transports, and supply boats to bypass the batteries on the bluff — had been in progress ever since the return of the army from Arkansas Post, but Sherman, who had assigned a thousand men a day to the digging job, was not sanguine of results. "The river is about full and threatens to drown us out," he was complaining as he sloshed about in a waste of gumbo, with the rain coming down harder every week. "The ground is wet, almost water, and it is impossible for wagons to haul stores from the river to camp, or even horses to wallow through." Conversely, as if to preserve a balance of optimism, Grant's expectations rose with the passage of time. In early March he wired Halleck: "The canal is near completion.... I will have Vicksburg this month, or fail in the attempt." But this was the signal for disaster. "If the river rises 8 feet more, we would have to take to the trees," Sherman had said, and presently it did. The dam at the upper end of the cut gave way, and the water, instead of scouring out a channel — as had been expected, or anyhow intended — spread all over the lower end of the peninsula, forcing the evacuation of the troops from their flooded camps, with the resultant sacrifice of many horses and much equipment. "This little affair of ours here on Vicksburg Point is labor lost," Sherman reported in disgust, announcing the unceremonious end of the third experiment.

But Grant already had a fourth in progress. Fifty-odd miles above Vicksburg, just west of the river and south of the Arkansas line, lay Lake Providence, once a bend of the Mississippi but long since abandoned by the Old Man in the course of one of his cataclysmic whims. Though the lake now was land-locked, separated moreover from the river by a levee, Bayou Baxter drained it sluggishly westward into Bayou Macon, which in turn flowed into the Tensas River, just over a hundred winding miles to the south. Still farther down, the Tensas joined the Ouachita to form the Black, and the Black ran into the Red, which entered the Mississippi a brief stretch above Port Hudson. Despite its roundabout meandering, a distance of some 470 miles, this route seemed to Grant to offer a chance, once the levee had been breached to afford access to Lake Providence and the intricate system of hinterland bayous and rivers, for a naval column to avoid not only the Vicksburg batteries but also those below at Warrenton and Grand Gulf. Accordingly, two days after his arrival at Young's Point, he sent an engineer detail to look into the possibilities indicated on the map, and the following week, in early February, he went up to see for himself. It seemed to him that "a little digging" — "less than one-quarter," he said, of what Sherman had done already on the old canal — "will connect the Mississippi and Lake, and in all probability will wash a channel in a short time." If so, the way would be open for a bloodless descent, at the end of which he would join Banks for a combined attack on Port Hudson, and once that final bastion had been reduced the Confederacy would

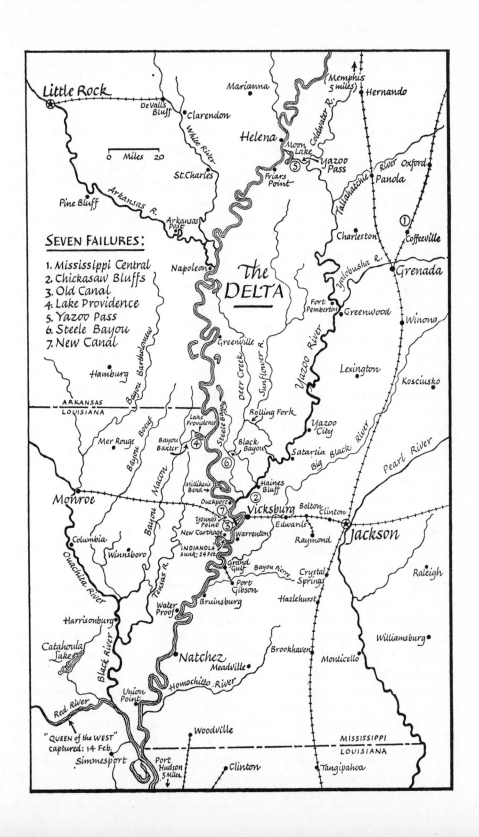

Little Rock

De Vall's Bluff
Clarendon
Marianna
(Memphis 5 miles)
Hernando

St. Charles
Helena
Moon Lake
Coldwater R.
Yazoo Pass
Tallahatchie River
Oxford
Panola

Friars Point
Charleston
①
Coffeeville

Pine Bluff
Arkansas R.
Arkansas Post
Napoleon
THE DELTA
Fort Pemberton
Greenwood
Yazoo River
Grenada
Yalobusha R.
Winona

0 Miles 20

SEVEN FAILURES:
1. Mississippi Central
2. Chickasaw Bluffs
3. Old Canal
4. Lake Providence
5. Yazoo Pass
6. Steele Bayou
7. New Canal

Hamburg
Greenville
Deer Creek
Sunflower R.
Lexington
Kosciusko

ARKANSAS
LOUISIANA
Bayou Bartholomew
Lake Providence
Rolling Fork
Yazoo City

Mer Rouge
Bayou Bœuf
④
Steele Bayou
Black Bayou
Satartia
Big Black River

Bayou Baxter
⑥
Haines Bluff
Pearl River

Bayou Macon
Milliken's Bend
Duckport
②
Vicksburg
Bolton
Clinton

Monroe
⑦
Young's Point
③
New Carthage
Warrenton
Edwards
Jackson

Columbia
Winnsboro
INDIANOLA sunk; 24 Feb.
Grand Gulf
Bayou Pierre
Crystal Springs
Raymond
Raleigh

Tensas R.
Port Gibson
Hazlehurst

Ouachita River
Water Proof
Bruinsburg
Brookhaven
Williamsburg

Harrisonburg
Black River
Monticello

Catahoula Lake
Natchez
Meadville

Red River
Union Point
Homochitto River

"QUEEN of the WEST" captured; 14 Feb.
Woodville
MISSISSIPPI
LOUISIANA

Simmesport
Port Hudson 5 miles
Clinton
Tangipahoa

have been cut in two and the Great Lakes region would have recovered its sorely missed trade connection with the Gulf. Impressed by this vista, Grant sent at once for McPherson to come down with a full division and get the project started without delay. "This bids fair to be the most practicable route for turning Vicksburg," he told him in the body of the summons.

He could scarcely have assigned the task to an officer better prepared to undertake it. McPherson, who was thirty-three and a fellow Ohioan, had been top man in the West Point class of '53 and had returned to the academy as an engineering instructor; he also had worked on river and harbor projects in the peacetime army, and had served at the time of Shiloh, when he was a lieutenant colonel, as chief engineer on Grant's staff. His advancement since then had been rapid, though not without some grousing, on the part of line officers he had passed on his way up the ladder, that a man who had never led troops in a major action should be given command of a corps. Sherman, on the other hand, considered him the army's "best hope for a great soldier," not excepting Grant and himself; "if he lives," he added. A bright-eyed, pleasant-faced young man, alternately bland and impulsive, McPherson came quickly down from Memphis with one of his two divisions and set to work at once. Without waiting for the levee to be cut, he horsed a small towboat overland, launched it on the lake, and got aboard for a reconnaissance — with the result that his high hopes took a sudden drop. The Bayou Baxter outlet led through an extensive cypress brake, and what could be found of its channel, which was but little at the present flood stage, was badly choked with stumps and snags that threatened to knock or rip the bottom out of whatever came their way. He put his men to work with underwater saws, but it was clear that at best the job would be a long one, if not impossible. Besides, Grant now saw that, even if a passage could be opened in time to be of use, he would never be able to get together enough light-draft boats to carry his army down to the Red River anyhow. McPherson and his staff meanwhile enjoyed something of a holiday, taking a regimental band aboard the little steamer for moonlight excursions, to and from the landing at one of the lakeside plantation houses which turned out to have a well-stocked cellar. Soldiers too found relaxation in this quiet backwater of the war, mainly in fishing, what time they were not taking turns on the underwater saws. By early March it was more or less obvious that nothing substantial was going to come of this fourth attempt to take or bypass Vicksburg, but Grant declared, later and rather laconically: "I let the work go on, believing employment was better than idleness for the men."

All seven of these experiments, four of which by now had gone by the board, anticipated some degree of co-operation from the navy. For the most part, indeed, they were classically amphibious, depending as much on naval as on army strength and skill. But if Porter, whatever his other shortcomings — one acquaintance called him "by all odds the greatest humbug of the war" — was not the kind of man to withhold needed help, neither was he the kind to be satisfied with a supporting role if he saw even an outside chance at stardom. And he believed he saw one now: had seen it, in fact, from the outset, and had already made his solo entrance on the stage. One of the two main reasons for attempting the reduction of Vicksburg and Port Hudson — in addition, that is, to opening a pathway to New Orleans and the Gulf — was to choke off rebel traffic along and across the nearly three hundred miles of river that flowed between them, particularly that segment of it tangent to the mouth of Red River, the main artery of trade connecting the goods-rich Transmississippi's far-west region with the principal Confederate supply depots in Georgia and Virginia. To accomplish this, the admiral perceived, it would not be absolutely necessary to capture either of the two bastions anchoring opposite ends of the long stretch of river. All that was needed, really, was to control what lay between them, and this could be done by sending warships down to knock out whatever vestiges of the rebel fleet remained and to establish a sort of internal blockade by patrolling all possible crossings. In early February, accordingly, while Sherman's men were still digging their way across soggy Vicksburg Point and Grant was steaming upriver for a preliminary look at cypress-choked Lake Providence, Porter gave orders which put his plan in the way of execution.

First off, this would require a run past the batteries on the bluff, and he gave the assignment to the steam ram *Queen of the West*, which had done it twice before, back in July, in an unsuccessful attempt to come to grips with the *Arkansas*. She was one of the navy's best-known vessels, having led the ram attack at the Battle of Memphis, where she had been commanded by her designer and builder, Colonel Charles Ellet, Jr., who had died of the only wound inflicted on a Northerner in that one-sided triumph. His son, nineteen-year-old Colonel Charles R. Ellet — who, as a medical cadet, had gone ashore in a rowboat, accompanied by three seamen, to complete the Memphis victory by raising the Stars and Stripes over the post office — had succeeded his uncle, Brigadier General A. W. Ellet, who had succeeded the first Ellet as commander of the ram fleet, as skipper of the *Queen*. Patched up from the two poundings she had taken from Vicksburg's high-perched guns, and fitted out now with guns of her own for the first time — previously she had depended solely on her punch — she made her run at daybreak, February 4, taking an even dozen hits, including two in the hull but none below the water line, and pulled up at a battery Sherman had established on the west bank, just around the bend, for the protection of his diggers. Above the town, two nights later, Porter set adrift a barge loaded with 20,000 bushels of coal, which made it downstream on schedule and without mishap, apparently not having been spotted by the lookouts on the bluff. "This gives the ram nearly coal enough to last a month," the admiral proudly informed Secretary Welles, "in which time she can commit great havoc, if no accident happens to her."

Though at first it seemed an unnecessary flourish — he knew the rebels had nothing afloat to match the *Queen* — that final reservation was prophetic. Setting out on the night of February 10, accompanied by an ex-Confederate steamboat, the *DeSoto*, which had been captured by the army below Vicksburg, Ellet began his career as a commerce raider in fine style, slipping past the Warrenton batteries undetected and going to work at once on enemy shipping by destroying skiffs and flatboats on both banks. He burned or commandeered hundreds of bales of cotton, taking some aboard for "armoring" the wheelhouse, destroyed supply trains heavily loaded with grain and salt pork being sent to collection points, and in reprisal for a sniper bullet, which struck one of his sailors in the leg, burned no less than three plantation houses, together with their outbuildings, apparently undismayed even when one planter's daughter sang "The Bonny Blue Flag" full in his face as the flames crackled. His greatest single prize, however, was the corn-laden packet *Era No. 5*, which he captured after passing Natchez and entering the Red River. But at that point, or just beyond it — seventy-five miles from the mouth of the river and with Alexandria in a turmoil less than half that far ahead — he and the *Queen* ran out of luck. On Valentine's Day, approaching Gordon's Landing, where a battery of guns had been reported, the ram stuck fast on a mud flat and was taken suddenly under fire by enemy gunners who yelled with delight at thus being offered a stationary target at a range of four hundred yards. In short order the boat's engine controls were smashed, her escape-pipe shot away, her boiler fractured. As she disappeared in hissing clouds of steam — one survivor later claimed to have avoided scalding his lungs because "I had sufficient presence of mind to cram the tail of my coat into my mouth" — officers and men began to tumble bales of cotton over the rail, then leap after them into the river, clinging to them in hope of reaching the *DeSoto* or the *Era*, a mile below. By now it was every man for himself, including the wounded, and the youthful skipper was not among the last to abandon the *Queen* in favor of a downstream ride astride a bale of cotton.

Picked up by the *DeSoto*, Ellet and the others were alarmed to discover that in the excitement she had unshipped both rudders and become unmanageable; so they set her afire and abandoned her, too, in favor of the more recently captured *Era*. Their career as raiders had lasted just four days. From now on, their only concern was escape, which seemed unlikely because of reports that the Confederates had at Alexandria a high-speed steamboat, the *William H. Webb*, which would surely be after them as soon as the news arrived upriver. She mounted only one gun, they had heard, and would never have dared to tackle the *Queen*, but now the tables were more or less turned; the pursuers became the pursued. "With a sigh for the poor fellows left behind, and a hope that our enemies would be merciful," a survivor wrote, "the prow of the *Era* was turned toward the Mississippi." They made it by daylight, after a race through stormy darkness unrelieved except for blinding flashes of lightning, and started north up the big river, heaving overboard all possible incidentals, including rations, in an attempt to coax more speed from their unarmed boat. Next morning, February 16, just below Natchez, with the *Webb* reportedly closing fast on their stern, they were startled to see an enormous, twin-stacked vessel bearing down on them from dead ahead. Their dismay at the prospect of being ground between two millstones was relieved, however, when the lookout identified her as the *Indianola*. The latest addition to the ironclad fleet and the pride of the Federal inland-waters navy, she mounted two great 11-inch smoothbores forward and a pair of 9-inch rifles amidships, casemated between her towering sidewheel-boxes, while for power she boasted four engines, driving twin screws in addition to her paddles, and she had brought two large barges of coal along, one lashed to starboard and one to port, to insure a long-term stay on the previously rebel-held 250-mile stretch of river above Port Hudson. Porter had sent her down past the Vicksburg batteries three nights ago, intending for her to support the *Queen* and thus, as he said, "make matters doubly sure."

Learning from Ellet that the *Queen* had been lost, Lieutenant Commander George Brown, captain of the *Indianola*, decided at once to proceed downriver, accompanied by the *Era*. Presently they sighted the *Webb*, in hot pursuit, and once more the tables were turned; for the *Webb* took one quick look at the iron-clad monster and promptly made use of her superior speed to withdraw before coming within range of those 11-inch guns, two short-falling shots from which only served to hurry her along, as one observer said, "for all the world like a frightened racehorse." Brown gave chase as far as the mouth of Red River, up which the rebel vessel disappeared, but there he called a halt, Porter having warned him not to venture up that stream without an experienced pilot, which he lacked. While Brown continued on patrol, guarding against a re-emergence of the *Webb*, Ellet took off northward in the *Era* with the unpleasant duty of informing Porter that he had lost the *Queen*. Two days later, still on patrol at the mouth of the Red, Brown received astounding news. The Confederates had resurrected the *Queen of the West*, patching up her punctured hull and repairing her fractured steam drum. Even now, in company with the skittish *Webb* and two cottonclad boats whose upper decks were crowded with sharpshooters, she was preparing to come out after the *Indianola*. Brown thought it over and decided to retire.

He would have done better to leave without taking time to think it over; the fuze was burning shorter than he knew. However, he was in for a fight in any event because of the two coal barges, which he knew would decrease his upstream speed considerably, but which he was determined to hold onto, despite the fact that the *Indianola*'s bunkers were chock-full. Partly this decision was the result of his ingrained peacetime frugality, but mostly it was because he wanted to have plenty of fuel on hand in case Porter complied with his request, forwarded by Ellet, that another gunboat be sent downriver as a replacement for the *Queen*. Brown left the mouth of the Red on Saturday, February 21, and stopped for the night at a plantation landing up the Mississippi to take on a load of cotton bales, which he stacked around the ironclad's low main deck to make her less vulnerable to boarders. Next morning he was off again in earnest, all four engines straining to offset the drag of the two barges lashed alongside. He did not know how much of a head start he had, but he feared it was not enough. In point of fact, it was even less than he supposed; for the four-boat Confederate flotilla, including the resurrected *Queen*, set out after him at about the same hour that Sunday morning, ninety miles astern of the landing where the *Indianola* had commandeered the cotton. The race was on.

It was not really much of a race. Major Joseph L. Brent, commanding the quartet of rebel warships, each of which was in the charge of an army captain, could have overtaken Brown at almost anytime Tuesday afternoon, the 24th, but he preferred to wait for darkness, which would not only make the aiming of the ironclad's big guns more difficult but would also give the Grand Gulf batteries a chance at her as she went by. Held to a crawl though she was by the awkward burden of her barges, the *Indianola* got past that danger without mishap; but Brown could see the smoke from his pursuers' chimneys drawing closer with every mile as the sun declined, and he knew that he was in for a fight before it rose again. He also knew by now that no reinforcing consort was going to join him from the fleet above Vicksburg, in spite of which he held doggedly to his barges, counting on them to give him fender protection from ram attacks. As darkness fell, moonless but dusky with starlight, he cleared for action and kept half of his crew at battle stations: "watch and watch," it was called. At 9.30 he passed New Carthage, which put him within thirteen miles of the nearest west-bank Union battery, but by that time the rebel boats were in plain sight. Abreast of Palmyra Island, heading into Davis Bend — so called because it flowed past the Confederate President's Brierfield Plantation — Brown swung his iron prow around to face his pursuers at last, thus bringing his heavy guns to bear and protecting his more vulnerable stern.

As the *Queen* and the *Webb* came at him simultaneously, the former in the lead, he fired an 11-inch shell point-blank at each. Both missed, and the *Queen* was on him, lunging in from port with such force that the barge on that side was sliced almost in two. Emerging unscathed from this, except for the loss of the barge, which was cut adrift to sink, the *Indianola* met the *Webb* bows on, with a crash that knocked most of both crews off their feet and left the Confederate with a gash in her bow extending from water line to keelson, while the Federal was comparatively unhurt. Nevertheless the *Webb* backed off and struck again, crushing the remaining barge so completely as to leave it hanging by the lashings. Meanwhile the *Queen*, having run upstream a ways to gain momentum, turned and came charging down, striking her adversary just abaft the starboard wheelhouse, which was wrecked along with the rudder on that side, and starting a number of leaks along the shaft. Likewise the *Webb*, having gained momentum in the same fashion, brought her broken nose down hard and fair on the crippled ironclad's lightly armored stern, starting the timbers and causing the water to pour in rapidly. All this time the *Indianola* had kept throwing shells into the smoky darkness, left and right, but had scored only a single hit on the *Queen*, which did no considerable damage to the boat herself though it killed two and wounded four of her crew. Brown, having done his worst with this one shot, was now in a hopeless condition, scarcely able to steer and with both of his starboard engines flooded. After waiting a while in midstream until the water had risen nearly to the grate-bars of the ironclad's furnaces, planning thus to avoid her capture by making sure that she would sink, he ran her hard into the more friendly west bank and hauled down his colors just as the two cottonclads came alongside, crowded with yelling rebels prepared for boarding. Quickly they leaped down and attached two ropes by which the steamers could haul the *Indianola* across the river to the Confederate-held east bank, barely making it in time for her to sink in ten feet of water. As soon as they got their prisoners ashore they went to work on the captured dreadnought, intending to raise her, as they had raised the *Queen of the West* the week before, for service under the Stars and Bars.

Though he had heard the heavy nighttime firing just downriver, Porter did not know for certain what had happened until two days later, when a seaman who had escaped from the *Indianola* during her brief contact with the western bank came aboard his flagship *Black Hawk* and gave him an eyewitness account of the tragedy. Coming as it did on the heels of news of the loss of the *Queen* — which in turn had been preceded, two months back, by the destruction of the *Cairo* — the blow was hard, especially since it included the information that the *Queen* had been taken over by the enemy and had played a leading part in the defeat of her intended consort, which was now about to be used in the same manner as soon as the rebels succeeded in getting her afloat. What made it doubly hard, for Porter at any rate, was the contrast between his present gloom and his recent optimism. "If you open the Father of Waters," Assistant Navy Secretary G. A. Fox had wired the acting rear admiral in response to reports of his progress just two weeks ago, "you will at once be made an admiral; besides we will try for a ribboned star.... Do your work up clean," Fox had added, "and the public will never be in doubt who did it. The flaming army correspondence misleads nobody. Keep cool, be very modest under great success, as a contrast to the soldiers." At any rate, such strain as there had been on Porter's modesty was removed by the awareness that all he had really accomplished so far — aside from the capture of Arkansas Post, which had had to be shared with the army — was the loss of three of his best warships, two of which were now in enemy hands. What filled his mind just now was the thought of what this newest-model ironclad, the former pride of the Union fleet, could accomplish once she went into action on the Confederate side. Supported as she would be by the captured ram, she might well prove invincible in an upstream fight. In fact, any attempt to challenge her en masse would probably add other powerful units to the rebel flotilla of defected boats, since any disabled vessel would be swept helplessly downstream in such an engagement. Far from opening the Father of Waters, and gaining thereby a ribboned star and the permanent rank of admiral, Porter could see that he would be more likely to lose what had been won by his predecessors. Besides, even if he had wanted to launch such an all-out attack, he had no gunboats in the vicinity of Vicksburg now; they had been sent far upriver to co-operate in another of Grant's ill-fated amphibious experiments.

Porter was inventive in more ways than one, however, and his resourcefulness now stood him in good stead. If he had no available ironclad, then he would build one — or anyhow the semblance of one. Ordering every man off the noncombatant vessels to turn to, he took an old flat-bottomed barge, extended its length to three hundred feet by use of rafts hidden behind false bulwarks, and covered it over with flimsy decking to support a frame-and-canvas pilothouse and two huge but empty paddle-wheel boxes. A casemate was mounted forward, with a number of large-caliber logs protruding from its ports, and two tall smokestacks were erected by piling barrels one upon another. As a final realistic touch, after two abandoned skiffs were swung from unworkable davits, the completed dummy warship was given an all-over coat of tar. Within twenty-four hours, at a reported cost of $8.63, the navy had what appeared, at least from a distance, to be a sister ship of the *Indianola*. Belching smoke from pots of burning tar and oakum installed in her barrel stacks, she was set adrift the following night to make her run past the Vicksburg batteries. They gave her everything they had, but to no avail; her black armor seemingly impervious to damage, she glided unscathed past the roaring guns, not even deigning to reply. At daybreak she grounded near the lower end of Sherman's canal, and the diggers pushed her off again with a cheer. As she resumed her course downriver, the *Queen of the West,* coming up past Warrenton on a scout, spotted the dark behemoth in the distance, bearing down with her guns run out and her deck apparently cleared for action. The ram spun on her heel and sped back to spread the alarm: whereupon — since neither the *Queen* nor the broken-nosed *Webb* was in any condition for another fight just yet — all four of the Confederate vessels made off southward to avoid a clash with this second ironclad. Aboard the *Indianola,* still immobile and now deserted by her new friends, the lieutenant in charge of salvage operations was for holding onto her and fighting it out, despite repeated orders for him to complete her destruction before she could be recaptured. At a range of about two miles, the dreadnought halted as if to look the situation over before closing in for the bloody work she was bent on. Still the lieutenant held his ground until nightfall, when he decided to comply with the instructions of his superiors. After heaving the 9-inch rifles into the river, he laid the 11-inch smooth-bores muzzle to muzzle and fired them with slow matches. When the smoke from this had cleared, he came back and set fire to what was left, burning the wreckage to the water line and ending the brief but stormy career of the ironclad *Indianola.*

Next morning, seeing the black monster still in her former position, some two miles upriver — one observer later described her as "terrible though inert" — a party of Confederates went out in a rowboat to investigate. Drawing closer they recognized her for the hoax she was, and saw that she had come to rest on a mudbank. Nailed to her starboard wheelhouse was a crudely lettered sign. "Deluded people, cave in," it read.

"Then, too," Grant added, continuing the comment on his reasons for keeping McPherson's men sawing away at the underwater stumps and snags clogging the Bayou Baxter exit from Lake Providence even after he knew that, in itself, the work was unlikely to produce anything substantial, "it served as a cover for other efforts which gave a better prospect of success." What he had in mind — in addition, that is, to Sherman's canal, which was not to be abandoned until March — was a fifth experimental project, whose starting point was four hundred tortuous miles upriver from its intended finish atop the Vicksburg bluff. In olden days, just south of Helena and on the opposite bank, a bayou had afforded egress from the Mississippi; Yazoo Pass, it was called, because it connected eastward with the Coldwater River, which flowed south into the Tallahatchie, which in turn combined with the Yalobusha, farther down, to form the Yazoo. Steamboats once had plied this route for trade with the planters of the delta hinterland. In fact, they still steamed up and down this intricate chain of rivers, but only by entering from below, through the mouth of the Yazoo River; for the state of Mississippi had sealed off the northern entrance, five years before the war, by constructing across the mouth of Yazoo Pass a levee which served to keep the low-lying cotton fields from going under water with every rise of the big river. Now it was Grant's notion that perhaps all he needed to do, in order to utilize this old peacetime trade route for his wartime purpose, was cut the levee and send in gunboats to provide cover for transports, which then could be unloaded on high ground — well down the left bank of the Yazoo but short of Haines Bluff, whose fortifications blocked an ascent of that river from below — and thus, by forcing the outnumbered defenders to come out into the open for a fight which could only result in their defeat, take Vicksburg from the rear. Accordingly, at the same time he ordered McPherson down from Memphis to Lake Providence, he sent his chief topographical engineer, Lieutenant Colonel James H. Wilson, to inspect and report on the possibility of launching such an attack by way of Yazoo Pass.

Wilson, described by a contemporary as "a slight person of a light complexion and with rather a pinched face," was enthusiastic from the start. An Illinois regular, only two years out of West Point and approaching his twenty-sixth birthday, he recently had been transferred from the East, where he had served as an aide to McClellan at Antietam, and he had approached his western assignment with doubts, particularly in regard to Grant, whose "simple and unmilitary bearing," as the young man phrased it, made a drab impression by contrast with the recent splendor of Little Mac, whose official family had included an Astor and two genuine French princes of the blood. But in this case familiarity bred affection; Wilson soon was remarking that his new commander was "a most agreeable companion both on the march and in camp." What drew him more than anything, however, was the trust Grant showed in sending him to take charge of the opening phase of this fifth and latest project for the reduction of the Gibraltar of the West. After a bit of preliminary surveying and shovel work, he wasted no time. On the evening of February 3 — while Ellet prepared to take the *Queen* past the Vicksburg bluff at daybreak and Grant himself was about to head upriver for a first-hand look at Lake Providence — Wilson mined and blew the levee sealing the mouth of Yazoo Pass. The result was altogether spectacular, he reported, "water pouring through like nothing else I ever saw except Niagara." After waiting four days for the surface level to equalize, east and west of the cut, he boarded a gunboat, steamed "with great ease" into Moon Lake, a mile beyond, and "ran down it about five miles to where the Pass leaves it." Hard work was going to be involved, he wrote Grant's adjutant, but he was confident of a large return on such an investment. Grant was infected at once with the colonel's enthusiasm. Wilson already had with him a 4500-man division from Helena; now a second division was ordered to join him from there. Presently, when he reported that he had got through to the Coldwater, McPherson was told to be prepared to follow with his whole corps. "The Yazoo Pass expedition is going to prove a perfect success," Grant informed Elihu B. Washburne, his home-state Representative and congressional guardian angel.

Hard work had been foreseen, and that was what it took. Emerging from Moon Lake, Wilson found the remaining twelve-mile segment of the pass sufficiently deep but so narrow in some places that the gunboat could not squeeze between giant oaks and cypresses growing on opposite banks. These had to be felled with axes, a patience-testing business but by no means the most discouraging he encountered. Warned of his coming, the Confederates had brought in working parties of slaves from surrounding plantations and had chopped down other trees, some of them more than four feet through the bole, so that they lay athwart the bayou, ponderous and apparently immovable. Undaunted, Wilson borrowed navy hawsers long enough to afford simultaneous handholds for whole regiments of soldiers, whom he put to work snaking the impediments out of the way. They did it with such ease, he later remarked, that he never afterwards wondered how the Egyptians had lifted the great stones in place when they built the Pyramids; enough men on a rope could move anything, he decided. Still, he had no such span of time at his disposal as the Pharaohs had had, and this was at best a time-consuming process. February was almost gone before he reached the eastern end of the pass. South of there, however, he expected to find clear sailing. The Coldwater being "a considerable stream," he reported, vessels of almost any length and draft could be sent from the Mississippi into the Tallahatchie in just four days. And so it proved when a ten-boat flotilla, including two ironclads, two steam rams, and six tinclads — the 22 light transports were to come along behind — tried it during the first week in March. In fact, it was not until the warships were more than a hundred miles down the winding Tallahatchie, near its junction with the Yalobusha, that Wilson realized he was in for a great deal more trouble, and of a kind he had not encountered up to now.

The trouble now was the rebels themselves, not just the various obstructions they had left in his path before fading back into the swamps and woods. Five miles above Greenwood, a hamlet at the confluence of the rivers, they had improvised on a boggy island inclosed by a loop of the Tallahatchie a fort whose parapets, built of cotton bales and reinforced with sandbags, were designed not only to deflect heavy projectiles but also to keep out the river itself, which had gone well past the flood stage when the Yankees blew the levee far upstream. Fort Pemberton, the place was called, and it had as its commander a man out of the dim Confederate past: Brigadier General Lloyd Tilghman, who had fought against Grant and the ironclads under similar circumstances at Fort Henry, thirteen months ago. Exchanged and reinstated, he was determined to wipe out that defeat, though the odds were as long and the tactical situation not much different. His immediate superior, Major General W. W. Loring, was also a carry-over from the past, and as commander of the delta subdepartment he intended to give the Federals even more trouble than he had given Lee and Jackson in Virginia the year before, which was considerable. A third relic on the scene was the former U.S. ocean steamer *Star of the West*, whose name had been in the scareheads three full months before the war, when the Charleston batteries fired on her for attempting the relief of Sumter. Continuing on to Texas, she had been captured in mid-April by Van Dorn at Indianola and was in the rebel service as a receiving-ship at New Orleans a year later, when Farragut provoked her flight up the Mississippi and into the Yazoo to avoid recapture. Here above Greenwood she ended her days afloat, but not her career, for she was sunk in the Tallahatchie alongside Fort Pemberton, blocking the channel and thus becoming an integral part of the outer defenses of Vicksburg. Three regiments, one from Texas and two from Mississippi, were all the high command could spare for manning the breastworks and the guns, which included one 6.4-inch rifle and half a dozen smaller pieces. This was scarcely a formidable armament with which to oppose 11-inch Dahlgrens housed in armored casemates, but on March 11 — while northward a long column of approaching warships and transports sent up a winding trail of smoke, stretching out of sight beyond the heavy screen of woods — the graybacks were a determined crew as they sighted their guns up the straight stretch of river giving down upon the fort.

Lieutenant Commander Watson Smith, who had charge of the ten-boat Union flotilla, was by now in a state of acute distress; he had never experienced anything like this in all his years afloat. Coming through Yazoo Pass into the Coldwater and down the Tallahatchie, all of which were so narrow in places that the gunboats had to be warped around the sharper bends with ropes, one tinclad had shattered her wheel and was out of action, while another had lost both smokestacks. All the rest had taken similar punishment in passing over rafts of driftwood or under projecting limbs that came sweeping and crashing along their upper works. The most serious of these mishaps was suffered when the *Chillicothe*, one of the two ironclads, struck a snag and started a plank in her bottom, which had to be held in place by beams shored in from the deck above. Smith's distress was greatly increased this morning, however, when this same unlucky vessel, at the head of the column, rounded the next-to-final bend leading down to the Yazoo and was struck hard twice on the turrets by high-velocity shells from dead ahead. She pulled back to survey the damage and fortify with cotton bales, then came on again that afternoon, accompanied by the other ironclad, the *De Kalb*. She got off four rounds at 800 yards and was about to fire a fifth — the loaders had already set the 11-inch shell in the gun's muzzle and were stripping the patch from the fuze — when a rebel shell came screaming through the port; both projectiles exploded on contact, killing 2 and wounding 11 of the gun crew. The two ironclads withdrew under urgent orders from Smith, whose distress had increased to the point where, according to Porter's subsequent report, he was showing "symptoms of aberration of mind."

Twice more, on the 13th and the 16th — without, however, attempting to close the range — the ironclads tried for a reduction of the fort at the end of that tree-lined stretch of river, as straight and uncluttered as a bowling alley: with similar results. Unable to maneuver in the narrow stream, the two boats took a terrible pounding, but could do little more than bounce their big projectiles off the resilient enemy parapet. The infantry, waiting rearward in the transports, gave no help at all; for the flooded banks made debarkation impossible, and any attempt at a small-boat attack — even if such boats had been available, which they were not — would have been suicidal. By the time the third day's bombardment was over, both ironclads were badly crippled; the *De Kalb* had lost ten of her gun-deck beams and her steerage was shot to pieces, while the luckless *Chillicothe* had more of her crew felled by armor bolts driven inward, under the impact of shells from the hard-hitting enemy rifle, to fly like bullets through the casemate. On March 17, in an apparent moment of lucidity, Smith ordered the flotilla to withdraw. Everyone agreed that this was the wisest course: everyone but Wilson, who complained hotly to Grant that the issue had not been pressed. "To let one 6½-inch rifle stop our navy. Bah!" he protested, and put the blame on "Acting Rear Admiral, Commodore, Captain, Lieutenant-Commander Smith" and the other naval officers. "I've talked with them all and tried to give them backbone," he said, "but they are not confident."

Returning up the Coldwater two days later — while Loring and Tilghman were celebrating the repulse in victory dispatches sent downriver to Vicksburg — the disconsolate Federals met the second Helena division on its way to reinforce them under Brigadier General Isaac Quinby, who outranked all the brass at hand and was unwilling to retreat without so much as a look at what stood in the way of an advance. So the expedition turned around and came back down again. Stopping short of the bend leading into the bowling alley, the men aboard the transports and gunboats slapped at mosquitoes and practiced their marksmanship on alligators, while Quinby conducted a boggy twelve-day reconnaissance which finally persuaded him that Smith had been right in the first place. Besides, even Wilson was convinced by now that the game was not worth the candle, for the rebels had brought up another steamboat which they were "either ready to sink or use as a boarding-craft and ram," and it seemed to the young colonel that they were "making great calculations 'to bag us' entire." He agreed that the time had come for a final departure. This began on April 5 and brought the Yazoo Pass experiment to a close. Being, as he said, "solicitous for my reputation at headquarters," Wilson ended a letter to Grant's adjutant with a request for the latest staff gossip, and thought to add: "Remember me kindly to the general."

His fears, though natural enough in an ambitious young career officer who had failed in his first independent assignment, were groundless. For unlike Porter, who no sooner learned the details of the Tallahatchie nightmare than he relieved Watson Smith of duty with the fleet and sent him North — where presently, by way of proving that his affliction had been physical as well as mental, he died in a delirium of fever and chagrin — Grant did not hold the collapse of this fifth experiment against his subordinate, but rather, when Wilson returned at last to Young's Point after an absence of more than two months, welcomed him back without reproach into the fold. By then the army commander had a better appreciation of the problems that stood in the way of an amphibious penetration of the delta, having been involved simultaneously in a not unsimilar nightmare of his own. In point of fact, however, no matter how little he chose to bring it to bear, Porter had even greater occasion for such charity, since he had been more intimately involved, not only as the author but also as the on-the-scene director of this latest fiasco, the sole result of which had been the addition of a sixth to the sequence of failures designed for the reduction of Vicksburg.

Left with time more or less on his hands after the downriver loss of two of his best warships, and being anxious moreover to offset the damage to his reputation with an exploit involving something less flimsy than a dummy ironclad, the admiral pored over his charts and made various exploratory trips up and down the network of creeks and bayous flowing into the Yazoo River below Haines Bluff, whose guns he had learned to respect back in December. Five miles upstream from its junction with the Mississippi, the Yazoo received the sluggish waters of Steele Bayou, and forty miles up Steele Bayou, Black Bayou connected eastward with Deer Creek, which in turn, at about the same upstream distance and by means of another bayou called Rolling Fork, connected eastward with the Sunflower River. That was where the payoff came within easy reach; for the Sunflower flowed into the Yazoo, fifty miles below, offering the chance for an uncontested high-ground landing well above the Haines Bluff fortifications, which then could be assaulted from the rear or bypassed on the way to the back door of Vicksburg. Though the route was crooked and the distance great — especially by contrast; no less than two hundred roundabout miles would have to be traversed by the column of gunboats and transports in order to put the troops ashore no more than twenty air-line miles above their starting point — Porter was so firmly convinced he had found the solution to the knotty Vicksburg problem that he called at Young's Point and persuaded Grant to come aboard the *Black Hawk* for a demonstration. Steaming up the Yazoo, the admiral watched the tree-fringed north bank for a while, then suddenly to his companion's amazement signaled the helm for a hard turn to port, into brush that was apparently impenetrable. So far, high water had been the curse of the campaign, but now it proved an asset. As the boat swung through the leafy barrier, which parted to admit it, the leadsman sang out a sounding of fifteen feet — better than twice the depth the ironclads required. Formerly startled, Grant was now convinced, especially when Porter informed him that they were steaming above an old road once used for hauling cotton to the river. Practically all the lower delta was submerged, in part because of the seasonal rise of the rivers, but mostly because of the cut Wilson had made in the levee, four hundred miles upstream at Yazoo Pass; a tremendous volume of water had come down the various tributaries and had spread itself over the land. It was Porter's contention, based on limited reconnaissance, that as a result all those creeks and bayous would be navigable from end to end by vessels of almost any size, including the gunboats and transports selected to thread the labyrinth giving down upon the back-door approach to Vicksburg. Infected once more with contagious enthusiasm, Grant returned without delay to Young's Point, where he issued orders that same night for the army's share in what was known thereafter as the Steele Bayou expedition.

Sherman drew the assignment, along with one of his two divisions of men who just that week had been flooded out of their pick-and-shovel work on the doomed canal, and went up the Mississippi to a point where a long bend swung eastward to within a mile of Steele Bayou. On the afternoon of March 16, after slogging across this boggy neck of land, he made contact with the naval units, which had come up by way of the Yazoo that morning. As soon as he got his troops aboard the waiting transports the column resumed its progress northward, five ironclads in the lead, followed by four all-purpose tugs and a pair of mortar boats which Porter, not knowing what he might encounter in the labyrinth ahead, had had "built for the occasion." With his mind's eye fixed on permanent rank and the ribboned star Fox had promised to try for, the admiral was taking no chances he could avoid. All went well — as he had expected because of his preliminary reconnaissance — until the gunboats approached Black Bayou, where the unreconnoitered portion of the route began. This narrow, four-mile, time-forgotten stretch of stagnant water was not only extremely crooked, it was also filled with trees. Porter used his heavy boats to butt them down, bulldozer style, and hoisted them aside with snatch blocks. This was heavy labor, necessarily slow, and as it progressed the column changed considerably in appearance. Overhead branches swept the upper decks of the warships, leaving a mess of wreckage in the place of boats and woodwork. Occasionally, too, as Porter said, "a rude tree would throw Briarean arms" around the stacks of the slowly passing vessels, "and knock their bonnets sideways." After about a mile of this, Sherman's men were put to work with ropes and axes, clearing a broader passage for the transports, while the sturdier ironclads forged ahead, thumping and bumping their way into Deer Creek, where they resumed a northward course next morning.

But this was worse in several ways, one of them being that the creek was even narrower than the bayou. If the trees were fewer, they were also closer together, and vermin of all kinds had taken refuge in them from the flood; so that when one of the gunboats struck a tree the quivering limbs let fall a plague of rats, mice, cockroaches, snakes, and lizards. Men were stationed about the decks with brooms to rid the vessels of such unwelcome boarders, but sometimes the sweepers had larger game to contend with, including coons and wildcats. These last, however, "were prejudiced against us, and refused to be comforted on board," the admiral subsequently wrote, "though I am sorry to say we found more Union feeling among the bugs." To add to the nightmare, Deer Creek was the crookedest stream he had ever encountered: "One minute an ironclad would apparently be leading ahead, and the next minute would as apparently be steering the other way." Along one brief stretch, less than half a mile in length, the five warships were steaming in five quite different directions. Moreover, this was a region of plantations, which meant that there were man-made obstacles such as bridges, and though these gave the heavy boats no real trouble — they could plow through them as if they were built of matchsticks — other impediments were more disturbing. For example, hearing of the approach of the Yankees, the planters had had their baled cotton stacked along both creekbanks and set afire in order to keep it out of the hands of the invaders: with the result that, from time to time, the gunboats had to run a fiery gauntlet. The thick white smoke sent the crews into spasms of coughing, while the heat singed their hair, scorched their faces, and blistered the paint from the vessels' iron flanks.

So far, despite the crowds of field hands who lined the banks to marvel at the appearance of ironclads where not even flat-bottomed packets had ventured before, Porter had not seen a single white man. He found this odd, and indeed somewhat foreboding. Presently, however, spotting one sitting in front of a cabin and smoking a pipe as if nothing unusual were going on around him, the admiral had the flagship stopped just short of another bridge and summoned the man to come down to the landing; which he did — a burly, rough-faced individual, in shirt sleeves and bareheaded; "half bulldog, half bloodhound," Porter called him. When the admiral began to question him he identified himself as the plantation overseer. "I suppose you are Union, of course?" Porter said. "You all are so when it suits you." "No, by God, I'm not, and never will be," the man replied. "As to the others, I know nothing about them. Find out for yourself. I'm for Jeff Davis first, last, and all the time. Do you want any more of me?" he added; "for I am not a loquacious man at any time." "No, I want nothing more with you," Porter said. "But I am going to steam into that bridge of yours across the stream and knock it down. Is it strongly built?" "You may knock it down and be damned," the overseer told him. "It don't belong to me." Catching something in his accent, Porter remarked: "You're a Yankee by birth, are you not?" "Yes, damn it, I am," the man admitted. "But that's no reason I should like the institution. I cut it long ago." And with this he turned on his heel and walked away. Porter had the skipper ring "Go ahead fast," and the ironclad smashed through the bridge about as easily as if it had not been there. When he looked back, however, to see what impression this had made on the overseer, he saw him seated once more in front of the cabin, smoking his pipe, not having bothered even to turn his head and watch. Deciding that the fellow "was but one re-move from a brute," Porter was disturbed by the thought that "there were hundreds more like him" lurking somewhere in the brush. At any rate, he fervently hoped that Sherman's men — particularly one regi-ment, which had the reputation of being able to "catch, scrape, and skin a hog without a soldier leaving the ranks" — would "pay the apostate Yankee a visit, if only to teach him good manners."

Under the circumstances, even aside from the necessary halts, half a mile an hour was the best speed the ironclads could make on this St Patrick's Day. Nightfall overtook them a scant eight miles from the morning's starting point. Twelve miles they made next day, but the in-creased speed increased the damage to the boats, including the loss of all the skylights to falling debris, and when they stopped engines for the night, Porter heard from up ahead the least welcome of all sounds: the steady chuck of axes, informing him that the rebels were warned of his coming. He wished fervently for Sherman, whose men were still at work in Black Bayou, widening a pathway for their transports, and con-soled himself with the thought that the red-haired general would be along eventually; "there was only one road, so he couldn't have taken the wrong one." For the present, however, he did what he could with what he had, sending the mortar boats forward in the darkness; and when their firing stopped, so had the axes. Next morning, March 19, he pushed on. Despite the delay involved in hoisting the felled trees aside, he made such good progress that by nightfall he was within half a mile of the entrance to Rolling Fork. At daybreak he steamed north again, but the flagship had gone barely two hundred yards when, just ahead and extending all the way across the creek, the admiral saw "a large green patch . . . like the green scum on ponds." He shouted down from the bridge to one of the admiring field hands on the bank: "What is that?" "It's nuffin but willers, sah," the Negro replied, explaining that in the off season the plantation workers often went out in skiffs and canoes to cut the willow wands for weaving baskets. "You kin go through dat lak a eel."

That this last was an overstatement — based on a failure to realize that, unlike skiffs and canoes, the gunboats moved *through* rather than *over* the water, and what was more had paddle wheels and overlapping plates of armor — Porter discovered within a couple of minutes of giving the order to go ahead. Starting with a full head of steam, the ironclad made about thirty yards before coming to a dead stop, gripped tightly by the willow withes, not unlike Gulliver when he woke to find himself in Lilliputian bonds. The admiral called for hard astern; but that was no good either; the vessel would not budge. Here was a ticklish situation. The high creekbanks rendered the warships practically helpless, for their guns would not clear them even at extreme elevation. Not knowing what he would do if the Confederates made a determined boarding attack, Porter fortified a nearby Indian mound with four smoothbore howitzers and put the flagship's crew over the side with knives and hooks and orders to cut her loose, twig by twig. It was slow work; "I wished ironclads were in Jericho," he later declared. Just then his wish seemed about to be fulfilled. The shrill shrieks of two rifle shots, which he recognized as high-velocity Whitworths, were followed at once by a pair of bursts, abrupt as blue-sky thunder and directly over the mound. Suddenly, in the wake of these two ranging shots — within six hundred yards of Rolling Fork and less than ten miles from clear sailing down the broad and unobstructed Sunflower River — two six-gun rebel batteries were firing on the outranged smoothbores from opposite directions, and the naval commander was shocked to see his cannoneers come tumbling down the rearward slope of the mound, seeking cover from the rain of shells. Continuing to hack at the clinging willows, he got his mortars into counterbattery action and, with the help of half a dollar, persuaded a "truthful contraband" (so Porter termed him later, but just then he called him Sambo; which drew the reply, "My name aint Sambo, sah. My name's Tub") to attempt to get a message through to Sherman and his soldiers, wherever downstream they might be by now. "Dear Sherman," the note began: "Hurry up, for Heaven's sake."

Tub reached Sherman on Black Bayou late that night, having taken various short cuts, and Sherman started northward before daylight, accompanied by all the troops on hand. Retracing the messenger's route through darkness, they carried lighted candles in their hands as they slogged waist-deep through swamps and canebrakes. "The smaller drummer boys had to carry their drums on their heads," the general afterwards recalled, "and most of the men slung their cartridge boxes around their necks." All the following day they pushed on, frequently losing their way, and into darkness again. At dawn Sunday, March 22, they heard from surprisingly close at hand the boom of Porter's mortars, punctuated by the sharper crack of the Whitworths. Presently they encountered rebels who had got below the ironclads and were felling trees to block their escape downstream. Sherman chased them from their work and pushed on. Soon he came within sight of the beleaguered flotilla, but found it woefully changed in appearance. After finally managing to extricate the willow-bound flagship with winches, Porter had unshipped the rudders of all five gunboats and was steaming backward down the narrow creek, fighting as he went. He had not only heard the sound of axes in his rear; what was worse, he had suddenly realized that the Confederates might dam the creek upstream with cotton bales and leave him stranded in the mud. The arriving bluecoats ran the snipers off — they were not actually so numerous as they seemed; just industrious — and came up to find the admiral on the deck of the flagship, directing the retreat from behind a shield improvised from a section of smokestack. "I doubt if he was ever more glad to meet a friend than he was to see me," Sherman later declared. For the present, though, he asked if Porter wanted him to go ahead and "clean those fellows out" so the navy could resume its former course. "Thank you, no," the admiral said. He had had enough, and so had Sherman, who complained hotly that this was "the most infernal expedition I was ever on." As Porter subsequently put it, "The game was up, and we bumped on homeward."

All the way downstream, from Deer Creek through Black Bayou, the sailors took a ribbing from the soldiers who stood along the banks to watch them go by, in reverse and rudderless. "Halloo, Jack," they would call. "How do you like playing mud turtle?" "Where's all your masts and sails, Jack?" "By the Widow Perkins, if Johnny Reb hasn't taken their rudders away and set them adrift!" But an old forecastleman gave as good as he got. "Dry up!" he shouted back at them. "We wa'n't half as much used up as you was at Chickasaw Bayou." So it went until the gunboats regained Steele Bayou and finally the mouth of the Yazoo, where they dropped anchor — those that still had them — and were laid up for repairs. Within another week they were supplied with new chimneys and skylights and woodwork; they glistened with fresh coats of paint, and according to Porter, "no one would have supposed we had ever been away from a dock-yard." By then, too, the officers had begun to discuss their share in this sixth of Grant's Vicksburg failures with something resembling nostalgia. There was an edge of pride in their voices as they spoke of the exploit, and some even talked of being willing to go again. But they did so, the admiral added, much "as people who have gone in search of the North Pole, and have fared dreadfully, wish to try it once more."

Despite the high hopes generated during the preliminary re-connaissance up Steele Bayou, Grant was no more discouraged by this penultimate failure, reported in no uncertain terms by a disgusted Sherman, than he had been by the preceding five. Now as before, he already had a successive experiment in progress, which served to distract the public's attention and occupy his mind and men. Besides, for once, he had good news to send along to Washington with the bad — the announcement of the first real success achieved by Federal arms on the river since his arrival in late January — although his pleasure in reporting it was considerably diminished by the fact that it had been accomplished not in his own department but in Banks's, not by the army but by the navy, and not by Porter but by Farragut.

Banks himself had been having troubles that rivaled Grant's, if not in number — being limited by a lack of corresponding ingenuity and equipment in his attempts to come to grips with the problem — then at any rate in thorniness. Port Hudson was quite as invulnerable to a frontal assault as Vicksburg, so that here too the solution was restricted to two methods: either to attack the hundred-foot bluff from the rear or else to go around it. He worked hard for a time at the latter, seeking a route up the Atchafalaya, into the Red, and thence into the Mississippi, fifty miles above the Confederate bastion. At first this appeared to be ready-made for his use, but it turned out to be impractical on three counts. 1) He had only one gunboat designed for work on the rivers; 2) a large portion of the Atchafalaya basin was under water as a result of breaks in the neglected levees; and 3) he became convinced that to leave the rebel garrison alive and kicking in his rear would be to risk, if not invite, the recapture of New Orleans. This last was so unthinkable that it no sooner occurred to him than he abandoned all notion of such an attempt. As for attacking Port Hudson from the rear, he perceived that this would be about as risky as attacking it from the front. Knowing nothing of Grant's success or failure upriver, except the significant fact that something must have happened to delay him, Banks did not know but what the Confederates would be free to concentrate against him from all directions, including the north, as soon as he got his troops ashore; which would mean, at best, that he would lose his siege train in a retreat from superior numbers, and at worst that he would lose his army. Thus both methods of approaching a solution to the problem seemed to him likely to end in disaster; he did not know what to do, at least until he could get in touch with Grant upstream. Consequently, he did nothing.

This reverse approach, with its stress on what the enemy might do to him, rather than on what he intended to do to the enemy, had not been Grant's way of coming to grips with the similar problem, some three hundred miles upstream; nor was it Farragut's. The old sea dog —

approaching sixty-two, he was Tennessee-born and twice married, both times to Virginians, which had caused some doubt as to his loyalty in the early months of the war — had surmounted what had seemed to be longer odds below New Orleans the year before, and he was altogether willing to try it again, "army or no army." In early March, when he received word that the rebels, by way of reinforcing their claim to control of the whole Red River system, along with so much of the Mississippi as ran between Vicksburg and Port Hudson, had captured the steam ram *Queen of the West*, he took the action as a challenge to personal combat; especially when they emphasized it by sinking and seizing the ironclad *Indianola*, which for all he knew was about to join the *Queen* in defying the flag she once had flown. He promptly assembled his seven wooden ships off Profit's Island, seven miles below Port Hudson, intending to take them past the fortified heights for a showdown with the renegade boats upriver. He had with him the three heavy sloops-of-war *Hartford*, *Richmond*, and *Monongahela*, the old side-wheeler *Mississippi*, and three gunboats. All were ocean-going vessels, unarmored but mounting a total of 95 guns, mostly heavy — the flagship *Hartford* alone carried two dozen 9-inch Dahlgrens — with which to oppose the 21 pieces manned by the Confederates ashore. This advantage in the weight of metal would be offset considerably, however, by the plunging fire of the guns on the hundred-foot bluff and by the five-knot current, which would hold the ships to a crawl as they rounded the sharp bend at its foot. In an attempt to increase the speed and power of his slower and larger ships, Farragut gave instructions for the three gunboats to be lashed to the unengaged port sides of the three sloops; the *Mississippi*, whose paddle boxes would not allow this, would have to take her chances unassisted. It was the admiral's hope that the flotilla would steam past undetected in the moonless darkness, but a greenhorn chaplain, watching the gun crews place within easy reach "little square, shallow, wooden boxes filled with sawdust, like the spittoons one used to see in country barrooms," was shocked to learn that the contents were to be scattered about the deck as "an absorbent" to keep the men from slipping in their own blood, when and if the guns began to roar and hits were scored. At 9.30 p.m. March 14, the prearranged signal — two red lights described by the same impressionable chaplain as "two distinct red spots like burning coals" — appeared just under the stern of the flagship in the lead, and the run began.

At first it went as had been planned and hoped for. Undetected, unsuspected, the *Hartford* led the way up the long straight stretch of river leading due north into the bend that would swing the column west-southwest; she even cleared the first battery south of town, her engines throbbing in the darkness, her pilot hugging the east bank to avoid the mudflat shallows of the point across the way. Then suddenly the night was bright with rockets and the glare of pitch-pine bonfires ignited by west-bank sentinels, who thus not only alerted the gun crews on the bluff, but also did them the service of illuminating their targets on the river down below. The fight began as it were in mid-crescendo. Still holding so close to the east bank that the men on her deck could hear the shouts of the enemy cannoneers, the flagship opened a rolling fire which was taken up in turn by the ships astern. The night was misty and windless; smoke settled thick on the water, leaving the helmsmen groping blindly and the gunners with nothing to aim at but the overhead muzzle flashes. In this respect the *Hartford* had the advantage, steaming ahead of her own smoke, but even she had her troubles, being caught by the swift current and swept against the enemy bank as she turned into the bend. Helped by her gunboat tug, she backed off and swung clear, chugging upstream at barely three knots, much damaged about her top and spars, but with only three men hit. Attempting to follow, the *Richmond* was struck by a plunging shot that crashed into her engine room and caromed about, cracking both port and starboard safety valves and dropping her boiler pressure below ten pounds. Too weak to make headway, even with the assistance of the gunboat lashed to her flank, she went with the current and out of the fight, leaking steam from all her ports, followed presently by the *Monongahela*, which suffered the same fate when her escort's rudder was wedged by an unlucky shot, one of her own engines was disabled by an overheated crankpin, and her captain was incapacitated by a shell that cut the bridge from under him and pitched him headlong onto the deck below. Between them, the two sloops and their escorts lost 45 killed and wounded before they veered out of range downriver. But the veteran frigate *Mississippi* — Commodore Matthew Perry's flagship, ten years ago, when he steamed into Tokyo Bay and opened Japan to the Western world — took the worst beating of the lot, not only from the Confederates on the bluff, but also from the gunners on the *Richmond*, who, not having gotten the word that the sloop had turned in the opposite direction, fired at the flashes of the side-wheeler's guns as they swept past her. Blind in the smoke, pounded alike by friend and foe, the pilot went into the bend and put the ship hard to larboard all too soon: with the result that she ran full tilt onto the mudflats across the way from the fuming bluff. Silhouetted against the glare of bonfires and taking hit after hit from the rebel guns, she tried for half an hour to pull loose by reversing her engines, but to no avail. Her captain ordered her set afire as soon as the crew — 64 of whom were casualties by now — could be taken off in boats, and it was only through the efforts of her executive, Lieutenant George Dewey, that many of her wounded were not roasted, including a badly frightened ship's boy he found hiding under a pile of corpses. Burning furiously, the *Mississippi* lightened before dawn and drifted off the flats of her own accord, threatening to set the other repulsed vessels afire as she passed unmanned among them and piled up at last on the head of Profit's Island, where she exploded with what an observer called "the grandest display of fireworks I ever witnessed, and the costliest."

It had been quite a costly operation all around. Thirty-five of the flotilla's 112 casualties were dead men — only two less than had been killed in the venture below New Orleans by a force almost three times as large — and of the seven ships that had attempted to run Port Hudson, one was destroyed and four had been driven back disabled. As a box score, this gave the Confederates ample claim to the honors of the engagement; but the fact remained that, whatever the cost, Farragut had done what he set out to do. He had put warships north of the bluff on the Mississippi, and he was ready to use them to dispute the rebel claim to control of the 250 miles of river below Vicksburg. Dropping down at dawn to just beyond range of Port Hudson's upper batteries, he fired the prearranged three-gun signal to let the rest of the flotilla know that he was still afloat, then set out upriver and anchored next morning off the mouth of the Red, up which he learned that the renegade *Queen* and the fast-steaming *Webb* had taken refuge after their flight from Porter's dummy ironclad. Both were too heavily damaged, as a result of their ram attacks on the *Indianola*, to be able to fight again without extensive repairs. So he heard; but he was taking no chances. Lowering the *Hartford*'s yards to the deck, he lashed them there and carried a heavy anchor chain from yard tip to yard tip, all the way round, to fend off attackers. Still unsatisfied, he improvised water-line armor by lashing cypress logs to the sides of the vessel and slung hawsers from the rigging, thirty feet above the deck, with heavy netting carried all the way down to the rail to frustrate would-be boarders. Then, accompanied by her six-gun escort *Albatross*, the *Hartford* — whose own builders would scarcely have recognized her, dressed out in this manner — set out northward, heading for Vicksburg in order to open communications with the upper fleet.

Passing Grand Gulf on March 19 the two ships came under fire that cost them 2 more killed and 6 more wounded, almost three times the number they had lost five nights ago; otherwise they encountered no opposition between Port Hudson and the point where they dropped anchor next morning, just beyond range of the lower Vicksburg batteries. Porter was up Steele Bayou, but conferring that afternoon with Grant and A. W. Ellet, the ram fleet commander, Farragut asked that he be reinforced by units from the upper flotilla. Ellet volunteered to send two of his boats, the *Switzerland* and the *Lancaster*, respectively under C. R. Ellet, the former captain of the *Queen*, and his uncle Lieutenant Colonel J. A. Ellet. They made their run at first light, March 25. The *Lancaster* was struck repeatedly in her machinery and hull, but she made it downstream, where a week's patchwork labor would put her back in shape to fight again. Not so the *Switzerland;* she received a shell in her boilers and others which did such damage to her hull that she went to pieces and sank, affording her nineteen-year-old skipper another ride on a bale of cotton. Unperturbed, Grant reported her loss as a blessing in disguise, since it served to reveal her basic unfitness for combat: "It is almost certain that had she made one *ram* into another vessel she would have closed up like a spy-glass, encompassing all on board."

In point of fact, whatever the cost and entirely aside from his accustomed optimism, he and all who favored the Union cause had much to be joyful about. As a result of this latest naval development, which would establish a blockade of the mouth of the Red and deny the rebels the use of their last extensive stretch of the Mississippi, Farragut had cut the Confederacy in two. The halves were still unconquered, and seemed likely to remain so for no one knew how long, but they were permanently severed one from the other. When the *Hartford* and the *Albatross* passed Port Hudson and were joined ten days later below Vicksburg by the steam ram *Lancaster*, the cattle and cereals of the Transmississippi, together with the goods of war that could be smuggled in through Mexico from Europe, became as inaccessible to the eastern South as if they were awaiting shipment on the moon.

This was not to say, conversely, that the Mississippi was open throughout its length to Federal commerce or even to Federal gunboats; that would not be the case, of course, until Vicksburg and Port Hudson had been taken or abolished. Continuing his efforts to accomplish this end, or anyhow his half of it, Grant was already engaged in the seventh of his experiments — which presently turned out to be the seventh of his failures. Work on the canal across the base of Vicksburg Point having been abandoned, he sent an engineering party out to find a better site for such a project close at hand. Receiving a report that a little digging south of Duckport, just above Young's Point, would give the light-draft vessels access to Roundaway Bayou, which entered the main river at New Carthage, well below the Vicksburg and Warrenton batteries, Grant gave McClernand's men a turn on the picks and shovels. For once, however, he had no great hope that much would come of the enterprise, even if it went as planned — only the lightest-draft supply boats would be able to get through; besides, there would still be the Grand Gulf batteries to contend with — and for once he was right. Even this limited success depended on a rise of the river; whereupon the river, perverse as always, began to fall, leaving Grant with a seventh failure on his hands.

"This campaign is being badly managed," Cadwallader Washburn, a brigadier in McPherson's corps, informed his congressman brother Elihu in Washington. "I am sure of it. I fear a calamity before Vicksburg. All Grant's schemes have failed. He knows that he has got to do something or off goes his head. My impression is that he intends to attack in front." (Washburn's fears were better founded than he knew. Grant had just written a long letter to Banks, reviewing his lack of progress up to now, and in it he had stated flatly: "There is nothing left for me but to collect my strength and attack Haines Bluff. This will necessarily be attended with much loss, but I think it can be done." On April Fools' Day, however, accompanying Porter up the Yazoo for a reconnaissance of the position, he decided that such an attack "would be attended with immense sacrifice of life, if not defeat," and abandoned the notion, adding: "This, then, closes out the last hope of turning the enemy by the right.") Nor were others, farther removed from the scene of action, more reticent in giving their opinion of the disaster in store for the Army of the Tennessee. For example Marat Halstead, editor of the *Cincinnati Commercial,* addressed his friend the Secretary of the Treasury on the matter: "You do once in a while, don't you, say a word to the President, or Stanton, or Halleck, about the conduct of the war? Well, now, for God's sake say that Genl Grant, entrusted with our greatest army, is a jackass in the original package. He is a poor drunken imbecile. He is a poor stick sober, and he is most of the time more than half drunk, and much of the time idiotically drunk.... Grant will fail miserably, hopelessly, eternally. You may look for and calculate his failures, in every position in which he may be placed, as a perfect certainty. Don't say I am grumbling. Alas! I know too well I am but feebly outlining the truth." Alarmed, Chase passed the letter on to Lincoln with the reminder that the *Commercial* was an influential paper, and the indorsement: "Reports concerning General Grant similar to the statements made by Mr Halstead are too common to be safely or even prudently disregarded." Lincoln read it with a sigh. "I think Grant has hardly a friend left, except myself," he told his secretary, and when a delegation came to protest Grant's alleged insobriety he put these civilians off with the remark, "If I knew what brand of whiskey he drinks I would send a barrel or so to some other generals." About this time a Nebraska brigadier, in Washington on leave from Vicksburg, called on the President and the two men got to talking. "What I want, and what the people want, is generals who will fight battles and win victories," Lincoln said. "Grant has done this, and I propose to stand by him."

The evidence was conflicting. Some said the general never touched a drop; others declared that he was seldom sober; while still others had him pegged as a spree drinker. "He tries to let liquor alone but he cannot resist the temptation always," a Wisconsin brigadier wrote home. "When he came to Memphis he left his wife at LaGrange, and for several days after getting here was beastly drunk, utterly incapable of doing anything. Quinby and I took him in charge, watching him day and night and keeping liquor away from him." According to this witness, the bender was only brought to an end when "we telegraphed to his wife and brought her on to take care of him." On the other hand, Mary Livermore — later famous as a suffragette — led a Sanitary Commission delegation down to Young's Point to investigate the rumors, and it was her opinion that the general's "clear eye, clean skin, firm flesh, and steady nerves ... gave the lie to the universal calumnies then current concerning his intemperate habits." Still unsatisfied, Stanton sent the former Brook Farm colonist and Greeley journalist Charles Dana down the Mississippi, ostensibly as an inspector of the pay service, but actually as a spy for the War Department. He arrived in early April, became in effect a member of the general's military family, and soon was filing reports that glowed with praise not only of Grant but also of Sherman and McPherson, declaring that in their "unpretending simplicity" the three Ohioans were "as alike as three peas." McClernand did not fare so well in these dispatches; for if Dana acquired a fondness for the army commander's friends, he also developed a dislike for his enemies. Later he summed up his findings by describing Grant as "the most modest, the most disinterested, and the most honest man I ever knew, with a temper that nothing could disturb and a judgment that was judicial in its comprehensiveness and wisdom. Not a great man except morally; not an original or brilliant man, but sincere, thoughtful, deep, and gifted with courage that never faltered."

Aside from the rhetoric here included, practically all of the general's soldiers would have agreed with this assessment of his character and abilities, even though it was delivered in the wake of seven failures. "Everything that Grant directs is right," one declared. "His soldiers believe in him. In our private talks among ourselves I never heard a single soldier speak in doubt of Grant." According to a New York reporter, this was not only because of "his energy and disposition to do something," it was also because he had "the remarkable tact of never spoiling any mysterious and vague notions which [might] be entertained in the minds of the privates as to the qualities of the commander-in-chief. He confines himself to saying and doing as little as possible before his men." Another described him as "a man who could be silent in several languages," and it was remarked that, on the march, he was more inclined to talk of "Illinois horses, hogs, cattle, and farming, than of the business actually at hand." In general he went about his job, as one observer had stated at the outset, "with so little friction and noise that it required a second look to be sure he was doing anything at all." One of his staff officers got the impression that he was "half a dozen men condensed into one," while a journalist, finding him puzzling in the extreme because he seemed to amount to a good deal more than the sum of all his parts, came up with the word "unpronounceable" as the one that described him best. Grant, he wrote, "has none of the soldier's bearing about him, but is a man whom one would take for a country merchant or a village lawyer. He had no distinctive feature; there are a thousand like him in personal appearance in the ranks. . . . A plain, unpretending face, with a comely, brownish-red beard and a square forehead, of short stature and thick-set. He is we would say a good liver, and altogether an unpronounceable man; he is so like hundreds of others as to be only described in general terms." The soldiers appreciated the lack of "superfluous flummery" as he moved among them, "turning and chewing restlessly the end of his unlighted cigar." They almost never cheered him, and they did not often salute him formally; rather, they watched him, as one said, "with a certain sort of familiar reverence." Present discouragements were mutual; so, someday, would be the glory. Somehow he was more partner than boss; they were in this thing together. "Good morning, General," "Pleasant day, General," were the usual salutations, more fitting than cheers or hat-tossing exhibitions; "A pleasant salute to, and a good-natured nod from him in return, seems more appropriate." All these things were said of him, and this: "Here was no McClellan, begging the boys to allow him to light his cigar on theirs, or inquiring to what regiment that exceedingly fine-marching company belonged. . . . There was no nonsense, no sentiment; only a plain business man of the republic, there for the one single purpose of getting that command over the river in the shortest time possible."

Yet the fact remained that he and they were into their third month of camping almost within the shadow of the Vicksburg bluff, and all they had accomplished so far was the addition of five to their previous two failures; they were still not "over the river." However, as the flood waters receded, defining the banks of the bayous and even the network of greasy-looking roads hub deep in mud, there were rumors that Grant was evolving an entirely new approach to the old problem. "As one after another of his schemes fail," Congressman Washburne heard from his brigadier brother — who had dropped the final euphonious "e" from his surname, presumably as superfluous baggage for a soldier — "I hear that he says he has a plan of his own which is yet to be tried [but] in which he has great confidence." Just what this was Grant would not say, either to subordinates or superiors, but his staff observed that he spent long hours in the former ladies' cabin of his headquarters boat the *Magnolia*, blueing the air with cigar smoke as he pored over maps and tentative orders, not so much inaccessible ("I aint got no business with you, General," they heard one caller tell him; "I just wanted to have a little talk with you, because folks will ask me if I did") as removed, withdrawn behind a barrier of intense preoccupation. After several days of this, McPherson came into the cabin one evening, glass in hand, and stood facing Grant across the work-littered desk. "General, this won't do," he said. "You are injuring yourself. Join us in a few toasts, and throw this burden off your mind." Mrs Livermore, for one, would have been horrified, but what followed would have quickly reassured her. Grant looked up, smiled, and replied that whiskey was not the answer; if McPherson really wanted to help him, he said, he could give him a dozen cigars and leave him alone. McPherson did so, and Grant returned to brooding over his papers, still seeking a way to come to grips with the Confederates in their hilltop citadel.

Death of a Soldier

PIERRE GUSTAVE TOUTANT BEAUREGARD WAS
as flamboyant by nature as by name, and over the course of the past
two years this quality, coupled all too often with a readiness to lay
down the sword and take up the pen in defense of his reputation with
the public, had got him into considerable trouble with his superiors,
who sometimes found it difficult to abide his Creole touchiness off the
field of battle for the sake of his undoubted abilities on it. Called "Old
Bory" by his men, though he was not yet forty-five, the Hero of Sumter had twice been relieved of important commands, first in the East,
where he had routed McDowell's invasion attempt at Manassas, then in
the West, where he had saved his badly outnumbered army by giving
Halleck the slip at Corinth, and now he was back on the scene of his
first glory in Charleston harbor. Here, as elsewhere, he saw his position
as the hub of the wheel of war. Defying Union sea power, Mobile on
the Gulf and Wilmington, Savannah, and Charleston on the Atlantic remained in Confederate hands, and of these four it was clear at least to
Beauregard that the one the Federals coveted most was the last, variously referred to in their journals as "the hotbed of treachery," "the
cradle of secession," and "the nursery of disunion." Industrious as always, the general was determined that this proud South Carolina city
should not suffer the fate of his native New Orleans, no matter what
force the Yankees brought against it. Conducting frequent tours of inspection and keeping up as usual a voluminous correspondence — a
steady stream of requisitions for more guns and men, more warships
and munitions, nearly all of which were returned to him regretfully unfilled — he only relaxed from his duties when he slept, and even then
he kept a pencil and a note pad under his pillow, ready to jot down any
notion that came to him in the night. "Carolinians and Georgians!" he
exhorted by proclamation. "The hour is at hand to prove your devotion to your country's cause. Let all able-bodied men, from the seaboard

to the mountains, rush to arms. Be not exacting in the choice of weapons; pikes and scythes will do for exterminating your enemies, spades and shovels for protecting your friends. To arms, fellow citizens! Come share with us our dangers, our brilliant success, or our glorious death."

Two approaches to Charleston were available to the Federals. They could make an amphibious landing on one of the islands or up one of the inlets to the south, then swing northeastward up the mainland to move upon the city from the rear; or they could enter through the harbor itself, braving the massed batteries for the sake of a quick decision, however bloody. Twice already they had tried the former method, but both times — first at Secessionville, three months before Beauregard's return from the West in mid-September, and again at Pocotaligo, one month after he reassumed command — they had been stopped and flung back on their naval support before they could gather momentum. This time he thought it probable that they would attempt the front-door approach, using their new flotilla of vaunted ironclads to spearhead the attack. If so, they were going to find they had taken on a good deal more than they expected; for the harbor defenses had been greatly improved during the nearly two years that had elapsed since the war first opened here. Fort Moultrie, Castle Pinckney, and Fort Sumter, respectively on Sullivan's Island, off the mouth of the Cooper River, and opposite the entrance to the bay, had not only been strengthened, each in its own right, but now they were supported by other fortifications constructed at intervals along the beaches and connected by a continuous line of signal stations, making it possible for a central headquarters, itself transferrable, to direct and consolidate their fire. First Beauregard, then Pemberton, and now Beauregard again — both accomplished engineers and artillerists, advised moreover by staffs of specialists as expert as themselves — had applied all their skill and knowledge to make the place as nearly impregnable as military science and Confederate resources would allow. A total of seventy-seven guns of various calibers now frowned from their various embrasures, in addition to which the harbor channels were thickly sown with torpedoes and other obstructions, such as floating webs of hemp designed to entangle rudders and snarl propellers. Not content with this, the sad-eyed little Creole had not hesitated to dip into his limited supply of powder in order to improve the marksmanship of his cannoneers with frequent target practice. Like his idol Napoleon he believed in a lucky star, but he was leaving as little as possible to chance; for which reason he had set marker buoys at known ranges in the bay, with the corresponding elevations chalked on the breeches of the guns. As a last-ditch measure of desperation, to be employed if all else failed, he encouraged the organization of a unit known as the Tigers, made up of volunteers whose assignment was to hurl explosives down the smokestacks of such enemy ships as managed to break through the ring of fire and approach the fortress walls or the city docks. The ironclads might indeed be invincible; some said so, some said not; but one thing was fairly certain. The argument was likely to be settled on the day their owners tested them in Charleston harbor.

This was not to say that Beauregard had abandoned all notion of assuming the offensive, however limited his means. He had at his disposal two homemade rams, the *Palmetto State* and the *Chicora*, built with funds supplied by the South Carolina legislature and the Ladies' Gunboat Fair. The former mounted an 80-pounder rifle aft and an 8-inch shell gun on each broadside, while the latter had two 9-inch smoothbores and four rifled 32-pounders. Both were balky and slow, with cranky, inadequate engines and armor improvised from boiler plate and railroad iron, but as January drew to a close the general was determined to put them to the test by challenging the blockade squadron off the Charleston bar. Orders were handed Flag Officer Duncan Ingraham on the 30th, instructing him to make the attempt at dawn of the following day. Beauregard meanwhile had in mind a more limited offensive of his own, to be launched against the 9-gun screw steamer *Isaac Smith*, which had been coming up the Stono River almost nightly to shell the Confederate camps on James and John's islands. That night he lay in wait for her with batteries of field artillery, allowed her to pass unchallenged, then took her under fire as she came back down. The opening volley tore off her stack, stopped her engines, riddled her lifeboats, and killed eight of her crew. Her captain quickly surrendered himself and his ship and the 94 survivors, including 17 wounded. Repaired and rechristened, the *Smith* became the *Stono* and served under that name as part of Charleston's miniature defense squadron, the rest of which was already on its way across the bay, under cover of darkness, in accordance with Ingraham's orders to try his hand at lifting the Union blockade.

Palmetto State and *Chicora*, followed by three steam tenders brought along to tow them back into the harbor in case their engines failed, were over the bar and among the wooden-walled blockaders by first light. Mounting a total of one hundred guns, the Federal squadron included the 1200-ton sloop-of-war *Housatonic*, two gunboats, and seven converted merchantmen. A lookout aboard one of these last, the 9-gun steamer *Mercedita*, was the first to spot the misty outline of an approaching vessel. "She has black smoke!" he shouted. "Watch, man the guns! Spring the rattle! Call all hands to quarters!" This brought the captain out on deck, clad only in a pea jacket. When he too spotted the stranger, nearer now, he cupped his hands about his mouth and called out: "Steamer, ahoy! You will be into us! What steamer is that?" It was the *Palmetto State*, but for a time she did not deign to answer. Then: "Halloo!" her skipper finally replied, and with that the ram put her snout into the quarter of the *Mercedita* and fired her guns. Flames went up from the crippled steamer. "Surrender," the rebel captain yelled up, "or I'll sink you!" The only answer was a cloud of oily smoke shot through with steam. "Do you surrender?" he repeated. This brought the reply, "I can make no resistance; my boiler is destroyed!" "Then do you surrender?" "Yes!" So the *Palmetto State* backed off, withdrawing her snout, and turned to go to the help of the *Chicora*, which meanwhile had been serving the 10-gun sidewheel steamer *Keystone State* in much the same fashion. Riddled and aflame, the Federal hauled down her flag to signify surrender, then ran it up again and limped out to sea as the two rams moved off in the opposite direction. At the far end of the line, the *Housatonic* and the gunboats held their station, thinking the racket had been provoked by a blockade runner venturing out. By full daylight the two improvised ironclads were back in Charleston harbor, their crews accepting the cheers of a crowd collected on the docks.

Beauregard was elated by the double coup. Quick to claim that the blockade had been lifted, at least for a time, he took the French and Spanish consuls out to witness the truth of his words that "the outer harbor remained in the full possession of the two Confederate rams. Not a Federal sail was visible, even with spyglasses." Next day the blockaders were back again, presumably too vigilant now to permit him to risk another such attempt, but he did not admit that this detracted in the slightest from the brilliance of the exploit. He bided his time, still improving his defenses for the all-out attack which he believed was about to be launched. "Already six monitors . . . are in the waters of my department, concentrating about Port Royal, and transports with troops are still arriving from the North," he reported in mid-March. "I believe the drama will not much longer be delayed; the curtain will soon rise." Three more weeks went past before his prediction was fulfilled. Then on Monday, April 6, the day after Easter — it was also the first anniversary of Shiloh and within a week of the second anniversary of the opening of the war in this same harbor — not six but nine brand-new Union ironclads, some single- and some double-turreted, crossed the Charleston bar and dropped anchor in the channel, bringing their great 15-inch guns to bear on the forts and batteries Beauregard had prepared for their reception. The curtain had indeed risen.

Rear Admiral Samuel Du Pont had the flag. It was he who, back in early November of 1861, had conceived and executed the elliptical attack on Port Royal, thereby giving the North its first substantial victory of the war, and it was hoped by his superiors — his desk-bound superiors in Washington, that is, for he had no superiors afloat — that he would repeat the triumph here in Charleston harbor. Son of a wealthy New York importer and nephew of an even wealthier Delaware powder maker, the admiral was approaching sixty, a hale, well-set-up aristocrat with a dignified but genial manner and a growth of luxuriant whiskers describing a bushy U about his chops and under his clean-shaven mouth and chin, all of which combined to give at least one journalist the impression that he was "one of the stateliest, handsomest, and most polished gentlemen I have ever seen." Gideon Welles admired him, too; up to a point. "He is a skillful and accomplished officer," the Secretary confided in his diary. "Has a fine address, [but] is a courtier with perhaps too much finesse and management." This edge of mistrust was returned by the man who was its object. It seemed to Du Pont, whose enthusiasm had been tempered by close association, that the Navy Department was suffering from an affliction which might have been diagnosed as "ironclads on the brain."

This had not always been the case, particularly in the days when John Ericsson was trying to persuade the brass to give him authority for construction of the *Monitor.* Grudgingly, despite grave objections, they had finally let him go ahead with a contract which stipulated that he would not be reimbursed in case of failure. But after Hampton Roads and the draw engagement that put an end to the overnight depredations of the *Merrimac,* the Department not only reversed itself, but went all-out in the opposite direction. Ericsson received an order for half a dozen sister ships of the one already delivered, and other builders were engaged for the construction of twenty-one more, of various shapes and sizes. Assistant Secretary Fox was especially enthusiastic, informing Du Pont that after he had used the new-fangled warships to reduce Charleston he was to move on to Savannah, then send them down to the Gulf to give Mobile the same treatment. Ironclads were trumps, according to Fox. He told Ericsson he had not "a shadow of a doubt as to our success, and this confidence arises from a study of your marvelous vessels." The Swede was less positive. "The most I dare hope is that the contest will end without loss of that prestige which your ironclads have conferred upon the nation abroad," he replied, adding the reminder: "A single shot may sink a ship, while a hundred rounds cannot silence a fort." Unwilling to have his confidence undermined or his ebullience lessened, Fox assured a congressional committee that the monitors (such was the generic name, adopted in honor of the first of what was intended to be a long line of invincible vessels) could steam into southern harbors, flatten the defenses, and emerge unscathed. His only note of caution was injected into a dispatch addressed to Du Pont. "I beg of you," he pleaded, "not to let the Army spoil it." He wanted the show to be all Navy, with the landsmen merely standing by to be ferried in to pick up the pieces when the smoke cleared. In late March, having gained nothing from nudging Porter with the promise of a ribboned star and permanent promotion, he informed Du Pont that it was up to him to make up for the reverses lately suffered in the West: "Farragut has had a setback at Port Hudson and lost the noble old *Mississippi.* It finally devolves upon you by great good fortune to avert the series of disasters that have fallen upon our Navy. That you will do it most gloriously I have no misgivings whatever."

In point of fact, Du Pont by this time had misgivings enough for them both. What was more, these doubts were shared by a majority of his ironclad skippers — and with cause. Near the mouth of the Ogeechee River, just beyond the Georgia line, the Confederates had constructed as part of the Savannah defenses a 9-gun earthwork called Fort McAllister, which Du Pont decided to use as a sort of test range to determine how well the monitors would do, offensively and defensively, under fire. He gave the reduction assignment to the *Montauk*, which meant that he was giving the best he had; for her captain was Commander John L. Worden, who had skippered the *Monitor* in her fight with the *Merrimac*. Worden made his first attack on January 27 and, after expending all his ammunition in a four-hour bombardment, withdrew undamaged despite repeated hits scored by the guns of the fort, which was not silenced. Returning February 1 he tried again, with like results. Neither the ship nor the fort had done much damage to the other, aside from the concussive strain on the eardrums of the *Montauk*'s crew from the forty-six hits taken on her iron decks and turret. A third attack, February 27, was more fruitful, although not in the way intended. Finding the rebel cruiser *Nashville* aground beyond Fort McAllister, Worden took her under long-range fire with his 11- and 15-inch guns, set her ablaze, and had the satisfaction of watching her destruction when her magazine exploded. Struck only five times by the guns of the fort, the ironclad pulled back without replying, well satisfied with her morning's work, only to run upon a torpedo which blew such a hole in her bottom that she had to be beached in the mud at the mouth of the river. While she was undergoing repairs that soon restored her to full efficiency, three more monitors came down from Port Royal on March 3 and tried their hand with an eight-hour bombardment of the fort: with similar results. Neither silenced or seriously damaged the other, and the ironclads withdrew to try no more.

Fruitless though the experiment had been in positive results — aside, that is, from the fortunate interception of the *Nashville* — a lesson had been learned, on the negative side, as to the capabilities of the monitors. "Whatever degree of impenetrability they might have," Du Pont reported, "there was no corresponding degree of destructiveness as against forts." He felt much as one sailor had felt on a test run. "Give me an oyster-scow!" the man had cried. "Anything — only let it be of wood, and something that will float over instead of under the water." Most of the captains were of a similar mind, and when they looked beyond the present to the impending future, their doubts increased. If these vaunted engines of destruction could not humble a modest 9-gun sand fort, what could they hope to accomplish against multi-gunned bastions like Sumter and Moultrie? They asked the question and shook their heads. "I do not feel as sure as I could wish," one skipper admitted, while another was more positive in expressing his reservations. "I begin to rue the day I got into the iron clad business," he wrote home.

Still, orders were orders, and as April came in Du Pont completed his final preparations for the attack. In addition to his flagship the *New Ironsides*, a high-bulwarked 3500-ton frigate whose ponderous armor and twenty heavy guns mounted in broadside made her the most powerful battleship in the world, he had eight low-riding monitors, mounting one or two guns each in revolving turrets: which meant that, in all, he would be opposing 77 guns ashore with 33 afloat. These odds were rather evened by the fact that the naval guns, in addition to being mounted on moving targets, which made them far more difficult to hit, were heavier in caliber and threw about an equal weight of metal. Other odds were irreducible, however, one being that in order to reach the city from the sea his ships would have to steam for seven winding miles in a shoal-lined channel, much of which had been fiendishly obstructed and practically all of which was exposed to the plunging fire of forts whose gun crews had been anticipating for months this golden opportunity to disprove the claim that monitors were indestructible. On April 2, despite increasing doubts and reservations, Du Pont left Port Royal and reached Edisto Island, twenty-odd miles below the entrance to Charleston harbor, before nightfall. There the ships were cleared for action, the exposed armor of their decks and turrets covered over with slippery untanned hides and their bulwarks slopped with grease to lessen the "bite" of enemy projectiles. (That at least was the hoped-for effect, when the vessels should come under fire. The more immediate result, however, was that they stank fearfully under the influence of the Carolina sun.) On the 5th — Easter Sunday — they cleared North Edisto and crossed the Charleston bar next morning. Du Pont had intended to attack at once, but finding the weather hazy, which as he said "prevent[ed] our seeing the ranges," he decided to drop anchors and wait for tomorrow, in hopes that it would afford him better visibility. (It would also afford the same for the gunners in the forts; but Du Pont was not thinking along these lines, or else he would have made a night attack.) Finally, against his better judgment — and after much prodding from above, including jeers that he had "the slows" and taunts that identified him as a sea-going McClellan, overcautious and too mindful of comparative statistics — he was going in.

Tomorrow — April 7 — brought the weather he thought he wanted, and soon after noon the iron column started forward, the nine ships moving in single file, slowly and with a certain ponderous majesty not lost on the beholders in the forts. Originally the admiral had intended to lead the way in the flagship, but on second thought he decided to take the center position from which "signals could be better made to both ends of the line," so that the resultant order of battle was *Weehawken, Passaic, Montauk, Patapsco; New Ironsides; Catskill, Nantucket, Nahant, Keokuk.* There was an exasperating delay of about an hour when the lead monitor's heavy anchor chain became entangled with the bootjack raft designed to protect her bow from torpedoes; then the column resumed its forward motion, passing Morris Island in an ominous silence as the rebel cannoneers on Cummings Point held their fire. As the ships approached the inner works, however, the Confederate and Palmetto flags were hoisted over Sumter and Moultrie, while bands on the parapets struck up patriotic airs and the guns began to roar in salute. Captain John Rodgers of the *Weehawken,* spotting the rope obstructions dead ahead, commanded the helmsman to swing hard to starboard in order to avoid becoming entangled in the web and immobilized under the muzzles of guns whose projectiles were already hammering the monitor like an anvil. This was well short of the point at which Du Pont had intended to open fire, however, and the result was that the whole line was thrown into confusion by the abrupt necessity, confronting each ship in rapid sequence, of avoiding a collision with the ship ahead. Moreover, as the *Weehawken* turned she encountered a torpedo which exploded directly under her. "It lifted the vessel a little," Rodgers later reported, "but I am unable to perceive that it has done us any damage."

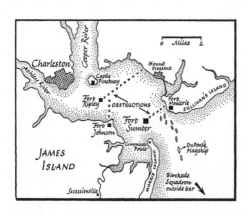

Aboard the flagship, with her deeper draft, the confusion was at its worst. When she lost headway she had to drop her anchor to keep from going aground, and as she hung there, trying to get her nose into the tide, she received two disconcerting butts from two of the monitors astern as they swept past in response to her signal to move up and join the action. Hoisting anchor at last, the *Ironsides* chugged forward a short distance, only to have to drop it again in order to avoid piling up on a shoal. This brought her, unbeknownst, directly over a huge submerged torpedo which the Confederates had fashioned by packing an old boiler with explosives and connecting it to an observation post ashore, to be used to detonate the charge at the proper time. Now the proper time was very much at hand; the rebel electrician later said that if he himself had been allowed to spot the Yankee flagship he could not have placed her more precisely where he wanted her. However, his elation quickly faded, turning first to dismay and then to disgust, when the detonating mechanism failed time after time to send a spark to the underwater engine of destruction. Meanwhile, happily unaware that he and his ship were in mortal danger of being hoisted skyward in sudden flame and smoke, Du Pont signaled the monitors to "disregard motions of commander in chief" and continue to press the attack without his help. The *Ironsides,* as one of her surgeons complained, was as completely out of the fight as if she had been moored to a dock in the Philadelphia Navy Yard, but this did not prevent her taking long-range punishment from the rebel guns. Presenting if not the closest, then at any rate the largest and least mobile target in the harbor, she was struck no less than ninety-five times in the course of the engagement. Despite the din, according to one of her officers, "the sense of security the iron walls gave to those within was wonderful, a feeling akin to that which one experiences in a heavy storm when the wind and hail beat harmlessly against the windows of a well-protected house."

No such feeling was experienced by the crews of the monitors, the officer added; "for in their turrets the nuts that secured the laminated plates flew wildly, to the injury and discomfiture of the men at the guns." Up closer, they were harder hit. "The shots literally rained around them," a correspondent wrote, "splashing the water up thirty feet in the air, and striking and booming from their decks and turrets." The flagship was a mile from Sumter, the nearest monitors about half that far, but the captain of the twin-turreted *Nahant* quickly found what it would cost to close the range. "Mr Clarke, you haven't hit anything yet," he protested to the ensign in charge of the 15-inch gun, which was throwing its 420-pound shells at seven-minute intervals. When the young man replied, "We aint near enough, Captain," the skipper went into a rage. "Not near enough? God damn it," he cried, "I'll put you near enough! Starboard your helm, Quartermaster!" As the ship came about, a rebel projectile slammed against the sight-slit, killing the helmsman and mangling the pilot. "Retire! Retire!" the captain shouted. Others caught it as hard or harder, with similar results: smokestacks perforated, turrets jammed, decks ripped up, guns knocked out of action. The only effect on the enemy a journalist could see, examining the brick northeast face of Sumter through his glasses, was that of "increasing pock marks and discolorations on the walls, as if there had been a sudden breaking out of cutaneous disease." But there was no corresponding slackening of fire from within the fort, whose cannoneers were jubilant over the many hits they scored. Frenzied at being kept from a share in the fun of pummeling the ironclads, Confederates locked in the Moultrie guardhouse screamed above the roar of the bombardment: "For God's sake, let us come out and go to the guns!"

After peering through the drifting smoke for about two hours, Du Pont was told that it was nearly 5 o'clock. "Make signal to the ships to drop out of fire," he said quietly. "It is too late to fight this battle tonight. We will renew it early in the morning." Below decks, when the gun captains received word of this decision, they sent up an urgent request that they be allowed to fire at least one broadside before retiring. It was granted, and as the *Ironsides* turned to steam down the channel an eight-gun salvo was hurled at Moultrie, the only shots she fired in the course of the engagement. This brought the total to an even 150 rounds expended by the flotilla, and of these 55 were scored as hits. The Confederates, on the other hand, had fired 2209, of which no less than 441 had found their mark, despite the fact that the targets had not only been comparatively small, and moving, but had also been mostly submerged. That this was remarkably effective shooting Du Pont himself began to appreciate when the retiring monitors came within hailing distance of the flagship and he got a close-up look at their condition. The first to approach was the *Keokuk*, limping badly. Last in and first out, she had ventured nearest to Sumter's 44 guns, and she had the scars of 90 point-blank hits to prove it. She was "riddled like a colander," one witness remarked, "the most severely mauled ship one ever saw." That night, in fact, she keeled over and sank at her anchorage off Morris Island. Others also had been roughly handled; *Weehawken* had taken 53 hits, *Nantucket* 51, *Patapsco* 47, *Nahant* 36, *Passaic* 35, *Catskill* 20, and *Montauk* 14. In general, the damage suffered was in inverse ratio to the individual distance between them and the rebel guns, and none had been closer than 600 yards.

The admiral's intention to "renew [the battle] early in the morning" was modified by the sight of his crippled monitors. Five of the eight were too badly damaged to be able to engage if ordered, and of these five, one would sink before the scheduled time for action. Equally conclusive were the reports and recommendations of the several captains when they came aboard the flagship that evening. "With your present means," John Rodgers advised, "I could not, if I were asked, recommend a renewal of the attack." The redoubtable Worden was no less emphatic. "After testing the weight of the enemy's fire, and observing the obstructions," he reported, "I am led to believe that Charleston cannot be taken by the naval force now present, and that had the attack been continued [today] it could not have failed to result in disaster." This gave Du Pont pause, and pausing he reflected on the risks. Here was no New Orleans, where the problem had been to run the fleet through a brief, furious gauntlet of fire in order to gain a safe haven above the forts and place a defenseless city under the muzzles of its guns; this was Charleston, whose harbor, in the words of a staff officer, "was a *cul-de-sac*, a circle of fire not to be passed." The deeper you penetrated the circle, the more you were exposed to destruction from its rim. Moreover, as the admiral saw the outcome, even if he pressed the attack "in the end we shall retire, leaving some of our ironclads in the hands of the enemy, to be refitted and turned against our blockade with deplorable effect." This last was unthinkable — though he thought about it in his cabin all night long. By daybreak he had made up his mind. "I have decided not to renew the attack," he told his chief of staff. "We have met with a sad repulse; I shall not turn it into a great disaster."

Next afternoon he recrossed the bar. "I attempted to take the bull by the horns, but he was too much for us," he admitted to the army commander whose troops had been standing by to pick up the pieces. By the end of the week the flotilla again was riding at anchor inside Port Royal, swarmed over by armorers hammering the vessels back into shape. The admiral knew the reaction in Washington would be severe, coming as it did on the heels of such great expectations, but he also knew that he had the support of his monitor captains, who stood, as one of them said, "like a wall of iron" around his reputation, agreeing with his chief of staff's opinion that "Admiral Du Pont never showed greater courage or patriotism than when he saved his ships and men, and sacrificed himself to the clamor and disappointment evoked by his defeat." In point of fact, however, part of the expressed disappointment, if not the outright clamor, occurred within the fleet itself. A chief engineer was clapped in arrest for complaining in his ship's mess that the attack had not been pressed to the victory point, and at least one junior officer remarked wryly that "the grim sort of soul like Farragut was lacking." Welles and Fox, though hot enough at the outcome and in no doubt at all as to where the blame lay, were considerably hampered in their criticisms by the political necessity for delay in bringing the matter out into the open with the publication of the adverse battle reports. After all, it was they — especially Fox — who had announced that the monitors were irresistible, and contracts already had been signed for the delivery of eighteen more of the expensive naval monsters. Two weeks after the repulse, Welles was attempting to shrug it off by telling his diary: "I am by no means confident that we are acting wisely in expending so much strength and effort on Charleston, a place of no strategic importance."

The grapes had soured for him; but not for Beauregard. The Louisiana general's only regrets were that the boiler-torpedo had not gone off beneath the *Ironsides* and that the Yankees had slunk away without attempting a renewal of the assault, which he felt certain would have been even more decisively repulsed. In a congratulatory address to his troops, his enthusiasm knew no bounds. He spoke of "the stranded, riddled wreck" of the *Keokuk*, whose big guns now were part of the harbor defenses, and of the ignominious flight of "her baffled coadjutors," whose defeat had reinspired world-wide confidence in the ultimate and glorious triumph of the Confederate cause. In his official report to Richmond, though — for he had recently confided to a friend that, from now on, he was adopting a more restrained style in his dispatches, in order to counteract a rumor that he was prone to exaggerate his accomplishments — the little Creole, with his bloodhound eyes, his swarthy face, and his hair brushed forward in lovelocks at the temples, contented himself for the most part with factual observations. "It may be accepted, as shown," he wrote, "that these vaunted monitor batteries, though formidable engines of war, after all are not invulnerable or invincible, and may be destroyed or defeated by heavy ordnance, properly placed and skillfully handled." However, in the glow and warmth of congratulations being pressed upon him, including one that he had made Sumter "a household word, like Salamis and Thermopylae," he could not resist the temptation to add a closing flourish to the report: "My expectations were fully realized, and the country, as well as the State of South Carolina, may well be proud of the men who first met and vanquished the iron-mailed, terribly armed armada, so confidently prepared and sent forth by the enemy to certain and easy victory."

✖ 2 ✖

Though he grew snappish at the first report that the fleet had been repulsed — "Hold your position inside the bar near Charleston," he instructed Du Pont in a message sent posthaste down the coast; "or, if you shall have left it, return to it, and hold it till further orders" — Lincoln was in a better frame of mind for the reception of bad news than he had been for months. The reason for this was that he had just returned from a five-day Easter vacation combined with a highly satisfactory inspection of the Army of the Potomac, whose tents were pitched along the Rappahannock in the vicinity of Falmouth. The visit was a heartening experience, not only because it showed him that the condition of the troops was excellent, but also because it abolished his main previous doubt as to the fitness of the man he had appointed as their commander. After saying, "Now there is Joe Hooker. He can fight. I think that is pretty well established," Lincoln had added: "But whether he can 'keep tavern' for a large army is not so sure." If the trip down the bay had done nothing else, it had reassured the President on that score. Fighting Joe had taken hold with a vengeance, and the results were plain to see on the faces and in the attitude of the men. Fredericksburg and the Mud March, though the letters of the former were embroidered on the rippling blue of their regimental colors, were no longer even a part of their vocabulary.

Hooker could indeed keep tavern. Within a week of his assumption of command he jolted the commissary department by ordering the issue of rations expanded to include fresh vegetables and soft bread; he supervised a thorough cleanup of the unsanitary camps, shrinking the overlong sick lists in the process, and he instituted a liberal system of furloughs which, combined with a tightening of security regulations, did much to reduce desertion. "Ah! the furloughs and vegetables he gave!" one infantryman still marveled years later, "How he did understand the road to the soldier's heart!" In the midst of all this welcome reform, army paymasters came down from Washington with bulging satchels and surprised the troops with six months' back pay. It was no wonder another veteran recalled that "cheerfulness, good order, and military discipline at once took the place of grumbling, depression, and want of confidence." Idleness, that breeder of discontent, was abolished by a revival of the old-time grand reviews, with regiment after regiment swinging past the reviewing stand so that when the men executed the command "eyes right" they saw their chieftain's clean-shaven face light up with pleasure at seeing their appearance improved by their diurnal spit-and-polish preparations. Unit pride, being thus encouraged, increased even more when Hooker, expanding the use of the so-called Kearny patch — a device improvised by the late Phil Kearny, about this time last year, to identify the men of his division in the course of their march up the York-James peninsula — ordered the adoption of corps insignia of various shapes, cut from red, white, or blue cloth, thus indicating the first, second, or third division, and stitched to the crown of the caps of the troops, so that he and they could tell at a glance what corps and division a man was gracing or disgracing, on duty or off. Moreover, after the gruff and dish-faced Pope and the flustered and fantastically whiskered Burnside, Hooker himself, by the force of his personality and the handsomeness of his presence, infused some of the old McClellan magnetism into the reviving army's ranks. "Apollo-like," a Wisconsin major called the forty-eight-year-old Massachusetts-born commander, and a visiting editor wrote of him as "a man of unusually handsome face and elegant proportions, with a complexion as delicate and silken as a woman's." Another remarked, along this same line, that the general looked "as rosy as the most healthy woman alive."

Some claimed that this glow, this rosiness, had its origin in the bottle (the men themselves apparently took pride in the assertion;

> *"Joe Hooker is our leader —*
> *He takes his whiskey strong!"*

they sang as they set off on practice marches) while other dissenters from the prevalent chorus of praise, although admitting that the general was "handsome and picturesque in the extreme," directed attention to what one of them called his "fatally weak chin." Still others believed they detected inner flaws, below the rosy surface. "He could play the best game of poker I ever saw," a former West Coast intimate recollected, "until it came to the point when he should go a thousand better, and then he would flunk." But the harshest judgment of all came from a cavalry officer, Charles F. Adams, Jr. According to this son of the ambassador to England, the new commander was "a noisy, low-toned intriguer" under whose influence army headquarters became "a place to which no self-respecting man liked to go, and no decent woman could go. It was a combination of barroom and brothel." Young Adams' own "tone" was exceptionally high, which made him something less than tolerant of the weakness of others — particularly the weaknesses of the flesh, from which he himself apparently was exempt — but in support of at least a part of the accusation was the fact that, from this time on, the general's surname entered the language as one of the many lower-case slang words for prostitute. As for the rest, however, a friend who was with him almost daily insisted that Hooker had gone on the wagon the day he took command. Headquarters might have some of the aspects of a barroom, as Adams said, but according to this observer the general himself did not imbibe.

The fact was, it did indeed appear that he as well as the army had experienced a basic change of character. Much of his former bluster was gone; he had even acquired a dislike for his *nom-de-guerre*, though perhaps this was largely because the story was beginning to get around that he had come by it as the result of an error made in a New York composing room during the Peninsula Campaign, when a last-minute dispatch arrived from the front with additional news involving his division. "Fighting — Joe Hooker," the follow-up was tagged, indicating that it was to be added to what had gone before, but the typesetter dropped the dash and it was printed as a separate story, under the resultant heading. The nickname stuck despite the general's objections. "Don't call me Fighting Joe," he said. "[It] makes the public think that I am a hot-headed, furious young fellow, accustomed to making furious and needless dashes at the enemy." Nor was this the only change in Hooker. All his military life, at West Point, in Mexico, and in the peacetime army — from which he had resigned in 1853, after sixteen years of service, in order to take up California farming and civil engineering, only to fail at both so utterly that when news came that the war had begun his friends had to pass the hat to get up money for his fare back East — he had been quick to resent the authority and criticize the conduct of his superiors. Just recently, he had sneered at the President and the Cabinet as a flock of bunglers and had asserted that what the country needed was a dictator, making it more or less clear that the man he had in mind for the job was himself. Now, though, all that had gone by the board. He had not even resented Lincoln's "beware of rashness. Beware of rashness" letter, calling him to account for his derogations while appointing him to command the army. Soon afterwards, in the privacy of his tent, Hooker read the letter to a journalist, only taking exception to the charge that he had "thwarted" Burnside. "The President is mistaken. I never thwarted Burnside in any way, shape, or manner," he broke off reading to say — though even now he could not resist adding: "Burnside was pre-eminently a man of deportment. He fought the battle of Fredericksburg on his deportment; he was defeated on his deportment; and he took his deportment with him out of the Army of the Potomac, thank God." He returned to the letter, and when he had finished reading it he folded it and put it back into his breast pocket, as if to emphasize the claim that he had taken it to heart. "That is just such a letter as a father might write to his son," he mused aloud, and the reporter thought he saw tears beginning to mist the general's pale blue-gray eyes. "It is a beautiful letter," Hooker went on, "and although I think he was harder on me than I deserved, I will say that I love the man who wrote it." Again he paused. Then he said, "After I have got to Richmond I shall give that letter to you to have published."

This last, variously phrased as "When I get to Richmond" or "After we have taken Richmond," cropped up more frequently in his talk as the spirit and strength of his army grew, and it was one of the few things that struck Lincoln unfavorably when he arrived for his Easter visit. "If you get to Richmond, General —" he remarked at their first conference, only to have Hooker break in with "Excuse me, Mr President, but there is no 'if' in this case. I am going straight to Richmond if I live." Lincoln let it pass, though afterwards he said privately to a friend: "That is the most depressing thing about Hooker. It seems to me that he is over-confident." Presently, however, as the inspection tour progressed, he began to see for himself that the general's ready assurance was solidly based on facts and figures. Even after the detachment of Burnside's old corps — which took with it, down the coast to Newport News, whatever resentment its members might be feeling as a result of the supersession of their former chief — Hooker still had seven others, plus a newly consolidated corps of cavalry, including in all no less than twenty divisions of infantry and three of horsemen, here on the Rappahannock, with a present-for-duty total of 133,450 effectives, supported by seventy batteries of artillery with a total of 412 guns. Across the way, the Confederates had less than half as many men and a good deal less than half as many guns, and Hooker not only knew the approximate odds, he was also preparing to take advantage of them. On the eve of Lincoln's arrival he had put his corps commanders on the alert by ordering all surplus baggage sent to the rear, and he had warned the War Department to have siege equipment ready for shipment to him in front of the rebel capital. In addition to 10,000 shovels, 5000 picks, 5000 axes, and 30,000 sandbags, he wanted authentic maps of the Richmond defenses, to be used in laying out saps and parallels, and he requested that a flotilla of supply boats be kept standing by at all times, ready to deliver 1,500,000 rations up the Pamunkey River as soon as the army got that far. He did not say "if," he said "as soon as," and when this was repeated at Falmouth on Easter Sunday Lincoln shook his head in some perplexity. He admired determination and self-reliance, especially in a military man, but he also knew there was such a thing as whistling in the dark. He had known men — John Pope, for one — who assumed those qualities to hide their doubts, not only from their associates but also from themselves. In fact, the louder a man insisted that there was no room for doubt in his make-up, the more likely he was to belong to the whistler category, and Lincoln feared that Hooker's brashness might be assumed for some such purpose. "It is about the worst thing I have seen since I have been down here," he remarked.

Most of what he saw he found encouraging, however. He agreed with Hooker's estimation of the army as "the finest on the planet," and he particularly enjoyed the temporary relief the visit afforded him from the day-to-day pressure of White House paperwork and the importunities of favor-seekers. Not that he was entirely delivered from the latter. Now that the career officers had him where they could get at him, out of channels and yet with no great strain on their ingrained sense of propriety, they did not neglect the opportunity. Even so stiff a professional as Meade, whose testiness had caused his troops to refer to him as "a God-damned old goggle-eyed snapping turtle," could not resist the chance to curry favor, difficult though he found it to unbend. "In view of the vacant brigadiership in the regular army," he wrote his wife, "I have ventured to tell the President one or two stories, and I think I have made decided progress in his affections." But this was all comparatively mild and even enjoyable — even the stories — in contrast to what the Chief Executive had left behind, and presently would be returning to, in Washington. What was more, his wife and younger son, who accompanied him on the outing, appeared to enjoy it every bit as much as he did. Mary Lincoln responded happily to the all-too-rare opportunity of being with her husband, in and out of office hours, and playing the role of First Lady in a style she considered fitting. Riding one day through a camp of Negro refugees, who crowded about the presidential carriage and lifted their children overhead for a look at the Great Emancipator, she asked her husband how many of "those piccaninnies" he supposed were named Abraham Lincoln. "Let's see," he calculated. "This is April, 1863. I should say that of all those babies under two years of age perhaps two thirds have been named for me." Mrs Lincoln, who enjoyed the notion — it was fairly customary in her native Bluegrass for slaves to name their offspring for the master — smiled. But ten-year-old Tad had an entirely different notion of what was fun. He wanted to see some real, live rebels. And Lincoln obliged him. Proceeding one blustery morning to Stafford Heights, they looked across the Rappahannock and down into the ruined streets of Fredericksburg, where the army had staged its two-day carnival before crossing the "champaign tract" to be brought up short in front of the sunken road at the foot of Marye's Heights, and to Tad's delight they saw floating from the eaves of one of the town's few unwrecked houses the Stars and Bars. Nearby, moreover, alongside a tall scorched chimney like a monument erected to commemorate a home, stood two sentinels: genuine, armed graybacks, though one of them —

perversely, as if to lessen Tad's pleasure — wore a light-blue U. S. Army overcoat. Their voices faint with distance, they began yelling across the river at the Yankee spectators, something about Fort Sumter and the ironclads being "licked," which brought an officer out of one of the Fredericksburg bomb-proofs to investigate the shouting. He took out his binoculars, beginning to sweep the opposite heights, and when he spotted the presidential group he paused, adjusted the focus, and peered intently. Whether or not he recognized the tall form, made still taller by the familiar stovepipe hat, they never knew; but at any rate he seemed to. He lowered the glasses and struck an attitude of dignity, then removed his wide-brimmed hat, made a low, formal bow, and retired.

For the Confederates across the way — less than 60,000 in all, including the punctilious officer and the two sentinels, one of whom had been lucky enough to scavenge a Yankee overcoat to put between him and the chill of Virginia's early spring — there had been no corresponding improvement, but rather a decline, in the quantity as well as the quality of the supplies provided by their government. The basic daily ration at this time consisted of a quarter-pound of bacon, often rancid, and eighteen ounces of cornmeal, including a high proportion of pulverized cob, supplemented about every third day by the issue of ten pounds of rice to each one hundred men, along with an occasional few peas and a scant handful of dried fruit when it was available, which was seldom. "This may give existence to the troops while idle," Lee complained to the War Department, "but [it] will certainly cause them to break down when called upon for exertion." Scurvy had begun to appear, and though he attempted to combat this by sending out details to gather sassafras buds, wild onions, and such antiscorbutics — together with other, more substantial windfalls, unofficial and in fact illegal; "Ah, General," he chided Hood, "when you Texans come about, the chickens have to roost mighty high" — Lee felt, as he said, "painfully anxious lest the spirit and efficiency of the men should become impaired, and they be rendered unable to sustain their former reputation or perform the service necessary for our safety."

Yet their morale was as high as ever, if not higher: not only because they managed to forget, or at least ignore, their hunger pangs by staging regimental theatricals and minstrel shows, attending the mammoth prayer meetings which were a part of the great religious revival that swept like wildfire through the army at this time, and organizing brigade-size snowball battles which served much the same purpose on this side of the river as Hooker's grand reviews were serving on the other; but also because they could look back on a practically uninterrupted series of victories which they had grounds for believing would be continued, whatever the odds. In the ten months Lee had been in command of the Army of Northern Virginia, including the past three spent in winter quarters, they had fought no less than thirteen battles, large and small, and in all but one of these — South Mountain, where they had been outnumbered ten to one — they had maintained the integrity of their position from start to finish, and in all but one other — Sharpsburg, where the odds were never better than one to three and mostly worse — they had dominated the field when the smoke cleared. Although they had generally assumed the more costly tactical role of the attacker, they had inflicted more than 70,000 casualties, at a cost of less than 50,000 of their own, and had captured about 75,000 small arms while losing fewer than one tenth as many. In guns, the advantage was greatest of all in this respect; losing 8, they had taken 155. ("I declare," a North Carolina private said as his Federal captors were taking him rearward through their lines. "You-uns has got about as many of them 'U.S.' guns as we have.") The over-all result was confidence, in Lee and in themselves, and a pride that burned fiercely despite privation and grim want. One Confederate, writing home, expressed amazement at the contrast between the army's bedraggled appearance in camp and its efficiency in combat. He marveled at the spirit of his companions, "so ragged, slovenly, sleeveless, without a superfluous ounce of flesh upon their bones, with wild matted hair, in mendicants' rags — and to think when the battle-flag goes to the front how they can and do fight!" Nor was praise of Lee's scarecrow heroes limited to those who stood in his army's ranks. An exchanged Union officer, returning to his own lines this spring after a term spent beyond them as a captive, put his first-hand observations on the record in a letter home. "Their artillery horses are poor, starved frames of beasts, tied to their carriages and caissons with odds and ends of rope and strips of raw hide; their supply and ammunition trains look like a congregation of all the crippled California emigrant trains that ever escaped off the desert out of the clutches of the rampaging Comanche Indians. The men are ill-dressed, ill-equipped, and ill-provided, a set of ragamuffins that a man is ashamed to be seen among, even when he is a prisoner and can't help it. And yet they have beaten us fairly, beaten us all to pieces, beaten us so easily that we are objects of contempt even to their commonest private soldiers, with no shirts to hang out the holes of their pantaloons, and cartridge-boxes tied around their waists with strands of rope."

Lee himself could silence grousing with a jest. "You ought not to mind that," he reassured a young officer who complained about the toughness of some biscuits; "they will stick by you the longer." He referred in much the same tone of levity to the threats made by his new opponent, who had no sooner taken charge of the blue army than he began showing signs of living up to his nickname, Fighting Joe. "General Hooker is obliged to do something," the gray commander wrote home in early February. "I do not know what it will be. He is playing the Chinese game, trying what frightening will do. He runs out his guns, starts wagons and troops up and down the river, and creates an excitement generally. Our men look on in wonder, give a cheer, and all again subsides *in statu quo ante bellum*." When nothing came of all this show of force before the month was out, Lee expressed a wry impatience. "I owe Mr F. J. Hooker no thanks for keeping me here," he told his wife. "He ought to have made up his mind long ago what to do." At the same time, though, he was warning subordinates that the bluecoats would "make every effort to crush us between now and June, and it will require all our strength to resist them." His confidence, while as firm as that of the men he led, did not cause him to ignore the present odds or the fact that if they continued to lengthen they would stretch beyond endurance. Within a month of the destructive but fruitless repulse of the Federal host that ventured across the river in mid-December, he made his warning explicit in a dispatch to the Secretary of War. "More than once have most promising opportunities been lost for want of men to take advantage of them, and victory itself has been made to put on the appearance of defeat because our diminished and exhausted troops have been unable to renew a successful struggle against fresh numbers of the enemy. The lives of our soldiers are too precious to be sacrificed in the attainment of successes that inflict no loss upon the enemy beyond the actual loss in battle." And he added, with a new note of bitterness which had come with the sack of Fredericksburg and the issuance of the Emancipation Proclamation: "In view of the vast increase of the forces of the enemy, of the savage and brutal policy he has proclaimed, which leaves us no alternative but success or degradation worse than death, if we would save the honor of our families from pollution [and] our social system from destruction, let every effort be made, every means be employed, to fill and maintain the ranks of our armies, until God in his mercy shall bless us with the establishment of our independence."

Instead of an increase, what followed hard on the heels of this appeal was a drastic reduction of his fighting strength, beginning January 14 with the detachment of D. H. Hill to contest the further invasion of the crusty Tarheel general's home state, presaged by the Federals' mid-December advance on Goldsboro. Lee himself went to Richmond two days later to confer with Davis on this and other problems, but had to hurry back to the Rappahannock on the 18th — the eve of his fifty-sixth birthday — when the high-level council of war was disrupted by news that Burnside's army was astir in its camps around Falmouth. As it turned out, all that came of this was the Mud March and Joe Hooker's elevation; Lee detached Robert Ransom's demi-division, which had played a leading role in Longstreet's defense of the sunken road the month before, and sent it south to North Carolina, as he had agreed to do at the interrupted strategy conference. Shortly afterwards, however, word came that Burnside's old corps had boarded transports at Aquia Landing and steamed down Chesapeake Bay to Hampton Roads. It seemed likely that these men were being returned to the scene of their year-old triumph below Norfolk, with instructions to extend their conquest eastward to the Weldon Railroad, Lee's vital supply connection with the factories and grainfields of Georgia and the Carolinas, or to Petersburg, whose fall would give them access to the back door of the capital itself. This two-pronged menace could not be ignored, whatever risk might be involved in attempting to contest it by a further weakening of the Rappahannock line. On February 15 the dismemberment of Longstreet's corps was resumed. Pickett's division was hastened south to Richmond; Hood's followed two days later, accompanied by Old Peter himself, who was charged with the defense of the region beyond the James. These two divisions combined with the troops already there would give him 44,000 men in all, whereas the Federals had 55,000 on hand, exclusive of the corps that presumably was about to join them from Hampton Roads. It was at best a chancy business for the Confederates, north and south of their threatened capital; for even if these blue reinforcements arrived, as was expected momentarily, the command on the south side of the James would be no worse outnumbered than the one on the south side of the Rappahannock, now that more than a fourth of the latter's strength had been subtracted in favor of the former. All Lee could do in this extremity was urge Longstreet to be ready to hurry northward, if possible — that is, if he could find a way to disengage without inviting the destruction of his command or the capture of Richmond — as soon as he got word that Hooker had left off playing the Chinese game and was on the move in earnest. "As our numbers will not admit of our meeting [the enemy] on equality everywhere," the gray commander wrote his detached lieutenant in mid-March, "we must endeavor, by judicious dispositions, to be enabled to make our troops available in any quarter where they may be needed [and] after the emergency passes in one place to transfer them to any other point that may be threatened."

With fewer First Corps troops on hand than had departed, he was down to 58,800 effectives and 170 guns, to be used in opposing a good deal better than twice as many of both. He was almost precisely aware of his opponent's numerical preponderance, not only because of information he received from spies beyond the northern lines, but also because he read the northern papers, one of which was quite specific on the point. Quoting Hooker's medical director, this journal showed 10,777 men on the current sick list, and then went on to state that the sick-well ratio was 67.64 per 1000. By computation Lee arrived at a figure close to 160,000. (Awesome though this total was, it was even a bit low. In late March the Federal commander, lumping teamsters, cooks, and other extra-duty personnel with all the rest, reported an "aggregate present" of 163,005.) Against such odds, and with the knowledge that Hooker would choose the time and place of attack, Lee's only hope

for salvation was superior generalship — his own and that of his chief
subordinates — coupled with the valor of his soldiers and the increased
efficiency of his army. To help achieve this last, he reorganized the artillery into battalions of four four-gun batteries each, four of which battalions were attached to each of the two corps, with two more in general reserve. His hope was that this arrangement, besides strengthening
the close-up support of the infantry on the defensive, would provide
the "long arm" with a flexibility that would permit a more rapid massing
of fire from several quarters of the field at once, either for counterbattery work or for softening an enemy position as a prelude to attack.
Whether such measures would produce the desired effect remained to
be seen in combat, but another innovation required no testing, its effectiveness being apparent even to a casual eye. This was a legacy left by
Longstreet on his departure beyond the James: left, indeed, not only to
the Army of Northern Virginia, but also to military science, since in
time it would be recognized as perhaps the Confederacy's main contribution to the art of war, which was never the same thereafter.

In mid-January, while Lee was away on his brief trip to Richmond, Old Peter had been left in command on the Rappahannock by
virtue of his seniority. His corps, still intact at the time, occupied the
northern half of the position, from Hamilton's Crossing to Banks Ford,
five miles above Fredericksburg, while Jackson's occupied the rest, from
Massaponax Creek down to Port Royal, twenty miles below the town.
Lee had no sooner left than Longstreet invited Stonewall to inspect the
First Corps defenses, and what the grim Virginian saw when he arrived

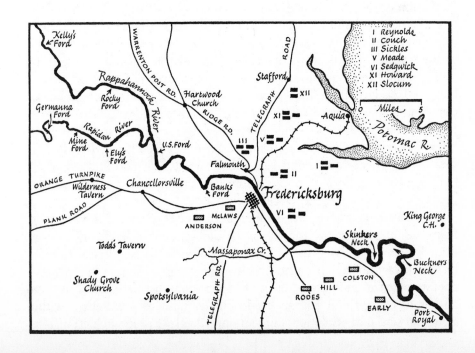

was in the nature of a revelation. Located so as to dominate the roads and open ground, the fieldworks had been designed for use by a skeleton force which could hold them against a surprise attack until supports came up from the reserve. There was nothing new about that; Lee had conceived and used intrenchments for the same purpose on the Peninsula, nearly a year ago. The innovation here involved was the traversed trench. Formerly such works had been little more than long, open ditches, with the spoil thrown forward to serve as a parapet, which gave excellent protection from low-trajectory fire from dead ahead but were vulnerable to flank attack and the lateral effect of bursting shells. To offset these two disadvantages — particularly the latter, intensified by the long-range rifled cannon of the Federals, firing from positions well beyond the reach of most Confederate batteries — Longstreet's engineers had broken the long ditches into quite short, squad-sized rifle trenches, staggered in depth, disposed for mutual support, and connected by traverses which could be utilized against flank attacks and afforded solid protection from all but direct artillery hits. Jackson took a careful look, then returned to his own lines, where the dirt began at once to fly anew. From such crude beginnings, fathered by the necessity for defending a fixed position against a greatly superior foe, grew the highly intricate field fortifications of the future. Presently the whole Rappahannock line, from Banks Ford to Port Royal, was thus protected throughout its undulant, winding, 25-mile length, and when Old Peter left next month with more than half of his men, so well had he and they designed and dug, Lee did not find it necessary to reinforce the two-division remnant by shifting troops from Jackson. "The world has never seen such a fortified position," a young Second Corps artillerist declared some weeks later. "The famous lines at Torres Vedras could not compare with them. ... They follow the contour of the ground and hug the bases of the hills as they wind to and from the river, thus giving natural flanking arrangements, and from the tops of the hills frown the redoubts for sunken batteries and barbette batteries *ad libitum*, far exceeding the number of our guns; while occasionally, where the trenches take straight across the fields, a redoubt stands out defiantly in the open plain to receive our howitzers." Hooker might, as Lee said, "make every effort to crush [the defenders] between now and June," but he was going to find it a much harder job, from here on out, if he tried anything like the approach his predecessor had adopted in December.

On the face of it, that seemed unlikely; Hooker did not resemble Burnside in manner any more than he did in looks. Clearly, if he continued to develop along the lines he had followed so far, Lee was going to have a far thornier problem on his hands, even aside from the lengthened numerical odds, than any he had overcome in frustrating the two all-out offensives that had succeeded his repulse of McClellan, within sight and sound of Richmond, nine months back. The new chieftain's reorganization of his mounted force was a case in point; "Hooker *made* the Federal cavalry," an admiring trooper later declared. Formerly parceled out, regiment by regiment, to infantry commanders whose handling of them had been at best inept, whether in or out of combat, the three divisions — 11,500 strong, with about 13,000 horses — were grouped into a single corps under Brigadier General George Stoneman, a forty-year-old West Pointer, all of whose previous service had been with the mounted arm, before and during the present war, except for a brief term as an infantry corps commander, in which capacity he had won a brevet for gallantry at Fredericksburg. His current rank was one grade below that of the other seven heads of corps; Hooker was withholding promotion until Stoneman proved that he could weld his inherited conglomeration of horsemen into an effective striking force. That was his basic task, and he seemed well on the way toward pushing it to fulfillment, helped considerably by the fact that, after nearly two years in the saddle, the early blue-jacket volunteers — formerly sneered at by their fox-hunt-trained opponents as "white-faced clerks and counter jumpers" who scarcely knew the on side from the off — were becoming seasoned troopers, no longer mounted on crowbait nags fobbed off on the government by unprincipled contractors, but on strong-limbed, sound-winded, well-fed animals who, like their riders, had learned the evolutions of the line and had mastered the art of survival in all weathers.

This improvement came moreover at a time of crisis for the gray cavalry on the opposite bank of the Rappahannock. Not only was there a critical shortage of horses in the Army of Northern Virginia; there was also the likelihood that those on hand, survivors for the most part of a year of hard campaigning, would die for lack of forage. This second danger increased the threat implicit in the first. So clean had the region been swept of fodder that such few remounts as could be found outside the immediate theater of war could not be brought northward. For example, four hundred artillery horses procured that winter in Georgia had to be kept in North Carolina because they could not be foraged with the army, all but a dozen of whose batteries had already been withdrawn from the lines in order to save the animals from starvation. A man could subsist, at least barely, on a couple of pounds of food a day, whereas a horse required about ten times that amount, and this was a great deal more than the rickety single-track railroad from Richmond could bring forward, even if that much grain had been available there. The result was that the cavalry's activity was severely limited. Brigadier General Wade Hampton's brigade, for instance — the first of Stuart's three, which contained in all about 5000 men — had staged three highly successful small-scale raids, deep in the Federal rear at Dumfries and Occoquan, immediately before and after the Battle of Fredericksburg, returning with some 300 captives and their mounts, mostly unwary vedettes picked up in the course of the gray column's advance by starlight, together with a sizeable train of mule-drawn wagons loaded with captured stores, including 300 pairs of badly needed boots — a real windfall. But the end result of these three coups was that Hampton's underfed horses were so utterly broken down by their exertions that the whole brigade had to be sent south to recover, thus weakening Lee still further at a time when he expected Hooker to make up his mind to come booming over the river any day.

Stuart chafed under the restriction thus imposed. His one exploit this winter was an 1800-trooper raid on Fairfax Courthouse, fifteen miles from the Federal capital, beginning the day after Christmas and ending New Year's Day; but all it earned him — in contrast to the enormously successful forays by Forrest and Morgan, launched simultaneously in the West — was 200 mounted prisoners, 20 wagons, and the contents of a dozen sutler stalls; which scarcely made up for the wear and tear of the long ride. Though as usual he made the most of the adventure in his report, it was followed by two months spent in winter quarters, where he was obliged to give less attention to the fast-developing enemy cavalry than to the problem of finding forage for his hungry horses. In such surroundings, though he sought diversion for himself and his men in regimental balls and serenades, the plumed hat, red-lined cape, and golden spurs lost a measure of their glitter, at least in certain eyes. "Stuart carries around with him a banjo player and a special correspondent," one high-ranking fellow officer remarked. "This claptrap is noticed and lauded as a peculiarity of genius, when in fact it is nothing else but the act of a buffoon to attract attention." Down to two brigades after Hampton's departure — one under W. H. F. Lee, called "Rooney," and the other under Fitzhugh Lee, respectively the commanding general's son and nephew — Jeb was obliged to take his pleasure at second hand, from the occasional exploits of subordinates and even ex-subordinates. Among the latter was Captain John S. Mosby, a former cavalry scout who had been given permission in January to recruit a body of partisans for operations in the Loudoun Valley, part of a region to be known in time as "Mosby's Confederacy," so successful were he and his Rangers in bedeviling and defeating the bluecoats sent there to capture or destroy him. Twenty-eight years old and weighing barely 125 pounds, the slim, gray-eyed Virginian first attracted wide attention by his capture, at Fairfax on a night in early March, of Brigadier General E. H. Stoughton, a Vermont-born West Pointer, together with two other officers, 30 men, and 58 horses. Mosby, who at present had fewer men than that in his whole command, entered the general's headquarters, stole upstairs in the darkness, and found the general himself asleep in bed. Turning down the covers, he lifted the tail of the sleeper's nightshirt and gave him a spank on the behind.

"General," he said, "did you ever hear of Mosby?"

"Yes," Stoughton replied, flustered and half awake; "have you caught him?"

"He has caught you," Mosby said, by way of self-introduction, and got his captive up and dressed and took him back through the lines, along with virtually all of his headquarters guard, for delivery to Fitzhugh Lee the following morning at Culpeper.

Fitz Lee, a year younger than the clean-shaven Mosby, though he disguised the fact behind an enormous shovel beard that outdid even Longstreet's in length and thickness, could appreciate a joke as well as the next man, and in this case he could appreciate it perhaps a good deal better, since he and the captive Vermonter had been schoolmates at the Point. Besides, he was in an excellent frame of mind just now, having returned the week before from a similar though less spectacular exploit involving still another fellow cadet of his and Stoughton's: New York-born Brigadier General W. W. Averell, who commanded the second of Stoneman's three divisions. Young Lee was sent by his uncle to investigate a rumor that Hooker was about to repeat McClellan's strategy by transferring his army to the Peninsula. Crossing the Rappahannock well upstream at Kelly's Ford on February 24, Lee's 400-man detachment pushed on to the Warrenton Post Road, then down it, penetrating the blue cavalry screen to the vicinity of Hartwood Church, eight miles short of Falmouth. Here the graybacks encountered their first serious opposition in the form of the 3d Pennsylvania Cavalry, Averell's old regiment before his promotion to divisional command. Lee promptly charged and routed the Keystone troopers, capturing 150 of them at a cost to himself of 14 killed and wounded. Then, having secured the information he had come for — Hooker, whose headquarters were a scant half-dozen miles away by now, obviously was planning no such move as had been rumored — Lee successfully withdrew without further incident, leaving behind him a note for his former schoolmate, whose entire division had been turned out, along with two others of infantry, in a vain attempt to intercept the raiders and avenge the defeat of one of its best regiments. The note was brief and characteristic. "I wish you would put up your sword, leave my state, and go home," Fitz told his old friend, adding in reference to the speed with which the bluecoats had retreated when attacked: "You ride a good horse, I ride a better. Yours can beat mine running." The close was in the nature of a challenge. "If you won't go home, return my visit and bring me a sack of coffee."

Averell returned the visit within three weeks, and he took care to bring along a sack of coffee in his saddlebags. What was more, he repaid the call in force, splashing through the shallows of Kelly's Ford on the morning of March 17 with 3000 troopers. Lee had fewer than 1000 at the time, but his pickets put up such a scrap at the crossing that Averell, though he was pleased to have captured about two dozen of them in the skirmish, persuaded himself that it would be wise to leave a third of his force there to protect his rear, thereby of his own accord reducing the odds to only a little better than two to one. Also, being aware of his old schoolmate's impulsive nature, he halted about midmorning, less than a mile beyond the river, dismounted his men, and took up a strong defensive position behind a stone wall crossing a pasture on the farm of a family named Brooks. Sure enough, at noon Lee came riding hard from Culpeper and attacked without delay, his lead regiment charging dragoon-style, four abreast. The result, as the defenders poured a hot fire from behind their ready-made breastworks, was a quick and bloody repulse. Averell cautiously followed it up, but was struck again, one mile north, with like results. While the blue riders held their ground, the Confederates crossed Carter's Run and reassembled; whereupon the two commands settled down to long-range firing across the creek, relieving the monotony from time to time with limited charges and counter-

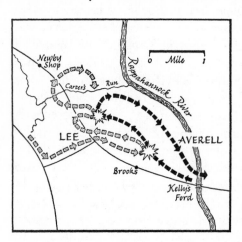

charges which did nothing to alter the tactical stalemate. This continued until about 5.30, when Averell, having learned from captured rebels that Stuart and his crack artillerist Pelham were on the field, decided that the time had come for him to recross the Rappahannock. "My horses were very much exhausted. We had been successful so far. I deemed it proper to withdraw." So he stated later in his report. However, before terminating the requested "visit" he took care to observe the amenities by leaving the sack of coffee Lee had asked for, together with a note: "Dear Fitz. Here's your coffee. Here's your visit. How do you like it? Averell."

The truth was, Fitz did not much like it. Though he could, and did, claim victory on grounds that he had remained in control of the field after the enemy withdrew, this was not very satisfactory when he considered that the Federals could make the same claim with regard to every similar Confederate penetration, including his own recent raid on Hartwood Church and Stuart's dazzling "rides" the year before. Then too, there was the matter of casualties. Suffering 133, Lee had inflicted only 78, or not much over half as many. If this was a victory, it was certainly a strange one. But there was more that was alarming about this St Patrick's Day action: much more, at least from the southern point of view. For the first time on a fair field of fight — the two-to-one odds were not unusual; moreover, they had been the source of considerable underdog glory in the past — Confederate cavalry had fallen back repeatedly under pressure from Federal cavalry. Nothing could have demonstrated better the vast improvement of this arm of the Union war machine, especially when it was admitted that only Averell's lack of the true aggressive instinct, which twice had left the rebel horsemen unmolested while they reformed their broken ranks, had kept the blue troopers from converting both repulses into routs. Unquestionably, this proof that the Federal cavalry had come of age, so to speak, meant future trouble for the men who previously had ridden around and through and over their awkward opponents almost at will. . . . Nor was that all either. This light-hearted exchange of calling cards, accompanied in one case by the gift of a pound of coffee, had its more immediate somber consequences, too. After all, a man who died on this small field was every bit as dead as a man who died in the thunderous pageantry of Fredericksburg, and his survivors were apt to be quite as inconsolable in their sorrow. They might possibly be even more inconsolable, since their grief did not take into account the battle or skirmish itself, but rather the identity of the man who fell. What made Kelly's Ford particular in this respect was that it produced one casualty for whom the whole South mourned.

One of Averell's reasons for withdrawing had been the report that Stuart was on the field. It was true, so far as it went; Jeb was there, but he had brought no reinforcements with him, as Averell supposed; he had come to Culpeper on court-martial business, and thus happened to be on hand when the news arrived that bluecoats were over the river. Similarly, the day before, John Pelham had left cavalry headquarters to see a girl in Orange, so that he too turned up in time to join Fitz Lee on the ride toward Kelly's Ford; "tall, slender, beautifully proportioned," a friend called the twenty-three-year-old Alabamian, and "as grand a flirt as ever lived." With his own guns back near Fredericksburg — including the brass Napoleon with which he had held up the advance of a whole Federal division for the better part of an hour — he was here supposedly as a spectator, but anyone who knew him also knew that he would never be content with anything less than a ringside seat, and would scarcely be satisfied even with that, once the action had been joined. And so it was. When the first charge was launched against the stone wall, the young major smiled, drew the sword which he happened to be wearing because he had gone courting the night before, and waved it gaily as he rode hard to overtake the van. "Forward! Forward!" he cried. Just then, abrupt as a clap of blue-sky thunder, a shell burst with a flash and a roar directly overhead. Pelham fell. He lay on his back, full length and motionless, his blue eyes open and the smile still on his handsome face, which was unmarked. Turning him over, however, his companions found a small, deep gash at the base of his skull, just above the hair line, where a fragment of the shell had struck and entered. When Stuart, who had ridden to another quarter of the field, heard that his young chief of artillery was dead he bowed his head on his horse's neck and wept. "Our loss is irreparable," he said.

Others thought so, too: three girls in nearby towns, for instance, who put on mourning. Word spread quickly throughout the South, and men and women in far-off places, who had known him only by reputation, received with a sense of personal bereavement the news that "the gallant Pelham" had fallen. Robert Lee, who had attached the adjective to the young gunner's name in his report on their last great battle, made an unusual suggestion to the President. "I mourn the loss of Major Pelham," he wrote. "I had hoped that a long career of usefulness and honor was still before him. He has been stricken down in the midst of both, and before he could receive the promotion he had richly won. I hope there will be no impropriety in presenting his name to the Senate, that his comrades may see that his services have been appreciated, and may be incited to emulate them." Davis promptly forwarded the letter, with the result that Pelham was promoted even as he lay in state in the Virginia capitol. For once, the Senate had acted quickly, and the dead artillerist, who just under two years ago had left West Point on the eve of graduation in order to go with his native state, went home to Alabama as Lieutenant Colonel Pelham.

At this time of grief, coupled with uncertainty as to the enemy's intentions, Lee fell ill for the first time in the war. A throat infection had settled in his chest, giving him pains that interfered with his sleep and made him testy during his waking hours. By the end of March his condition was such that his medical director insisted that he leave his tent and take up quarters in a house at Yerby's, on the railroad five miles south of Fredericksburg. He did so, much against his wishes, and complained in a home letter that the doctors were "tapping me all over like an old steam boiler before condemning it." After the manner of most men unfamiliar with sickness, he was irritable and inclined to be impatient with those around him at such times (which in turn provoked his staff into giving him the irreverent nickname "the Tycoon") but he never really lost the iron self-control that was the basis of the character he presented to the world. Once, for example, when he was short with his adjutant over some administrative detail, that officer drew himself up with dignity and silently defied his chief; whereupon Lee at once got hold of himself and said calmly, "Major Taylor, when I lose my temper don't let it make you angry." Nor did his illness detract in any way from the qualities which, at the time of his appointment to command, had led an acquaintance to declare: "His name might be Audacity. He will take more desperate chances, and take them quicker, than any other general in this country, North and South." Confirmation of these words had come in the smoke and flame of the Seven Days, in the fifty-mile march around Pope with half of an outnumbered army, and in the bloody defense of the Sharpsburg ridge with his back to a deep river. Yet nothing gave them more emphasis than his reaction now to the early-April news that Burnside's old corps, after lingering all this time at Newport News, was proceeding west to join its old commander, who had been assigned to head the Department of the Ohio. This signified trouble for Johnston and Bragg in Tennessee, since it probably meant that these troops would reinforce Rosecrans. At Charleston, moreover, Beauregard even now was under what might well be an irresistible attack by an ironclad fleet, with thousands of bluecoats waiting aboard transports for the signal to steam into the blasted harbor and occupy the city. Lee's reaction to this combination of pressures, sick though he was, and faced with odds which he knew were worse than two to one here on the Rappahannock, was to suggest that, if this bolstering of the Union effort down the coast and in the West indicated a lessening of the Union effort in the East, the Army of Northern Virginia should swing over to the offensive. "Should Hooker's army assume the defensive," he wrote the Secretary of War on April 9, "the readiest method of relieving the pressure on General Johnston and General Beauregard would be for this army to cross into Maryland." The wretched condition of the roads, plus the cramping shortage of provisions and transportation, made such a move impossible at present, he added; "But this is what I would recommend, if practicable."

Such audacity, though ingrained and very much a part of the nature of the man, was also based on the combat-tested valor of the soldiers he commanded. He knew there was nothing he could ask of them that they would not try to give him, and he believed that with such a spirit they could not fail; or if they failed, it would not be their fault. "There never were such men in an army before," he said this spring. "They will go anywhere and do anything if properly led." And if his admiration for them was practically boundless, so too was his concern. "His theory, expressed upon many occasions," a staff officer later wrote, "was that the private soldiers — men who fought without the stimulus of rank, emolument, or individual renown — were the most meritorious class of the army, and that they deserved and should receive the utmost respect and consideration." Not one of them ever appealed to him without being given a sympathetic hearing, sometimes in the very heat of battle, and he turned down a plan for the formation of a battalion of honor because he did not believe there would be room in its ranks for all who deserved a place there. Quite literally, nothing was too good for them in the way of reward, according to Lee, and this applied without reservation. To him, they all were heroes. One day he saw a man in uniform standing near the open flap of his tent. "Come in, Captain, and take a seat," he said. When the man replied, "I'm no captain, General; I'm nothing but a private," Lee told him: "Come in, sir. Come in and take a seat. You ought to be a captain."

· · ·

Lincoln apparently felt much the same way about the enlisted men in blue. One correspondent observed that at the final Grand Review, staged on the last full day of his Falmouth visit, "the President merely touched his hat in return salute to the officers, but uncovered to the men in the ranks." Seated upon a short, thick-set horse with a docked tail, the tall civilian in the stovepipe hat and rusty tailcoat presented quite a contrast to the army commander, who wore a dress uniform and rode his usual milk-white charger. A Maine soldier noticed Hooker's "evident satisfaction" as the long blue files swung past in neat array, and spoke of "the conscious power shown on his handsome but rather too rosy face," whereas another from Wisconsin remarked that "Mr Lincoln sat his cob perfectly straight, and dressed as he was in dark clothes, it appeared as if he was an exclamation point astride of the small letter *m*." He seemed oddly preoccupied with matters far removed from the present martial business of watching the troops pass in review. This was shown to be the case when he turned without preamble to Major General Darius N. Couch, the senior corps commander, and asked: "What do you suppose will become of all these men when the war is over?" Couch was somewhat taken aback; his mind had not been working along those lines; but he said later, "It struck me as very pleasant that somebody had an idea that the war would sometime end."

Four days of intimate acquaintance with the Army of the Potomac had indicated to Lincoln, despite the blusterous symptoms of overconfidence on the part of the man beside him on the big white horse — despite, too, the rumored repulse of the ironclads at Charleston, the loss of the Union foothold on Texas, the upsurge of guerillas in Missouri, the apparent stalemate in Middle Tennessee, and Grant's long sequence of failures in front of Vicksburg — that the end of the war might indeed be within reach, once Hooker decided the time had come for a jump-off. Morale had never been higher, the Chief Excutive found by talking with the troops in their renovated camps and hospitals. Moreover, the reorganizational shake-up seemed to have brought the best men to the top. Sumner and Franklin were gone for good, along with the clumsy Grand Division arrangement which had accomplished little more than the addition of another link to the overlong chain of command, and of the seven major generals now at the head of the seven infantry corps, less than half — Couch, Reynolds, and Henry W. Slocum had served in the same capacity during the recent Fredericksburg fiasco, while the remaining four were graduates of the hard-knocks school of experience and therefore could be presumed to have achieved their current eminence on merit. Daniel E. Sickles, the only nonregular of the lot, had taken over from Stoneman after that officer's transfer to the cavalry; Meade had succeeded Dan Butterfield, who had moved up to the post of army chief of staff; John Sedgwick had inherited the command of W. F. Smith, now in charge of Burnside's old corps on its way out to Ohio; Oliver O. Howard, who had lost an arm last year on the Peninsula, had replaced Sigel when that general, already miffed because Hooker had been promoted over his head, resigned in protest because his corps, being next to the smallest of the seven, was incommensurate with his rank. Lincoln had known most of these men before, but in the course of the past four days he had come to know them better, with the result that he felt confident, more confident at any rate than he had felt before, as to the probable outcome of a clash between the armies now facing each other across the Rappahannock. In fact his principal admonition, in a memorandum which he prepared in the course of his visit — perhaps on this same April 9 of the final Grand Review, while Lee was recommending to his government that the Army of Northern Virginia swing over to the offensive in order to break up the menacing Federal combinations — was that "our prime object is the enemy's army in front of us, and is not . . . Richmond at all, unless it be incidental to the main object." Having observed from Stafford Heights the strength of the rebel fortifications, he did not think it would be wise to "take the disadvantage of attacking [Lee] in his intrenchments; but we should continually harass and menace him, so that he shall have no leisure or safety in sending away detachments. If he weakens himself, then pitch into him."

One further admonition he had, and he delivered himself of it the following morning as he sat with Hooker and Couch before departing for Aquia Landing, where the steamer was waiting to take him and his party back to Washington. "I want to impress upon you two gentlemen," he said, "in your next fight, put in all your men." He pronounced the last five words with emphasis, perhaps recalling that in the December fight a good half of the army had stood idle on the left while the conflict wore toward its bloody twilight finish on the right, and then he was off to join his wife and son for the boat ride up the Potomac. Although the trip unquestionably had done him good, providing him with a rare chance to relax, it was after all no more than an interlude in the round of administrative cares, a brief recess from the importunities of men who sought to avail themselves of the power of his office. When a friend remarked that he was looking rested and in better health as a result of his visit to the army, Lincoln replied that it had been "a great relief to get away from Washington and the politicians. But nothing touches the tired spot," he added.

✗ 3 ✗

Longstreet, on his own at last — at least in a manner of speaking — was finding no such opportunities for glory beyond the James as his fellow corps commander Jackson had found the year before, on detached service out in the Shenandoah Valley. There Stonewall had not only added a brisk chapter to military history and several exemplary paragraphs to future tactics manuals, but had also earned for himself, according to admirers, the one thing his senior rival, according to detractors, wanted more than anything on or off the earth: a seat among the immortals in Valhalla. However, this southside venture, being a different kind of thing, seemed quite unlikely to be productive of any such reward. Designed less for the gathering of laurels than for the gathering of the hams and bacon which for generations had made and would continue to make the Smithfield region famous, it was aimed at satisfying the hunger of the stomach, rather than the hunger of the soul. What was more, throughout his ten weeks of "independent" command, Old Peter was obliged to serve three masters — Davis, Seddon, and Lee — who saddled him with three separate, simultaneous, and sometimes incompatible assignments: 1) the protection of the national capital, threatened by combinations of forces superior to his own, 2) the gathering of supplies in an area that had been under Federal domination for nearly a year, and 3) the disposition of his troops so as to be able to hurry them back to the Rappahannock on short notice. To these, there presently was added a fourth, the investment of Suffolk, which had more men within its fortifications than he could bring against them. The wonder, under such conditions as obtained, was not that he failed in part, but that he succeeded to any degree at all in fulfilling these divergent expectations.

In Richmond itself there had been no talk of failure at the outset, only a feeling of vast relief as the battle-hardened divisions of Hood and Pickett arrived to block the approach of blue forces reported to be gathering ominously, east and southeast of the city, beyond the rim of intrenchments mainly occupied by part-time defenders recruited in the emergency from the host of clerks and other government workers who had escaped conscription up to now. One of these, an industrious diarist, influenced perhaps by a far-fetched sense of rivalry — or perhaps by the fact that in the past six months, since Lee's army had set out northward after Pope, he had forgot what a combat soldier looked like — thought the First Corps veterans "pale and haggard" when he saw them on February 18, slogging through snow deposited calf-deep in the streets by a heavy storm the night before. Four days later, however, Seddon wrote Lee that their "appearance, spirit, and cheerfulness afforded great satisfaction," not only to the authorities but also to the fretful populace. "General Longstreet is here," the Secretary added, "and under his able guidance of such troops no one doubts as to the entire security of the capital." On February 25 he appointed the burly Georgian commander of the Department of Virginia and North Carolina, which was created by combining the three departments of Richmond, Southern Virginia, and North Carolina, respectively under Major Generals Arnold Elzey, Samuel G. French, and D. H. Hill, together with the independent Cape Fear

River District under Brigadier General W. H. C. Whiting, who was charged with protecting Wilmington from attack by land or water. Longstreet's total number of men present for duty, including those in the two divisions he brought with him, plus Ransom's demi-division forwarded earlier, was 44,193 of all arms, mostly scattered about the two states in ill-equipped and poorly administered garrisons of defense. Already outnumbered by the Federals on hand — whose current strength of 50,995 effectives he considerably overestimated — he was alarmed by reports, received on the day he assumed command, that transports were arriving daily in Hampton Roads, crowded to the gunwales with reinforcements for the intended all-out drive on Richmond. So far, they had unloaded an estimated "40,000 or 50,000" troops at Newport News, he wired Lee, and there were rumors that Joe Hooker himself had been seen at Fort Monroe, presaging the early arrival of the balance of the Army of the Potomac.

In such alarming circumstances, and schooled as he had been in strategy under Lee, Old Peter reasoned that the time had come for him to attack, if only by way of creating a diversion. As he put it, "We are much more likely to succeed by operating ourselves than by lying still to await the enemy's time for thorough preparations before he moves upon us." However, it was in the attempted application of this commendable principle that his troubles really began; for it was then that he came face to face with the fact that the exercise of independent command, especially in the armies of the Confederacy, involved a good deal more than a knowledge of tactics and logistics. Like him, his three ranking subordinates were West Pointers in their early or middle forties, and like him, too, they had their share of temperamental peculiarities — as he discovered when he issued instructions for a joint attack on New Bern. Held by the Federals for nearly a year now, the town had been the base for their mid-December advance against the Wilmington & Weldon Railroad, sixty miles away at Goldsboro, and it was Longstreet's belief that an attack on both banks of the Neuse River, farther down, would pinch off the blue garrison and expose it to capture or destruction. His plan was for Hill to move against the place with his whole command, reinforced by one of Whiting's two brigades, which would give him about 14,000 men in all. Hill was altogether willing, having recently excoriated the Yankee invaders by calling upon his infantry to "cut down to 6 feet by 2 the dimensions of the farms which these plunderers propose to appropriate." But Whiting was not, even though the brigade asked for was Ransom's, detached from the First Corps and forwarded to him only the month before. In response to Longstreet's call for "half your force and as many more as can be spared from the Wilmington garrison," along with one of his three long-range Whitworth guns, Whiting — a brilliant thirty-nine-year-old Mississippian who, three years after Old Peter had finished near the bottom of the

West Point class of '42, had not only graduated at the top of his class, but had done so with the highest marks any cadet had ever made — promptly wrote: "I perceive you are not acquainted with this vicinity. . . . So far from considering myself able to spare troops from here, I have applied for and earnestly urged that another brigade be sent here immediately. The works here are by no means completed and I need the services of every man I can raise."

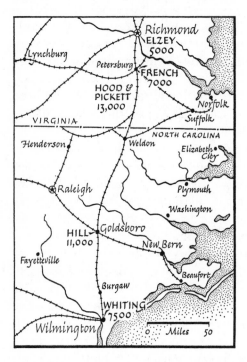

The result was that Hill moved against New Bern without the help of Whiting's men or the loan of the precious long-range gun, and though he converted what was to have been an attack into a demonstration — it was March 14, the anniversary of the fall of the town to the Federals as a follow-up of their capture of Roanoke Island — even that was repulsed decisively when the defenders towed gunboats up the river from Pamlico Sound and opened a scorching fire against the Confederates on both banks, inflicting 30-odd casualties at a cost of only 6. Back in Goldsboro two days later, Hill was furious. "The spirit manifested by Whiting has spoiled everything," he protested in his report. As he saw it, the proper correction for this was for the government to keep its word that he would be given command of all the troops in the state, including those at Wilmington, in which case he would be able to bend the fractious Whiting to his will. "I have received nothing but contemptuous treatment from Richmond from the very beginning of the war," he complained hotly, "but I hope they will not carry matters so far as to perpetuate a swindle." Longstreet, receiving his caustic friend's report, sought to protect him from the wrath of their superiors. "I presume that this was not intended as an official communication," he replied, "and have not forwarded it. I hope that you will send up another account of your trip." Hill neither insisted that the document stand nor offered to withdraw it, but he declined to submit a new or expurgated account of what Old Peter referred to as his "trip."

For all his obstreperous ways of protesting the injustice he saw everywhere around him, Hill was only one among the many when it came to presenting his chief with problems. Arnold Elzey, in charge of the Richmond defenses north of the James, had only recently returned to duty after a long and painful convalescence from the face wound he had suffered at Gaines Mill. A Marylander, he originally had had the last name Jones, but had dropped it in favor of his mother's more distinctive maiden name. Erratic and moody, perhaps because of his disfigurement and the internal damage to his mouth which made his words scarcely intelligible, he was said to be drinking heavily — a particular yet not uncommon type among the casualties of war, injured as much in pride as in body. At any rate, neither he nor his command could be counted on for anything more than the desperate last-ditch resistance that was his and their assignment. Moreover, Longstreet had no high opinion of the abilities of Sam French, who was charged with the defense of Petersburg, that vital nexus of rail supply lines connecting Virginia and the deeper South. A New-Jersey-born adoptive Mississippian and a veteran of the Mexican War, French had attained high rank without distinction in the field of the present conflict, and Old Peter had the usual combat officer's prejudice in this and other such cases he encountered when he crossed the James. Because of Lee's policy of quietly getting rid of men he found unsatisfactory, not by cashiering them but by transferring them to far or adjoining theaters where he considered their shortcomings would cost their country less, Longstreet might have thought he was back with the old Army of the Potomac, as it had been called before the advent of Lee and its transfiguration into the Army of Northern Virginia, so familiar were the faces of many of the officers he found serving under him when he took over his new department. All too many of those faces reflected failure, and all too many others identified men who were inexperienced in combat.

Not that there appeared to be any considerable need for such experience just now. Foraging operations were in full swing, with commissary details scouring the countryside and sending back long trains of wagons heavily loaded with hams and bacon, side meat, salted fish, and flour and cornmeal, all of which were plenteous in the region. Increasingly, as the Federals failed to press their rumored drive on Richmond, the removal of such badly needed stores was becoming the prime concern of the department commander and his troops.

On March 17 their work was interrupted by a dispatch from Lee. Bluecoats were over the Rappahannock at Kelly's Ford; Longstreet was to hurry north with Hood and Pickett to help drive them back. Before he could obey, however, the order was countermanded. The threat had been no more than a cavalry raid; the enemy troopers had retired. Old Peter returned to his foraging duties with new zeal. Now that the nearer counties had been picked clean, he wanted to move eastward into those beyond the Blackwater and Chowan Rivers, out of reach for the past year because of the Union occupation. He figured that if the Yankees could be driven back within their works and held there for a reasonable length of time, his commissary agents — unhampered by the enemy and aided by the citizens of those regions, who had remained intensely loyal to the Confederacy through long months when they might have thought themselves forsaken — would be able to effect a quick removal of the stores. However, this was at best a risky business for him to undertake. He would not only have to keep his two most effective divisions ready to disengage on short notice, in order to be able to speed them north on call from Lee; he would also have to detail a considerable portion of his force for commissary duties behind the lines if he was to accomplish the main purpose underlying his reason for advancing in the first place. In short, with these two disadvantages added to the fact that he was outnumbered before he even began, he would be reversing the required two-to-one numerical ratio between the two parties engaged in siege operations. But he decided to give the thing a try in any event, for the sake of all those thousands of slabs of bacon and barrels of herring awaiting removal from areas previously inaccessible to the soldiers who were fighting here and elsewhere for their eventual deliverance from the blue forces now in occupation.

He made his plans accordingly. Hood and Pickett would join French for a movement against Suffolk, which would serve the double purpose of bringing the fertile Blackwater-Chowan watersheds within the grasp of his commissary agents and of blocking the path of a Federal drive on Petersburg from the lower reaches of the James. Nor was that all. Hill — reinforced at last by Ransom's brigade, pried loose from Whiting over that general's violent protest that he was being stripped of two thirds of his infantry on the eve of an all-out assault on Wilmington by the ironclad fleet Du Pont was assembling at Port Royal — would move simultaneously against Washington, North Carolina, the Tar River gateway to a region which was lush with agricultural produce and gave access to the fisheries of upper Pamlico Sound. This lower movement under Hill, while equally rich in foraging possibilities, was more in the nature of a diversion, favoring the main effort against Suffolk, which would be under Longstreet's personal direction. It was Old Peter's hope that the Unionists, being threatened in two places at once, would not only be prevented from strengthening either at the expense of the other, but would also be thrown off balance by the expectation of additional strikes, all down the long perimeter of their coastal holdings. Though he made it clear at the outset, to his superiors as well as to his subordinates, that both advances were intended to be no more than demonstrations, staged primarily to drive the bluecoats within their works so that his foraging details would be free to scour the area unmolested, he did not overlook the possibility of taking advantage of any opening the enemy might afford. Food for Lee's soldiers was his main concern, but he intended to draw blood, too — despite the numerical odds — whenever and wherever the tactical risk appeared slight enough to justify grasping the nettle. "The principal object of the expedition was to draw out supplies for our army," he reminded the War Department after the movement against Suffolk was under way. "I shall confine myself to this unless I find a fair opportunity for something more."

Hill took off first, however, advancing so rapidly from Goldsboro that on March 30 he had Washington invested before the Federal department commander, Major General John G. Foster, had a chance to reinforce its 1200-man garrison. With ten times that many troops on hand, the Confederates would have little trouble keeping the defenders penned up, but Hill did not believe their capture would be worth the casualties he would suffer in an assault. Consequently, while his foragers were busily rounding up hogs and cattle, he continued to hover about the place, making threatening gestures from time to time in the face of highly accurate fire from gunboats anchored off the town. His chief worry was that Foster — one of Burnside's three aggressive brigadiers in last year's smashing attack on Roanoke Island — would order an advance against his rear by the Union force at New Bern, only thirty miles away. As the siege progressed through the first week in April he vibrated with alternate emotions of jubilation and despair, much to the confusion of Longstreet, who scarcely knew what to make of his lieutenant's fluctuant dispatches. "Up to the 2d instant," he replied from Petersburg on April 7, apparently in something of a daze, "you gave me no reason to hope that you could accomplish anything. . . . Then came your letter of the 2d, which was full of encouragement and hope. . . . After your letter of the 2d came one of the 4th, which I believe was more desponding than your previous letters. . . . Your letter of the 5th revives much hope again." Old Peter was understandably confused, but in point of fact Hill was doing much better than he knew or would admit. Not only were large quantities of supplies moving swiftly back to Goldsboro for forwarding to Richmond and the Rappahannock line, but Foster was reacting exactly as the Confederates had hoped he would do to their pretense of great strength and earnestness. Drawing in his horns in expectation of being struck next at almost any point in his department, he left Hill's commissary agents a clear field for exploitation. "I am confident," he warned Halleck on Easter Sunday, "that heavy operations will be necessary in this state, and that the most desperate efforts are and will continue to be made to drive us from the towns now occupied."

At any rate Longstreet's main concern was centered presently on matters closer at hand than Hill's pendulum swings from gloom to elation down on the banks of the Tar. On April 9 — the day Lee recommended an advance into Maryland as the best Confederate strategy for contesting the over-all Union menace, East and West, and also the day Hooker staged the last of the Grand Reviews in honor of Lincoln's Falmouth visit — First Corps troops moved out of their camps near Petersburg and took up the march southeastward in the direction of the lower Blackwater crossings less than twenty miles from Suffolk, which the Federals had been fortifying ever since they occupied it formally in September. Two divisions were quartered there now, under Major General John J. Peck and Brigadier General George W. Getty, with a combined total of 21,108 effectives. Hood, Pickett, and French had 20,192 between them; but Peck, estimating the rebel strength at "40,000 to 60,000 men," reacted much as Foster had done, ten days ago, to Hill's advance on Washington. Calling in all his detachments from the surrounding countryside, he skirmished briefly along the Blackwater to gain time for a concentration, then fell back on Suffolk, where he buttoned himself up tightly. While his troops were at work improving the intrenchments, he notified his superiors at Fort Monroe and Washington that he was prepared to fight to the last man, despite the enemy's "great preponderance of artillery as well as other branches." Longstreet moved up deliberately. On April 11 he invested the town, taking the bluecoats under fire from the opposite bank of the Nansemond River while extending his right southward all the way to Dismal Swamp. Behind this long, concave front, which he held with a minimum number of men in order to provide details for his all-important foraging operations, commissary officers were soon busy purchasing everything in sight that a man could eat or wear. Long trains of wagons, piled high with goods and forage, soon were grinding westward amid a din of cracking whips, ungreased axles, and teamster curses. After unloading at newly established dumps along the Petersburg & Norfolk Railroad, they returned eastward, rattling empty across the muddy landscape, for new loads. Day and night, to Longstreet's considerable satisfaction — as well as to that of the hungry men on the Rappahannock, whose rations improved correspondingly — the shuttle work continued. Supplies appeared inexhaustible in this region scarcely touched by war till now.

Meanwhile, by way of keeping up the bluff, the troops on line were demonstrating noisily, as if in preparation for an assault on the blue intrenchments across the way. Although the duty was mostly dull, there were occasional incidents that provided all the excitement a man could want, and more. For instance, there was the affair at Fort Huger, an old Confederate redoubt constructed originally as part of the Suffolk defenses but abandoned by the Federals when they took over. As it turned out, they showed wisdom by this action. On April 16, French moved five guns and three companies of infantry into the fort on the far left of his line, intending to deny enemy gunboats the use of the adjoining Nansemond River. Three nights later, however, six companies of Connecticut infantry crossed the river, a quarter of a mile upstream, and swooped down in a surprise attack that captured the works, along with all five of the guns and 130 officers and men. Joined before dawn by the other four companies of their regiment, they held the place all the following day and returned to their own lines after dark, taking along the captured men and guns. Longstreet had scarcely had time to absorb the news of this setback when he heard from Hill that the Washington siege had been abandoned on the same day Fort Huger was occupied by French. Two weeks had sufficed for the removal of most of the stores from the region; so that when, at the end of that span, the Federals succeeded in running in two ships to replenish the supplies of the garrison, Hill decided the time had come for him to withdraw. Back at Goldsboro before the week was out, he praised his troops for their "vigilance on duty and good behavior everywhere." His scorn he reserved for home-guarders, especially those of lofty rank, whose avoidance of combat duty he blamed for his lack of the strength required to drive the detested Yankees not only "into their rat holes at New Bern and Washington," but into Pamlico Sound as well. "And such noble regiments they have," he sneered at these stay-at-home Tarheel warriors. "Three field officers, four staff officers, ten captains, thirty lieutenants, and one private with a misery in his bowels. . . . When our independence is won, the most trifling soldier in the ranks will be more respected, as he is now more respectable, than an army of these skulking exempts."

Longstreet accepted vexation far more philosophically. Even the overrunning of Fort Huger, though it showed, as he said, "a general lack of vigilance and prompt attention to duties," did not arouse his ire. "Many of the officers were of limited experience," he concluded his report of the affair, "and I have no doubt acted as they thought best. I do not know that any of them deserve censure. This lesson, it is hoped, will be of service to us all." Others reacted differently as the Suffolk siege wore on. Hood, for example, had small use for this buttoned-up style of warfare. "Here we are in front of the enemy again," he wrote Lee toward the end of April. "The Yankees have a very strong position, and of course they increase the strength of their position daily. I presume we shall leave here so soon as we gather all the bacon in the country." Boyishly the Kentucky-born Texan added: "When we leave here it is my desire to return to you. If any troops come to the Rappahannock please don't forget me." Thirty-one and a bachelor, Hood was bored. But that could scarcely be said of his fellow division commander Pickett. This thirty-eight-year-old widower, a handsome if rather doll-faced man with long chestnut eurls which he anointed regularly with perfume, was in the full flush of a sunset love affair with a southside girl not half his age. LaSalle Corbell was her name; he styled her "the charming Sally" — his dead wife had been called Sally, too — and wrote her ardent letters signed "Your Soldier" despite the fact that he saw her almost nightly, riding up to her home at Chuckatuck by twilight and back to his lines before the first red glow of dawn. When Longstreet at last began to frown on this inattentiveness to duty, not to mention the abuse of horse-flesh, Pickett tried to persuade the corps adjutant, Major G. Moxley Sorrel, to give him permission to take off without Old Peter's knowledge.

Sorrel, who did not approve of what he called "such carpet-knight doings in the field," declined to accept the responsibility for what might happen in Pickett's absence, and referred him back to Longstreet. "But he is tired of it and will refuse," the ringleted Virginian protested. "And I must go; I must see her. I swear, Sorrel, I'll be back before anything can happen in the morning." Sorrel still said no; but recalling the scene years later he added that "Pickett went all the same. Nothing could hold him back from that pursuit."

Increasingly, as spring wore on and the end of the campaign drew near — he himself had set a May 3 closing date by notifying Richmond on April 19 that two more weeks would suffice for draining the region of its stores — Longstreet grew dissatisfied: not so much with what he had done, which was after all considerable, as with the thought of what he had not done. While it was true that he had carried out, practically to the letter, his difficult triple assignment — that is, he had kept the Yankees out of Petersburg, he had secured enormous quantities of previously inaccessible supplies, and he had kept his First Corps troops on the alert for a swift return to Lee — it was also painfully true that he had accomplished nothing that would compare in tactical brilliance with even the smallest battlefield victory scored by Jackson out in the Valley a year ago. As a result, the taking of Suffolk, along with its thousands of bluecoats and tons of matériel, began to appeal to him more and more as a fitting end to these two months of detached service. Moreover, as the notion grew more attractive in his mind's eye, it also began to appear more feasible to his military judgment, despite the fact that the Federals inside the place were stronger now, by some 9000 reinforcements brought in from Hampton Roads, than they had been at the outset. There were several ways of assessing this last, however, and one was that the grandeur of the triumph would be in direct ratio to the plumpness of the prize. Accordingly, Old Peter wrote to Lee, telling him what he had in mind and asking if he could not be sent the rest of his corps in order to assure the success of his assault on the blue intrenchments. Foreseeing objections — as well he might — he suggested that Lee, if need be, could fall back to the line of the Annas, though it was his own conviction that one corps would be able to stand fast on the Rappahannock in the event of an attack. Lee replied on April 27 that Hooker was far too strong, and just now far too active, for him to consider a further weakening of his army. In fact, he countered by asking his lieutenant if he could spare him any of the troops in North Carolina. But he certainly did not veto the proposal for ending the southside siege with an assault. "As regards your aggressive movement upon Suffolk," he wrote, "you must act according to your good judgment. If a damaging blow could be struck there or elsewhere of course it would be advantageous." He added some doubts as to whether the game would be worth the candle in this case, but Longstreet could see in the letter a relaxation of the urgency for keeping his First Corps divisions practically uncommitted in order to have them ready to hurry north on short notice. Consequently, while his foraging crews kept busy, hauling out the last of the precious wagonloads of hogs and corn and herring, he turned his thoughts to tactical details of the assault that would cap the climax by adding the one element — glory — so far lacking in a campaign already productive of much else.

Three days later, however — April 30 — his plans were shattered by a wire from Adjutant General Cooper in Richmond, quoting a dispatch just received from Lee. Hooker was over the Rappahannock in great strength, above as well as below Fredericksburg, Lee had announced, "and it looks as if he was in earnest." Cooper's instructions to Longstreet were brief and to the point: "Move without delay your command to this place to effect a junction with General Lee."

Longstreet inquired by telegraph whether this meant that he was to abandon his wagons, still scattered about on foraging operations, and risk a quick withdrawal of his men, which would bring out the Federals hot on his heels. By no means, Cooper replied on May Day. What had been intended was for him "to secure all possible dispatch without incurring loss of trains or unnecessary hazard of troops." Having thus avoided going off half-cocked, Old Peter turned to the always difficult task of designing a disengagement. After the wagons had been called in and sent rearward, orders were issued on May 2 for all the troops to withdraw from the intrenchments the following evening and retire westward under cover of darkness, burning bridges and felling trees in their wake to discourage pursuit. This came off on schedule, and after some sharp skirmishing by rear-guard elements, the whole command was across the Blackwater by sundown of the 4th. Leaving French to defend that line, Hood and Pickett moved to Petersburg next day. Dawn of the 6th found them on the march for the James, leg-weary but eager, and Longstreet himself was in Richmond before noon, making preparations to speed both divisions northward by rail for a share in the great battle reportedly still raging along the near bank of the Rappahannock. All this ended the following day, however, when he received a wire from Lee: "The emergency that made your presence so desirable has passed for the present, so far as I can see, and I desire that you will not distress your troops by a forced movement to join me, or sacrifice for that purpose any public interest that your sudden departure might make it necessary to abandon."

�҉ 4 ✗

"Go forward, and give us victories," Lincoln had written, and that was what Hooker had in mind when he crossed the Rappahannock. Nor was that all. "I not only expected victory," he would recall when the smoke had cleared, "I expected to get the whole [rebel] army." That this had indeed been his intention was confirmed by his chief of staff, who also declared in retrospect that the real purpose of the campaign had been "to destroy the army of General Lee where it then was." Earlier, on the eve of committing what he called "the finest body of soldiers the sun ever shone on," Fighting Joe had expressed his resolution in terms that were even more expansive. "My plans are perfect," he announced, "and when I start to carry them out, may God have mercy on Bobby Lee; for I shall have none."

Just what those plans were he was not saying, even to those whose task it would be to translate them into action. In point of fact, however, they were influenced considerably by the man who had preceded him in command. In addition to having demonstrated the folly of launching headlong attacks against prepared intrenchments — intrenchments which, incidentally, had been enormously strengthened and extended since December — Burnside had explored, at least on paper, several other approaches to the problem of how to prise the rebels loose from their works and come to grips with them in the open, where the advantage of numbers would be likely to decide the issue in favor of the Union. Now he had departed, taking "his deportment with him out of the Army of the Potomac, thank God," but Hooker could remember how the lush-whiskered general had stressed the need for secrecy and then proceeded to talk with all and sundry about his plans, with the result that his opponent's only surprise had been at his foolhardiness. So the new commander, who, by ordinary, was anything but a close-mouthed man, profited in reverse from his predecessor's example. He kept his plans to himself.

Not that he did not have any; he did, indeed, and he did not care who knew it, so long as the particulars remained hidden. These too had been inherited, however, for the most part. Originally, like Burnside on the eve of his bloody mid-December commitment, Hooker had planned to cross the Rappahannock well below Fredericksburg; but this had two serious disadvantages. It would uncover the direct route to Washington, which he knew would distress Lincoln, and it would have to be announced to the Confederates in advance by the laying of pontoons. Upstream, on the other hand, the river narrowed and was comparatively shallow. There were fords in that direction — Banks Ford, five miles above the town, and United States Ford, seven miles farther west — behind which he could mass and conceal his troops in order to send them splashing across in a rush that would smother the south-bank gray outpost detachments, thus forcing Lee to face about and meet his assailants without the advantage of those formidable intrenchments. This had been Burnside's intention in the campaign that ground to a soggy halt in January, but Hooker, by waiting for the advent of fair weather, had greatly

reduced the likelihood of the movement's coming to any such premature and ignominious end. Besides, there would be tactical embellish-
ments, designed to increase the Federal chances for an all-out victory.

Principal among these was a plan for taking advantage of the recently demonstrated improvement of the blue cavalry. With Stoneman
outnumbering Stuart better than three to one — just over 11,500 sabers
opposed to just under 3500 — it was Hooker's belief that if his troopers
crossed the river in strength they would be able to have things pretty
much their own way in the Confederate rear. Damage to Lee's communications and supply lines, coupled with strikes at such vital points as
Gordonsville and Hanover Junction, might throw him into sudden retreat; in which case the Federal infantry, coming down on the run from
the upstream crossings, would catch him in flight, strung out on the
roads leading southward, and destroy him. No one so far in this war had
been able to throw Lee into such a panic, it was true, but the reason for
this might be that no one had dared to touch him where he was tender.
At any rate Hooker thought it worth a try, and he had his adjutant general draw up careful instructions for Stoneman. His entire corps, less one
brigade but accompanied by all 22 of its guns, was to cross Rappahannock Bridge, thirty miles above Fredericksburg, not later than 7 a.m.
on April 13, "for the purpose of turning the enemy's position on his left,
throwing the cavalry between him and Richmond, isolating him from his
supplies, checking his retreat, and inflicting on him every possible injury
which will tend to his discomfiture and defeat." Lest there be any doubt
that the cavalry chief was to be vigorous in his treatment of the fleeing
Lee, the adjutant then broke into what might one day have become the
model for a pregame Rockne pep talk: "If you cannot cut off from his
column large slices, the general desires that you will not fail to take small
ones. Let your watchword be fight, fight, fight, bearing in mind that
time is as valuable to the general as rebel carcasses."

Stoneman and his 10,000 chosen troopers, along with their 22
guns and a train of 275 wagons containing enough additional food and
forage to sustain them for nine days beyond the lines, were poised for a
crossing at the specified hour. One brigade had already forded the river
a few miles above Rappahannock Bridge, with instructions to come
sweeping down and clear out the rebel horsemen watching from across
the way. But as the three divisions stood to their mounts, awaiting the
order that would send them about their task of cutting slices large and
small from Lee's retreating column, rain began to patter and then to
drum, ominously reminiscent of the downpour that had queered the
Mud March. Now as then, roads became quagmires and the river began
to swell, flooding the fords and tugging at the shaky pilings of the
bridge. Stoneman decided to wait it out. Recalling the brigade that had
crossed, he wired headquarters that his rolling stock was stalled. Hooker
replied that he was to shuck his guns and wagons and proceed without

them. Stoneman said he would, and set dawn of the 15th as his new jump-off time. Then the wire went dead. Hooker, having promised to keep the President posted on the progress of the movement, struck an optimistic note in a dispatch sent to Washington on that date: "I am rejoiced that Stoneman had two good days to go up the river, and was able to cross it before it had become too much swollen. If he can reach his position [deep in the enemy rear] the storm and mud will not damage our prospects." Lincoln was not so sure. It was his belief, he replied within the hour, that "General S. is not moving rapidly enough to make the expedition come to anything. He has now been out three days, two of which were unusually fair weather, and all three without hindrance from the enemy, and yet he is not 25 miles from where he started. To reach his point he still has 60 to go, another river (the Rapidan) to cross, and will be hindered by the enemy. By arithmetic, how many days will it take him to do it? . . . I greatly fear it is another failure already."

His fears were confirmed the following day when a courier reached Falmouth with a letter from upstream. "I cannot say what has been the state of affairs away from this vicinity," Stoneman wrote, "but here, at the hour of my last dispatch, the condition of things may be judged of when I tell you that almost every rivulet was swimming, and the roads next to impassable for horses or pack-mules. . . . The railroad bridge has been partly carried away by the freshet. The river is out of its banks, and was still on the rise a few hours ago. . . . My dispatch [setting a new date for the crossing] was based upon the expectation that we were to be favored with a continuation of fair weather. It certainly was not predicated upon the expectation of being overtaken by one of the most violent rainstorms I have ever been caught in." There was much else by way of explanation and excuse, including the news that three men and several horses had been drowned that morning while attempting to cross what had been a nearly dry stream bed the day before. But the gist of the long letter came about midway: "The elements seem to have conspired to prevent the accomplishment of a brilliant cavalry operation."

Hooker was disappointed. He told Stoneman to stay where he was, keep up his reserve supply of rations, and be ready to take off southward "as soon as the roads and rivers will permit." However, the rain showed no sign of a real letup. For nearly two weeks it kept falling, with only a few fair days mixed in to mock the army's immobility, and all this time Hooker was champing at the bit, anxious to put his troops in motion for the kill. As the days went by, his bitterness increased. He began to doubt that Stoneman and the cavalry were up to carrying out the mission he had assigned them; he began, in fact, to see room for improvement in the plans he had called perfect. Since he had the Confederates outnumbered better than two to one — as he knew by reports from the excellent intelligence service he had established as part of his staff — he had a rare chance to attack them, front and back, with separate columns each of which would be superior to the gray mass clamped between them. Instead of 10,000 cavalry, he would put 60,000 infantry and artillery in Lee's immediate rear, blocking his retreat while the other 60,000 pounded his front and the troopers far in his rear slashed at his lines of supply and communication. Isolated and surrounded, prised out of his intrenchments and grievously outnumbered, Lee would be pulverized; Hooker would "get the whole army." It was a pleasant thing to contemplate, not only because of its classic tactical simplicity, but also because it would involve what might be called poetic justice, a turning of the tables on the old fox who so often had divided his own army, but without the advantage of numbers, in hopes of destroying the very soldiers who now were about to destroy him.

What was more, as Hooker pored over his maps to plan the logistical details of the proposed envelopment, he found that the terrain seemed made to order for just such a maneuver. Banks Ford was stoutly defended from across the way, the rebels having honeycombed the dominant south-bank heights with trenches that formed the left-flank anchor of their line, and U. S. Ford was guarded nearly as heavily by an intrenched outpost detachment; besides which, the recent rains had swollen them both well past wading depth, so that his previous design to seize them in a sudden, splashing rush was now impractical. On the other hand Kelly's Ford, fifteen miles above the junction of the Rappannock and the Rapidan, which occurred just over a mile above U. S. Ford, was lightly held, unfortified, and comparatively shallow. Although crossing there would call for a long approach march and would involve another river crossing when the column reached the Rapidan, the advantages greatly outweighed the drawbacks. For one thing, Kelly's Ford was far enough out beyond the enemy flank to give hope that, with luck, the march and perhaps both crossings could be accomplished before the rebs knew what was afoot, and for another it would afford a covered approach, along excellent roads traversing a wooded region known locally as the Wilderness, to within striking distance of the Confederate rear. Moreover, as the column moved eastward along the south bank of the Rappahannock it would uncover both U.S. and Banks Fords, which would not only shorten considerably its lines of supply and communication, thereby making it possible for the two halves of the blue army to reinforce each other quickly if an emergency arose in either direction, but would also give the flankers, in the case of the Banks Ford defenses, control of high ground that dominated much of the present rebel line of fortifications; Lee would be obliged to come out into the open, whether he wanted to or not. All this sounded fine to Hooker. Admittedly he was about to engage in the risky business of dividing his army in the presence of the enemy, but Lee had proved on more than one occasion that the profits more than justified the risk, even though he had done so with the numerical odds against him; whereas with Hooker it would be the other way around. It was this last that gave him substantial reason to hope for the Cannae which so far, and for all his vaunted skill in battle, had eluded Lee.

Translating theory into action, Fighting Joe sent orders on April 26 for the corps of Slocum, Howard, and Meade to march for Kelly's Ford at sunrise the following morning. They were to be in position there not later than 4 p.m. of the 28th, at which time they were to head south for the Rapidan, cross that river at Ely's and Germanna Fords, and take the roads leading southeast to the Orange Turnpike, then proceed due east along it to a position covering a crossroads hamlet called Chancellorsville, eight miles west of Lee's line and less than half that far from the ragged eastern rim of the Wilderness. Couch — minus Gibbon's division, which could not be moved just yet because its Falmouth camp was in plain view of the enemy on Marye's Heights — was to march at dawn of the 29th to a position in the rear of Banks Ford and stand ready to throw pontoons for a crossing as soon as Slocum's advance flanked the rebels out of the trenches across the way. Meanwhile, with 60,000 Federal soldiers marching against the Confederate rear, the corps of Sedgwick, Reynolds, and Sickles, aggregating another 60,000, would move down to the riverbank south of Fredericksburg, near the point of Frank-

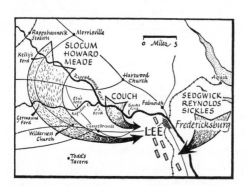

lin's crossing in December, where they would establish a west-bank bridgehead on the 29th for the purpose of demonstrating against Lee's front, thus distracting his attention from what would be going on behind him and keeping him in doubt as to where the heaviest blow would fall. Stoneman would add to the confusion by striking first at the Virginia Central Railroad, then eastward along it to the Richmond, Fredericksburg & Potomac, where he was to harass and slow down the gray army if it attempted to escape the jaws of the blue vise by falling back on its threatened capital. Still mindful of the need for secrecy, Hooker enjoined the generals with the upstream column to regard the "destination of their commands as strictly confidential." Apparently his left hand was to be kept from knowing what his right hand was about, but he lifted the veil a little by telling Sedgwick, who was in charge of the downstream column, to carry the enemy works "at all hazards" in case Lee detached "a considerable part of his force against the troops operating . . . west of Fredericksburg." Whether the main attack would be delivered against the enemy's front or his rear — that is, by Sedgwick's 60,000 or by Slocum's — remained to be seen. At the critical moment, probably on the 30th but certainly by May Day, Hooker would ride to Chancellorsville, make his estimate of the situation, and then, like an ambidextrous boxer, swing with either hand for the knockout.

The upstream march began on schedule Monday, April 27, despite a slow drizzle that threatened to undo the good which three days of fair weather had done the roads. Slogging toward Hartwood Church and Morrisville, where they would turn off south for Kelly's Ford, the veterans chanted as they trudged:

> "*The Union boys are moving on the left and on the right,*
> *The bugle call is sounding, our shelters we must strike;*
> *Joe Hooker is our leader, he takes his whiskey strong,*
> *So our knapsacks we will sling, and go marching along.*"

Sweating under fifty to sixty pounds of weight, which included eight days' rations, a pair of blankets, a thick wool overcoat, and forty rounds of ammunition each, they interpreted the word "sling" as they saw fit, shedding knapsacks by the roadside to be gleaned by civilian scavengers — "ready finders," the army called them — who moved in their wake and profited from their prodigality. Hooker's administrative sensibilities were offended by the waste, but he was consoled by the fact that the march was otherwise orderly and rapid in spite of the showers, which fortunately left off before midday without softening the roads. In response to a wire that afternoon from a fretful Lincoln — "How does it look now?" — he managed to be at once reticent and reassuring: "I am not sufficiently advanced to give an opinion. We are busy. Will tell you all soon as I can, and have it satisfactory." Riding next day up to Morrisville, through rain that had come on again to slow the march and throw it several hours behind schedule, he was pleased all the same to note that the column had turned south for the Rappahannock, and he sent an aide ahead with a message urging Slocum to make up for lost time: "The general desires that not a moment be lost until our troops are established at or near Chancellorsville. From that moment all will be ours."

He sounded buoyant, and presently he had cause for feeling even more so. By dusk the head of the flanking column was approaching Kelly's Ford, and Hooker received word from his chief of staff at Falmouth that Couch had his two divisions in position behind Banks Ford, as ordered, and was improving the waiting time by extending the telegraph to U.S. Ford, in case that proved to be a better point for crossing. Sedgwick had been delayed by the rain, Butterfield added, but he had his three corps on the march and would begin throwing five pontoon bridges across the river below Fredericksburg on schedule in the morning. Moreover, though the weather had been too gusty to permit spy-glass observation from the bobbing gondolas of Professor T. S. C. Lowe's two balloons, the ruse of leaving Gibbon's division in its exposed camp seemed to have worked as intended; Lowe reported that, from what he could see, the Confederate trenches "appeared to be occupied as usual," indicating that Lee almost certainly had no intimation that the various Federal columns were on the move for positions from which to accomplish his destruction. All this was about as encouraging as could be, but Hooker, being painfully familiar with the tricks of the old fox across the way, was leaving as little as possible to chance. He wired Lowe to send a balloon up anyhow, despite the wind and darkness, "to see where the enemy's campfires are," not forgetting to add: "Someone acquainted with the position and location of the ground and of the enemy's forces should go up."

By the time the Professor — the title was complimentary; his official designation was "Chief of Aeronauts, Army of the Potomac," and his basic uniform was a voluminous linen duster — got a balloon up into the windy night for a look at the rebel campfires, Howard's corps was over the Rappahannock, crossing dry-shod on a pontoon bridge just completed by the engineers, and had taken up a position on the south bank to guard against a surprise attack while the other two corps were crossing. Slocum came over at dawn, followed by Meade, who struck out southeastward for Ely's Ford; then Howard fell in behind Slocum, who had already headed south for Germanna Ford. Behind all three came Stoneman, a full day late and complaining bitterly that the alert order had not allowed him time to call in his 10,000 horsemen from their camps around Warrenton. He set out for Raccoon Ford, ten miles west of Germanna, for a descent on the Virginia Central in the vicinity of Louisa Courthouse, leaving Hooker a single 1000-man brigade of three slim regiments to accompany the infantry on the march and another 500 troopers to guard the deserted north-bank camps and installations. The foot soldiers pushed ahead, stepping fast but warily now; for it was here in the V of the rivers that Pope, for all his bluster, had nearly come to grief in August. Neither column encountered any real difficulty, however, in the course of its daylong hike to the Rapidan. Nor did Slocum's run into much trouble after it got there. His advance guard, splashing its way through the chest-deep water, surprised a drowsy 100-man rebel detachment at Germanna, capturing a number of graybacks before they knew what was upon them. Finding timbers collected here on the south bank for the construction of a bridge, the jubilant bluecoats set to work and put them to use in short order, with the result that the rest of their corps, and all of Howard's, made a second river crossing without having to wet their socks.

Meade's troops had no such luck. Though he too encountered no opposition in the V, his march to Ely's was longer than Slocum's to Germanna, and he found no bridge materials awaiting him at its end.

Coming down to the ford at sunset the advance guard plunged across the cold, swift-running Rapidan, chased off the startled pickets on the opposite bank, and set to work building fires to light the way for the rest of the corps approaching the crossing in the dusk. Regiment by regiment the three road-worn divisions entered the foam-flecked, scrotum-tightening water and emerged to toil up the steep south bank, which became increasingly slippery as the slope was churned to gumbo by the passage of nearly 16,000 soldiers, all dripping wet from the armpits down. Once across, they gathered about the fires for warmth, some in good spirits, some in bad, each arriving cluster somewhat muddier than the one before, but all about equally wet and cold. By midnight the last man was over. Low in the east, the late-risen moon, burgeoning toward the full, had the bruised-orange color of old gold, and while all around them the whippoorwills sang plaintively in the moon-drenched woods, the men lay rolled in their blankets, feet to the fire, catching snatches of sleep while awaiting the word to fall back into column. Meade had them on the go again by sunup of the last day of April, still marching southeast, but now through an eerie and seemingly God-forsaken region; the Wilderness, it was called, and they could see why. Mostly a tangle of second-growth scrub oak and pine, choked with vines and brambles that would tear the clothes from a man's back within minutes of the time he left the road, it was interrupted briefly at scattered points by occasional small clearings whose abandoned cabins and sag-roofed barns gave proof, if such was needed, that no amount of hard work could scratch a living from this jungle. To make matters worse, rebel cavalry slashed at the column from time to time, emerging suddenly from ambush, then back again, apparently for the purpose of taking prisoners who would identify their units. Meade did not like the look of things any better than the men did. He rode with the van and set a rapid pace, wanting to get them out of here, and for once they were altogether willing. Chancellorsville was less than half a dozen miles from the ford, and though it was still a good three miles short of open country where he could deploy his troops and bring his guns to bear, he remembered that Hooker had said that once the flankers were "established" in that vicinity, "all will be ours."

Arriving about an hour before noon, still without having encountered anything more than token resistance from the enemy cavalry and none at all from the famed, hard-marching rebel infantry, he found that for all its grand-sounding name the crossroads hamlet — if it could be called even that — consisted of nothing more than a large, multi-chimneyed brick-and-timber mansion, with tall slim pillars across its front supporting a double-decked veranda, and three or four outbuildings scattered about the quadrants of the turnpike intersection. There was, however, a hundred-acre clearing, which seemed expansive indeed after what he had just emerged from and would re-enter when he moved on, and there were also four ladies, of various ages and in bright spring dresses, who likewise were a relief of sorts despite their show of pique at having to receive unwelcome guests. At any rate, Meade's spirits rose as he waited for Slocum and Howard, whose troops had the longer march today. Much that he previously had not understood, mainly because of Hooker's refusal to give out details of his plan — "It's all right" had been his usual and evasive reply to questions from commanders of all ranks — suddenly became much clearer to Meade, now that he was within a half-day's march of Lee's rear without its having cost him anything more than the handful of men gobbled up by the graybacks in the course of his plunge through the heart of the Wilderness. Now that he believed he saw the whole design, his dourness gave way to something approaching exaltation. By 2 o'clock, when Slocum arrived at the head of his two-corps column, Meade was fairly beside himself. "This is splendid, Slocum," he cried, displaying an exuberance that seemed all the more abandoned because it was so unlike him; "hurrah for Old Joe! We are on Lee's flank and he doesn't know it."

What he wanted now, he added with no slackening of enthusiasm, was to push on eastward without further delay, at least another couple of miles before nightfall, "and we'll get out of this Wilderness." Slocum felt much the same way about it. But while they talked a courier arrived with a dispatch signed by Butterfield, relaying an order from Hooker: "The general directs that no advance be made from Chancellorsville until the columns are concentrated. He expects to be at Chancellorsville tonight."

Somewhat crestfallen, and nearly as puzzled now as he had been before he saw what he had believed was the light, Meade went about the business of getting his troops into bivouac. Slocum and Howard were doing the same when presently, at about 4.30 and true to his word, Fighting Joe himself came riding up on his big white horse, cheered lustily by the men along the roadside, and explained the logic behind the restraining order. The easterly advance along the turnpike had already flanked the rebels out of their U.S. Ford defenses, permitting Couch to sidle upstream for a crossing there instead of at Banks Ford, where the defenders were still in occupation; he was on the march for Chancellorsville even now, and Gibbon had been alerted to join him from Falmouth with his third division. This would put four whole corps in the Confederate rear, as had been intended from the start, but the northern commander had it in mind to do even more by way of cinching the victory already within reach. Sedgwick's bridgehead having been established across the river below Fredericksburg with a minimal resistance from the rebels on the heights — who thus were clamped securely between two superior Union forces which now could reinforce each other, rapidly and at will, by way of U.S. Ford — Hooker had decided to summon Sickles from the left to add the weight of his corps to the blow about to be delivered against the more vulnerable enemy rear. His arrival tonight or tomorrow morning would bring the striking force up to a strength of 77,865 effectives within the five corps. With three regiments of cavalry added, along with several batteries detached from the artillery reserve, engineer troops, and headquarters personnel, the total would reach about 80,000 of all arms, who then could be flung in mass against Lee's rear to accomplish his destruction with a single May Day blow.

Meade was considerably reassured; he saw in fact, or believed he saw, a brighter light than ever. A rare attention to detail — pontoons in place on time, road space properly allotted to columns on the march, surprise achieved through ruse and secrecy — had made possible, at practically no cost at all, one of the finest maneuvers in military history. Now this same attentiveness, with regard to the massing of troops for the ultimate thrust, would also make possible one of the grandest victories. Sure enough, Couch arrived before nightfall and went into bivouac a mile north of the crossroads; Sickles sent word that he was on the way. Once more careful planning had paid off. A New York *Herald* correspondent who had accompanied the flankers shared the pervading optimism. "It is rumored that the enemy are falling back toward Richmond," he wrote, "but a fight tomorrow seems more than probable. We expect it, and we also expect to be victorious." Hooker expected it, too, because he knew the rumor to be untrue. Sedgwick, from his low-lying, close-up position south of Fredericksburg, and Professor Lowe, from the gondola of one of his big yellow balloons riding high over Stafford Heights, had both assured him that the Confederates still occupied the ridge beyond the town. Reynolds, in fact, had reported to headquarters this afternoon that he believed some of the troops in his front had just arrived from Richmond: which brought the reply, "General Hooker hopes they are from Richmond, as the greater will be our success."

His spirits were high, and so were those of his men, who cheered him to the echo, especially when a congratulatory order was read to them that evening in their camps around Chancellorsville: "It is with heartfelt satisfaction that the commanding general announces to the army that the operations of the last three days have determined that our enemy must either ingloriously fly, or come out from behind his defenses and give us battle on our own ground, where certain destruction awaits him."

★ ★ ★

Battle on his "own ground" — setting aside for the moment the question of whether any part of the Old Dominion could ever properly be so termed in relation to the man Lee called Mr F. J. Hooker — was exactly what Stonewall Jackson had been aching to give him for the past three months. "We must make this campaign an exceedingly active one," the Virginian declared as spring approached. "Only thus can a weaker country cope with a stronger. It must make up in activity what it lacks in strength." Fredericksburg, for all its one-sided tactical brilliance, had been a strategic disappointment to him, and he hoped to compensate for this in the great battle he knew would be fought as soon as the Federals decided the time had come for them to attempt another Rappahannock crossing. "My trust is in God," he said quietly, seated one day in his tent and musing on the future. But then, anticipating the hour when the blue host would venture within his reach, his patience broke its bounds and he rose bristling from his chair, eyes aglow. "I wish they would come!" he cried.

These past three months had been perhaps the happiest of his military life. In fact, despite his eagerness to interrupt any or all of them with bloodshed, February, March, and April, following as they did his thirty-ninth birthday in late January, had been idyllic, at least by Jacksonian standards. Aside from administrative concerns, such as the usual spate of court-martials and the preparation of battle reports, grievously neglected up to now because he had been too busy fighting to find time for writing — the total was fourteen full-scale battles in the previous eight months, with the reduction and capture of Harpers Ferry added for good measure — his principal occupation was prayer and meditation, relieved from time to time by evenings of unaccustomed social pleasure. His quarters, an office cottage on the grounds of a Moss Neck estate, were comfortable to the point of lavishness, which prompted Jeb Stuart to express mock horror at the erstwhile Presbyterian deacon's evident fall from spirituality, and Lee himself, in the course of a particularly fine meal featuring oysters, turkey, and a waiter decked out in a fresh white apron, taunted the high-ranking guests and their host with the remark that they were merely playing at being soldiers; they should come and dine with him, he said, if they wanted to see how a real soldier lived. Stonewall took the raillery and the chiding in good part, at once flustered and delighted. But the best of the idyl came at its close. The last nine days, beginning April 20, were spent with the wife he had not seen in just over a year and the five-month-old daughter he had never seen at all.

He had moved by then, back into his tent near Hamilton's Crossing, which did much to reduce the Calvinistic twinges. "It is rather a relief," he said, "to get where there will be less comfort in a room." But for the occasion of the long-anticipated visit he accepted the hospitality of the Yerby house, in which Lee had stayed for a time under doctor's orders, and was given a large room, with no less than three beds, where he could be alone with his wife and get to know the baby. Outside duty hours, the couple took walks in the woods and along the heights overlooking the Fredericksburg plain whose December scars were beginning to be grassed over. It was the happiest of times for them both. The days went by in a rush, however, for there in full view across the way were the enemy guns and the yellow observation balloons, reminders that the idyl was likely to have a sudden end. And so it was. Dawn, Wednesday, April 29; booted feet on the stairs and a knock at the bedroom door; "That looks as if Hooker were crossing," Jackson said. He drew on some clothes and went out, was gone ten minutes, and then returned to finish dressing. The visit was over, he told Anna as he buckled on his sword. He would come back if he could, but if he could not he would send an aide to see her to the train. After a last embrace, and a last long look at the baby, he was gone. Presently the staff chaplain arrived to tell her the general would not be coming back. While she was packing she began hearing the rattle of musketry from down by the river. It grew louder behind her, all the way to Guiney Station, where she boarded an almost empty train for Richmond.

Lee expressed even less surprise when an aide sent by Jackson came into his tent before sunup to give him the news. Still abed, Lee said teasingly: "Captain, what do you young men mean by waking a man out of his sleep?" Hooker had thrown his pontoons near the site of the lower December crossing, the aide replied; he was over the river in force. "Well, I thought I heard firing," Lee said, "and I was beginning to think it was time some of you young fellows were coming to tell me what it was all about. You want me to send a message to your good general, Captain? Tell him that I am sure he knows what to do. I will meet him at the front very soon."

Shortly afterwards, peering through rifts in the early morning fog, he saw for himself that the Federals had one bridge down and others under construction, all near the point now known as Franklin's Crossing, just over a mile below the town. They did not attempt an advance across the plain, but seemed content to stay within their bridgehead, at least for the present, covered by the long-range guns on Stafford Heights. Resisting the temptation to attack while the build-up was in progress, Lee decided to make his defense along the ridge, as he had done in December. Accordingly, he told Jackson to bring up the rest of his corps from below, and ordered the reserve artillery to leave its rearward camps and move forward into line. In notifying Richmond of these developments, although he knew it was unlikely that the two detached divisions would arrive in time for a share in the battle now shaping up, he requested that Longstreet be alerted for a return from Suffolk as soon as possible. Before noon, the situation was complicated by a dispatch from Stuart, informing Lee that a blue force of about 14,000 infantry and six guns had crossed at Kelly's Ford and appeared to be headed for Gordonsville. This was corrected a few hours later, however, when the cavalry commander sent word that the enemy column had turned in the direction of Ely's and Germanna Fords; so far, Jeb added, he had taken prisoners from three different Union corps, though he did not say whether he thought all three were present in full strength. In reaction, Lee sent instructions for Stuart to move eastward at once and thus avoid being cut off from headquarters. This would leave the Federal cavalry free to operate practically unmolested against his lines of supply; yet, bad as that was, it was by no means as bad as having to fight blind when he and the greatly superior Federal main body came within grappling distance of each other, here on Marye's Heights or elsewhere. Just after sundown a third courier arrived to report the bluecoats across both Rapidan fords. Though Lee still had no reliable information as to the strength of this flanking column, it was clear by now that some part of Hooker's army — a considerable part, for all he knew — was in the Confederate rear and moving closer, hour by hour. Whatever its strength, the threat it offered was too grave to be ignored. Nor did he ignore it. Two brigades of Richard Anderson's division were already at U.S. Ford; Lee instructed him to draw them in and move the others rearward to meet them in the vicinity of Chancellorsville, where the roads leading south and east from Ely's and Germanna Fords came together, "taking the strongest line you can and holding it to the best advantage." To McLaws, who commanded Longstreet's other remaining division, went orders alerting him for a possible westward march, in case it turned out that Anderson was not strong enough to stop the blue columns last reported to be moving in his direction. Anderson pulled out of the line at 9 o'clock, and after a three-hour march through driving rain informed headquarters that his division was concentrated near Chancellorsville by midnight. Knowing that his rear was protected at least to this extent, Lee turned in to rest for tomorrow.

Morning of the 30th disclosed a total of five bridges spanning the river below Fredericksburg. Though the bluecoats had enlarged their west-bank foothold, they showed no disposition to advance. In fact, they were intrenching their perimeter — as if in expectation, not of delivering, but of receiving an attack. Jackson, for one, was eager to give it to them, whereas Lee preferred to draw them farther away from their heavy guns on Stafford Heights. Both men thus reacted as they had done to the similar situation in December; but this time Lee offered to defer to his lieutenant's judgment. "If you think you can effect anything," he said, "I will give orders for the attack." While Stonewall went about conducting a more thorough examination of the bridgehead, preparatory to moving against it, Lee received another cavalry report that the Federals were advancing eastward from Germanna Ford, along the Orange Turnpike, while a substantial train of wagons and artillery was across Ely's Ford with a heavy infantry escort, following in the wake of the column that had crossed at that point the night before. A little later — it was now past noon — Anderson sent word that he had taken up a good defensive position east of Chancellorsville, along the near fringe of the Wilderness, and was preparing to resist the blue advance. So far, all he had seen of the enemy were cavalry outriders, he added, but he thought he was going to need support when the infantry came up. Lee replied at 2.30 that Anderson was to dig in where he was, providing hasty fortifications not only for his own division but also for McLaws', which was on call to join him in case it was needed. "Set all your spades to work as vigorously as possible," Lee urged, and sent him some engineers to assist in drawing his line, as well as a battalion of artillery from the reserve. Then he turned back to see how Jackson was doing.

The fact was, Jackson was not doing so well, at least by his own interpretation. A careful reconnaissance had shown the enemy bridgehead to be stronger than he had supposed; he regretfully admitted that an assault would be unwise. Lee took out his binoculars for a better look at the bluecoats massed on the plain below and on the heights beyond the river. He took his time, evaluating reports while he peered. There was by now much disagreement among his officers as to whether Hooker was planning to deliver his heaviest blow from upstream or down. Presently, however, Lee returned the glasses to their case and snapped it shut with a decisive gesture. "The main attack will come from above," he said.

Having made this estimate of the situation he proceeded to act on it with an urgency required by the fact that a farther advance by the Federals approaching his rear would put them between him and Richmond, in which case he would have no choice except to retreat. He might have to do so anyhow, under the menace of Hooker's skillful combinations, but he was determined, now as always, to yield no ground he saw any chance of holding. His decision, then — announced in orders which he retired to his tent to write and issue soon after nightfall — was to turn on the rearward Union column with a preponderance of his badly outnumbered army, leaving a skeleton force to defend his present position against a possible frontal assault by the blue mass on the plain. Early's division of Jackson's corps drew the latter assignment, reinforced by a brigade from McLaws, whose other three brigades were to proceed at once to join Anderson in the intrenchments he was digging four miles east of Chancellorsville. Jackson was to follow McLaws with his remaining three divisions "at daylight tomorrow morning . . . and make arrangements to repulse the enemy." This would give Lee a total of 45,000 troops, plus Stuart when he came up, to block the path of the enemy columns moving eastward through the Wilderness, and barely 10,000, including the artillery reserve, to hold the Fredericksburg ridge, which by tomorrow would have become his rear. The risks were great, but perhaps no greater than the odds that led him to accept them. At any rate, if it came to a simultaneous fight in both directions, he would have the advantage of interior lines, even though he would have gained it by inviting annihilation.

McLaws pulled back at midnight, leaving Barksdale's Mississippians behind for a possible repetition of their mid-December exploit. Early spread his lone division all up and down the five-mile stretch of intrenchments from Marye's Heights to Hamilton's Crossing, mindful of Lee's admonition that he was to keep up a bristling pretense of strength and aggressive intentions. Jackson, told to move at daylight, was on the march by 3 a.m. Riding ahead of his troops he arrived soon after sunrise at Tabernacle Church, the left-flank anchor of Anderson's newly established line, which McLaws was busy extending northward to the vicinity of Duerson's Mill, covering Banks Ford. His instructions were to "make arrangements to repulse the enemy," and to Stonewall this meant, quite simply, to attack him. If he had no orders to proceed beyond this point, neither did he have any to remain here. Besides, there was no enemy in sight except an occasional scampering blue horseman in brief silhouette against the verdant background of the Wilderness. Before he could repulse the enemy he would have to find him, and the obvious way to find him would be to go where he was — reportedly, four miles dead ahead at Chancellorsville. So he told Anderson and McLaws to leave off digging and get their men in motion. He would go forward with them. If they ran into trouble up ahead, and it was clear by now that trouble was what they definitely were going to find in that direction, his three divisions would soon be up to lend support.

It was about 11 o'clock of a fine May Day morning by the time they got their troops into march formation and set out, preceded by clouds of skirmishers. The advance was by two main roads, the turnpike on the right and the plank road on the left; McLaws took the former, Anderson the latter, accompanied by Jackson himself. Almost as soon as they entered the green hug of the Wilderness, McLaws made contact with the enemy advancing on the turnpike. At 11.20 the first gun of the meeting engagement boomed. Then others began to roar in that direction. Jackson's instructions were for both divisions to keep pushing west until they ran into something solid. Presently he received a dispatch from Stuart, who was near at hand. "I will close in on the flank," Jeb wrote, "and will help all I can when the ball opens.... May God grant us victory." Stonewall replied, "I trust that God will grant us a great victory." But he added, by way of showing what he had in mind to reinforce his trust: "Keep closed on Chancellorsville."

★ ★ ★

Hooker too had started forward at 11 o'clock, so that the meeting engagement occurred about midway between Chancellorsville and Tabernacle Church. Sickles having come up that morning, the northern commander was set to throw a five-corps Sunday punch. This was no time for wild blows, however, and he made his preparations with the same concern for detail as before. Slocum would advance along the plank road on the right, supported by Howard; Meade would take the left, along the turnpike, supported by Couch; Sickles would remain in general reserve, on call to add the extra weight that might be needed in either direction. Nor was Fighting Joe committing the amateur's gaffe of forgetting he had another hand to box with. Orders had gone the previous evening to Sedgwick: "It is not known, of course, what effect the advance will have upon the enemy, and the general commanding directs that you observe [Lee's] movements with the utmost vigilance, and, should he expose a weak point, attack him in full force and destroy him." This was made even more specific by instructions sent to Sedgwick as the advance got under way. No matter whether the rebels weakened their Fredericksburg line or not, he was "to threaten an attack in full force at 1 o'clock and to continue in that attitude until further orders. Let the demonstration be as severe as can be," Hooker added, "but not an attack," unless of course the enemy afforded a real opening, in which case the earlier instructions would obtain and Sedgwick would go for a left-hand knockout.

Slocum and Meade stepped off smartly, much encouraged by a circular prescribing the order of march and closing: "After the movement commences, headquarters will be at Tabernacle Church." It sounded as if Hooker meant business this time. Also it made considerable tactical sense, for the turnpike and the plank road, after branching off from one another at Chancellorsville, converged near that objective. Out of the woods at last, the two lead corps would be concentrated for the final lunge, supported by Howard, Couch, and Sickles, who would follow close behind. For more than half the distance, however, these two main Wilderness arteries diverged: with the result that as the two columns moved eastward, hemmed in by the dense jungle of stunted trees and brambly underbrush, they lost contact with each other. As an additional complication, Meade had one division on the pike and two on the River Road, which curved northward to outflank the rebel intrenchments at Banks Ford; so that here, too, contact was quickly lost. Two miles from its crossroads starting point, out of touch with Slocum on the right and the rest of its own corps on the left, the division on the turnpike came under fire from enemy skirmishers as it plodded up a long slope whose crest would bring the eastern rim of the Wilderness in view. It so happened that this division, commanded by Major General George Sykes, could lay substantial claims to being the sturdiest in the Army of the Potomac, two of its three brigades being composed exclusively of U.S. regulars, while the third was made up of battle-hardened New York volunteers who had stood fast on Henry Hill and thereby saved the fleeing remnant of Pope's army from utter destruction at Bull Run. As steady now as then, they went smoothly into attack formation and drove the rebel skirmishers back to the crest of the low ridge. There, however, they came upon the Confederate main body, long gray lines of infantry supported by clusters of guns that broke into a roar at the sight of bluecoats. Calling a halt, Sykes sent back word that he was badly in need of help. Then, as the gray mass started forward, overlapping both of his open flanks, he began a rearward movement down the pike, dribbling casualties as he went. What would be known as the Battle of Chancellorsville had opened.

Couch was already coming up with Major General Winfield S. Hancock's division, which he threw into the line at once to stabilize the situation preparatory to resuming the advance. Before this last could be accomplished, however, a courier arrived with orders from Hooker: "Withdraw both divisions to Chancellorsville." Couch was amazed. Here he was, as he later said, with "open country in front and the commanding position," yet his chief was telling him to retire. Sykes and Hancock were equally puzzled. They too wanted to push ahead in accordance with the original instructions. With their approval, Couch sent an aide to inform Hooker that the situation was under control and the troops were about ready to continue their drive along the pike. Off to the right, a mounting bank of smoke and the rumble of guns told them that Slocum was likewise engaged and seemed to be holding his own, while Meade's other two divisions apparently had encountered no resistance at all on the left. But within half an hour the aide returned with a peremptory repetition of the order: Pull back to Chancellorsville without delay. Couch considered outright disobedience. Brigadier General G. K. Warren, chief engineer of the army, urged him to adopt just such a course while he himself rode back to explain its advantages to Hooker. He spurred rearward; but as soon as he left, Couch's West-Point-inculcated instinct for obedience took over. Complying with the order to retire, he withdrew the two divisions, first Sykes, then Hancock. The disengagement had been completed, except for two rear-guard regiments still in line, when a third message arrived from Hooker: "Hold on until 5 o'clock." Evidently Warren had stated his case persuasively, but Couch by now was disgusted. "Tell General Hooker he is too late," he replied testily. "The enemy are already on my right and rear. I am in full retreat."

In point of fact, his right was more seriously threatened than he knew. Slocum, followed as closely by Anderson as Couch himself was being followed by McLaws, had already fallen back down the plank road in accordance with similar instructions from headquarters. Meade too was backtracking by now, but unpursued, having encountered nothing substantial in the way of resistance on the left. As a result he was even more astounded than Couch had been at receiving the order to withdraw. Within sight of Duerson's Mill, he had been within easy reach of Banks Ford, control of which would shorten greatly the lines of supply and communication between the army's divided wings. To be told to fall back under such circumstances, with clear going to his front and his lines extending along the crest of the eastward rise, was more exasperating than anything he had encountered up to now. Once again Hooker had built up his hopes only to dash them with a peremptory order which not only called for a halt, as before, but also insisted on a retirement. Meade was furious. "If he thinks he can't hold the top of a hill, how does he expect to hold the bottom of it?" the Pennsylvanian stormed as he complied with the instructions to fall back.

That was about 2 o'clock. All three corps commanders were hard put to understand what had come over Fighting Joe in the scant three hours since they had set out from the crossroads they now were under orders to return to. At the outset, with the announcement that his headquarters would be leapfrogged four miles forward while the movement was in progress, he had seemed confident of delivering a knockout blow. Then suddenly, at the first sputter of musketry on the turnpike, he had abandoned all his aggressive intentions and ordered everything back for a defense of Chancellorsville, deep in the Wilderness. Why? They did not know, but already they were beginning to formulate theories which they and others down the years would enlarge on. For one thing, that excellent intelligence section back at Falmouth was hard at work, forwarding information disturbing enough to jangle the nerves of the steadiest man alive. According to one rebel deserter, brought in for interrogation the night before, Longstreet's whole corps had left Suffolk, presumably by rail, and had "gone to Culpeper," which would place it directly in rear of the Union flanking column and scarcely a day's march away. The prisoner added "that Lee said it was the only time he should fight equal numbers," which if true was alarming in the extreme, considering all the old fox had been able to accomplish with inferior numbers in the past. Another deserter — "from New York state originally; an intelligent man," Butterfield commented — avowed that Hood's division was already with Lee; he knew this, he said, because he had "asked the troops as they passed along." One of the two informers must be lying, at least so far as Longstreet's location was concerned. Indeed, both might be lying; it was not unusual for the Confederates to send out bogus "deserters" to confuse an opponent with misleading information. But the fact was, Lee was not reacting to his present predicament at all as he ought to be doing if he was heavily outnumbered. He was reacting, in fact, as if the numerical advantage was with him even more than either deserter claimed. And just what that reaction was Hooker had learned shortly after Meade and Slocum left him. Until that time, Professor Lowe's balloons had been fogbound high over Stafford Heights, but all of a sudden the weather faired, permitting the aeronaut to tap out a steady flow of information regarding the panorama now spread out before his eyes. He could see various rebel columns in motion, he wired Hooker at 11 o'clock, but the largest of these was "moving on the road toward Chancellorsville." This tallied with the intelligence summation forwarded shortly thereafter by Butterfield. Completing his tabulation of the Confederate order of battle, the chief of staff declared: "Anderson, McLaws, A. P. Hill, and Hood would, therefore, be in your front."

It also explained — all too clearly — the sudden clatter of musketry and the boom of guns, first down the turnpike, then down the plank road, not long after the two columns set out eastward through the forest. In part, as well, it accounted for Hooker's reaction, which in effect was a surrendering of the initiative to Jackson, who plunged deeper into the Wilderness in pursuit. But there was a good deal more to it than this: a good deal more that was no less valid for being less specific. Perhaps Hooker at last had recalled Lincoln's admonition, "Beware of rashness." Perhaps at this critical juncture he missed the artificial stimulus of whiskey, which formerly had been part of his daily ration but which he had abjured on taking command. Perhaps he mistrusted his already considerable accomplishment in putting more than 70,000 soldiers in Lee's immediate rear, with practically no losses because he had met practically no resistance. It had been altogether too easy; Lee must have wanted him where he was, or at any rate where he had been headed before he called a halt and ordered a pull-back. Or perhaps it was even simpler than that. Perhaps he was badly frightened (not physically frightened: Hooker was never that: but morally frightened) after the manner of the bullfighter Gallo, who, according to Hemingway, "was the inventor of refusing to kill the bull if the bull looked at him in a certain way." This Gallo had a long career, featuring many farewell performances, and at the first of these, having fought the animal bravely and well, when the time came for killing he faced the stands and made three eloquent speeches of dedication to three distinguished aficionados; after which he turned, sword in hand, and approached the bull, which was standing there, head down, looking at him. Gallo returned to the barrera. "You take him, Paco," he told a fellow matador; "I don't like the way he looks at me." So it was with Hooker, perhaps, when he heard that Lee had turned in his direction and was, so to speak, looking at him. Lowe had signaled at noon that the rebels were "considerably diminished" on the heights behind Fredericksburg. Consequently, at 2 o'clock, Fighting Joe wired Butterfield: "From character of information have suspended attack. The enemy may attack me — I will try it. Tell Sedgwick to keep a sharp lookout, and attack if can succeed." In effect, now that Lee had turned his attention westward, Hooker was telling Sedgwick: "You take him, Paco. I don't like the way he looks at me."

None of this perturbation showed in his manner, however, when the returning generals confronted him at the Chancellor house, which he had taken over as his headquarters. "It's all right, Couch; I've got Lee just where I want him," he said expansively. "He must fight me on my own ground." Couch had a cold eye for this blusterous performance. "The retrograde movement had prepared me for something of the kind," he wrote years later, "but to hear from his own lips that the advantages gained by the successive marches of his lieutenants were to culminate in fighting a defensive battle in that nest of thickets was too much. . . . I retired from his presence with the belief that my commanding general was a whipped man."

Whether or not this was the case remained to be seen. For the present, the order was for the army to intrench itself along lines prescribed with the usual attention to detail. On the map they resembled a double-handled dipper. Couch and Slocum, with two divisions each in the vicinity of Chancellorsville — Gibbon had stayed at Falmouth after all — formed the cup, bulging south of the crossroads to include some comparatively high ground known as Fairview. The cup was just over a mile wide at the rim, tapering slightly toward the base, and just under a mile deep. Sickles' three divisions were in reserve, poised for a leap into the cup or a quick march out either of the handles, which were between two and three miles long and extended generally northeast and due west. Meade's three divisions connected the eastern lip of the cup with the Rappahannock, his left resting on a bend of the river south of U. S. Ford, which thus was covered. Howard's three divisions, the dipper's western handle, extended out the turnpike past Wilderness Church, where the plank road came in from the southwest, and thus presumably could block the approach of an enemy moving up from that direction. The troops worked into the night with picks and shovels, intrenching the six-mile line from flank to flank. At 2 a.m. Couch, Slocum, and Howard reported themselves satisfied that their respective sectors could be held against assault. Advantageously disposed along Mineral Spring Run, a small boggy creek that covered his front and rendered his position doubly secure, Meade had reported the same thing earlier. Hooker, with his accustomed thoroughness, seemed to have allowed for all eventualities before he retired to a bedroom in the crossroads mansion to sleep and store up strength for whatever tomorrow was going to bring.

He hoped it would bring an all-out Confederate attack; or so at least he had been saying, all afternoon and evening. "The rebel army is now the legitimate property of the Army of the Potomac," he announced to the officers gathered about him in the May Day sunshine on the Chancellor veranda. The fact that nearly all of his cavalry had ridden well beyond his reach, while nearly all of Lee's was in what Hooker called "my immediate presence," did not seem to him a cause for alarm, but rather an advantage, "which I trust will enable Stoneman to do a land-office business in the interior. I think the enemy in his desperation will be compelled to attack me on my own ground. . . . I am all right." Thus he wired the Washington authorities, thinking that such information, besides relieving the President's concern, might "have an important bearing on movements elsewhere." If the other Union armies would only keep step with this one, the war would soon be over and done with — won. As the daylight hours wore on and his intrenchments were extended, still with no full-scale rebel assault, his show of confidence reached its zenith. He feared nothing and he wanted it known; not even the artillery of heaven. "The enemy is in my power," he exulted, "and God Almighty cannot deprive me of them." In the late afternoon he issued another circular for the encouragement of subordinates: "The major general commanding trusts that a suspension in the attack today will embolden the enemy to attack him."

⚔ 5 ⚔

Lee and Jackson met at sundown, on the plank road just over a mile southeast of Chancellorsville, for the purpose of deciding how best to go about giving Hooker what he claimed he wanted. They began their conference on the road itself, at the junction where a trail came in from Catharine Furnace, a rural ironworks on Lewis Creek a mile and a half to the west, but they withdrew presently into a nearby clump of pines when a Federal sharpshooter began ranging in on them from a perch in a tree just up the road, beyond the line along which Anderson's and Slocum's pickets were keeping up a rackety contention. Seated side by side on a log, the two men continued their discussion in the May Day twilight, the gray-bearded elder impeccably dressed as always, his neat gray tunic devoid of trappings except for the three unwreathed stars on each side of the turned-down collar, and the younger wearing the rather gaudy uniform which had provoked such hoots and catcalls on the day of Fredericksburg. Reconnoitering on the right this afternoon, Lee had found the terrain unpromising, hemmed in as it was by a bend of the Rappahannock, and the few heavily wooded approaches well guarded by troops already dug in along the far side of a marsh. To attempt to come to grips with them in that quarter, he said, would be to invite destruction. How about the center and the left? Jackson had not been far to the west, but he had made a long-range examination of the enemy lines in front of Chancellorsville itself and had found the blue-coats disposed three-deep, hard at work with picks and shovels, and supported by many batteries of artillery. However, he was inclined to believe that the question of how to get at Hooker, here in the Wilderness tomorrow, was largely academic. The ease with which he had repulsed the advancing Union columns today made him suspect that their recoil was prelude to a withdrawal. "By tomorrow morning there will not be any of them on this side of the river," he declared.

Lee shook his head. So far he had deferred to Stonewall's judgment, but not in this. Though he too was puzzled by his opponent's sudden, turtle-like reaction to moderate pressure, he was convinced that Hooker was planning to make his main effort right here. Anyhow, even if that were not the case, they must prepare to deal with him tomorrow

on even the outside chance that he would still be in his present intrenched position. Without quite giving over his belief that dawn would
show the forest empty to their front, Jackson could not disagree with
the logic of Lee's contention; besides which, he found the prospect so attractive as to overrule his inclination to think that it would not be offered. For him, as for his commander, to "deal with" Hooker meant to
attack him. But how? And where? One possibility was that the Federal
center might not appear as stout to a close-up view as it had seemed from
a distance. The two generals accordingly dispatched an engineer officer
from each of their staffs to go take a look at the intrenchments there and
report on what they saw.

From this time on, Lee and Jackson gave little attention to any-
While this night reconnaissance was in progress, and while Lee
and Jackson continued to speculate on ways of bringing the blue
army's current excursion to a violent close, Jeb Stuart came jingling up
from Catharine Furnace in fulfillment of his promise to "help all I can
when the ball opens." Glad as he was to see his friend Stonewall decked
out in the handsome uniform he had given him, he deferred comment in
favor of some interesting information which had just come to hand. According to Fitzhugh Lee, who had ridden west to scout it, Hooker's
right flank was "in the air" on the Orange Turnpike, wide open to attack
from that direction. Though this was news of a kind to set both him and
his chief lieutenant on tremble, the southern commander suppressed his
excitement to ask whether roads were available for a covered approach
to that critical point by troops in large numbers. Stuart replied that he
did not know but he would do what he could to find out, and with that
he swung back onto his horse and rode off westward, his red-lined cape
and cinnamon whiskers glistening in the light of the new-risen moon.

From this time on, Lee and Jackson gave little attention to anything but the possibility of launching the suggested flank attack. When
the two engineers returned to announce that the Union center was too
strongly intrenched to be assaulted, Lee received the anticlimactic report with a nod and kept peering at a map spread on his knees; he peered
so intently, indeed, that he seemed to be trying to make it give him information which it did not contain. "How can we get at those people?"
he asked, half to himself and half to Jackson, who replied in an equally
distracted manner, as he too searched the map for roads that were not
on it: "You know best. Show me what to do, and we will do it." Finally, Lee traced a fingertip westward along the map from their present
location, as if to sketch in an ideal route past the front of the enemy position, then northward to intersect the turnpike, where the latter veered
abruptly east to address the Union flank end-on. In naval parlance, he was
crossing Hooker's T. That would be the movement, he said; Jackson
would lead it and Stuart would cover his march. Smiling, Jackson stood
erect and saluted. "My troops will move at 4 o'clock," he said. In his
eagerness, he not only seemed unable to remain seated, he also seemed to

have forgotten his prediction that Hooker would clear out before sunup. Lee checked him with a reminder. If there was any doubt about this next morning, he said, Jackson could open from an exposed position with a couple of guns, then judge by the response as to whether the blue army was still behind its Wilderness fortifications.

There was much to be done between now and sunrise: especially by Jackson, to whom Lee had left the choice of a route, the composition of the force to be employed, and the decision as to when and in what manner the flank attack would be delivered. But what both men needed for the present, at the close of a strenuous day and on the eve of what promised to be an even more strenuous morrow, was a few hours' sleep: again especially Jackson, who had demonstrated on several occasions — the Seven Days, for one — that without at least a minimum of profound rest he would be reduced to a state of somnambulism. They lay down where they were, in separate quarters of the grove, spreading their saddle blankets on the pine needles for a bed and using their saddles for a pillow. Both were soon asleep, but Lee was wakened presently by an officer he had sent to look into conditions on the turnpike to the north. "Ah, Captain, you have returned, have you?" he said, and he sat up slowly. "Come here and tell me what you have learned on the right." It was the same young man from Jackson's staff who had wakened him two mornings ago to tell him Hooker was crossing; J. P. Smith was his name, a divinity student before the war. He hesitated, in awe of the general whose massive features and gray beard looked so imposing in the moonlight, but as he leaned forward the seated man put an arm about his shoulder and drew him down by his side while he finished his report. Lee thanked him and then, still retaining his grip, began to chide him by saying that he regretted that Smith and the other "young men about General Jackson" had not done a better job today of locating and silencing an enemy battery that had held up the advance. Young men nowadays, he declared in the accents of Nestor, were a far remove from the young men of his youth. The captain, seeing, as he later said, that the general "was jesting and disposed to rally me," broke away from the hold Lee tried to retain on his shoulder. As he moved off through the moonlit pines he could hear the Virginian laughing heartily there in the Wilderness where many men now sleeping would be laid in their graves tomorrow and the next day and the next, blue and gray alike, as a result of instructions he had given just before he himself lay down, in apparently excellent spirits, to rest for what he knew was coming with the dawn.

When Lee woke he saw the gaunt figure of Jackson bending over a small fire a courier had built. Rising, he joined him and the two sat on a couple of hardtack boxes the Federals had left behind the day before. It was already past 4 o'clock, the hour set for the column to move out, but Jackson explained that he was awaiting the return of his staff chaplain, who once had had a church hereabouts and was familiar with the region. For this reason he had sent him, together with a skilled cartographer, to explore the roads leading west from Catharine Furnace and then north to the plank road, up which he expected to make his strike. The two sat talking, warming their hands at the meager fire, until the glimmer of dawn showed the staff officers returning from their scout. Major Jedediah Hotchkiss, the cartographer, approached the generals and spread his map on another hardtack box which he placed between them. It was obvious from his manner, before he said a word, that he had found the route he had been seeking, and as he spoke he traced it on the map: first due west to the furnace, then due south, away from the enemy, along a trail that gradually turned back west to enter the Brock Road, which ran northward to the plank road and the turnpike. However, he explained that the column must not turn north at this point, since that would bring it within sight of a Federal signal station at Fairview, but south again for a short distance to another road leading north and paralleling the Brock Road, which it rejoined a couple of miles above in some heavy woods just short of its junction with the plank road. That way, practically the entire route — some ten miles in length from their present position and firm enough throughout to support wagons and artillery — would be screened from the eyes of enemy lookouts. Completing his exposition, Hotchkiss looked from one to another of the generals, both of whom kept their eyes fixed on the map for what seemed to him an inordinately long time. Finally Lee spoke, raising his head to look at his lieutenant: "General Jackson, what do you propose to do?" Jackson put out his hand and retraced, with a semicircular motion of his wrist, the route just drawn. "Go around here," he said. Lee kept looking at him. "What do you propose to make this movement with?" he asked, and Jackson promptly replied: "With my whole corps."

Now there was a pause while Lee absorbed the shock the words had given him. "What will you leave me?" he asked. The question was rhetorical; he already knew the answer. But Jackson answered it anyhow, as readily as before. "The divisions of Anderson and McLaws." This meant that he would have better than 30,000 soldiers off to the rear and on the flank, necessarily out of contact with the enemy and the rest of his own army for most of the day, while Lee would be left with scarcely half as many troops planted squarely across the path of a greatly superior blue host which might resume its forward movement at any minute. However, having weighed the odds — which had to include the by no means improbable chance that Hooker might learn what was afoot and react accordingly — the southern commander made and announced his decision. "Well, go on," he said.

While they talked the sun had reddened the east, and now it broke clear, fiery above the treetops back toward Fredericksburg, where Early was facing odds almost as long as Lee's would be when the flanking column left. Jackson informed his chief that the march would be led by D. H. Hill's old division, now under Brigadier General Robert Rodes; next would come his own old division, commanded by its senior brigadier, Raleigh Colston; A. P. Hill's division would bring up the rear. He would take all his artillery with him, dispersed along the column, and depend on Stuart to cover his advance. Lee took notes on this, then retired to write the necessary orders while his lieutenant went about making preparations to move out. As Jackson rode past one brigade camp the lounging veterans rose to cheer him, but seeing what one of them later called "battle in his haste and stern looks," they merely gazed at him and wondered what exertion he was about to require of them. The preliminary dispositions were a time-consuming business, involving the extraction of some units already committed, but at last they were completed. Shortly before 8 o'clock, the lead regiment — Georgians who had fought under him in every battle since McDowell, the prologue to the Valley Campaign, which had opened exactly a year ago today with his descent through Brown's Gap to put his troops aboard the cars for Staunton — turned off the plank road and set out westward for Catharine Furnace and Hooker's right. Though he was four hours behind the starting time he had set the night before, Stonewall did not appear to be disturbed by the delay. He was alert but not impatient, one observer remarked, and spoke tersely "as though all were distinctly formed in his mind and beyond all question." Under the lowered bill of his cap, the battle light was already shining fiercely in his pale blue eyes.

Lee came up and joined him at the turn-off where the sniper had tried to draw a bead on them at sunset. Both mounted — Lee on Traveller, a tall dapple gray, and Jackson on stocky, ox-eyed Little Sorrel — they spoke briefly against a background of skirmish fire which had begun to sputter along the two-mile front now occupied exclusively by Anderson and McLaws, with just over 15,000 troops between them. Nothing in Lee's manner showed the strain involved in gambling that his opponent, whether or not he became aware in the meantime of what was happening in his front and on his flank, would not exploit his five-to-one numerical advantage by launching an all-out attack — frontal or otherwise; either would be about equally destructive — before the widely divided Confederate wings were reunited. Moreover, Lee was proceeding not only on the assumption that Jackson could gain and strike the Union flank before the bluecoats recovered from their current puzzling lethargy, here in the Wilderness or back in front of Marye's Heights; he was also proceeding on the belief, or at any rate the hope, that Hooker would be completely unstrung by the explosion on his right. Nothing less would serve. For if Hooker could absorb and then recover from the shock, he might still take the offensive against the outnumbered and divided graybacks to the west and south, or signal eastward for an assault upon the thinly held Fredericksburg ridge in Lee's immediate rear. This was, in short, the longest gamble of a career which had been crowded with risks throughout the eleven months since Lee first took command at Seven Pines. Now, their brief conversation ended, the two men parted, the elder to stay, the other to go. As they did so, the dark-bearded younger general raised his arm and pointed west, in the direction he was headed. Lee nodded, and Stonewall rode off into the forest, out of sight.

Fighting Joe had been up for hours, conducting a flank-to-flank inspection of his lines. "How strong! How strong!" he marveled as he examined the hastily improvised but elaborate fortifications: particularly those out on the right, where so many of the regiments were composed of foreign-born troops who performed such labor with Germanic thoroughness and a meticulous attention to detail rivaling Hooker's own. Wherever he went this morning, tall in the saddle and rosy-looking, flushed with confidence and trailing a kite-tail of staff officers behind his big white high-stepping horse, the soldiers cheered him lustily, delighted to see their commander sharing with them the rigors of the field. His mood was as expansive as before; more so, in fact; and with cause. For he had received, the night before, a report from a trusted operative just in from Richmond, who not only had documentary evidence that Lee was receiving barely 59,000 daily rations, but also reported that the southern commander could hope for no reinforcements except from Longstreet, both of whose divisions — despite the contrary fabrications passed on by yesterday's rebel deserters — were still in front of Suffolk. This last was confirmed by Peck himself, who wired that he had taken prisoners from Hood and Pickett that same day. In reaction, Hooker's last move before retiring had been to direct that Reynolds' corps be detached from Sedgwick and sent to join him here at Chancellorsville. When it arrived — as it should do before long, the summons having been issued at 1.55 this morning — he would have better than 90,000 men on hand to repulse the attack Lee seemed to be preparing to deliver against the bulging center of the Union line. If the old fox really believed what he was rumored to have said the day before, that this "was the only time he should fight equal numbers," he was in for a large surprise. What Fighting Joe was planning was Fredericksburg in reverse, with Lee in the role of Burnside, and himself in the role of Lee: except that this time, when the attackers were exhausted and bled white as a result of their attempts to storm his fortifications, he would be in a position to swing over to the offensive that had been impossible for the Confederates, back in December, because of their numerical inferiority and the guns on Stafford Heights. Hereabouts there were no heights for Lee to mass his guns on, only the blinding and restricting thickets, and Hooker had men aplenty for the delivery of an all-out counterattack and the administration of the

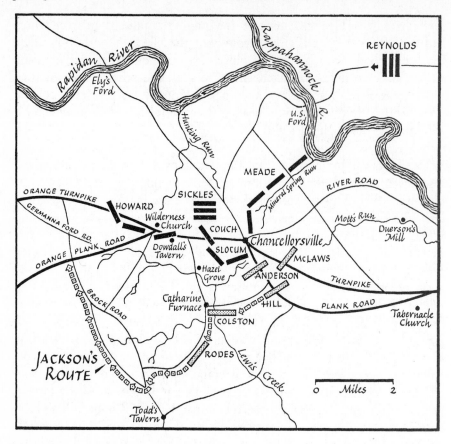

windup *coup de grâce* which would end the final spasmodic twitch of the dying rebel army.

He was in excellent spirits when he got back to headquarters at 9 o'clock to find a courier waiting for him from Brigadier General David Birney, commander of a division Sickles had sent out to some unoccupied high ground southwest of Fairview — Hazel Grove, it was called on the map — for a look at what the graybacks might be up to. According to the information brought back by the courier, they were up to a great deal. Hazel Grove afforded a clear but limited view of Catharine Furnace, less than one mile south, and the advancing bluecoats had spotted a rebel column moving due south of there along a stretch of road that disappeared into the woods. Apparently endless, the column included infantry, artillery, wagons, and ambulances; Birney thought it must signify an important development in the enemy's plans. Hooker agreed. In fact, after referring to his map, which showed that the road in question veered west beyond the screen of trees, he believed he knew just what that development was. The Confederates were in retreat, probably on Gordonsville, where Stoneman must have struck by now, severing one of their two main supply lines. However, on the off-chance that Lee was attempting at this late date to come up with something out of his bag of tricks, Hooker decided it would be wise to warn Howard of what was going on, and he sent him a message advising him to be vigilant in protecting the western flank: "We have good reason to suppose that the enemy is moving to our right. Please advance your pickets for purposes of observation as far as may be safe to obtain timely information of their approach." He might have followed to see for himself that his instructions were carried out, but presently a dispatch arrived from Howard, sent before his own had been received, stating that he too had sighted the rebel column "moving westward on a road parallel with this," and adding, of his own accord: "I am taking measures to resist an attack from the west." It was clear that Howard required no supervision to assure that he did his duty; he had performed it before he was even told what it was, thereby leaving Hooker free to concentrate on the question of pursuit.

In this connection he thought again of Sedgwick, who had been kept by a faulty telegraph connection from getting yesterday's instructions until the hour was too late for an attack. First Sickles and now Reynolds had been detached from the downstream force, but Sedgwick's was the largest corps in the army. With Gibbon's division still available at Falmouth, he had close to 30,000 effectives, plus the support of the long-range guns on Stafford Heights, and though Professor Lowe had reported earlier that a hard wind was bumping him around so much he could not use his telescope, the headquarters intelligence section informed Hooker that only Early's division remained on the Fredericksburg ridge. Accordingly, he directed Butterfield to pass the word along to Sedgwick and authorize him to attack if there was "a reasonable expectation of success." Meanwhile Hooker kept his staff busy preparing orders designed to put the whole army on Lee's trail if he still appeared to be in retreat next morning. A circular issued at 2.30 instructed corps commanders to load up with forage, provisions, and ammunition so as "to be ready to start at an early hour tomorrow." By the time this was distributed, reports had begun to come in from Sickles, who had been given permission at noon to advance with two divisions to investigate the movement Birney had spotted from Hazel Grove. He sent back word that he had pierced the rebel column near Catharine Furnace, capturing men and wagons, but that practically all of it had moved westward beyond his reach by now. Hooker took fire at this, his confidence soaring: Lee was unquestionably in full retreat, intending to follow the heavily escorted train with the Confederate main body. At 4.30 the jubilant Federal commander wired Butterfield to order Sedgwick to throw his entire force across the river, "capture Fredericksburg and everything in it, and vigorously pursue the enemy." Previous instructions had been discretionary, and so were these; but Hooker made it clear that a fine opportunity lay before him. "We know that the enemy is fleeing, trying to save his trains," he added. "Two of Sickles' divisions are among them."

As might have been expected with the rebel column filing through the woods to the army's front, there was a good deal of excitement along the outpost lines. Couriers and even unit commanders began to turn up at the Chancellor house with frantic, sometimes near-hysterical warnings of an impending flank attack. Staff officers had all they could do to keep some of them — especially one persistent artilleryman with the lowly rank of captain, who claimed to have ridden out and seen the graybacks massing — from bothering Hooker himself with their perturbations. When these men finally could be made to understand that the high command was already aware of the alleged danger and had taken steps to meet it in case it developed, they returned to their units, most of them feeling rather sheepish at having presumed to believe they knew more than their superiors. Others, however, remained unconvinced: particularly those through whose ranks the rebel prisoners had been taken rearward after their capture near Catharine Furnace. They were Georgians, hale-looking men in neat butternut clothes, and for the most part they seemed cheerful enough, considering their plight. They had come over, they replied to taunts, to help "eat up them eight-day rations." But some were surly and in no mood to be chided. Told by a bluecoat, "We'll have every mother's son of you before we go away," one snapped back: "You'll catch hell before night." Another was more specific as to how calamity was to be visited upon them, and by whom. "You think you've done a big thing just now," he said, "but wait till Jackson gets around on your flank." This seemed to its hearers well worth passing on to headquarters, but when they went there to report it they were told to return to their outfits; Lee was in retreat, no matter what the butternut captives said, and Hooker was making plans even now for an orderly pursuit.

Far out on the right flank, as the shadows lengthened toward 5 o'clock and beyond, Howard's men were taking it easy. They had seen no action so far in the campaign, but that was much as usual; they had seen little real action anywhere in the war, save for a great deal of marching and countermarching, and were in fact a sort of stepchild corps, collectively referred to by the rest of the army as "a bunch of Dutchmen." Indeed, nothing demonstrated more conclusively Hooker's lack of concern for his western flank than the fact that he had posted these men here. Mostly New Yorkers and Pennsylvanians, large numbers of them were immigrants, lately arrived and scarcely able to speak English; "Hessians," their enemies called them, with a contempt dating back to the days of the Revolution. Schurz, Steinwehr, and Schimmelfennig were three of their generals, while their colonels had names such as Von

Gilsa, Krzyzanowski, Einsiedel, Dachrodt, and Schluemback. Howard himself was by no means popular with them, despite his sacrifice of an arm to the cause and a record of steady progress up the ladder of command. After his maiming, a year ago at Fair Oaks, he had returned to lead a brigade at Antietam and a division at Fredericksburg, both with such distinction that now — to the considerable displeasure of men whose proudest boast had been "I fights mit Sigel" and who rather illogically put the blame for their hero's departure on his successor — he had a corps. He had had it, in fact, exactly a month today; but in his anxiety to make good he not only had borne down hard on discipline, he also had tried to influence the out-of-hours activities of his troops by distributing religious tracts among them. The latter action was resented even more than the former, for many of the men were freethinkers, lately emerged from countries where the church had played a considerable part in attempting their oppression, and they drew the line somewhere short of being preached at, prayed over, or uplifted. The result of all this, and more, was that army life was not a happy one for them or their commander, whose ill-concealed disappointment at their reaction to his attempt to play the role of Christian Soldier only served to increase their mistrust and dislike of him, empty sleeve and all.

Today was one of the better days, however, with a minimum of work, no drill whatsoever, and a maximum of rest. Extended for more than a mile along the turnpike west of Dowdall's Tavern, an oversized cabin just east of the junction where the plank road came in from the southwest, they lounged behind the elaborate southward-facing breastworks Hooker himself had admired. Like his chief, Howard was convinced that he was onto the rebel strategy, which seemed to him to be designed to cover a retreat with a pretense of strength and boldness. He too rejected various cries of wolf, including those from an outpost major who sent back a stream of frantic messages from beyond the flank, all patterned after the first at 2.45: "A large body of the enemy is massing in my front. For God's sake make disposition to receive him!" At the outer end of the intrenched line, two guns were posted hub-to-hub on the pike itself, facing west, and two regiments of infantry — not over 900 men in all — were disposed at right angles to the road, strung out northward from the point where the guns were posted. These two regiments and guns were all the flank protection Howard had provided after notifying Hooker that he was "taking measures to resist an attack from the west," but he considered them ample, since nothing could approach him from that direction except along the turnpike, covered by the two guns, or through a tangle of second-growth timber and briery underbrush which he had pronounced impenetrable. Moreover, there was a half-mile stretch of unoccupied ground between his left and Slocum's right, marking the former position of his one reserve brigade, which had been detached in the midafternoon and still had not returned from its mission of guarding Sickles' flank in the course of his advance from Hazel Grove. This gap was critical. Though it went unnoticed, or at any rate unfilled, it meant that if anything struck Howard a hard enough blow from the west, he would be in much the same predicament as a man attempting to sit on a chair he did not know had been removed.

That, or something like that, was what happened. Not long after 5 o'clock, with some regiments already eating supper and others lounging about while waiting for it, their rifles neatly stacked, the troops at the far end of the line were alarmed and then amused to see large numbers of deer break out of the thickets to the west and come bounding toward them, accompanied by droves of rabbits darting this way and that in the underbrush, as if pursued by invisible beaters. The men cheered and hallooed, waving their caps at the startled forest creatures, until presently something else they heard and saw froze the laughter in their throats. Long lines of men in gray and butternut, their clothes ripped to tatters by the briers and branches, were running toward them through the "impenetrable" thickets. They were screaming as they came on, jaws agape, and their bayonets caught angry glints from the low-angled sun pouring its beams through the reddened treetops and over their shoulders.

★ ★ ★

For all its explosive force, its practically complete surprise, and its rapid gathering of momentum, Stonewall's flank attack was launched with only about two hours of daylight left for the accomplishment of the destruction he intended. One of the two main reasons for this tardiness was that the start itself had been late, and the other was that the finish was delayed by an extension of the march. Between these two untoward extremes, however, all went smoothly, despite attempted enemy interruptions. The roads, described by one of the marchers as "just wet enough to be easy to the feet and free from dust," were narrow but firm, so that the column was elongated but its progress was not impeded. Like his men, who were enthused by a sense of adventure before they had even had time to guess what the adventure was going to be, Jackson was in excellent spirits, and though he did not push them to the limit of their endurance as he had done so often in the past, being concerned for once to conserve their energy for the work that lay ahead, he took care to deal with emergencies in a manner that would not hold up the main body. For instance, when the head of the column came under fire from a section of guns just north of Catharine Furnace, he detached the lead regiment of Georgians, with instructions for them to block a possible infantry probe at that point, and had the remaining units double-time across the clearing, being willing to suffer whatever incidental losses this involved rather than to burn more daylight by taking a roundabout route. Similarly A. P. Hill, whose division did not clear the starting point until well after 11 o'clock, dropped off his two rear brigades to assist the hard-pressed Georgians — forty of them had been captured and most of the rest were about to be captured — in fending off an infantry attack launched by the Federals just as he was approaching the furnace about noon, and forged ahead with his other four brigades. Far in the lead and quite unmindful of his rear, which he left to look out for itself after making the original provision, Jackson kept the main body on the go. "Press forward. Press forward," he urged his subordinate commanders. Including 1500 attached cavalry and 2000 artillerymen in support of his 70 regiments of infantry, Stonewall had better than 31,000 effectives in the column, and his only regret was that he did not have more. "I hear it said that General Hooker has more men than he can handle," he remarked in the course of the march. "I should like to have half as many more as I have today, and I should hurl him into the river!"

His eyes glowed at the thought, and presently they had occasion to blaze even more fiercely, not only at a thought, but also at what was actually spread before them. About 2 o'clock, as he approached the Orange Plank Road — the intended objective, up which he expected to turn the column northeastward for an attack that would strike the Orange Turnpike just west of Dowdall's Tavern, where Hooker's flank presumably was anchored — he was met by Fitz Lee, who approached from the opposite direction, drew rein alongside Little Sorrel, and announced with a barely suppressed excitement that explained his lack of ceremony: "General, if you will ride with me, halting your column here out of sight, I will show you the enemy's right." The two officers, accompanied by a single courier so as not to increase the risk of detection, rode past the plank road intersection, then turned off eastward through the trees to a little hill which they climbed on horseback. From the summit, parting the curtain of leaves, Stonewall saw what had provoked the excitement Lee would still be feeling, years later, when he came to write about it: "What a sight presented itself before me! Below, and but a few hundred yards distant, ran the Federal line of battle . . . with abatis in front and long lines of stacked arms in the rear. Two cannon were visible in the part of the line seen. The soldiers were in groups in the rear, laughing, smoking, probably engaged, here and there, in games of cards and other amusements indulged in while feeling safe and comfortable, awaiting orders. In rear of them were other parties driving up and butchering beeves." As he observed the peaceful scene, Jackson's mind was on a different kind of butchery. According to Lee, "his eyes burned with a brilliant glow, lighting his sad face. His expression was one of intense interest; his face was colored slightly with the paint of the approaching battle, and radiant in the success of his flank movement."

The salient fact was that Hooker's flank was as completely "in the air" as had been reported the night before, but that an attack up the plank road, such as had been intended, would strike it at an angle, about midway, rather than end-on; which would not do. Correction of this, however, called for a two-mile extension of the march in order to get beyond the farthest western reach of the Union intrenchments and approach them on the perpendicular. That meant a further delay of at least an hour, to which of course would be added the time required to form the three divisions for assault. With the sun already well past the overhead — by now, in fact, the hands of his watch were crowding 2.30 — there might not be enough daylight left for the execution of his plans. But Jackson did not hesitate beyond the few minutes it took him to make a careful examination of what was spread before his eyes. Seeing his lips moving as he looked at the enemy soldiers down below, Lee assumed that he was praying. If this was so, there was no evidence of it in his voice as he turned to the courier and snapped out an order for him to take back to the head of the column, halted on the Brock Road to await instructions: "Tell General Rodes to move across the plank road, halt when he gets to the old turnpike, and I will join him there." The courier took off. Jackson turned for a final look at the lounging bluecoats, disposed as they were for slaughter, then "rode rapidly [back] down the hill, his arms flapping to the motion of his horse, over whose head it seemed, good rider as he was, he would certainly go." Lee saw him thus; then he too turned and followed, somewhat chagrined that he had not received the thanks he had expected in return for making a discovery which not only would save many Confederate lives but also had made possible what gave promise of being the most brilliant tactical stroke of Stonewall's career.

Jackson had already forgotten him, along with practically everything else preceding the moment when his mind became fixed on what he was going to do. Retracing his horse's steps back down the Brock Road he passed Rodes, who had his men slogging northward for the turnpike, and returned to the plank road intersection, where he met and detached Colston's lead brigade — his own old First Manassas outfit, the Stonewall Brigade — to advance a short distance up the plank road and take position at a junction where the road from Germanna Ford came in from the northwest. With his rear and right flank thus screened and protected, he took a moment to scrawl a note briefly explaining the situation to Lee, who he knew must be fretting at the delay. "I hope as soon as practicable to attack," he wrote, and added: "I trust that an ever kind Providence will bless us with great success." The note was headed, "Near 3 p.m."; time was going fast. He hurried northward to the turnpike, overtook Rodes, and gave him the instructions he had promised. Rodes accordingly moved eastward on the pike for about a mile — unopposed and apparently unobserved, although this brought

him within 1000 yards of the western knuckle of Howard's intrenchments — then formed his division along a low, north-south ridge. Four
brigades were in line, two to the right and two to the left, extending
about a mile in each direction from the turnpike, which would be the
guide for the assault. The fifth brigade took position behind the extreme
right, and Colston's remaining three brigades prolonged this second line
northward, 200 yards in rear of the first. Jackson's orders were that the
charge would be headlong. Under no circumstances was there to be even
a pause in the advance. If a first-line brigade ran into trouble, it was to
call for help from the brigade in its immediate rear, without taking time
to notify either division commander. The main thing, he emphasized as
he spoke to his subordinates in turn, was to keep rolling, to keep up the
pressure and the scare.

Maneuvering the stretched-out column off the road and into a
compact mass, like a fist clenched for striking, was a time-consuming
business, however, especially when it had to be done in woods so dense
that visibility scarcely extended beyond the limits of a single regiment.
Also there was the problem of fatigue. Though by ordinary standards
the march had been neither long nor hard — an average dozen miles in
an average eight hours — none of the troops had had anything to eat
since breakfast, and many of them had not had even that. Hunger made
them trembly. Moreover, there had been a tormenting shortage of water all along the way, and the men were spitting cotton as they filed into
position to await the signal that would send them plunging eastward
through the thickets to their front. They knew now, for certain, what
they had only assumed before: Hooker's flank lay dead ahead and they
were about to strike it. But the waiting was long. It was 4.30 by the time
Colston had formed in rear of Rodes, and Hill was not yet off the road.
Another half hour sufficed to get Little Powell's two leading brigades
into position in rear of Colston's left, while the center two were coming
forward on the turnpike; but the last two were miles back down the
road, delayed by their rear-guard action at Catharine Furnace. Jackson
waited as long as he could, watch in hand. Rodes stood beside him, waiting too; he was a V.M.I. graduate, just past his thirty-fourth birthday,
and like his chief a former professor of mathematics. Tall and slender, a
Virginia-born Alabamian with a tawny mustache that drooped below
the corners of his mouth, he had fought well in almost every major battle since First Manassas, taking time off only for wounds, but he
would be leading a division in combat for the first time today. At 5.15 —
an hour and a half before sundown — Jackson looked up from his
watch. His proposed third line was not half formed, but he and the sun
could wait no longer.

"Are you ready, General Rodes?"

"Yes sir."

"You can go forward then."

He spoke calmly, almost matter-of-factly; yet what followed within the next quarter hour approximated pandemonium. Crashing through the half-mile screen·of brush and stunted trees, whose thorns and brittle, low-hanging limbs quickly stripped the trail-blazing skirmishers near-naked, the long lines of Confederates broke suddenly into the clear, where the sight of the enemy brought their rifles to their shoulders and the quavering din of the rebel yell from their throats; "that hellish yell," one bluecoat called it, though Jackson himself had once referred to the caterwaul as "the sweetest music I ever heard." He was getting his fill of such music now. All across the nearly two-mile width of his front, the woods and fields resounded with it as the screaming attackers bore down on the startled Federals, who had just risen to whoop at the frightened deer and driven rabbits. Now it was their turn to be frightened — and driven, too. For the Union regiments facing west gave way in a rush before the onslaught, and as they fled the two guns they had abandoned were turned against them, hastening their departure and increasing the confusion among the troops facing south behind the now useless breastworks they had constructed with such care. These last, looking over their shoulders and seeing the fugitives running close-packed on the turnpike immediately in their rear, took their cue from them and began to pull out, too, in rapid succession from right to left down the long line of intrenchments, swelling the throng rushing eastward along the road. Within twenty minutes of the opening shots, Howard's flank division had gone out of military existence, converted that quickly from organization to mob. The adjoining division was sudden to follow the example set. Not even the sight of the corps commander himself, on horseback near Wilderness Church, breasting the surge of retreaters up the turnpike and clamping a stand of abandoned colors under the stump of his amputated arm while attempting to control his skittish horse with the other, served to end or even slow the rout. Bareheaded and with tears in his eyes, Howard was pleading with them to halt and form, halt and form, but they paid him no mind, evidently convinced that his distress, whether for the fate of his country or his career or both, took no precedence over their own distress for their very lives. Some in their haste drew knives from their pockets and cut their knapsack straps as they ran, unburdening themselves for greater speed without taking the time to fumble at buckles, lest they be overtaken by the horde of tatterdemalion demons stretching north and south as far as the eye could follow and screaming with delight at the prospect of carnage.

Jackson was among the pursuers, riding from point to point just in rear of the crest of the wave, exultant. "Push right ahead," he told his brigadiers and colonels, and as he spoke he made a vigorous thrusting gesture, such as a man would make in toppling a wall. When a jubilant young officer cried, "They are running too fast for us. We can't keep up with them!" he replied sternly: "They never run too fast for me, sir. Press them, press them!" It was 6.30 by now; the sun was down behind the rearward treetops. Dowdall's Tavern lay dead ahead, and from the east the answering thunder of guns and clatter of musketry told Stonewall that Lee had heard or learned of the attack and was applying pressure to keep the tottering Union giant off balance, even though he could scarcely hope to break through the endless curve of fortifications south and east of Chancellorsville. Here to the west, on the other hand, whenever a clump of bluecoats more stalwart than their fellows tried to make a stand, they found themselves quickly outflanked on the left and right by the overlapping lines of the attackers, and they had to give way in a scramble to avoid being surrounded. Every time Jackson heard the wild yell of victory that followed such collapses he would lift his head and smile grimly, as if in thanks to the God of battle. Conversely, whenever he came upon the bodies of his own men, lying where panicky shots had dropped them, he would frown, draw rein briefly, and raise one hand as if blessing the slain for their valor. A staff officer later remarked, "I have never seen him so well pleased with the progress and results of a fight."

On through sundown his pleasure was justified by continuing success, and presently it was increased. By 7 o'clock, with darkness settling fast in the clearings and the woods already black, his triumph over Howard was complete as the Federals gave way around Dowdall's Tavern and began their flight across the reserveless gap that yawned between them and the rest of the blue army. On the right, just south of the turnpike, there was a meeting engagement with a column of Union cavalry, which resulted in its repulse, and enemy guns were booming on Fairview Heights, firing blind to discourage pursuit, but Jackson did not believe there was anything substantial between him and the loom of forest screening Chancellorsville itself, just over a mile ahead. The only deterrent beyond his control was the darkness, and soon there was not even that. As if in response to a signal from the southern Joshua, the full moon came up, huge and red through the drifting smoke, then brightened to gold as it rose to light the way for pursuit. Many times in the past Stonewall had ached to launch a night attack; now he not only had the chance, he believed it was downright necessary if he was to prevent the enemy from recovering from the shock and attempting to turn the tables on the still-divided Confederates. Two immediate objectives he had in mind. One was to strike deep in Hooker's rear, cutting him off from U.S. Ford so as to prevent his escape across the Rappahannock, and the other was to reunite with Lee for a combined assault on the bluecoats who thus would be hemmed in for slaughter. It was more or less obvious by now that Rodes and Colston had done their worst, at least for the present; they would need a breathing spell in which to regain control of their troops, hopelessly mingled in a single wave that was already ebbing because of exhaustion; but Hill's four brigades were still intact, available as a reserve, and Jackson was determined to use them for a moonlight advance along the pike and up the roads leading northeastward to the single river crossing in Hooker's rear. Soon he found Little Powell and gave him his instructions. There was no studied calmness about him now, such as there had been three hours ago when he told Rodes he could go forward. His excitement was evident to everyone he met, and his sense of urgency was communicated with every word he spoke, including those in the orders he gave Hill: "Press them! Cut them off from the United States Ford, Hill. Press them!"

Hooker by then was doing all he could to avert disaster, but for the better part of an hour after the first wave of attackers struck and crumpled the tip of his western wing — three miles from the Chancellor gallery where he sat chatting amiably with members of his staff — he had been under the tactical disadvantage of not even knowing that he had been surprised. Because of acoustic peculiarities of the terrain and the cushioning effect of brush and trees, the roar of battle reached him but faintly and indirectly. He and his aides supposed that the racket, such as it was, came from down around Catharine Furnace, a couple of miles to the south, and were exchanging conjectures as to the havoc Sickles must be making among Lee's trains in that direction. Just before sundown, however, one of the officers strolled out to the road and casually gazed westward. "My God — here they come!" the others heard him shout. Then they saw for themselves what he meant. A stumbling herd of wild-eyed men, the frantic and apparently unstoppable backwash of Howard's unstrung corps, was rushing eastward, filling the pike from shoulder to shoulder. Fighting Joe reacted fast. At hand was Sickles' third division — his own in the days before his elevation to corps and army command — left in reserve when the other two moved south; Hooker ordered it to wheel right and stem the rout. "Receive them on your bayonets! Receive them on your bayonets!" he cried, not making it clear whether he meant the demoralized Dutchmen or the rebels somewhere in their rear, as he rode westward through the failing light and into the teeth of the storm.

At Hazel Grove, sealed off from the uproar which by now was just over a mile away, a regiment of Pennsylvania cavalry received at about this same time, between sunset and moonrise, orders to join Howard near Wilderness Church. With no suggestion of urgency in the message and no hint that a clash had occurred, let alone a retreat, the troopers mounted and set out northwestward on a trail too narrow for anything more than a column of twos. They rode at a walk, talking casually among themselves, their weapons sheathed, until they approached the turnpike: at which point the major in command barely had time to cry, "Draw sabers! Charge!" before they ran spang into a whole Confederate division moving eastward through darkness that all of a sudden was stitched with muzzle flashes and filled with yells and twittering bullets. One side was about as startled as the other. The riders managed to hack their way out of the melee, though by the time they reassembled in the moonlight back near Chancellorsville a good many saddles had been emptied and a number of troopers had been captured, along with their unmanageable horses.

For blue and gray alike, whether mounted or afoot, the meeting engagement had some of the qualities of a nightmare too awful to be remembered except in unavoidable snatches. But for other Union soldiers, east of there, such an experience would have been counted almost mild in comparison with the one they blundered into a few hours later, in which blue was pitted not only against gray, but also against blue. Down around Catharine Furnace, deep in enemy territory, Dan Sickles knew nothing of what had been happening until well past sundown, when he heard the roar of batteries massed on the heights at Hazel Grove and Fairview, far in his rear. Informed at last of the enemy flank attack, which placed his two divisions precariously between the superior halves of the rebel army and thus exposed him to the danger of being pinched off and surrounded, he pulled hurriedly back to Hazel Grove — unhindered, so far, but by no means out of the trap whose jaws seemed likely to snap shut at any moment. By now it was past 9 o'clock, and except for occasional bellows by the 22 guns posted here and the 34 at Fairview, the firing had died to a mutter. Placing one division on the left and the other on the right of a trail leading northward through the forest, Sickles prepared to continue his march to the comparative safety of the turnpike. He had scarcely set out, however, before the two columns lost the trail and drifted apart, one veering east and the other west, with the result that they ran into horrendous trouble in both directions. The division on the left angled into a line of Confederates, alert behind hastily improvised intrenchments, while the one on the right stumbled into a similar line along which one of Slocum's divisions was deployed. Both broke into flames on contact, and a three-sided fight was in progress as suddenly as if someone had thrown a switch. Caught in what a participant called "one vast square of fire," Sickles' troops milled aimlessly, throwing bullets indiscriminately east and west. Shouts of "Don't fire! We're friends!" brought heavier volleys from both sides of the gauntlet, and consternation reached a climax when rival batteries started pumping shell and canister into the frantic mass hemmed thus between the lines. Somehow, though, despite the darkness and confusion, Sickles finally managed to effect a withdrawal southward, in the direction he had come from. By midnight he had what was left of his two divisions back at Hazel Grove, where the men bedded down to wait for daylight, barely four hours off, and restore their jangled nerves as best they could.

Elsewhere along his contracted line — albeit the contraction had been accomplished more by Jackson's efforts than his own — Hooker saw to it that the rest of his army did likewise. He did not know what tomorrow was going to bring, but he intended to be ready for it. And in point of fact he had cause for confidence. Reynolds was over the river by now; his three divisions were available as a reserve. Even Howard's three, or anyhow a good part of them, had managed to reassemble in the vicinity of U.S. Ford, where they were brought to a halt after ricocheting northward off Lee's intrenchments east of Chancellorsville. Meade's three had been unaffected by the turmoil across the way. Couch and Slocum, under cover of the 56-gun barrage from Hazel Grove and Fairview, had adapted their four divisions to the altered situation, along with the one Sickles had left behind. Moreover, another brigade of cavalry was at hand, Averell having been called in from near Rapidan Station, where Stoneman had dropped him off, ostensibly to check Stuart's pursuit but actually, since there was no pursuit, to play little or no part in the southward raid. His total loss, after three days in enemy country, was 1 man killed and 4 wounded; Hooker was furious and relieved him on the spot. "If the enemy did not come to him, he should have gone to the enemy," Fighting Joe protested with unconscious irony. Apparently he could not see that this applied in his own case. He still depended on Sedgwick for the delivery of any blow that was to be struck, repeating in greater detail at 9 p.m. the instructions sent him earlier in the day. This time they were peremptory; Sedgwick was to "cross the Rappahannock at Fredericksburg on the receipt of this order." Leaving Gibbon to hold the town, he was to march at once on Chancellorsville and "attack and destroy any force he may fall in with on the road." This would bring him promptly into contact with Lee's rear, "and between us we will use him up. . . . Be sure not to fail." The pattern was unchanged. Now as before, Gallo-Hooker was leaving the confrontation of the bull to Paco-Sedgwick, while he himself stood fast behind the barrera to cheer him on.

Lulled by what one insomniac called "the weird, plaintive notes of the whippoorwills," who would not let even a battle the size of this one cancel their serenade to the full, high-sailing moon, the army slept. From point to point the Wilderness was burning — "like a picture of hell," a cavalryman said of the scene as he viewed it from a hilltop — but the screams of the wounded caught earlier by the flames had died away, together with the growl and rumble of the guns. It was midnight and the Army of the Potomac took its rest.

Though the Army of Northern Virginia was doing the same, west and south of the now one-handled Union dipper, it did so in an atmosphere of tragedy out of all ratio to the success it had scored today. Not only had Stonewall's plan for continuing the eastward drive by moonlight been abandoned, but Stonewall himself had been taken rearward, first on a stretcher and then in an ambulance, to a hospital tent near Wilderness Tavern, where even now, as midnight came and went, surgeons were laying out the probes and knives and saws they would use in their fight to save his life. Intimations of national tragedy, intensified by a sense of acute personal loss, pervaded the forest bivouacs as the rumor spread that Jackson had been wounded.

After telling Hill to bring his men forward in order to resume the stalled pursuit, he had proceeded east along the turnpike in search of a route that would intercept the expected blue retreat to U.S. Ford. As he and several members of his staff rode past the fringe of Confederate pickets, taking a secondary road that branched off through the woods on the left, they began hearing the sound of axes from up ahead, where the Federals were trimming and notching logs for a new line of breastworks. "General, don't you think this is the wrong place for you?" an officer asked. Jackson did not agree. "The danger is all over," he said. "The enemy is routed. Go back and tell A. P. Hill to press right on." Presently, though, with the ring of axes much nearer at hand, he drew rein and listened carefully. Then he turned and rode back the way he had come, apparently satisfied that the bluecoats, for all their frenzy of preparation, would be unable to resist what he intended to throw at them as soon as Hill got his troops into position. Soon he came upon Little Powell himself, riding forward with his staff to examine the ground over which he expected to advance, and the two parties returned together. To the pickets crouched in the brush ahead — North Carolinians whose apprehensiveness had been aroused by the meeting engagement, a short while ago, with the saber-swinging Pennsylvanians over on the turnpike — the mounted generals and their staffs, amounting in all to nearly a score of horsemen, must have had the sound of a troop of Union cavalry on the prowl or the advance element of a wave of attackers. At any rate that was the premise on which they acted in opening fire. "Cease firing! Cease firing!" Hill shouted, echoed by one of Jackson's officers: "Cease firing! You are firing into your own men!" Fortunately, no one had been hit by the sudden spatter of bullets, but the Tarheel commander believed he saw through a Yankee trick. "Who gave that order?" he cried. "It's a lie! Pour it into them, boys!" The boys did just that. Not only the pickets but the whole front-line battalion opened fire at twenty paces and with such devastating effect that the bodies of no less than fourteen horses were counted later in the immediate area.

Little Sorrel was not among them, having returned by then to the allegiance from which Stonewall had removed him, nearly two years ago, with his capture at Harpers Ferry. Frightened by the abrupt first clatter of fire from the pickets crouched in the brush ahead, he whirled and made a rearward dash through the woods. Jackson managed to turn him, though he could not slow him down, and was coming back west, his right arm raised to protect his face from low-hanging branches, when the second volley crashed. Once more Little Sorrel whirled and scampered toward the enemy lines, completely out of control now because his rider had been struck by three of the bullets, two in the left arm, which hung useless at his side, and one through the palm of the upraised hand, which he lowered and used as before, despite the pain, to turn the fear-crazed animal back toward his own lines. There one of the surviving officers, dismounted by the volley, caught hold of the horse's bridle and brought him to a stop, while another came up and braced the general in the saddle. He seemed dazed. "Wild fire, that, sir; wild fire," he exclaimed as he sat staring into the darkness lately stitched with muzzle flashes. All around them they could hear the groans and screams of injured men and horses. "How do you feel, General?" one of the officers asked, with the simplicity of great alarm, and Jackson replied: "You had better take me down. My arm is broken." They did so, finding him already so weak from shock and bleeding that he could not lift his feet from the stirrups. Freed at last of the restraining weight, Little Sorrel turned and ran for the third time toward the Union lines, and this time he made it. Meanwhile the two staffers laid the general under a tree. While one went off in search of a surgeon and the other was doing what he could to staunch the flow of blood from an artery severed in the left arm, just below the shoulder, Jackson began muttering to himself, as if in disbelief of what had happened. "My own men," he said.

That was about 9.30; the next two hours were a restless extension of the nightmare as Federal batteries at Fairview began firing, the gunners having spotted the moonlit confusion just over half a mile away. Presently the second of Jackson's two attendant staff officers returned through the storm of bursting shells with a regimental surgeon, who administered first aid and ordered the general taken rearward on a stretcher. This had to be done under artillery fire so intense that the bearers were forced to stop and lie flat from time to time, as much for Jackson's protection as their own. On several such occasions they almost dropped him, and once they did, hard on the injured arm, which made him groan with pain for the first time. At last they found an ambulance and got him back to the aid station near Wilderness Tavern, where his medical director, Dr Hunter McGuire, took one look at "the fixed, rigid face and the thin lips, so tightly compressed that the impression of the teeth could be seen through them," and ordered the patient prepared for surgery. "What an infinite blessing . . . blessing . . . blessing," Stonewall murmured as the chloroform blurred his pain. Then McGuire removed the shattered left arm, all but a two-inch stump. Coming out of the anesthetic, half an hour later — it was now about 3 o'clock in the morning — Jackson said that during the operation he had experienced "the most delightful music," which he now supposed had been the singing of the bone-saw. At that point, however, he was interrupted by a staff officer just arrived from the front. Tragedy had succeeded tragedy.

Hill had been incapacitated, struck in both legs by shell fragments, and had called on Jeb Stuart to take command instead of Rodes, the senior infantry brigadier, who until today had never led anything larger than a brigade. Stuart had come at a gallop from Ely's Ford, altogether willing. Knowing little of the situation and almost nothing of Stonewall's plans, however, he had sent to him for instructions or advice. Jackson stirred, contracting his brow at the effort. For a moment the light of battle returned to his eyes. Then it faded; his face relaxed. Even the exertion of thought was too much for him in his weakened condition. "I don't know — I can't tell," he stammered. "Say to General Stuart he must do what he thinks best."

Stuart would do that anyhow, of course, and so would Lee, who was informed at about this same time of the progress of the flank attack and the climactic wounding of his chief lieutenant. "Ah, Captain," he said; he shook his head; "Any victory is dearly bought which deprives us of the services of General Jackson, even for a short time." When the officer started to give him further details of the accident Lee stopped him. "Ah, don't talk about it. Thank God it is no worse." He was quick to agree, however, when the young man expressed the opinion that it had been Stonewall's intention to continue the attack. "Those people must be pressed today," Lee said decisively, and he put this into more formal language at once in a note to Stuart: "It is necessary that the glorious victory thus far achieved be prosecuted with the utmost vigor, and the enemy given no time to rally.... Endeavor, therefore, to dispossess them of Chancellorsville, which will permit the union of the army."

★ ★ ★

Hooker did not wait for Stuart or anyone else to dispossess him of Chancellorsville. He dispossessed himself. After establishing in the predawn darkness a secondary line of defense — a formidable V-shaped affair, with Reynolds deployed along Hunting Run, Meade at the southern apex, where the roads from Ely's and U.S. Fords came together in rear of army headquarters, and the fragments of Howard reassembled in Meade's old position along Mineral Spring Run, so that the flanks were anchored, right and left, on the Rapidan and the Rappahannock — he rode forward at first light, past the works still held by Couch and Slocum around Fairview, to confer in person with Sickles. Despite last night's horrendous experience of being mauled by foes and friends, Sickles had got his nerve back and was all for holding his ground; but Hooker would not hear of it, and ordered him to withdraw at once. It was this well-intentioned readjustment, designed to tidy up his lines and consolidate his defenses south of the vital crossroads, which resulted in his dispossession. Hazel Grove turned out to be the key to the whole advance position, since rebel artillery posted there could enfilade the intrenchments around Fairview, which in turn were all that covered Chancellorsville itself. The result was that everything south of the improvised V came suddenly unglued, and Hooker was left, scarcely twelve hours after his apparent delivery from the first, with a possible second disaster on his hands.

Stuart's advance, south of the turnpike and into the rising sun, coincided with Sickles' withdrawal, the final stages of which became a rout as the graybacks swarmed into Hazel Grove and overran the tail of the blue column. Immediately behind the first wave of attackers came the guns, 30 of them slamming away from the just-won heights at the Federals massed around Fairview, while another 30 assailed the western flank from a position near Howard's former headquarters, back out the pike, and 24 more were roaring from down the plank road to the southeast. Lee's midwinter reorganization of the Confederate long arm, for increased flexibility in close-up support, was paying short-term dividends this morning. Caught in the converging fire of these 84 guns, along with others west and south, the troops of Couch and Slocum were infected by the panic Sickles' men brought out of the smoke at Hazel Grove. North of the pike, sheltered by the breastworks Jackson had heard them constructing the night before, the bluecoats held fast against repeated assaults by the rebel infantry, but they were galled by the crossfire from batteries whose shots were plowing the fields around the crossroads in their rear and smashing their lines of supply and communication. Not even the Chancellor mansion, converted by now into a hospital as well as a headquarters by surgeons who took doors off their hinges and propped them on chairs for use as operating tables, was safe from the bombardment — as Hooker himself discovered presently, in a most emphatic manner. Shortly after 9 o'clock he was standing on the southwest veranda, leaning against one of the squat wooden pillars, when a solid projectile struck and split it lengthwise. He fell heavily to the floor, stunned by the shock. His aides gathered round and took him out into the yard, where they laid him on a blanket and poured a jolt of brandy down his throat. Revived by this first drink in weeks, Fighting Joe got up, rather wobbly still, and walked off a short distance, calling for his horse. It was well that he did, for just after he rose a second cannonball landed directly on the blanket, as if to emphasize the notion suggested by the first that the war had become an intensely personal matter between the Union commander and the rebel gunners who were probing for his life. He mounted awkwardly, suffering from a numbness on the side of his body that had been in contact with the shattered pillar, and rode for the rear, accompanied by his staff.

Despite the fact that he would succeed to command of the army in the event that its present chief was incapacitated, Couch knew nothing of Hooker's precipitate change of base until about 10 o'clock, when he received a summons to join him behind Meade's lines, where the apex of the secondary V came down to within a mile of the Chancellor house. Though he had his hands quite full just then — it was during the past half hour that the lines around Fairview had begun to come unglued in earnest — Couch told Hancock to take charge, and set out rearward in the wake of his chief, whom he found stretched out on a cot in a tent beside the road to U.S. Ford. "Couch, I turn the command of the army over to you," the injured general said, raising himself on one elbow as he spoke. However, his next words showed that he did not really mean what he had said. Whether or not he had control of himself at this point was open to question, but there was no doubt that he intended to retain control of the army. "You will withdraw it and place it in the position designated on this map," he added, indicating a field sketch with the V drawn on it to show where the new front lines would run. Couch perhaps was relieved to hear that he would not be given full control, along with full responsibility — "If he is killed, what shall I do with this disjointed army?" he had asked himself as soon as he heard that Hooker had been hurt — but others were hoping fervently that he would take charge; for he was known to be a fighter. "By God, we'll have some fighting now," a colonel said stoutly as Couch emerged from the tent. Meade looked inquiringly at his friend, hoping to receive at last the order for which he had been waiting all morning: Go in. Instead, Couch shook his head by way of reply and relayed Hooker's instructions for a withdrawal.

In any event, such instructions were superfluous by now except as they applied to Hancock, whose division was the only one still maintaining, however shakily, its forward position in a state that even approached cohesiveness. The choice, if the army's present disjointed condition allowed for any choice at all, lay not in whether or not to withdraw, as Hooker expressly directed, but in whether or not to counterattack and thus attempt to recover what had been lost by the retreat already in progress; which manifestly would be difficult, if not downright impossible, since the Confederates had just seized the heights at Fairview and with them domination of the open fields across which the troops of Sickles, Couch, and Slocum were streaming to find sanctuary within the line of breastworks to the north. Hancock's rear-guard division was having to back-pedal fast to keep from being cut off or overrun by a horde of butternut pursuers who were screaming as triumphantly now, and with what appeared to be equally good cause, as they had done when they bore down on Howard's startled Dutchmen yesterday. While Stuart pressed eastward, making his largest gains on the south side of the turnpike, Lee had been pushing north and west up the plank road and reaching out simultaneously to the left, past Catharine Furnace, for the anticipated hookup. It was his belief that the best and quickest way to accomplish the reunion of the two wings of his army would be to uncover Chancellorsville, after which it was his intention to launch a

full-scale joint assault that would throw Hooker back against the Rappahannock and destroy him.

For a time it looked as if that might indeed be possible in the ten
full hours of daylight still remaining. Never before, perhaps, had the
Army of Northern Virginia fought with such frenzy and exaltation,
such apparent confidence in its invincibility under Lee. Accompanied by
the roar of artillery from the dominant heights, McLaws and Anderson
moved steadily westward up the turnpike and the plank road, while
Rodes, Colston, and Henry Heth — the senior brigadier in Hill's division — plunged eastward along both sides of the turnpike, cheered on
by Stuart, who rode among them, jaunty in his red-lined cape, hoicking
them up to the firing line and singing at the top of his voice some new
words set to a familiar tune: "Old Joe Hooker, won't you come out the
Wilderness?" All advanced rapidly toward the common objective, east
and west, as the bluecoats faded back from contact. Shortly before 10.30
the two wings came together with a mighty shout in the hundred-acre
clearing around the Chancellor mansion, which had been set afire by the
bombardment. Lee rode forward from Hazel Grove, past Fairview, on
whose crown two dozen guns had been massed to tear at the rear of the
retreating enemy columns, and then into the yard of the burning house,
formerly headquarters of the Union army, where the jubilant Confederates, recognizing the gray-bearded author of their victory, tendered him
the wildest demonstration of their lives. "The fierce soldiers with their
faces blackened with the smoke of battle, the wounded crawling with
feeble limbs from the fury of the devouring flames, all seemed possessed
with a common impulse," a staff man later wrote. "One long, unbroken
cheer, in which the feeble cry of those who lay helpless on the earth
blended with the strong voices of those who still fought, rose high above
the roar of battle and hailed the presence of the victorious chief. He sat
in the full realization of all that soldiers dream of — triumph.... As I
looked upon him in the complete fruition of the success which his genius,
courage, and confidence in his army had won," the officer added, "I
thought that it must have been from such a scene that men in ancient
times rose to the dignity of gods."

In the midst of this rousing accolade a courier arrived with a dispatch from Jackson, formally reporting that the extent of his wounds
had compelled him to relinquish command of his corps. Lee had not
known till now of the amputation, and the news shook him profoundly.
His elation abruptly replaced by sadness, he dictated in reply an expression of regret. "Could I have directed events," he told his wounded
lieutenant, "I would have chosen for the good of the country to be disabled in your stead," and added: "I congratulate you upon the victory,
which is due to your skill and energy." This done, he returned to the
business at hand. He had, as he said, won a victory; but if it was to
amount to much more than the killing, as before, of large numbers of an

enemy whose reserves were practically limitless, the present advantage would have to be pressed to the point at which Hooker, caught in the coils of the Rappahannock and with the scare still on him, would have to choose between slaughter and surrender. Before this could be accomplished, however, or even begin to be accomplished by a resumption of the advance, the attackers themselves would have to be reorganized and realigned for the final sweep of the fields and thickets stretching northward to the river. Lee gave instructions for this to be done as quickly as possible, and while waiting got off a dispatch to Davis in Richmond. "We have again to thank Almighty God for a great victory," he announced.

His hope was that he would be sending another announcement of an even greater victory by nightfall. But just as he was about to order the attack, a courier on a lathered horse rode in from the east with news of a disaster. At dawn that morning, with a rush across the pontoon bridge they had thrown under cover of darkness, the Federals had occupied Fredericksburg. Sedgwick then had feinted at the thinly held defenses on the ridge beyond the town, first on the far left and then the right, by way of distracting attention from his main effort against the center. This too had been repulsed, not once but twice, before the weight of numbers told and the bluecoats swarmed up and over Marye's Heights. In accordance with previous instructions designed for such a crisis, Early had withdrawn southward to protect the army's trains at Guiney Station; but Sedgwick had not pursued in that direction. Instead, he had moved — was moving now — due west along the plank road, which lay open in Lee's rear. This was the worst of all possible threats, and the southern commander had no choice except to meet it at this worst of all possible times. Postponing the assault on Hooker, he detached McLaws to head eastward and delay Sedgwick, if possible, while Anderson extended his present right out the River Road to prevent a junction of the two Union forces in case Sedgwick managed to sidestep McLaws or brush him out of the way. By now it was close to 3 o'clock. Holding Rodes and Heth in their jump-off positions, Lee ordered Colston to move up the Ely's Ford Road in order to establish and maintain contact with Hooker, who might be emboldened by this new turn of events. "Don't engage seriously," Lee told Colston, "but keep the enemy in check and prevent him from advancing. Move at once."

Now as before, he was improvising, dividing his badly outnumbered army in order to deal with a two-pronged menace. While McLaws swung east to throw his 7000 soldiers in the teeth of Sedgwick's 20,000 or more, Lee would endeavor to hold Hooker's 80,000 in position with his own 37,000. When and if he managed to stabilize the situation — as Jackson had done, two days ago, with the advance beyond Tabernacle Church — he would decide which of the two enemy wings to leap at, north or east. Meanwhile, as usual, he was prepared to take advantage of any blunder his opponents might commit, and he was determined to recover the initiative. Above all, he kept his head and refused to take counsel of his fears. When an excited officer, alarmed by the threat to the army's rear, arrived with a lurid eyewitness account of the loss of Marye's Heights, Lee cut him short. "We will attend to Mr Sedgwick later," he said calmly.

What with the relentless depletion of his forces, siphoned off westward at the rate of a corps a day for the past two days, and the spate of discretionary orders, generally so delayed in transmission that the conditions under which they had been issued no longer obtained by the time they came to hand, John Sedgwick — "Uncle John" to his troops, a fifty-year-old bachelor New Englander with thirty years of army service, including West Point, the Mexican War, the Kansas border troubles, and frontier Indian uprisings, in all of which he had shown a good deal more of plodding dependability than of flash — had difficulty in maintaining the unruffled disposition for which he was beloved. Even the peremptory dispatch received last night, after the uproar subsided in the thickets across the way, had left him somewhat puzzled. Hooker told him to "cross the Rappahannock at Fredericksburg on receipt of this order," which was clear enough, so far as the words themselves went; but what did it mean? Surely the army commander knew he was already across the Rappahannock, and in fact had been across it for the past three days. . . . Deciding that it meant what it ought to mean, he told Gibbon, whose division was still at Falmouth, to cross the river at dawn and seize the west-bank town, preparatory to joining in the attack Sedgwick was planning to launch against the fortified ridge with his other three divisions. He had not taken part in the December battle, having been laid up with three wounds received at Antietam, but he knew well enough what Burnside had encountered on this ground. For a time, indeed, it appeared that Sedgwick was going to do no better, despite his usual methodical preparations. After feinting on the left and right, he sent ten regiments in mass against the sunken road at the foot of the heights where so many men had come to grief, five months ago, when two of Longstreet's divisions held this section of the line. Now, however, so well had the feints misled the defenders, all that were there were two slim regiments and sixteen guns. Even so, the first two assaults were bloodily repulsed. As the bluecoats dropped back into the swale for a breather, preparatory to giving the thing another try, the colonel of a Wisconsin regiment made a short speech to the men who would lead the third assault. "When the signal *forward* is given you will advance at double-quick," he told them. "You will not fire a gun and you will not stop until you get the order to halt." He paused briefly, then added: "You will never get that order."

The Badgers gulped, absorbing the shock of this, then cheered and went in fast, the other nine regiments following close on their heels. Beyond the stone wall to their front, Barksdale's two Mississippi regiments turned loose with everything they had, attempting to shatter the head of the column of assault, while four batteries of the Washington Artillery, a crack New Orleans outfit, broke into a frenzied roar on the ridge beyond. The attackers took their losses and kept going, over the wall and among the defenders with the bayonet, then across the sunken road and up the slope of Marye's Heights with scarcely a pause, staring directly into the muzzles of the flaming guns on the crest. These too were taken in a rush as the cannoneers got off a final volley and broke for the rear. Within half an hour, and at a cost of no more than 1500 casualties, Sedgwick had his flags aflutter on ground that Burnside had spent 6300 men for no more than a fairly close-up look at, back in December. The bluecoats went into a victory dance, hurrahing and thumping each other on the back in celebration of their triumph; whereas the Confederates, several hundred of whom had been captured, were correspondingly dejected or wrathful, depending on the individual reaction to defeat. One cannoneer, who had managed to get away at the last moment, just as the Union wave broke over his battery, was altogether furious. "Guns be damned!" he replied hotly when a reserve artillerist twitted him by asking where his guns were. "I reckon now the people of the Southern Confederacy are satisfied that Barksdale's Brigade and the Washington Artillery can't whip the whole damned Yankee army!"

Having broken Jubal Early's line and thrown him into retreat, Sedgwick would have enjoyed pursuing his West Point classmate down the Telegraph Road, but another classmate, Hooker himself, had forbidden this by insisting that he push westward without delay, so that between them, as Fighting Joe put it, they could "use up" Lee. Moreover, at 10 o'clock — less than an hour after being stunned by the split pillar, and at about the same time, as it turned out, that his forward defenses began to come unglued — Hooker had his adjutant send Sedgwick a dispatch reminding him of his primary mission: "You will hurry up your column. The enemy's right flank now rests near the plank road at Chancellorsville, all exposed. You will attack at once." This reached Sedgwick at about 11.30, amid the victory celebration on Marye's Heights, and he did what he could to comply. Leaving Gibbon to hold Fredericksburg in his rear, he began to prepare his other three divisions for the advance on Lee. It was a time-consuming business, however, to break up the celebration and get the troops into formation for the march. The lead division did not get started until 2 o'clock, and it was brought to a sudden halt within the hour, just over a mile from Marye's Heights, by the sight of Confederate skirmishers in position along a ridge athwart the road. Despite Hooker's assurance that Lee's flank was "all exposed," the graybacks seemed quite vigilant, and what was more they appeared to be present in considerable strength, with guns barking aggressively in support. Sedgwick was obliged to halt and deploy in the face of the resistance, at the cost of burning more daylight.

Slowly the rebels faded back, bristling as they went, leapfrogging their guns from ridge to ridge and flailing the pursuers all the time. Near Salem Church, a mile ahead and a mile short of the junction of the plank road and the turnpike, they stiffened. It was 4 o'clock by now; the day was going fast, and Sedgwick was still a good half-dozen miles from Chancellorsville. Without waiting for the others to come up, he sent the troops of his lead division forward on the run. At first they made headway, driving the graybacks before them, but then they encountered a heavy line of battle. Repulsed, they came streaming back across the fields. The second division was up by now, however, with the third not far behind, and between them they managed to check the pursuit, though by the time Sedgwick got them rallied and into attack formation the day was too far gone for fighting. Aware by now that he had run into something considerably stronger than a mere rear guard, he set up a perimetrical defense and passed the word for his 22,000 soldiers to bed down.

Today had been a hard day. Tomorrow gave promise of being even harder. He had set out to put the squeeze on Lee, but it had begun to seem to him that he was the one in danger now. All around him, south and east as well as west, he could hear enemy columns moving in the darkness. "Sedgwick scarcely slept that night," an observant soldier later recalled. "From time to time he dictated a dispatch to General Hooker. He would walk for a few paces apart and listen; then returning he would lie down again in the damp grass, with his saddle for a pillow, and try to sleep. The night was inexpressibly gloomy."

The night was inexpressibly gloomy, and he was in graver danger than he knew. All that had stood in his way at the outset, when he began his march from Marye's Heights, had been a single brigade of Alabamians, stationed for the past three days on outpost duty at Banks Ford, from which point their commander, Brigadier General Cadmus Wilcox, had shifted them, on his own initiative, when he learned that Early's defenses had been pierced. Determined to do what he could to protect Lee's unguarded rear, he had taken up a position athwart the plank road, spreading his men in the semblance of a stout line of skirmishers, and thus had managed to bluff Sedgwick into caution, delaying his advance until McLaws had had time to post his division near Salem Church and rock the charging bluecoats on their heels. As a result, when darkness ended the fighting here to the east of Chancellorsville, Lee had what he had been hoping for: a more or less stable situation and the opportunity, as he had said, to "attend to Mr Sedgwick." Early, he learned, had retreated only a couple of miles down the Telegraph Road, then had halted on finding that he was unpursued. Lee wrote him, just after sunset, that McLaws was confronting the Federals east of Salem Church; "If . . . you could come upon their left flank, and communicate with General McLaws, I think you would demolish them." A similar message went to McLaws, instructing him to co-operate with Early. "It is necessary to beat the enemy," Lee told him, "and I hope you will do it."

A dawn reconnaissance — Monday now: May 4 — showed Hooker's intrenchments well laid out and greatly strengthened overnight, the flanks securely anchored below and above the U.S. Ford escape hatch, and the whole supported by batteries massed in depth. While this discouraged attack, it also seemed to indicate that the Federals had gone entirely on the defensive in the region north of Chancellorsville. At any rate Lee proceeded on that assumption. Canceling a projected feeling-out of the enemy lines along Mineral Spring Run, he shifted half of Heth's division from the far left, beyond Colston and Rodes, to take up Anderson's position on the right, and ordered Anderson east to join with McLaws and Early in removing the threat to his rear. His plan, if daring, was simple enough. Stuart and the 25,000 survivors of Jackson's flanking column were given the task of keeping Hooker's 80,000 penned in their breastworks, while the remaining 22,000 Confederates disposed of Sedgwick, who had about the same number to the east. This last was now the main effort, and Lee decided to supervise it in person. Riding over to Salem Church at noon, he conferred with McLaws, who was awaiting Anderson's arrival before completing his dispositions for attack, and then proceeded east, skirting the southward bulge of Sedgwick's perimeter, to see Early. He found him on Marye's Heights, which he had reoccupied soon after sunrise, posting the remnant of Barksdale's brigade in the sunken road to resist another possible advance by Gibbon, who had retired into Fredericksburg. The plan of attack, as McLaws and Early had worked it out, was for Anderson to take up a position between them, confronting Sedgwick from the south, while they moved against him, simultaneously, from the east and west. The result, if all went well, would be his destruction. Lee gave his approval, though he saw that this would involve a good deal of maneuvering over difficult terrain, and rode back toward the center.

It was past 2 o'clock by now, and Anderson was not yet in position. Time was running out for Lee today, as it had done the day before for Sedgwick. Already he was finding what it cost him to be deprived even temporarily of the services of Jackson, of whom he would say before the week was over: "He has lost his left arm, but I have lost my right." More hours were spent examining the approaches and correcting the alignment of the columns so as to avoid collisions. While Anderson continued to balk, McLaws was strangely apathetic and Early floundered in the ravines across the way; it was 6 o'clock before all the troops were in position and the signal guns were fired. The fighting was savage

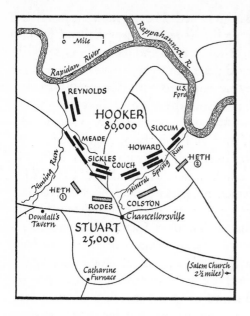

at scattered points, especially on Early's front, but McLaws got lost in a maze of thickets and scarcely made contact, either with the enemy or with Anderson, whose men added to the confusion by firing into each other as they advanced. Fog thickened the dusk and the disjointed movement lurched to a halt within an hour. Sedgwick had been shaken, though hardly demolished. Anxious to exploit his gains, such as they were, before the Federals reintrenched or got away across the river, Lee for the first time in his career ordered a night attack. While the artillery shelled Banks Ford in the darkness, attempting to seal off the exit, the infantry groped about in the fog, dog-tired, and made no progress. At first light, the skirmishers recovered their sense of direction, pushed forward, and found that the works to their front were empty; Sedgwick had escaped. Though his casualties had been heavy — worse than 4600 in all, including the men lost earlier — he had got his three divisions to safety across a bridge the engineers had thrown a mile below Banks Ford, well beyond range of the all-night interdictory fire.

Word came presently from Barksdale that Gibbon too had recrossed the river at Fredericksburg and cut his pontoons loose from the west bank. This meant that for the first time in three days no live, uncaptured bluecoats remained on the Confederate side of the Rappahannock except the ones intrenched above Chancellorsville; Lee had abolished the threat to his rear. Though he was far from satisfied, having failed in another of a lengthening sequence of attempts to destroy a considerable segment of the Union army, he had at least restored — and even improved — the situation that had existed yesterday, when he was preparing to give Hooker his undivided attention. Once more intent on destruction, he allowed the men of McLaws and Anderson no rest, but ordered them to take up the march back to Chancellorsville, intending for them to resume the offensive they had abandoned for Sedgwick's sake the day before. Stuart reported that the Federals, though still present in great strength behind their V, had made no attempt to move against him, either yesterday or so far this morning; yet Lee did what he could to hasten the march westward, not so much out of fear that Hooker would lash out at Stuart, whom he outnumbered better than three to one, as out of fear that he would do as Sedgwick had done and make his escape across the river before the Confederates had time to reconcentrate and crush him.

In point of fact, Lee's fears on the latter count were more valid than he had any way of knowing, not having attended a council of war held the night before at his opponent's headquarters. At midnight, while Sedgwick was beginning his withdrawal across the Rappahannock, Hooker had called his other corps commanders together to vote on whether they should do the same. Couch, Reynolds, Meade, Howard, and Sickles reported promptly, but Slocum, who had the farthest to come, did not arrive until after the meeting had broken up. Hooker put the question to them — remarking, as Couch would recall, "that his instructions compelled him to cover Washington, not to jeopardize the army, etc." — then retired to let them talk it over among themselves. Reynolds was much fatigued from loss of sleep; he lay down in one corner of the tent to get some rest, telling Meade to vote his proxy for attack. Meade did so, adding his own vote to that effect. Howard too was for taking the offensive; for unlike Meade and Reynolds, whose two corps had scarcely fired a shot, he had a reputation to retrieve. Couch on the other hand voted to withdraw, but made it clear that he favored such a course only because Hooker was still in charge. Sickles, whose corps had suffered almost as many casualties as any two of the other five combined, was in favor of pulling back at once, Hooker or no Hooker. Fighting Joe returned, was given the three-to-two opinion, and adjourned the council with the announcement that he intended to withdraw the army beyond the river as soon as possible. As the generals left the tent, Reynolds broke out angrily, quite loud enough for Hooker to overhear him: "What was the use of calling us together at this time of night when he intended to retreat anyhow?"

Their instructions were to cut whatever roads were necessary, leading from their present positions back to U.S. Ford, while the army engineers were selecting a strong inner line, anchored a mile above and a mile below the two pontoon bridges, for Meade's corps to occupy in covering the withdrawal. All were hard at work on their various assignments before dawn on the 5th, at which time Hooker crossed in person, accompanied by his staff. Then at noon, with the pull-back to the inner line completed, rain began to fall.

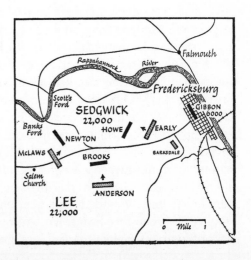

It fell in earnest, developing quickly into what one diarist called "a tremendous cold storm." By midnight the river had risen six feet, endangering the bridges and interrupting the retreat before more than a handful of regiments had reached the opposite bank. Cut off from Hooker, Couch believed he saw his chance. "We will stay where we are and fight it out," he announced. But peremptory orders arrived at 2 a.m. for the movement to be continued. One of the bridges was cannibalized to piece out the other, and the crossing was resumed. By midmorning Wednesday, May 6, it was completed. Except for the dead and missing, who would not be coming back, the army's week-long excursion south of the river had come full circle.

Lee was up by then, after being delayed by the storm the day before, but when his skirmishers pushed forward through the dripping woods they found the enemy gone. He lost his temper at the news and scolded the brigadier who brought it. "That is the way you young men always do," he fumed. "You allow those people to get away. I tell you what to do, but you won't do it!" He gestured impatiently. "Go after them, and damage them all you can!" But no further damage was possible; the bluecoats were well beyond his reach. At a cost of less than 13,000 casualties he had inflicted more than 17,000 and had won what future critics would call the most brilliant victory of his career, but he was by no means satisfied. He had aimed at total capture or annihilation of the foe, and the extent to which he had fallen short of this was, to his mind, the extent to which he had failed. Leaving a few regiments to tend the wounded, bury the dead, and glean the spoils abandoned by the Unionists on the field, he marched the rest of his army back through the rain-drenched Wilderness to Fredericksburg and the comparative comfort of the camps it had left a week ago, when word first came that the enemy was across the Rappahannock.

Back at Falmouth that evening, while his army straggled eastward in his wake, Hooker learned that Stoneman's raid, from which so much had been expected, had been almost a total failure. Intending, as he later reported, to "magnify our small force into overwhelming numbers," the cavalryman had broken up his column into fragments, none of which, as it turned out, had been strong enough to do more than temporary damage to the installations in Lee's rear. According to one disgusted trooper, "Our only accomplishments were the burning of a few canal boats on the upper James River, some bridges, hen roosts, and tobacco houses." Stoneman returned the way he had come, recrossing at Raccoon Ford on the morning of May 7, while other portions of his scattered column turned up as far away as Yorktown. His total losses, in addition to about 1000 horses broken down and abandoned, were 82 men killed and wounded and 307 missing. These figures seemed to Hooker to prove that Stoneman had not been seriously engaged, and it was not long before he removed him from command. However, his own casualties, while quite as heavy as anyone on his own side of the line could have desired — the ultimate total was 17,287, as compared to Lee's 12,821 — were equally condemning, though in a different way, since a breakdown of them indicated the disjointed manner in which he had fought and refrained from fighting the battle. Meade and Reynolds, for example, had lost fewer than 1000 men between them, while Sedgwick and Sickles had lost more than four times that number each. Obviously Lincoln's parting admonition, "Put in all your men," had been ignored. Hooker was quick to place the blame for his defeat on Stoneman, Averell, Howard, and Sedgwick, sometimes singly and at other times collectively. It was only in private, and some weeks later, that he was able to see, or at any rate confess, where the real trouble had lain. "I was not hurt by a shell, and I was not drunk," he told a fellow officer. "For once I lost confidence in Joe Hooker, and that is all there is to it."

In time that would become the registered consensus, but for the present many of his compatriots were hard put to understand how such a disaster had come about. Horace Greeley staggered into the *Tribune* managing editor's office Thursday morning, his face a ghastly color and his lips trembling. "My God, it is horrible," he exclaimed. "Horrible. And to think of it — 130,000 magnificent soldiers so cut to pieces by less than 60,000 half-starved ragamuffins!" An Episcopal clergyman, also in New York, could not reconcile the various reports and rumors he recorded in his diary that night. "It would seem that Hooker has beaten Lee, and that Lee has beaten Hooker; that we have taken Fredericksburg, and that the rebels have taken it also; that we have 4500 prisoners, and the rebels 5400; that Hooker has cut off Lee's retreat, and Lee has cut off Sedgwick's retreat, and Sedgwick has cut off everybody's retreat generally, but has retreated himself although his retreat was cut off.... In short, all is utter confusion. Everything seems to be everywhere, and everybody all over, and there is no getting at any truth." Official Washington was similarly confused and dismayed. When Sumner of Massachusetts heard that Hooker had been whipped, he flung up his hands and struck an attitude of despair. "Lost — lost," he groaned. "All is lost!" But the hardest-hit man of them all was Lincoln, whose hopes had had the longest way to fall. Six months ago, on the heels of Emancipation, he had foreseen clear sailing for the ship of state provided the helmsman kept a steady hand on the tiller. "We are like whalers who have been on a long chase," he told a friend. "We have at last got the harpoon into the monster, but we must now look how we steer, or with one flop of his tail he will send us all into eternity." Then had come Fredericksburg, and he had said: "If there is a worse place than Hell, I am in it." Now there was this, a still harder flop of the monster's tail, and Hooker and the Army of the Potomac had gone sprawling. Even before the news arrived, a White House caller had found the President "anxious and harassed beyond any power of description." Yet this was nothing compared to his reaction later in the day, when he reappeared with a telegram in his hand. "News from the army," he said in a trembling voice. The visitor read that Hooker was in retreat, and looking up saw that Lincoln's face, "usually sallow, was ashen in hue. The paper on the wall behind him was of the tint known as 'French gray,' and even in that moment of sorrow ... I vaguely took in the thought that the complexion of the anguished President's visage was like that of the wall." He walked up and down the room, hands clasped behind his back. "My God, my God," he exclaimed as he paced back and forth. "What will the country say? What will the country say?"

Within the ranks of the army itself, slogging down the muddy roads toward Falmouth, the reaction was not unlike the New York clergyman's. "No one seems to understand this move," a Pennsylvania private wrote, "but I have no doubt it is all right." He belonged to Meade's corps, which had seen very little fighting, and he could not quite comprehend that what he had been involved in was a defeat. All he knew for certain was that the march back to camp was a hard one. "Most of the way the mud was over shoe, in some places knee deep, and the rain made our loads terrible to tired shoulders." Others knew well enough that they had taken part in a fiasco. "Go boil your shirt!" was their reply to jokes attempted by roadside stragglers. Turning the matter over in their minds, they could see that Hooker had been trounced, but they could not see that this applied to themselves, who had fought as well as ever — except, of course, the unregenerate Dutchmen — whenever and wherever they got the chance. Mostly, though, they preferred to ignore the question of praise or blame. "And thus ends the second attempt on the capture of Fredericksburg," a Maine soldier recorded when he got back to Falmouth. "I have nothing to say about it in any way. I have no opinions to express about the Gen'ls or the men nor do I wish to. I leave it in the hands of God. I don't want to think of it at all."

★ ★ ★

Unquestionably, this latest addition to the lengthening roster of Confederate victories was a great one. Indeed, considering the odds that had been faced and overcome, it was perhaps in terms of glory the greatest of them all; *Chancellorsville* would be stitched with pride across the crowded banners of the Army of Northern Virginia. But its ultimate worth, as compared to its cost, depended in large measure on the outcome of Stonewall Jackson's present indisposition. As Lee had said on Sunday morning, when he first learned that his lieutenant had been wounded, "Any victory is dearly bought which deprives us of the services of General Jackson, even for a short time."

So far — that is, up to the time when Hooker threw in the sponge and the northern army fell back across the Rappahannock — Dr McGuire's prognosis had been most encouraging and the general himself had been in excellent spirits, despite the loss of his arm. "I am wounded but not depressed," he said when he woke from the sleep that followed the amputation. "I believe it was according to God's will, and I can wait until He makes his object known to me." Presently, when Lee's midday note was brought, congratulating him on the victory, "which is due to your skill and energy," Jackson permitted himself the one criticism he had ever made of his commander. "General Lee is very kind," he said, "but he should give the praise to God." Next day, May 4, with Sedgwick threatening the army's rear, he was removed to safety in an ambulance. The route was south to Todd's Tavern, then southeast, through Spotsylvania Court House, to Guiney Station, where he had met his wife and child, two weeks ago today, to begin the idyl that had ended with the news that Hooker was on the march. All along the way, country people lined the roadside to watch the ambulance go by. They brought with them, and held out for the attendants to accept, such few gifts as their larders afforded in these hard times, cool buttermilk, hot biscuits, and fried chicken. Jackson was pleased by this evidence of their concern, and for much of the 25-mile journey he chatted with an aide, even responding to a question as to what he thought of Hooker's plan for the battle whose guns rumbled fainter as the ambulance rolled south. "It was in the main a good conception, sir; an excellent plan. But he should not have sent away his cavalry. That was his great blunder. It was that which enabled me to turn him, without his being aware of it, and to take him by the rear." Of his own share in frustrating that plan, he added that he believed his flank attack had been "the most successful movement of my life. But I have received more credit for it than I deserve. Most men will think that I had planned it all from the first; but it was not so. I simply took advantage of circumstances as they were presented to me in the providence of God. I feel that His hand led me."

By nightfall he was resting comfortably in a cottage on the Chandler estate near Guiney Station. He slept soundly, apparently free from pain, and woke next morning much refreshed. His wounds seemed to give him little trouble; primary intention and granulation were under way. All that day and the next, Tuesday and Wednesday, he rested easy, talking mainly of religious matters, as had always been his custom in times of relaxation. The doctor foresaw a rapid recovery and an early return to duty. Then — late Wednesday night and early Thursday morning, May 7 — a sudden change occurred. McGuire woke at dawn to find his patient restless and in severe discomfort. Examination showed that the general faced a new and formidable enemy: pneumonia. He was cupped, then given mercury, with antimony and opium, and morphine to ease his pain. From that time on, as the drugs took effect and the pneumonia followed its inexorable course, he drifted in and out of sleep and fuddled consciousness. His wife arrived at midday, having been delayed by Stoneman's raiders, to find him greatly changed from the husband she had left eight days ago. Despite advance warning, she was shocked at the sight of his wounds, especially the mutilated arm. Moreover, his cheeks were flushed, his breathing oppressed, and his senses numbed. At first he scarcely knew her, but presently, in a more lucid moment, he saw her anxiety and told her: "You must not wear a long face. I love cheerfulness and brightness in a sickroom." He lapsed into stupor, then woke again to find her still beside him. "My darling, you are very much loved," he murmured. "You are one of the most precious little wives in the world." Toward evening, he seemed to improve. Once at least, in the course of the night, he appeared to be altogether himself again. "Will you take this, General?" the doctor asked, bending over the bed with a dose of medicine. Stonewall looked at him sternly. "Do your duty," he said. Then, seeing the doctor hesitate, he repeated the words quite firmly: "Do your duty." Still later, those in the room were startled to hear him call out to his adjutant, Alexander Pendleton, who was in Fredericksburg with Lee: "Major Pendleton, send in and see if there is higher ground back of Chancellorsville! I must find out if there is high ground between Chancellorsville and the river. . . . Push up the columns; hasten the columns! Pendleton, you take charge of that. . . . Where is Pendleton? Tell him to push up the columns." In his delirium he was back on the field of battle, doing the one thing he did best in all the world.

All that day and the next, which was Saturday, he grew steadily worse; McGuire sent word to Fredericksburg and Richmond that recovery was doubtful. Lee could not believe a righteous cause would suffer such a blow. "Surely General Jackson will recover," he said. "God will not take him from us now that we need him so much." The editor of the Richmond *Whig* agreed. "We need have no fears for Jackson," he wrote. "He is no accidental manifestation of the powers of faith and courage. He came not by chance in this day and to this generation. He was born for a purpose, and not until that purpose is fulfilled will his great soul take flight." Jackson himself inclined to this belief that he would be spared for a specific purpose. "I am not afraid to die," he said in a lucid moment Friday. "I am willing to abide by the will of my Heavenly Father. But I do not believe I shall die at this time. I am persuaded the Almighty has yet a work for me to perform." On Saturday, when he was asked to name a hymn he would like to hear sung, he requested "Shew Pity, Lord," Isaac Watts's paraphrase of the Fifty-first Psalm:

> *"Shew pity, Lord; O Lord, forgive;*
> *Let a repenting rebel live —"*

This seemed to comfort him for a time, but night brought a return of suffering. He tossed sleepless, mumbling battle orders. Though these were mostly unintelligible, it was observed that he called most often on A. P. Hill, his hardest-hitting troop commander, and Wells Hawks, his commissary officer, as if even in delirium he strove to preserve a balance between tactics and logistics.

Sunday, May 10, dawned fair and clear; McGuire informed Anna Jackson that her husband could not last the day. She knelt at the bedside of the unconscious general, telling him over and over that he would "very soon be in heaven." Presently he stirred and opened his eyes. She asked him, "Do you feel willing to acquiesce in God's allotment if He will you to go today?" He watched her. "I prefer it," he said, and she pressed the point: "Well, before this day closes you will be with the blessed Savior in his glory." There was a pause. "I will be the infinite gainer to be translated," Jackson said as he dozed off again. He woke at noon, and once more she broached the subject, telling him that he would be gone before sundown. This time he seemed to understand her better. "Oh no; you are frightened, my child. Death is not so near. I may yet get well." She broke into tears, sobbing that the doctor had said there was no hope. Jackson summoned McGuire. "Doctor, Anna informs me that you have told her I am to die today. Is it so?" When McGuire replied that it was so, the general seemed to ponder. Then he said, "Very good, very good. It is all right." After a time he added, "It is the Lord's day; my wish is fulfilled. I have always desired to die on Sunday."

At 1.30 the doctor told him he had no more than a couple of hours to live. "Very good; it's all right," Jackson replied as before, but more weakly, for his breathing was high in his throat by now. When McGuire offered him brandy to keep up his strength, he shook his head. "It will only delay my departure, and do no good," he protested. "I want to preserve my mind, if possible, to the last." Presently, though, he was back in delirium, alternately praying and giving commands, all of which had to do with the offensive. Shortly after 3 o'clock, a few minutes before he died, he called out: "Order A. P. Hill to prepare for action! Pass the infantry to the front.... Tell Major Hawks —" He left the sentence unfinished, seeming thus to have put the war behind him; for he smiled as he spoke his last words, in a tone of calm relief. "Let us cross over the river," he said, "and rest under the shade of the trees."

LIST OF MAPS

Maps drawn by George Annand, of Darien, Connecticut, from originals by the author. All are oriented north.

BIBLIOGRAPHICAL NOTE
The following bibliographical note was included with the full text of
THE CIVIL WAR: A Narrative—Fredericksburg to Meridian.

In the course of this second of three intended five-year stints, the third
of which will bring me to defeat and victory at Appomattox, my debt
has grown heavier on both sides of the line where the original material
leaves off, but most particularly on the near side of the line. Although
the *Official Records,* supplemented by various other utterances by the
participants, remain the primary source on which this narrative is based,
the hundredth anniversary has enriched the store of comment on that
contemporary evidence with biographies, studies of the conflict as a
whole, examinations of individual campaigns, and general broodings on
the minutiae—all of them, or anyhow nearly all of them, useful to the
now dwindling number of writers and readers who, surviving exposure
to the glut, continue to make that war their main historical concern. So
that, while I agree in essence with Edmund Wilson's observation that "a
day of mourning would be more appropriate," the celebration of the
Centennial has at least been of considerable use to those engaged, as I
am, in the process Robert Penn Warren has referred to as "picking the
scab of our fate."

Not that my previous obligations have not continued. They have
indeed, and they have been enlarged in the process. Kenneth P. Williams,
Douglas Southall Freeman, J. G. Randall, Lloyd Lewis, Stanley F. Horn,
Carl Sandburg, Bell I. Wiley, Bruce Catton, T. Harry Williams, Allan
Nevins, Robert S. Henry, Jay Monaghan, E. Merton Coulter, Clifford
Dowdey, Burton J. Hendrick, Margaret Leech are but a handful among
the many to whom I am indebted as guides through the labyrinth. With-
out them I not only would have missed a great many wonders along the

way, I would surely have been lost amid the intricate turnings and the uproar. Moreover, the debt continued to mount as the exploration proceeded: to Hudson Strode, for instance, for the extension of his *Jefferson Davis* at a time when the need was sore, and to Mark Mayo Boatner for his labor-saving *Civil War Dictionary.* Specific accounts of individual campaigns, lately published to expand or replace the more or less classical versions by Bigelow and others, have been of particular help through this relentless stretch of fighting. Edward J. Stackpole's *Chancellorsville,* for example, was used in conjunction with two recent biographies of the hero of that battle, Frank E. Vandiver's *Mighty Stonewall* and Lenoir Chambers' *Stonewall Jackson.* Similarly, for the Vicksburg campaign, there were Earl Schenck Miers's *The Web of Victory* and Peter F. Walker's *Vicksburg, a People at War,* plus biographies of the two commanders, *Pemberton, Defender of Vicksburg* and *Grant Moves South,* by John C. Pemberton and Bruce Catton. For Gettysburg, there were Clifford Dowdey's *Death of a Nation,* Glenn Tucker's *High Tide at Gettysburg,* and George R. Stewart's *Pickett's Charge.* For the battles around Chattanooga, there were Glenn Tucker's *Chickamauga* and Fairfax Downey's *Storming of the Gateway.* James M. Merrill's *The Rebel Shore,* Fletcher Pratt's *Civil War on Western Waters,* and Clarence E. Macartney's *Mr. Lincoln's Admirals* contributed to the naval actions, as Benjamin P. Thomas' and Harold M. Hyman's *Stanton* did to events in Washington. These too were only a few of the most recent among the many, old and new, which I hope to acknowledge in a complete bibliography at the end of the third volume, *Red River to Appomattox.* Other obligations, of a more personal nature, were carried over from the outset: to the John Simon Guggenheim Memorial Foundation, which extended my fellowship beyond the norm: to the National Park Service, whose guides helped me (as they will you) to get to know so many confusing fields: to the William Alexander Percy Memorial Library, in my home town Greenville, Mississippi, which continued its loan of the *Official Records* and other reference works: to Robert D. Loomis of Random House, who managed to keep both his temper and his enthusiasm beyond unmet deadlines: to Memphis friends, who gave me food and whiskey without demanding payment in the form of talk about the war. To all these I am grateful: and to my wife Gwyn Rainer Foote, who bore with me.

Other, less specific obligations were as heavy. The photographs of Mathew Brady, affording as they do a gritty sense of participation—of being in the presence of the uniformed and frock-coated men who fought the battles and did the thinking, such as it was—gave me as much to go on, for example, as anything mentioned above. Further afield, but no less applicable, Richmond Lattimore's translation of the *Iliad* put a Greekless author in close touch with his model. Indeed, to be complete, the list of my debts would have to be practically endless. Proust I believe has taught me more about the organization of material than even Gibbon has done, and Gibbon taught me much; Mark Twain and Faulkner would also have to be included, for they left their sign on all they touched, and in the course of this exploration of the American scene I often found that they had been there before me. In a quite different sense, I am obligated also to the governors of my native state and the adjoining states of Arkansas and Alabama for helping to lessen my sectional bias by reproducing, in their actions during several of the years that went into the writing of this volume, much that was least admirable in the position my forebears occupied when they stood up to Lincoln. I suppose, or in any case fervently hope, it is true that history never repeats itself, but I know from watching these three gentlemen that it can be terrifying in its approximations, even when the reproduction—deriving, as it does, its scale from the performers—is in miniature.

As for method, it may explain much for me to state that my favorite historian is Tacitus, who dealt mainly with high-placed scoundrels, but that the finest compliment I ever heard paid a historian was tendered by Thomas Hobbes in the foreword to his translation of *The Peloponnesian War,* in which he referred to Thucydides as "one who, though he never digress to read a Lecture, Moral or Political, upon his own Text, nor enter into men's hearts, further than the Actions themselves evidently guide him . . . filleth his Narrations with that choice of matter, and ordereth them with that Judgement, and with such perspicuity and efficacy expresseth himself that (as Plutarch saith) he maketh his Auditor a Spectator. For he setteth his Reader in the Assemblies of the People, and in their Senates, at their debating; in the Streets, at their Seditions; and in the Field, at their Battels." There indeed is something worth aiming at, however far short of attainment we fall.

—S.F.

INDEX

ABOUT THE AUTHOR

Shelby Foote was born in Greenville, Mississippi, and attended school there until he entered the University of North Carolina. During World War II he served in the European theater as a captain of field artillery. In the period after the war he wrote five novels: *Tournament, Follow Me Down, Love in a Dry Season, Shiloh,* and *Jordan County*. He was twice awarded a Guggenheim fellowship. A longtime resident of Memphis, Tennessee, he died in 2005 at the age of 88.

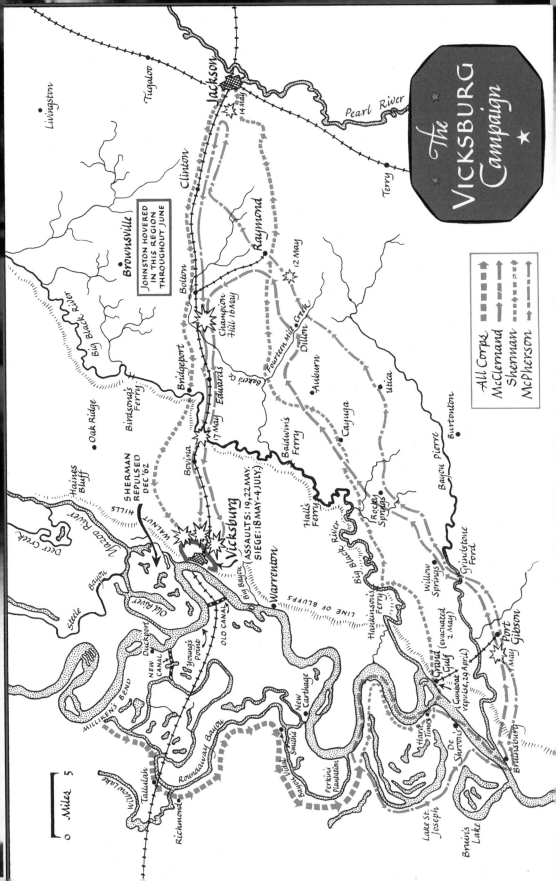

The Vicksburg Campaign

Pearl River

Livingston
Tugaloo
Jackson   14 May

Clinton
Brownsville

JOHNSTON HOVERED
IN THIS REGION
THROUGHOUT JUNE

Bolton
Raymond
12 May
Champion Hill 16 May
Baker's Cr.
Fourteen Mile Creek
Dillon
Edwards
17 May
Bridgeport
Birdsong's Ferry
Auburn
Utica
Baldwin's Ferry
Big Black River
Bovina
Cayuga
Bayou Pierre
Burtonton
Oak Ridge
HILLS
SHERMAN
REPULSED
DEC '62
Hall's Ferry
Rocky Springs
Willow Springs
Grindstone Ford
Haines Bluff
WALNUT
Vicksburg
ASSAULTS: 19, 22 MAY.
SIEGE: 18 MAY – 4 JULY.
Warrenton
Big Bayou
Big Black River
Hankinson's Ferry
Port Gibson
1 May
Deer Creek
Yazoo River
Old River
Old Canal
LINE OF BLUFFS
Grand Gulf (evacuated
2 May)
(Gunboat repulse, 29 April)
Duckport
New Canal
H Young's Point
Hard Times
De
Shroon's
Steele Bayou
MILLIKEN'S BEND
New Carthage
Smith's
Bruinsburg
Perkins
Plantation
Bayou Vidal
Richmond
Roundaway Bayou
Lake St. Joseph
Bruin's Lake
Willow
Talulah
Willow Lake

0   Miles   5

All Corps
McClernand
Sherman
McPherson